CHARACTER EXPRESSIONS

A FICTION WRITER'S THESAURUS OF FACIAL EXPRESSIONS

DAHLIA EVANS

For Mum

Contents

Chapter 5: Glare

Chapter 6: Glower

Chapter 7: Grimace

Chapter 8: Grin / Smile

Chapter 9: Leer

Chapter 14: Squint

Chapter 15: Stare

Chapter 16: Wince

Chapter 17: Wink

Chapter 18: Yawn

Appendix: Facial Expressions

Introduction

The use of facial expressions to convey a character's emotional state is a vital part of fiction writing. These facial expressions usually take the form of descriptive phrases or clauses. And while on the surface they may appear simple, there are literally thousands of ways these descriptions can be rendered. And that good reader is where this thesaurus comes in.

Character Expressions is the result of hundreds of hours of corpus study. Using a selection of bestselling novels from popular genres, I was able to compile a body of useful words and phrases that can be used in all forms of popular fiction writing. These entries will give you an almost endless supply of descriptive recipes that will last a lifetime.

How This Book Is Organized

The *Character Expressions* thesaurus is divided into 18 chapters, with each one focusing on a specific facial expression. There is also an additional appendix that highlights the many ways to describe the word *'expression'*.

Each chapter is broken up into two core sections. Section one is dedicated to the *noun form* of the entry, while section two focuses on the *verb form*. Within these sections there are subsections that show the many ways in which the word can be used.

Noun Form:

1. Noun Synonyms: This section lists similar words, as one might expect to find in a traditional thesaurus.

2. Adjectives: Numerous adjectives are given in alphabetical order. These adjectives appeared with the entry word in the corpus study. Therefore, they're what bestselling authors are using to describe the main entry word.

3. Noun + Prepositional Phrases: These entries include the noun form followed by a prepositional phrase (also called an *adjectival prepositional phrase*). As the name suggests, these phrases describe the noun. You will find some chapters have more listings than others. This is based on the corpus; some expressions are more popular than others in their use of adjectival prepositional phrases. In practice, these entries are used instead of *Adj + Noun*. For example, instead of writing: *'An uncertain frown,'* you could use: *'A frown of uncertainty.'*

4. Noun Phrases: This section lists noun phrases. In practice, these entries are typically used as a replacement for the single noun. For example, instead of writing: *'A frown crossed her forehead,'* you could write: *'The ghost of a frown crossed her forehead.'*

5. Verbs - Word as Subject: This section and the next are sorted by facial feature. There is also a standalone verb section in some chapters. Use this section when you want to describe the noun as the subject of a sentence.

6. Verbs - Word as Object: This section is used when you want to describe the main noun as an object of a verb, or the object of a preposition.

Note: An asterisk indicates that a particular entry doesn't fit 100%. That could be:

a) It isn't totally intransitive (for standalone).

b) It is used in the passive voice, or a passive way.

c) It should be used in a descriptive sense; For instance, using linking verbs, such as the forms of *be* (is/was/are etc.).

7. Noun Usage Examples: These sentences include examples which illustrate the use of the noun form, adjectives, adjectival prepositional phrases, and noun phrases.

Verb Form:

1. Verb Synonyms: Just like the noun synonyms, these verb synonyms are what you would typically find in a standard thesaurus.

2. Adverbs: These adverbs were found associated with the main verb during the corpus study. An asterisk signifies that the adverb almost always precedes the verb. All unmarked adverbs are typically used both before and after the verb.

3. Adverbials: These include adverbials of emotion, feeling, mental state, appearance, environment, and response. An asterisk is typically used to differentiate appearance types or other non-emotion types from the rest. Most entries are of the emotion or feeling variety.

4. Verb Usage Examples: These sentences include examples which illustrate the use of verbs, participle, gerunds, adverbs, and adverbials.

How To Use This Book

The best way to illustrate the use of the thesaurus is to give you an example.

Example: You have a female character who is feeling embarrassed. You want to convey this using a flush or blush.

Go to *Chapter 2: Flush/Blush* and dig around until you find a phrase or clause that sparks an idea in your mind.
    Now, you could just write something like:

Samantha flushed in embarrassment.

But, you may also want to be more visual, like so:

A flush of palest rose bloomed across Samantha's cheekbones.

Ultimately, it's up to you. In most cases, context and style will be the deciding factor. Another important factor is the type of genre you're writing. For example, thrillers tend to be less descriptive than romances. In any case, you will find exactly what you need in this thesaurus which has been compiled using all popular genres.
    Also, be sure to take some time to just read through each chapter as well as the appendix. This exercise will help hone your ability as a wordsmith.
    Finally, I want to thank you for purchasing *Character Expressions*. I hope this thesaurus helps you in all your future writing projects.

Warm Wishes,
Dahlia Evans

1
BLINK

1. Noun Form

1.1 – Noun Synonyms

a bat of eyelashes; a flicker of eyes; a fluttering of eyes; batting eyes; wink.

1.2 - Adjectives

A
accepting; adoring; affectionate; agitated; another; appreciative; arrogant; astonished.

B
batting; bewildered; big-eyed; blank; bleary; bored; brief.

C
calm; careless; complete; confused; contented; continuous; cool; curly-lashed; cursory.

D
dazed; deliberate; determined; disbelieving; dismissive; double; drowsy-eyed.

E
each; Eastwood-like; exaggerated.

F
faint; fast; few; flickering; flirtatious; forcible; frowning; frustrated; full.

G
gentle; good.

H
hard; hasty; heavy; horrifying; humiliated; hurried.

I

imperceptible; indolent; infinitesimal; innocent.

L

languid; languorous; last; lazy; light; little; lizard-like; long; long-lashed.

M

mere; merest; minute.

N

nervous; numerous.

O

obliging; occasional; ominous; one; one-eyed; owlish.

Q

quick.

R

rapid.

S

sad; sassy; second; seductive; several; sexy; sharp; shocked; short; simple; single; single-eyed; single-lidded; sleepy; slight; slow; slow-eyed; slow-motion; small; solid; speculative; squinty; startled; steady; stunned; subtle; sudden; sultry; surprised; surreptitious; swift.

T

tear-soaked; telltale; tense; terrific; theatrical; three; tiny; two.

U

uncertain; uneven; usual.

W

warning; weary; wet; wide-eyed; worried.

1.3 - Noun + Prepositional Phrases

blink of a pair of flat gray eyes*; blink of a twinkling eye*; blink of amazement; blink of an ebony eyelash*; blink of an eye*; blink of an eyelash*; blink of an eyelid*; blink of annoyance; blink of apology; blink of astonishment; blink of dense lashes*; blink of disappointment; blink of disbelief; blink of doubt; blink of false eyelashes*; blink of green eyes*; blink of happiness; blink of her beautiful eyes*; blink of her big brown eyes*; blink of her blue eyes*; blink of her dark lashes*; blink of her eye*; blink of her eyelids*; blink of her eyes*; blink of her false eyelashes*; blink of her feathery lashes*; blink of her heavily mascaraed eyelashes*; blink of her incredibly green eyes*; blink of her incredulous eyes*; blink of her lashes*; blink of her long black eyelashes*; blink of her long lashes*; blink of her lush lashes*; blink of her magnificent dark eyes*; blink of her silky lashes*; blink of her startled eyes*; blink of her turquoise eyes*; blink of her wide eyes*; blink of hesitation; blink of long lashes*; blink of long seductive lashes*; blink of naturally long eyelashes*; blink of obvious pleasure; blink of one thickly lashed eye*; blink of recognition; blink of shock; blink of something like surprise; blink of sooty lashes*; blink of surprise; blink of uncertainty; blink of vulnerability.

1.4 - Noun Phrases

a barrage of blinks; a couple of blinks; a flurry of blinks; a languid sort of blink; a lazy sort of blink; a number of blinks; a quick succession of blinks; a rapid series of blinks; a sleepy sort of blink; a tired kind of blink; another couple of blinks; the frequency of her blinks.

1.5 - Verbs: Blink as Subject

Eyes as Object
camouflage (the emotion) in (eyes); clear (the tears) from (eyes); cover (softness) in (eyes); hide (the tears) in (eyes); mask (the tears) in (eyes).

1.6 - Verbs: Blink as Object

Character (I / He / She) as Subject
give (him) (a blink); have (a blink); manage (a blink); miss (a blink)*; need (a blink); offer (him) (a blink); perform (a blink); register (a blink)*; see (a blink)*; steal (a blink); take (a blink).

Eyes as Subject
close in (a blink); close with (a blink); come down in (a blink); dip in (a blink); drift closed in (a blink); flicker with (a blink); give (a blink); greet (her) with (a blink); have (a blink); look away with (a blink); move in (a blink); narrow in (a blink); need (a blink); pull down in (a blink); shut in (a blink); snap closed in (a blink); venture (a blink).

NOUN USAGE EXAMPLES

Elle didn't so much as blink.

She gave an uncertain blink.

A blink was his only reaction to the insult.

Natasha merely performed a slow blink of her wide eyes before turning away.

Upon hearing her words, his eyes gave a blink of disbelief.

2. Verb Form

2.1 - Verb Synonyms

bat; flicker; flutter; nictate; nictitate; wink.

2.2 - Adverbs

A
abruptly; absently; actually*; adoringly; amazedly; amiably; angrily; anxiously; appealingly; approvingly; artlessly; automatically; awkwardly.

B
balefully; barely*; belatedly; bemusedly; bewilderedly; blankly; blearily; blindly; boldly; bravely; briefly; brightly; briskly.

C
calmly; carefully; cautiously; certainly*; challengingly; clearly; cluelessly; complacently; completely; confusedly; consciously; constantly; contentedly; continually; continuously; coquettishly; covertly; coyly; curiously.

D
dangerously; dazedly; defiantly; definitely*; deliberately; demandingly; demurely; desperately; desultorily; determinedly; dimly; disappointedly; disbelievingly; discreetly; disdainfully; distantly; distractedly; dizzily; dopily; dreamily; drowsily; drunkenly; dully; dumbly.

E

earnestly; enigmatically; enquiringly; erratically; exaggeratedly; experimentally.

F

faintly; fantastically; ferociously; fiercely; finally*; firmly; fitfully; foolishly; forcibly; forlornly; frantically; frenziedly; frowningly; fully; furiously; fuzzily.

G

gradually; groggily; guilelessly; guiltily.

H

happily; hardly*; hastily; haughtily; hazily; heavily; helplessly; hollowly; hurriedly.

I

immediately; impatiently; inanely; incredibly; incredulously; indifferently; indignantly; ingenuously; innocently; instantly; instinctively; involuntarily; irrationally; irresolutely; irritably.

L

languidly; lazily.

M

madly; mentally*; merely*; merrily; mindlessly; mistily; mockingly; momentarily; mutely; myopically.

N

nearly*; nervously; normally.

O

obligingly; obscenely; occasionally; only*; owlishly.

P

painfully; patently; patiently; peacefully; pleadingly; prettily; probably*; promptly*; properly; protestingly; proudly.

Q

questioningly; quickly; quizzically.

R

rapidly; rarely*; really*; reassuringly; reluctantly; repeatedly; reproachfully; resentfully; resolutely; rhythmically; robotically; ruthlessly.

S

sadly; saucily; savagely; scarcely; seductively; sensuously; seraphically; serenely; shamelessly; sharply; shortsightedly; shyly; simply*; sleepily; slightly; slowly; smilingly; smugly; softly; solemnly; stalwartly; staunchly; steadfastly; steadily; stubbornly; stupidly; successfully; suddenly; surprisedly; surreptitiously; suspiciously; sweetly; swiftly; sympathetically.

T

thoughtfully; tiredly; troubledly.

U

unashamedly; unbelievingly; uncertainly; uncomfortably; uncomprehendingly; uneasily; unhappily; unknowingly; unobtrusively; unseeingly; urgently; uselessly; usually*.

V

vacantly; valiantly; violently.

W

warily; weakly; wearily; wetly; whimsically; widely; wildly; wonderingly.

Y

yearningly.

2.3 - Adverbials of Emotion, Feeling, Mental State, Response, Manner, and Reaction to Environment

in a bemused fashion; in a combination of surprise and delight; in a combination of surprise and disappointment; in a daze; in a dazed and puzzled fashion; in a dazed fashion; in a dazed manner; in a dazed way; in a desperate attempt to clear her whirling mind; in a finely incredulous flutter; in a frenzy*; in a mesmerized fashion; in a mixture of astonishment and dismay; in a puzzled way; in a resigned sort of way; in a startled reaction to (...); in a vain attempt to focus; in a very self-satisfied rhythm; in abject disappointment; in absolute amazement; in acquiescence; in admiration; in agony; in agreement; in alarm; in amazement; in an appealing, sexy way; in an effort to clear her head; in an effort to clear her vision; in an effort to clear the glaze of confusion from her head; in an effort to focus her eyes; in an effort to focus his swimming senses; in an effort to hold back the tears*; in an effort to keep back tears*; in an effort to pull herself together; in an interested way; in anger; in anger and frustration; in anticipation of (...); in anxious hesitation; in apparent alarm; in apparent bewilderment; in apparent confusion; in appreciation; in astonished incredulity; in astonishment; in astonishment and confusion; in astonishment and dismay; in awe; in befuddled confusion; in bemused chagrin; in bemusement; in bewildered confusion; in bewilderment; in blurry disorientation; in charming confusion; in complete astonishment; in complete disconcertion; in complete disorientation; in concern; in confused embarrassment; in confusion; in confusion and astonishment; in confusion and disbelief; in confusion and embarrassment; in consternation; in dazed confusion; in dazed delight; in dazed disbelief; in dazed shock; in delight; in disbelief; in disconcertion; in disgruntled surprise; in dismay; in disorientation; in dispassionate surprise; in doubtful surprise; in embarrassment; in exaggerated confusion; in fascination; in feigned surprise; in final comprehension; in fleeting bewilderment; in frantic bemusement; in frantic confusion; in frowning uncertainty; in genuine astonishment; in groggy confusion; in growing confusion; in growing disconcertion; in guilty horror; in heavy-lidded surprise; in horrified disbelief; in hot-faced bewilderment; in incomprehension; in indignation; in innocent mischief; in irritation; in joy; in lazy cheer; in mild surprise; in mock astonishment; in mock innocence; in mock surprise; in momentary blindness*; in momentary confusion; in oblivious innocence; in obvious astonishment; in obvious bafflement; in obvious confusion; in obvious disbelief; in obvious surprise; in order to accustom her eyes to the light*; in order to keep awake*; in owl-like confusion; in owlish surprise; in pain; in panic; in panic and surprise; in protest; in pure astonishment; in pure disbelief; in pure innocence; in puzzlement; in rapid confusion; in rapid repetition*; in rapid succession*; in raw amazement; in reaction; in real alarm; in realization; in recognition; in recognition and surprise; in relief; in response; in response to (...); in shaken astonishment; in sheer bemusement; in sheer disbelief; in sheer shock; in sheer surprise; in shock; in shock and confusion; in shock and incomprehension; in shock and rejection; in shocked amazement; in shocked disbelief; in sleepy astonishment; in sleepy confusion; in sleepy surprise; in sloe-eyed shock; in slow motion*; in some bewilderment; in some confusion; in something close to disbelief; in something like shock; in startled fascination; in startled reaction; in startled surprise; in stunned amazement; in stunned confusion; in stunned delight; in stunned disbelief; in stunned horror; in stunned surprise; in stupefaction; in stupefied amazement; in stupefied, stunned silence; in sudden alarm; in sudden confusion; in sudden shock; in sudden uncertainty; in sudden wariness; in sudden, silent surprise; in surprise; in surprise and puzzlement; in surprised hurt; in surprised silence; in terror; in that way she had; in the abrupt glare*; in the beam of light thrown up into her face*; in the blaze of the sun*; in the blinding glare*; in the bright sun*; in the bright sunlight*; in the bright sunshine*; in the dazzling sunlight*; in the dim light*; in the dimness*; in the face of his vicious anger; in the glare; in the glare*; in the glaring sunlight*; in the gloom*; in the light*; in the radiance*; in the strong sunlight*; in the sudden brightness*; in the sudden light*; in the sunlight*; in the tropical sunlight*; in tired confusion; in total bewilderment; in total disbelief; in total surprise; in uncertainty; in unconcern; in understanding; in unfocused confusion; in unison*; in utter astonishment; in utter confusion; in utter shock; in utter surprise; in vague bewilderment; in vague surprise; in what appeared to be irritation; in what looked like astonishment; in what seemed like confusion; in what was essentially wordless shock; in what was obviously complete and utter confusion; in wide-eyed surprise; in wise acknowledgment; in wonder; in wonderment; with a frown; with admiration; with amazement; with an air of innocence; with astonishment; with bewilderment; with both eyes*; with calculated seductiveness; with catlike interest; with confusion; with consternation; with contentment; with delight; with disbelief; with dismay; with embarrassment; with exaggerated wonder; with fake innocence; with feigned innocence; with feigned surprise; with fury; with heart-wrenching appeal; with heavy satisfaction; with her good eye*; with horror; with interest; with nerves; with nervous confusion; with nervousness; with obvious surprise; with overplayed innocence; with pleasurable disbelief; with pleasure; with polite surprise; with puzzlement; with relief; with shock; with shock and pleasure; with slow purpose; with startled awareness; with startled reaction; with sudden comprehension and some other, unidentifiable emotion; with sudden realization; with surprise; with surprise and a slight feeling of panic; with surprised delight; with suspicious rapidity*; with the revelation; with the sudden brightness*; with total disbelief; with unmistakable urgency; with what looked like abject terror.

VERB USAGE EXAMPLES

Amy blinked furiously.

Michael blinked, stunned.

She blinked several times, unsure what to make of his outburst.

He blinked with slow purpose and squared his shoulders.

Cooper blinked in surprise.

2
FLUSH / BLUSH

1. Noun Form

1.1 - Noun Synonyms

a bloom of color; electrification; excitation; excitement; fever; fire; freshness; glow; heat; palpitation; pinkness; pulsation; quiver; radiance; red face; reddening; redness; rosiness; rouge; rubescence; rubicundity; ruddiness; thrill; throb; tingle; tingling; titillation; warmth.

1.2 - Adjectives

A
absurd; accompanying; added; additional; adorable; affronted; agonized; all-body; all-over; all-revealing; all-too-revealing; all-too-telling; amorous; anemic; angry; annoyed; annoying; another; answering; apricot; ardent; arousal-induced; aroused; attractive; awakened; awkward.

B
beautiful; becoming; beetroot; beetroot-red; belated; betraying; blistering; blood-red; blossom-red; boiling; boyish; brick-colored; brick-red; brief; bright; brilliant; burning.

C
carnation-colored; chagrined; charming; childish; clammy; cold; colorful; comely; coming; contented; cool; coral; corresponding; creamy; creeping; crimson; cruel; curious.

D
damning; damp; dangerous; dark; darkening; debilitating; deep; deep-pink; deep-red; deepening; defensive; defiant; definite; delectable; delicate; delicious; delighted; delightful; devastating; dewy; disconcerted; dismayed; distinct; distinctive; distressed; drowsy; dubious; dull; dulled; dusky; dying.

E

eager; earlier; ebbing; embarrassed; embarrassing; emotional; enchanting; endearing; enraged; enticing; erotic; euphoric; ever-reddening; excited; expectant; exquisite; extra.

F

fabulous; faint; faintest; familiar; fast; febrile; feminine; fever; fevered; feverish; fierce; fiery; flustered; fluttering; foreign; frantic; fresh; full; full-body; full-fledged; furious; further.

G

gargantuan; gauche; gentle; giddy; girlish; giveaway; glorious; glowing; gorgeous; gratified; great; growing; guilty; guilty-looking.

H

happy; hateful; head-to-toe; heady; healthy; healthy-looking; heated; heavy; hectic; heightened; helpless; hesitant; hideous; horrible; hostile; hot; humiliated; humiliating.

I

ignoble; immediate; impatient; imperceptible; increasing; incredible; incriminating; indignant; inevitable; inferno-like; infuriating; initial; instant; instinctive; intense; interesting; intriguing; involuntary; irritated.

L

light; little; livid; lovely; luminescent.

M

magnificent; merest; miserable; modest; morning; mortified; mortifying; mottled; mounting; mutinous.

N

naive; natural; nervous; new; nice.

O

occasional; odd; orange; orgasmic; outraged.

P

pained; painful; pale; palest; passion-induced; passionate; peach; peach-colored; peach-like; peachy; peculiar; peony; perceptible; permanent; persistent; pink; pinkened; pinkening; pinkish; pleasant; pleased; pleasurable; post-coital; post-orgasmic; powerful; pretty; prickly; private; pronounced; protesting.

Q

quick; quivering.

R

radiant; raging; rapid; rare; ravishing; raw; ready; real; rebellious; red; red-hot; reddish; regretful; renewed; resentful; responding; responsive; resultant; resulting; retrospective; revealing; ridiculous; ripe; rising; romantic; rose; rose-bloom; rose-colored; rose-pink; rose-tinged; rosy; rosy-pink; ruddy; rueful; russet.

S

saffron; sated; scalding; scarlet; schoolgirl; scorching; searing; self-betraying; self-conscious; sensitive; sensual; sensuous; sexual; sexy; shamed; shamefaced; shameful; sharp; shivery; shocked; shy; shy-girl; sick; silent; similar; sleepy; slight; slightest; slow; small; sobering; soft; speedy; spreading; stark; startled; steady; steamy; stinging; strange; stupid; subdued; subsequent; subtle; sudden; sullen; surprised; surprising; swarthy; sweeping; sweet; swift; swollen.

T

tangerine; tawny; telling; telltale; tender; terrible; thwarted; tingling; tiniest; tiny; tormented; tormenting; traitorous; treacherous; triumphant; turbulent; twin.

U

ugly; unaccountable; unaccustomed; unattractive; unbecoming; uncharacteristic; uncomfortable; uncontrollable; underlying; uneasy; unexpected; unfamiliar; ungovernable; unhappy; unhealthy; unlikely; unmistakable; unnatural; unpleasant; unruly; unsophisticated; untoward; unusual; unwanted; unwelcome; usual.

V

vague; velvety; vexed; violent; visible; vivid; vulnerable.

W

waning; warm; warming; warning; weird; whole-body; wild; wild-rose; wine-dark; wonderful; worried; wrathful.

1.3 - Noun + Prepositional Phrases

flush of a climax; flush of a first love; flush of a great happiness; flush of a guilt that (...); flush of a heavy drinker; flush of a higher emotion; flush of a peach; flush of a rose; flush of a swift embarrassment; flush of a wild rose; flush of a woman who (...); flush of abandon; flush of absolute fulfillment; flush of accomplishment; flush of achievement; flush of acute sexual awareness; flush of adoring thankfulness; flush of affront; flush of agonized awareness; flush of

15

alarm; flush of alcohol; flush of almond blossom; flush of almost uncontrollable rage; flush of almost youthful color; flush of an inner heat; flush of an unexpected kind; flush of anger; flush of anger and anxiety; flush of anger and embarrassment; flush of anger and mortification; flush of angry astonishment; flush of angry color; flush of angry embarrassment; flush of angry frustration; flush of angry heat; flush of angry resentment; flush of angry shame; flush of anguish and mortification; flush of annoyance; flush of annoyance and chagrin; flush of annoyed color; flush of answering warmth; flush of antagonism; flush of anticipation; flush of anticipatory desire; flush of anxiety; flush of apple blossom; flush of apricot; flush of ardor; flush of arousal; flush of arousal and embarrassment; flush of arrogant youth; flush of attraction; flush of awareness; flush of awareness and excitement; flush of awkwardness; flush of betraying color; flush of blood; flush of bright pink; flush of bright red; flush of burning color; flush of carnation; flush of chagrin; flush of clear embarrassment; flush of cold; flush of color; flush of completion; flush of compunction; flush of confused color; flush of confusion; flush of contentment; flush of corresponding warmth; flush of courage; flush of courageous effort; flush of crimson; flush of dark color; flush of dark red; flush of deep color; flush of deep crimson; flush of dejection; flush of delicate color; flush of delicate pink; flush of delight; flush of delight and warmth; flush of denial; flush of desire; flush of desire and anticipation; flush of desperation; flush of devotion; flush of disappointment; flush of discomfiture; flush of discomfort; flush of dismay; flush of distaste; flush of distress; flush of dull color; flush of dusky red; flush of dusty rose; flush of eagerness; flush of earnestness; flush of ecstasy; flush of elation; flush of embarrassed color; flush of embarrassed heat; flush of embarrassed recollection; flush of embarrassingly awkward heat; flush of embarrassment; flush of emotion; flush of emotions; flush of enjoyment; flush of enthusiasm; flush of envy; flush of euphoric enthusiasm; flush of excited attraction; flush of excitement; flush of exertion; flush of exhilaration; flush of extreme arousal; flush of fear; flush of fear and anger; flush of feeling; flush of feminine arousal; flush of feminine satisfaction; flush of fever; flush of fresh desire; flush of frustrated fury; flush of frustration; flush of fulfilled passion; flush of furious frustration; flush of furious red; flush of fury; flush of glory; flush of gratification; flush of growing sexuality; flush of guilt; flush of guilt and embarrassment; flush of guilt and grief; flush of guilt and shame; flush of guilty embarrassment; flush of guilty pleasure; flush of guilty red; flush of happiness; flush of health; flush of healthy color; flush of heat; flush of heat and anger; flush of heat and awareness; flush of heat and fury; flush of heated anger; flush of heated longing; flush of hectic color; flush of helpless anger; flush of her cheeks; flush of her climax; flush of her complexion; flush of her creamy skin; flush of her face; flush of her flawless skin; flush of her mistake; flush of her mouth; flush of her olive skin; flush of her pale skin; flush of her skin; flush of her smooth cheeks; flush of high delight; flush of high fever; flush of his angled cheekbones; flush of his cheekbones; flush of his dusky skin; flush of hope; flush of horror; flush of hot anger; flush of hot color; flush of hot embarrassment; flush of humiliated heat; flush of humiliation; flush of hurt and anger; flush of ill temper; flush of impatience; flush of inappropriate longing; flush of incipient enjoyment; flush of increasing rage; flush of indignant astonishment; flush of indignant color; flush of indignant disbelief; flush of indignation; flush of infatuation; flush of inspiration; flush of instant heat; flush of insult; flush of intimacy; flush of involuntary pleasure; flush of irrational hope; flush of irritation; flush of jealousy; flush of joy; flush of laughter; flush of lingering heat; flush of living pink; flush of longing; flush of love; flush of love and emotion; flush of love and passion; flush of love and pride; flush of lust; flush of male desire; flush of masculine shame; flush of mauve; flush of melting heat; flush of mingled shame and anger; flush of mortification; flush of mortified color; flush of mortified heat; flush of mortified pink; flush of need; flush of need and yearning; flush of nervous excitement; flush of newly awakened desire; flush of outrage; flush of overt desire; flush of overwhelming horror; flush of pain; flush of pained color; flush of palest rose; flush of panic; flush of passion; flush of peach; flush of perceived insult; flush of perspiration; flush of pink; flush of pink color; flush of pleasure; flush of pleasure and embarrassment; flush of pleasure and interest; flush of praise; flush of prickling awareness; flush of pride; flush of pride and pleasure; flush of pure and stunning red; flush of pure female pride; flush of pure pink; flush of pure pleasure; flush of pure shame; flush of rage; flush of rare color; flush of real embarrassment; flush of real resentment; flush of reassurance; flush of rebelliousness; flush of red; flush of release; flush of relief; flush of relief and warm gratitude; flush of remembered pleasure; flush of remorse and embarrassment; flush of remorse and shame; flush of resentment; flush of resistance; flush of response; flush of revelation; flush of rising hope; flush of rose; flush of roses; flush of rosy color; flush of ruddy color; flush of sadistic triumph; flush of satisfaction; flush of scarlet; flush of secret desire; flush of self-conscious color; flush of self-consciousness; flush of sensation; flush of sensual awareness; flush of sexual anticipation; flush of sexual arousal; flush of sexual awareness; flush of sexual desire; flush of sexual energy; flush of sexual excitement; flush of sexual intimacy; flush of sexual need; flush of sexual pleasure; flush of sexual satisfaction; flush of shame; flush of shame and anger; flush of shame and bitterness; flush of shame and embarrassment; flush of shame and humiliation; flush of shameful color; flush of shameful memory; flush of sheer pleasure; flush of shock; flush of shock and bewilderment; flush of shyness; flush of sleep; flush of soft color; flush of something akin to envy; flush of something hot and forbidden; flush of something hot and needy; flush of something like shame; flush of something which felt like guilt; flush of spring fever; flush of success; flush of surprise; flush of temper; flush of temperature; flush of the skin on her cheeks; flush of those high cheekbones; flush of those ruddy cheeks; flush of triumph; flush of triumph akin to a blush; flush of true love; flush of true pleasure; flush of ultimate joy; flush of unattractive color; flush of unbridled passion; flush of undeniable pleasure; flush of unease; flush of uneasiness; flush of uneasy color; flush of unhappiness; flush of unwanted pleasure; flush of unwelcome heat; flush of victory; flush of vivid color; flush of want; flush of warm color; flush of warm pleasure; flush of warmth; flush of wild apricot; flush of wild rose color; flush of wondering excitement; flush of youth.

1.4 - Noun Phrases

a betraying sort of flush; a bit of a flush; a defensive kind of flush; a glimpse of a flush; a hint of a flush; a rosy sort of flush; the beginnings of a hot flush; the betrayal of the flush; the deepening red of her flush; the deepening warmth of the flush; the distinct beginnings of a flush; the faint hint of flush; the faintest of flushes; the fascinating rise of a flush; the ghost of a flush; the heat of a flush; the heat of a fresh flush; the heat of a rising flush; the heat of her first flush; the hot burn of a flush; the hot color of a flush; the last vestiges of her flush; the origin of the flush; the remains of a flush; the rise of a flush; the sight of a faint flush; the sight of her deep flush; the slightest tinge of a flush; the sort of flush; the start of a guilty flush; the tinge of a flush; the warmth of her flush.

1.5 - Verbs: Flush as Subject

Standalone Verbs

abate; appear (again); bloom; burn; burn (hotter)*; come (again); come and go; creep (higher)*; darken; deepen; die away; die down; drain away; ebb; fade; get (darker)*; get (deeper)*; get (worse)*; go; grow; grow (darker)*; grow (deeper)*; grow (hotter)*; grow (worse)*; heighten; increase; intensify; linger; move (down)*; move (up)*; recede; remain; return; spread; subside; vanish; worsen.

Brow as Object

begin to creep from (neck) up to (brow); cover (her) from (brow to chin); cover (her) from (brow to jaw); stain (brow).

Cheekbones as Object

accentuate (cheekbones); accentuate (the high sweep) of (cheekbones); accentuate (the taut angle) of (high cheekbones); accentuate (the taut slant) of (high cheekbones); adorn (cheekbones); appear along (cheekbones); appear high on (cheekbones); appear on (cheekbones); appear under (cheekbones); arrow in slants down over (cheekbones); bloom across (cheekbones); bloom beneath (cheekbones); blotch (cheekbones); brush (the taut skin) across (cheekbones); burn across (the translucent skin) of (cheekbones); burn along (cheekbones); chase across (cheekbones); climb (the crest) of (cheekbones); coat (cheekbones); color (cheekbones); color (skin) high across (cheekbones); color (the curve) of (cheekbones); color (the line) of (cheekbones); cover (cheekbones); crawl along (cheekbones); creep along (cheekbones); creep along (the lines) of (cheekbones); creep beneath (cheekbones); creep over (cheekbones); creep up over (cheekbones); creep up under (cheekbones); crest (cheekbones); darken (cheekbones); darken (neck) and (cheekbones); darken (the curve) of (cheekbones); darken (the tanned skin) over (cheekbones); darken (the taut, bronzed skin) across (cheekbones); deepen along (cheekbones); deepen on (cheekbones); delineate (cheekbones); develop across (cheekbones); develop on (cheekbones); distribute (itself) in patches at (temples) and upon (cheekbones); drive high on (cheekbones); drop from (cheekbones); dust (cheekbones); emphasize (cheekbones); flare across (cheekbones); flare on (cheekbones); flare over (cheekbones); flirt with (the delicate lines) of (cheekbones); follow (cheekbones); give definition to (cheekbones); grow on (cheekbones); heat (cheekbones); heat (the skin) along (cheekbones); heighten (cheekbones); heighten (the slash) of (cheekbones); highlight (cheekbones); highlight (the slanted line) of (cheekbones); illuminate (cheekbones); irradiate (cheekbones); is high on (cheekbones)*; is mounted on (cheekbones)*; is over (cheekbones)*; is painted along (cheekbones)*; lick high across (cheekbones); lie across (cheekbones); lie along (cheekbones); lie along (the line) of (cheekbones); lie over (cheekbones); light (cheekbones); line (cheekbones); linger on (cheekbones); mantle (cheekbones); mark (cheekbones); mount (cheekbones); move over (cheekbones); outline (cheekbones); outline (the bold sweep) of (cheekbones); overlay (cheekbones); overlie (cheekbones); paint (itself) over (cheekbones); pinken (cheekbones); pool on (cheekbones); redden (cheekbones); return to (cheekbones); ride (cheekbones); ride high on (cheekbones); ride over (cheekbones); rim (cheekbones); rise along (cheekbones); rise high on (cheekbones); rise on (cheekbones); rise over (cheekbones); rise to (cheekbones); rise to accentuate (the exotic line) of (cheekbones); rise up along (cheekbones); run across (cheekbones); run along (cheekbones); run high along (cheekbones); run over (cheekbones); scorch along (cheekbones); score (cheekbones); scour (cheekbones); sculpt (cheekbones); sear (cheekbones); sear across (cheekbones); seem to color (the line) of (cheekbones); seem to crawl across (cheekbones); seep over (cheekbones); settle across (cheekbones); settle on (cheekbones); shadow (cheekbones); show along (cheekbones); show on (cheekbones); skid across (cheekbones); skim across (cheekbones); slash across (cheekbones); spear across (cheekbones); spread across (cheekbones); spread all over (cheekbones); spread along (cheekbones); spread high on (cheekbones); spread over (cheekbones); spread to (cheekbones); spring to (cheekbones); stain (cheekbones); start across (cheekbones); steal across (cheekbones); steal over (cheekbones); streak (cheekbones); streak across (cheekbones); streak up along (cheekbones); suffuse (cheekbones); suffused (the skin) over (cheekbones); sweep (cheekbones); sweep along (cheekbones); sweep over (cheekbones); tinge (cheekbones); tinge (the olive skin) covering (cheekbones); tint (cheekbones); tint (the taut skin) over (cheekbones); touch (cheekbones); underscore (cheekbones); warm (the sweep) of (cheekbones); wash across (cheekbones); wash over (cheekbones); wash up over (cheekbones); work (its way) over (cheekbones).

Cheeks as Object

add to (already red and chapped) (cheeks); appear along (the smooth contours) of (cheeks); appear and spread (like wildfire) across (cheeks); appear high on (cheeks); appear in (cheeks); appear on (cheeks); arrive on (cheeks); ascend (cheeks); begin at (neck) and reach up to tint (cheeks) and (forehead); begin at (the base of throat) and creep upward(s) to (cheeks); begin creeping into (cheeks); begin in (neck) and run all the way up into (cheeks); begin on (cheeks) and then race down; begin to burn (cheeks); begin to heat (cheeks); begin to make (its way) into (cheeks); begin to stain (cheeks); begin to steal into (cheeks); begin to tinge (cheeks); blanket (cheeks); blaze across (cheeks); blaze in (cheeks); bloom across (cheeks); bloom at (the tops) of (cheeks); bloom in (cheeks); bloom on (cheeks); bloom over (cheeks); break out beneath (the skin) on (cheeks); break out on (cheeks); brighten (cheeks); bring (a revealing rose pink) to (cheeks); bring (color) to (cheeks); bring pink to (cheeks); brush (cheeks); build in (cheeks); burn (cheeks); burn (like a rosy glow) in (cheeks); burn in (cheeks); burn into (cheeks); burn up (neck) and (cheeks); burst into flame upon (cheeks); career across (cheeks); carmine (cheeks); cascade through (cheeks); claim (cheeks); climb (cheeks); climb (neck) and (cheeks); climb from (throat) to (cheeks); climb into (cheeks); climb to (cheeks); climb up (cheeks); cling to (cheeks); cloud (cheeks); color (cheeks); come (unbidden) to (cheeks); come and go in (cheeks); come into (cheeks); come over (cheeks); come to (cheeks); come up in (cheeks); cover (cheeks); crawl into (cheeks); crawl over (cheeks); crawl up (cheeks); crawl up (neck) and (cheeks); creep across (cheeks); creep along (cheeks); creep from (neck) to (cheeks); creep high into (cheeks); creep into (cheeks); creep onto (cheeks); creep over (cheeks); creep through (cheeks); creep to (cheeks); creep up (cheeks); creep up (neck) to (cheeks); creep up (throat) and flood (cheeks); creep up into (cheeks); creep up over (cheeks); creep upward(s) from (neck) and spread across (cheeks); cross (cheeks); dance over (cheeks); darken (cheeks); darken (the angled line) of (cheeks); darken (the tan) of (cheeks); darken (the tightly stretched skin) across (cheeks); deepen (already ruddy) (cheeks); deepen (the color) in (cheeks); deepen (the color) of (cheeks); deepen in (cheeks); deepen on (cheeks); die from (cheeks); die out of (cheeks); drain from (cheeks); drain out of (cheeks); drift across (cheeks); drive away (the pallor) of (cheeks); dust (cheeks); ebb away from (cheeks); enhance (the perfect sweep) of (cheeks); enter (cheeks); explode on (cheeks); fade from (cheeks); fan across (cheeks); fan over (cheeks); fill (cheeks); fire in (cheeks); fire into (cheeks); flag (cheeks); flame (cheeks); flame (crimson) in (cheeks); flare in (cheeks); flood (cheeks); flood into (cheeks); flood over (cheeks); flood up (neck) and over (cheeks); flood up (neck) and scorch (cheeks); flood upward(s) over (cheeks); flood upward(s), over (throat) to (cheeks); flow over (cheeks); flow up (cheeks); flow up over (cheeks); form on (cheeks); gather along (cheeks); gather on (cheeks); gather under (cheeks); give (cheeks) a rosy tone; give (cheeks) an apricot glow; give (pale) (cheeks) a peachy warmth; glow on (cheeks); glow through (the tan) of (cheeks); go from (cheeks); grow in (cheeks); grow on (cheeks); heat (cheeks); heat (the soft skin) of (cheeks); heighten (cheeks); highlight (cheeks); hit (cheeks); infuse (cheeks);

invade (cheeks); irradiate (cheeks); is back in (cheeks)*; is bright red on (cheeks)*; is evident on (cheeks)*; is mounted to (cheeks)*; is painted across (cheeks)*; is visible on (cheeks)*; kiss (cheeks); land hard and fast upon (cheeks); leap to (cheeks); leave (cheeks); lend (cheeks) a rosy glow; lie across (cheeks); lie on (cheeks); lie under (the tan) of (cheeks); light (cheeks); light up (cheeks); linger on (cheeks); make (bright banners) in (cheeks); make (cheeks) ache; make (cheeks) darken; make (cheeks) darker; make (cheeks) feel hot; make (cheeks) glow; make (cheeks) grow pink; mantle (the broad line) of (cheeks); march up (throat) and (cheeks); mottle (cheeks); mount (cheeks); mount in (cheeks); move from (neck) to (cheeks); move over (cheeks); move up (cheeks); move up (throat) to tint (cheeks); move up to (cheeks); overlie (cheeks); overspread (cheeks); overtake (cheeks); paint (cheeks); pinken (cheeks); pour up (cheeks); put (two vivid spots of color) into (cheeks); race into (cheeks); reach (cheeks); reappear on (cheeks); recede from (cheeks); redden (cheeks); return to (cheeks); ride high in (cheeks); ride over (cheeks); rise (like a tide) along (cheeks); rise again in (cheeks); rise and arc across (cheeks); rise and fall in (cheeks); rise from (neck) to (cheeks); rise from (throat) and sting (cheeks); rise from (throat) to stain (cheeks); rise high on (cheeks); rise in (cheeks); rise into (cheeks); rise on (cheeks); rise on (throat) and (cheeks); rise over (cheeks); rise to (cheeks); rise to cover (cheeks); rise to wash (cheeks); rise toward(s) (cheeks); rise up (cheeks); rise up (neck) and flood into (cheeks); rise up (neck) and into (cheeks); rise up (neck) and spread into (cheeks); rise up (neck) to (cheeks); rise up (neck) to sting (cheeks); rise up and stain (cheeks); rise up in (cheeks); rise up over (cheeks); rise up to stain (cheeks); rouge (cheeks); run into (cheeks); run over (cheeks); run under (cheeks); run underneath (the skin) of (cheeks); run up (cheeks); run up (neck) and (cheeks); run up (neck) to color (cheeks); rush across (cheeks); rush into (cheeks); rush to (cheeks); rush up (cheeks); rush up to (cheeks); scald (cheeks); scorch (cheeks); scorch up (neck) and burn (cheeks); scour (cheeks); sear (cheeks); seem to creep into (cheeks); seep across (cheeks); seep into (cheeks); shoot from (toes) to (cheeks); singe (cheeks); skid from (throat) to (cheeks); skim (cheeks); slant across (cheeks); slash across (cheeks); slide over (cheeks); slide up (cheeks); speed to (cheeks); speed up (cheeks); speed up (throat) to singe (cheeks); spill over (cheeks); spread (its way) across (cheeks); spread across (cheeks); spread across (cheeks) and down (neck); spread all over (cheeks); spread down (cheeks); spread from (cheeks) down (neck); spread from (cheeks) to (neck); spread from (ears) to (cheeks); spread from (neck) to (cheeks); spread from (neck) up (cheeks); spread from (neck) up to (cheeks); spread from (throat) up (cheeks) to (hair line); spread into (cheeks); spread on (cheeks); spread out over (cheeks); spread over (cheeks); spread over (neck) and (cheeks); spread through (cheeks); spread to (cheeks); spread up (cheeks); spread up (neck) and into (cheeks); spread up (throat) and across (cheeks); spread up across (chin) and (cheeks); spread up over (cheeks); spread upward(s) from (throat) to (cheeks); spring to (cheeks); stain (cheeks); stain (neck) and (cheeks); start at (neck) and work (its way) up into (cheeks); start flooding (cheeks); start to crawl up (cheeks); start to creep up (cheeks); start up (cheeks); steal across (cheeks); steal into (cheeks); steal over (cheeks); steal through (cheeks); steal up (cheeks); steal up (neck) and (cheeks); steal up (neck) and bloom in (cheeks); steal up (throat) and flame (cheeks); steal up (throat) to stain (cheeks); steal up into (cheeks); sting (cheeks); storm to (cheeks); storm up (neck) and stain (cheeks); streak (cheeks); streak across (cheeks); streak up (cheeks); subside in (cheeks); suffuse (cheeks); surge from (throat) up into (cheeks); surge into (cheeks); surge up into (cheeks); swarm over (cheeks); sweep (cheeks); sweep across (cheeks); sweep into (cheeks); sweep over (cheeks); sweep up (cheeks); sweep up into (cheeks); sweep up over (cheeks); swept up (throat) and stain (cheeks) a tempting pink; threaten to darken (cheeks); threaten to scorch (cheeks); tinge (cheeks); tinge (throat) and wander to (cheeks); tingle on (cheeks); tint (cheeks); tint (cheeks) rose; touch (cheeks); travel down from (cheeks) and onto (neck); travel up (cheeks); travel up (neck) to color (cheeks); travel up to (cheeks); try to mount (cheeks); turn (cheeks) carnation pink; turn (cheeks) from peach to rose; turn (cheeks) hot; waft over (cheeks); warm (cheeks); wash (cheeks); wash into (cheeks); wash over (cheeks); wash up (neck) and burn into (cheeks); well (back) up in (cheeks); work (its way) into (cheeks); work (its way) up (neck) and into (cheeks); work (its way) up (neck) to (cheeks); work (its way) up (throat) and across (cheeks); work (its way) up (throat) to (cheeks); work (its way) up from (throat) to (cheeks); work (its way) up off (neck) onto (cheeks); work up (cheeks); zoom into (cheeks).

Face as Object

appear on (face); appear on (face) and (neck); bathe (face) with (glowing heat); begin to burn in (face); begin to show on (face); begin to spread over (face); begin to wash (face); bleed into (face); bloom (hotly) across (face); bloom on (face); bloom up (neck) and across (face); break over (face); bring (pale face) to life; burn (face); burn along (face); burn up (face); chase (the pallor) from (face); climb (face); climb from (neck) up to (face); climb into (face); climb over (face); climb up (face); climb up into (face); color (face); come and go on (face); come into (face); come over (face); come rushing back to (face); come to (face); come up into (face); cover (face); crawl up (face); crawl up (neck) and into (face); crawl up (throat) to (face); creep across (face); creep from (neck) to (face); creep into (face); creep over (face); creep through (face); creep up (face); creep up (neck) and over (face); creep up (neck) to (face); creep up into (face); creep up on (face); cross (face); darken (face); deepen on (neck) and (face); die away from (face); die out of (face); disappear from (face); drain from (face); emphasize (the triangular shape) of (face); engulf (face); faded from (face); fill (face); flame (face); flash across (face); flee through (face); flood (face); flow into (face); flow over (face); give (face) a warm glow; go from (face); grow in (face); grow on (face); heat (face); hit (face); inch (its way) across (face) and (neck); invade (face); join up (all the freckles) on (face); lash (face); light (face); light up (face); linger in (face); mantle (face); mottle (face); mount (face); mount in (face); move over (face); move up (chest) and into (face); overspread (face); paint (face); pass over (face); pinken (face); race over (face); race through (body) and up into (face); race up (neck) and (face); race up (throat) and across (face); rage across (face); recede from (face); redden (face); refuse to leave (face); return to (face); ride over (face); ride up (throat) to suffuse (face); rise (unbidden) in (face); rise beneath (the dark tan) of (face); rise from (chest) to (face); rise from (neck) into (face); rise from (throat) to (face); rise in (face); rise into (face); rise on (face); rise over (chest) and (face); rise over (face); rise to (face); rise to highlight (the lovely contours) of (face); rise up (face); rise up (neck) into (face); rise up over (face); roll up (neck) and onto (face); run into (face); run over (face); run up (face); run up into (face); rush into (face); rush to (face); rush up (face); scorch (face); sear (face); seep into (face); settle over (face); show beneath (the deep tan) of (face); show on (face); slide over (face); spread across (face); spread across (neck) and (face); spread from (neck) to (face); spread from (neck) up through (face); spread from (neck) up to bloom across (face); spread over (face); spread over (neck) and (face); spread over (throat) and (face); spread through (face); spread up (face); spread up (neck) and (face); spring into (face); stain (face); stain (throat) and (face); start at (neck) and creep up onto (face); start at (neck) and spread up to (face); start in (neck) and sweep into (face); start low on (throat) and work (its way) to (face); start on (chest) and move up to (face); start on (chest) and spread up (face); started at (toes) and race up to (face); steal across (face); steal into (face); steal into (the smooth olive) of (face); steal over (face); steal up (face); steal up over (face); steam up (face); sting (face); streak (face) unevenly; subside from (face); subside from (face) and (upper chest); suffuse (face) and (neck); surge into (face); surge into (face) and (neck); surge up (neck) and cover (whole face); sweep (face); sweep across (face); sweep into (face); sweep over (face); sweep up (face); sweep up (torso) and over (face); sweep up over (face); take (the pallor) from (face); take over (neck) and (face); threaten to cover (face); threaten to suffuse (face); tinge (face); tint (face); touch (face); travel up (neck) to (face); warm (face); wash over (face); wash up over (face); whip across (face); work (its way) up (face); work over (face).

Features as Object
accentuate (features); color (features); creep over (features); darken (features); edge (features); flood (features); passed over (features); redden (features); rise over (features); rise up over (features); spread across (features); spread over (features); stain (features); steal over (features); streak across (features); suffuse (features); sweep over (features); work over (features).

Forehead as Object
begin at (neck) and reach up to tint (cheeks) and (forehead); creep from (throat) to (forehead); creep up from (collar) all the way to (forehead); ease (its way) up from (neck) to (forehead); mount to (forehead); move from (toes) to (forehead); rise to (forehead); spread from (forehead) downward(s); weave (its way) up (forehead) and into (scalp).

Nose as Object

bloom across (the bridge) of (nose); color (the skin over the bridge) of (nose); spread over (nose); swamp (the dusting of freckles) over (nose).

Skin as Object

accentuate (the whiteness) of (skin); appear beneath (skin); begin to burn (skin); bloom beneath (skin); bloom on (skin); bloom over (skin); blossom across (skin); brush (skin); burn (skin); burn across (skin); burn beneath (skin); burn into (skin); burn over (skin); burn through (skin); burn under (skin); burn up under (skin); carmine (skin); climb into (skin); cling to (skin); color (skin); come over (skin); come under (skin); come up beneath (skin); come up under (skin); cover (skin); crawl across (skin); creep across (skin); creep along (skin); creep beneath (skin); creep into (skin); creep over (skin); creep under (skin); creep up (skin); creep up beneath (skin); creep up under (skin); darken (skin); deepen on (skin); deepen under (skin); die from (skin); drain from (skin); emphasize(the translucent quality) of (skin); engulf (skin); enhance (the peach bloom) of (skin); fade from (skin); feather (skin); flame up (skin); flood (skin); flood under (skin); from rising over (skin); from the surface of (skin) to the core of; gild (skin); give (skin) an almost opalescent sheen; glow beneath (skin); glow from (skin); glow under (skin); heat (skin); heat up (skin); illuminate (skin); infuse (a rosy glow) on (skin); infuse (skin); invade (skin); leave (skin); light (skin); light (skin) with (a rosy hue); linger (skin); make (milky skin) positively glow; make (skin) burn and tingle; make (skin) glow red; make (skin) less pale; make (skin) rosy; make (skin) tingle; mantle (skin); mark (skin); mount (skin); mount beneath (skin); mount under (skin); move under (skin); overlay (skin); pinken (skin); prickle (skin); prickle across (skin); race (its way) along (skin); race across (skin); recede from (skin); redden (skin); rise along (skin); rise below (skin); rise beneath (skin); rise on (skin); rise over (skin); rise to (skin); rise to color (skin); rise to enhance (the fair beauty) of (skin); rise under (skin); rise up (skin); rise up beneath (skin); rise up over (skin); rise up under (skin); roll over (skin); roll through (skin); run (like fire) across (skin); run along (skin); run helter-skelter over (skin); run oven (skin); run through (skin); run under (skin); run underneath (skin); run up beneath (skin); run up under (skin); scorch (skin); sear (skin); seem to light (skin) from the inside out; seep into (skin); seep through to (the outermost layer) of (skin); seep up under (skin); shade (skin); show through (skin); show under (skin); skim under (skin); slither across (skin); spread (like fire) over (skin); spread (rosily) across (skin); spread across (skin); spread along (skin); spread beneath (skin); spread out through (skin); spread over (skin); spread through (skin); spread under (skin); stain (skin); stained (skin); steal across (skin); steal into (skin); steal over (skin); steal under (skin); steal up under (skin); sting (skin); suffuse (skin); sweep (the pallor) from (skin); sweep over (skin); sweep up (skin); tinge (skin); tint (skin); tint (skin) slightly red; touch (skin); travel all over (skin); travel over (skin); turn (brown skin) somewhat ruddy; turn (skin) pink; turn (skin) to peaches and cream; turn pale (skin) to rose; turn the pale (skin) a vibrant pink; warm (every inch) of (skin); warm (skin); wash across (skin); wash over (skin); work (its way) across (skin).

1.6 - Verbs: Flush as Object

Character (I / He / She) as Subject
battle (a flush); bear (a flush); detect (a flush) rising; detect (a flush)*; experience (a flush); face (him) with (a flush); fight (a flush); fight back (a flush); fight off (a flush); flash (him) (a flush); give (a flush); give (him) (a flush); hide (a flush); prevent (a flush) rising; prevent (a flush) spreading; resist (a flush); sense (a flush) creeping up; show (him) (a flush); stifle (a flush); still (a flush); stop (a flush) rising; subdue (a flush); suppress (a flush); swallow (a flush).

Cheekbones or Character as Subject
(I) bear (a flush) high on (cheekbones)*; are highlighted with (a flush)*; are slashed with (a flush)*; are tinged with (a flush)*; carry (a flush); have (a flush).

Cheeks or Character as Subject
(color in cheeks) become (a flush); (color in cheeks) deepen to (a flush); (I) draw (a flush) to (cheeks)*; are alive with (a flush)*; are glazed with (a flush)*; are lit with (a flush)*; are pink with (a flush)*; are rosy with (a flush)*; are stained with (a flush)*; are suffused with (a flush)*; are tinged with (a flush)*; are touched with (a flush)*; bear (a flush); burn with (a flush); carry (a flush); flare with (a flush); glow with (a flush); grow hot with (a flush); grow warm with (a flush); have (a flush); have become tinged with (a flush); hold (a flush); register (a flush); show (a flush); start to burn with (a flush); warm with (a flush); wear (a flush).

Face or Character as Subject
(color of face) deepen to (a flush); (I) let (a flush) steal across (face)*; bear (a flush); burn with (a flush); darken in (a flush); darken with (a flush); fill with (a flush); glow with (a flush); heat with (a flush); is aglow with (a flush)*; is awash with (a flush)*; is infused with (a flush)*; is mantled with (a flush)*; is pink with (a flush)*; is rosy with (a flush)*; is stained (along the high cheekbones) with (a flush)*; is stained with (a flush)*; is suffused with (a flush)*; is tinged with (a flush)*; is tinted with (a flush)*; is wreathed in (a flush)*; light up with (a flush); redden into (a flush); show (a flush); turn to conceal (a flush); wear (a flush).

Skin as Subject
break out in (a flush); brighten with (a flush); darken with (a flush); deepen with (a flush); give way to (a flush); glow with (a flush); heat to (a flush); heat with (a flush); hold (a flush); is dark with (a flush)*; is honey-tinted with (a flush)*; is stained with (a flush)*; is suffused with (a flush)*; is tinged with (a flush)*; is touched by/with (a flush)*; redden in (a flush); respond with (a flush); wear (a flush).

NOUN USAGE EXAMPLES

She turned her head so he wouldn't see her guilty flush.

An embarrassed flush crept across his features.

He chuckled at the pink flush that spread across her cheeks.

A bright red flush exploded on her cheeks.

A flush of desire stole over her.

2. Verb Form

2.1 - Verb Synonyms

become red; bloom; burn; burn red; carmine; color; color up; crimson; flame; flare; flood with color; glow; go red; pink; pinken; redden; turn crimson; turn red; turn rosy; turn ruddy.

2.2 - Adverbs

A

abnormally; abruptly; absurdly; accidentally; actually*; acutely; adorably; alarmingly; angrily; appealingly; attractively; automatically; awfully; awkwardly.

B

beautifully; becomingly; betrayingly; boyishly; briefly; brightly; brilliantly.

C

certainly*; charmingly; clearly; completely; consciously; crossly.

D

daintily; dangerously; darkly; decidedly; decorously; deeply; defensively; defiantly; definitely; deliberately; delicately; deliciously; delightfully; deliriously; desperately; disappointingly; distinctly; dully.

E

easily; embarrassedly; embarrassingly; enchantingly; engagingly; enticingly; essentially*; excitedly; expectantly; exquisitely.

F

faintly; feverishly; fiercely; finely; frightfully; fully; furiously.

G

gently; gloriously; gradually; guiltily.

H

handsomely; happily; hardly; hastily; healthily; heatedly; heavily; hectically; helplessly; horribly; hotly.

I

immediately; increasingly; incredibly; indignantly; inexplicably; instantly; intensely; involuntarily; irritably.

L

largely; lightly.

M

madly; mentally*; merely*; miraculously; miserably; momentarily.

N

naturally; nearly*; nervously; newly; nicely; normally*.

O

obviously; oddly; only*; overly.

P

painfully; palely; permanently; pinkly; pleasantly; pleasingly; pleasurably; positively*; possibly*; prettily; probably*; promptly*.

Q

quickly; quietly.

R

rapidly; really*; remarkably; resentfully; revealingly; richly; ridiculously; romantically; rosily; ruefully.

S

searingly; self-consciously; sensually; sensuously; sheepishly; shyly; simply*; simultaneously; slightly; slowly; softly; sparsely; steadily; stormily; strangely; suddenly; sufficiently; surprisingly; suspiciously; sweetly.

T

tellingly; tensely; terribly; thoroughly; totally*.

U

unaccountably; unattractively; unbecomingly; uncertainly; uncharacteristically; uncomfortably; uncontrollably; uneasily; unexpectedly; unfalteringly; unhappily; unhealthily; unlikely*; unnaturally; unpleasantly; unusually; usually*.

V

violently; virtually*; visibly; vividly; vulnerably.

W

warmly; wildly; wonderfully.

2.3 - Adverbials of Emotion, Feeling, Mental State, Appearance, and Response

in a burst of self-deprecating amusement; in a cold sweat; in a most unbecoming way; in a rather boyish way; in acknowledgment of her mistake; in acknowledgment of the truth; in acute embarrassment; in agitation; in amazement; in an agony of shame; in anger; in angry embarrassment; in angry mortification; in annoyance; in anticipation; in anticipation and excitement; in both embarrassment and pride; in comprehension, and then shame; in confused wariness; in confusion; in delight; in denial; in disconcertion; in dismay; in distress; in ecstasy; in embarrassment; in embarrassment and anger; in embarrassment and horror; in guilty embarrassment; in guilty-looking embarrassment; in helpless reaction; in her cheekbones*; in her cheeks*; in her complexion*; in her face*; in her revealing fashion; in her skin*; in horror; in miserable embarrassment; in mortification; in outrage; in painful confusion; in painful self-consciousness; in pleased embarrassment; in pleased surprise; in pleasure; in pride; in reaction; in reaction (to the unexpected compliment); in remembrance; in response; in response (to the deliberate innuendo); in response (to the errant thought); in scarlet embarrassment; in shame; in silent outrage; in sleep; in spite of herself; in sudden anger; in sudden embarrassment; in the utmost confusion; in vexed embarrassment; in what must resemble guilt; with a brilliant happiness; with a burgeoning arousal; with a burst of angry color; with a combination of relief and anger; with a combination of shock and embarrassment; with a crazy excitement; with a crimson flood of color; with a dangerous sense of exhilaration; with a dark anger; with a deep anger; with a deep rosy color; with a delightful rosy glow; with a different sort of heat; with a dusky rose; with a feverish excitement; with a glorious warmth.; with a guilty stain; with a healthy color; with a heat she had no control over; with a heat that started deep inside and radiated outward; with a helpless mixture of embarrassment and excitement; with a hint of pink; with a hot rush of desire; with a kind of anger; with a lovely color; with a low, soft heat; with a mingling of guilt and desire; with a mixture of amusement and embarrassment; with a mixture of anger and embarrassment; with a mixture of embarrassment and annoyance; with a mixture of embarrassment and guilt; with a mixture of embarrassment and indignation; with a mixture of exertion and excitement; with a mixture of fear and excitement; with a mixture of fright and embarrassment; with a mixture of guilt and indignation; with a mixture of pleasure and embarrassment; with a mixture of pleasure and shyness; with a mixture of resentment and surprise; with a mixture of shyness and boldness; with a mounting excitement; with a new and bewitching excitement; with a pink glow; with a pretty and unfamiliar color; with a relieved triumph; with a renewed heat; with a rosy glow; with a ruddy hue; with a sense of self-reliance; with a shaming heat; with a silly feeling of pleasure; with a slight pink tinge; with a soft blush of peach color; with a soft glow; with a soft radiance; with a strange mixture of temper and embarrassment; with a sudden spurt of anger; with a suddenly hot embarrassment; with a thrumming need to touch and be touched; with a trace of fever; with a warm glow; with a warm glow of satisfaction; with a warm heat that started at her core; with absolute outrage; with achievement; with acute embarrassment; with adrenaline; with affronted modesty; with afterglow; with aggression; with agitation and excitement; with agonized self-consciousness; with almost childlike pleasure; with amusement; with an apricot stain; with an embarrassed confusion; with an embarrassed heat; with an embarrassed resentment; with an endearing mixture of innocence, shyness and desire; with an exquisite color; with an inner warmth she could not contain; with an intriguing mix of temper and desire; with an odd excitement; with an odd, embarrassed sensation; with an unbidden excitement; with an uncomfortable mixture of anxiety, excitement, and uncertainty; with an uncomfortable warmth; with an unexpected surge of anger; with an unwelcome heat; with anger; with anger and bitter with disappointment; with anger and disbelief; with anger and embarrassment; with anger and exertion; with anger and frustration; with anger and indignation; with anger and maybe a little bit of guilt; with anger and mortification; with anger and passion; with anger and self-contempt; with anger and shame; with angry awareness; with angry color; with angry emotion; with angry indignation; with angry mortification; with angry red; with angry triumph; with animation; with annoyance; with annoyance and a certain amount of embarrassment; with annoyance and embarrassment; with annoyance and what looked a great deal like panic; with annoyance.; with annoyed confusion; with answering warmth; with anticipated delight; with anticipation; with anxiety; with anxious color; with apparent embarrassment; with apparent pleasure; with apprehension; with arousal; with awareness; with awareness and caution; with barely contained rage; with barely controlled anger; with becoming color; with betraying color; with betraying heat; with bewilderment and then anger; with bitter shame; with black fury; with blood; with body heat; with both annoyance and embarrassment; with both irritation and insult; with both passion and immense satisfaction; with both pleasure and surprise; with boyish pleasure; with bright red; with brilliant color; with building excitement; with building temper; with bursting pride; with cautious triumph; with chagrin; with cold; with cold and excitement; with color; with concentration; with concern; with confusion; with confusion and anger; with confusion and half excitement; with confusion and hurt; with consternation; with consuming heat; with conviction; with coyness; with crimson; with dark blood; with dark color; with dark embarrassment; with dazed pleasure; with deep color; with deep embarrassment; with defensive anger; with defiance; with defiant embarrassment; with delicate color; with delight; with delight and relief; with delight and the hope that (...); with delighted surprise; with desire; with desire and longing; with determination; with disbelieving color; with discomfiture; with discomfort; with discomfort and guilt; with dismay; with displeasure; with distaste and embarrassment; with distress; with doubt; with dull red color; with eagerness; with eagerness and relief; with effort; with effort and annoyance; with effort and triumph; with either pleasure or embarrassment; with elation; with embarrassed amusement; with embarrassed color; with embarrassed heat; with embarrassed pleasure; with embarrassing color; with embarrassment; with embarrassment and anger; with embarrassment and annoyance; with embarrassment and anxiety; with embarrassment and fury; with embarrassment and guilt; with embarrassment and indignation; with embarrassment and irritation; with embarrassment and shame; with embarrassment and triumph; with emotion; with emotions; with enjoyment; with enthusiasm; with equal fury; with erotic heat; with even more color; with evident embarrassment; with excited color; with excited delight; with excited pleasure; with excitement; with excitement and happiness; with excitement and joy; with excitement and relief; with excitement and triumph; with exertion; with exertion and anger; with exertion and mortification; with exertion and triumph; with exhilaration; with expectation; with faint hope; with fear and exertion; with fear and worry; with feeling; with feminine pride; with fever; with fierce desire; with fierce passion; with fiery color; with fiery pride; with fire; with first love; with flattery and excitement; with fresh arousal; with fresh shame; with fresh spirit; with fruitless exertion; with frustration; with frustration and fury; with frustration and remorse; with furious color; with furious disbelief; with furious frustration; with further annoyance; with fury; with fury and embarrassment; with fury and frustration; with genuine pleasure; with girlish confusion; with glee; with glorious surprise; with glory; with good humor; with gratification; with gratitude; with growing exasperation; with guilt; with guilt and angry surprise; with guilt and embarrassment; with guilt and resentment; with guilt and self-contempt; with guilt and something more; with guilty annoyance; with guilty shame; with happiness; with happiness and excitement; with happiness and exertion; with harassment; with hatred; with heady heat; with healthy color; with

30

heat; with heat and anger; with heat and desire; with heat and embarrassment; with heat and exertion; with heat and pleasure; with heat and temper; with heat at the memory; with heated anger; with heated emotion; with hectic color; with heightened color; with high color; with high emotion; with high wild color; with high, angry color; with hope and shame; with horror; with hot angry color; with hot blood; with hot color; with humiliation; with humiliation and anger; with humor; with hunger; with hurt; with hurt embarrassment; with impatience; with importance; with impotent bad temper; with incredulous rage; with indecision; with indignant amusement; with indignant anger; with indignation; with indignation and disappointment; with indignation and something like alarm; with indignation or excitement; with inner heat; with instant color; with instant heat; with intense self-consciousness; with interest; with internal warmth; with involuntary pleasure; with irritation; with irritation and anger; with joy; with laughter; with laughter and happiness; with liquor and temper; with love; with love and desire; with lovely color; with male satisfaction; with memories of (...); with mind-blowing heat; with mingled dread and excitement; with mingled embarrassment and annoyance; with mingled embarrassment and pleasure; with mingled relief and dismay; with mingled temper and embarrassment; with miserable confusion and hurt anger; with mock indignation; with more delight than fear; with more than indignation; with more than the cold; with mortification; with mortification and anger; with mortification and shame; with mortified color; with much more than embarrassment; with need; with need and desire; with nerves; with nervous excitement; with nervous guilt; with nervousness; with newborn anger; with newfound confidence; with obvious desire; with obvious embarrassment; with obvious pleasure; with obvious relief; with optimism; with outrage; with outraged shock; with pain and anger; with pain and embarrassment; with pain as well as embarrassment; with painful embarrassment; with panic; with passion; with passion and a good deal of embarrassment; with passion and desire; with passion and embarrassment; with passion and fury; with passionate self-righteousness; with pink; with pink color; with pleased embarrassment; with pleased surprise; with pleasure; with pleasure and a little triumph; with pleasure and astonishment; with pleasure and exertion; with pleasure and happiness; with pleasure and incredulity; with pleasure and purpose; with pleasure and relief; with pleasure and surprise; with power; with pretty color; with pride; with pride and anger; with pride and excitement; with pride and happiness; with pride and pleasure; with pure abandon; with pure guilt; with quick anger; with quiet outrage; with rage; with rage and embarrassment; with rage and fury; with rage mingled with pain; with rare anger; with rare color; with reaction; with ready anger; with red; with red fury; with red-hot heat; with release; with relief; with remembered desire; with remembered heat; with remembered heat and humiliation; with remembered pain and outrage; with remembered pleasure; with remembrance; with remorse; with renewed anger; with renewed embarrassment; with renewed fury; with renewed outrage; with renewed rage; with resentment; with response; with restrained aggravation; with righteous anger; with righteous indignation; with rose; with rosy color; with ruddy color; with satisfaction; with scarlet; with secret passion; with self-conscious color; with self-consciousness; with self-consciousness and excitement; with self-disgust; with self-mockery; with sensation; with sensual heat; with sensual longing; with sexual arousal; with sexual desire; with sexual excitement; with sexual heat; with sexual satisfaction; with shame; with shame and a flicker of rebellion; with shame and humiliation; with shame and pain; with shamed embarrassment; with sheer pleasure; with sheer rage; with shock; with shock and pain; with shyness; with simmering lust; with sleep; with sleep and a slight temperature; with sleep and heat; with so much pleasure; with soft color; with soft pink; with some emotion she couldn't name; with something approaching shame; with something curiously akin to guilt; with something deeper than pleasure; with something like anticipation; with something like temper; with something other than anger; with something other than embarrassment now; with spirited indignation; with spots of color; with stirrings of resurging desire; with stunned pleasure; with stupid pride; with success; with success and newfound courage; with sudden anger; with sudden annoyance; with sudden anxiety; with sudden childish pleasure; with sudden color; with sudden embarrassment; with sudden excitement; with sudden guilt; with sudden heat; with sudden heat and sensitivity; with sudden horrified guilt; with sudden pleasure; with sudden shame; with sudden shock; with sudden triumph; with suppressed anger; with suppressed rage; with surprise; with surprise and embarrassment; with surprised pleasure; with suspense; with sympathy; with tears*; with telltale color; with telltale heat; with temper; with temper and embarrassment; with temper and insulted pride; with terrible heat; with the admission; with the bright-eyed look of a fever; with the cold; with the cold air; with the color of desire; with the confusion of her thoughts; with the dark blood of desire; with the dark tide of passion; with the dull heat of desire; with the effort; with the embarrassment of her thoughts; with the exertion of walking*; with the exhilaration of the moment; with the force of her anger; with the force of her conviction; with the force of her emotions; with the force of her rage; with the force of his desire; with the full force of her emotions; with the full force of his fury; with the heat of desire; with the heat of embarrassment; with the heat of her thoughts; with the heat of his fever; with the heat of passion; with the intensity of her feelings; with the memory; with the memory of humiliation; with the most gorgeous shade of pink; with the onrush of adrenalin to her veins; with the rosy blush of desire; with the rosy glow of desire; with the rosy glow of unbidden excitement; with the same heat burning inside her; with the same heat he could feel climb in him; with the shock of the thoughts that had crept into her mind; with the soft glow of pleasurable satisfaction; with the sting of shame; with the stirrings of pleasure; with the thrill of victory; with the tussle; with the unmistakable color of desire; with the weirdest mixture of pleasure and embarrassment; with tingling heat; with tingling pleasure; with trepidation; with triumph; with triumph and happiness; with triumphant pride; with turbulent emotion; with unaccustomed heat; with unbecoming color; with unbidden excitement; with uncertainty; with uncontrolled desire; with unexpected color; with unexpected pleasure; with unhidden delight; with unmistakable passion; with unmistakable pleasure; with unreasonable pride; with unusual anger; with unusual excitement; with vexation; with victory; with victory.; with violent rage; with vivid color; with wanting; with warm color; with warmth; with warmth and sleep; with warmth and surprise; with what had to be embarrassment; with what he was feeling; with what looked like agonized self-consciousness; with what looked like unusual embarrassment; with wild color; with wild heat; with wine and excitement.

VERB USAGE EXAMPLES

Kevin flushed in embarrassment.

The smooth skin beneath her cheekbones flushed pink.

She felt her face flush.

Willow flushed nervously when her name was announced over the loudspeaker.

Ashley flushed under the heat of his gaze.

3
FROWN

1. Noun Form

1.1 - Noun Synonyms

arabesque; channel(s); cleft; corrugation; crease(s); crimp(s); crinkle(s); deep V; depression(s); frown creases; frown furrows; frown grooves; frown lines; frown marks; furrow(s); groove(s); indentation(s); line(s); pleat; ridge(s); rut(s); seam(s); track(s); trench; trough; worry lines; wrinkle(s); vertical track(s).

1.2 - Adjectives

A

abrupt; absent; absentminded; absorbed; accusing; admonishing; adorable; adult; adult-like; affronted; aggravated; aggressive; aggrieved; agitated; agonized; alarmed; alarming; all-business; all-out; all-too-familiar; all-too-perceptive; ambiguous; amused; angry; anguished; annoyed; annoying; another; answering; anxiety-riddled; anxious; apologetic; appealing; appraising; apprehensive; appropriate; arrogant; assessing; astonished; astounded; attractive; austere; autocratic; automatic; awful.

B

bad-humored; bad-tempered; baffled; barest; beefy; beetling; beleaguered; belligerent; bemused; best; bewildered; bewildering; big; bitter; black; black-browed; blackening; blade; blank; bleak; bona-fide; boss-like; bossy; boyish; brief; brittle; brooding; broody; brotherly; business; business-like.

C

careworn; caring; casual; cautioning; cautious; censorious; censuring; certain; chagrined; challenging; characteristic; charming; chastising; chiding; child-like; chilling; chiseled; close-mouthed; cold; comical; commanding; commiserating; compassionate; concentrated; concentrating; concentration; concern-etched; concerned; condemnatory; condensed; confounded; confused; considerable; considering; constant; contemplative; contemptuous; continual; continuous; contrived; convincing; cool; corresponding; craggy; cranky-in-the-morning; creasing; crimson; critical; cross; crotchety; cryptic; curious; current; curt; customary; cute; cynical.

D

dainty; dangerous; dark; dark-as-the-devil; dark-browed; dark-eyed; darkening; darkling; daunting; dawning; dazed; decided; decisive; deep; deep-in-thought; deepening; defensive; defiant; definite; dejected; delectable; delicate; delicious; demanding; derisive; desperate; detectable; determined; different; dignified; dipped-in-vinegar; direct; disappearing; disappointed; disapproving; disbelieving; discerning; disconcerted; disconcerting; discontented; discouraging; disdainful; disgruntled; disgusted; dismayed; dismaying; dismissive; dispirited; displeased; dissatisfied; dissenting; distant; distinct; distracted; distracted-looking; distraught; distressed; distrustful; disturbed; disturbing; doctorly; doleful; don't-rub-it-in; doubtful; doubting; dour; downward; drawing; drawn; drunk; dubious; dusky.

E

earlier; earnest; effective; elderly; elegant; elicit; embarrassed; embittered; emphatic; enchanting; endearing; engraved; enigmatic; enormous; enquiring; etched; eternal; even; ever-deepening; ever-increasing; ever-present; every; exaggerated; exasperated; expected; expressive.

F

faint; fake; false; familiar; famous; fascinating; fast; fatalistic; fearsome; feigned; ferocious; fierce; fiery; fine; firm; first; fitful; fixed; flashing; flat-out; fleeting; flickering; flustered; focused; fond; forbidding; formidable; frantic; fretful; friendly; frosty; frustrated; full; full-blown; full-fledged; furious; furrowed; fused.

G

gathering; gentle; genuine; giant-sized; glaring; gloomy; glowering; good; good-natured; gorgeous; graceless; grave; gray; grim; grooved; grouchy; ground-dragging; growing; grown-up; grudging; grumpy; guarded.

H

habitual; half; half-asleep; half-bemused; half-convincing; half-hearted; half-perplexed; half-worried; happy; harassed; hard; harried; harsh; haughty; hazy; heavy; heavy-duty; helpless; hesitant; hooded; hopeless; horrible; horrified; hostile; huge; humorous; hurry-up; hurt.

I

I-don't-get-it; I-mean-business; icy; identical; ill-tempered; immediate; impatient; imperceptible; imperious; implacable; inappropriate; incipient; incomprehensible; inconvenienced; incredulous; indecisive; indignant; indiscernible; indomitable; indulgent; inevitable; inexplicable; inimical; initial; injured; inner; inquiring; inquisitive; inscrutable; instant; instinctive; intense; intent; interested; interrogative; intimidating; intrigued; introspective; involuntary; inward; ironic; irritable; irritated.

J

jealous; judgmental; judicial; justified.

K

killer; kind; kissable; knitted; knotted; knowing.

L

last; laughing; lazy; less-than-welcoming; lethal; light; lined; lingering; little; lop-sided; lowering.

M

maddening; make-believe; male; man-sized; man-style; marked; masculine; massive; matching; maternal; mean; meaningful; meditative; melancholy; men-are-from-Mars; menacing; mental; mere; microscopic; mighty; mild; minuscule; minute; miserable; mock; mock-ferocious; mock-puzzled; mock-reflective; mock-reproving; mock-serious; mock-stern; mocking; momentary; moody; morning; morose; mother-hen; motherly; mournful; muddled; mulish; multi-layered; mutinous; muzzy; mystified.

N

narrow; narrow-eyed; near; near-permanent; nervous; nervy; nettled; new; niggling; niggly; no-nonsense; non-committal; non-comprehending; normal; noticeable; notorious; now-familiar.

O

obvious; occasional; odd; off-putting; offended; ominous; open; out-and-out; outraged; overdone; own.

P

pained; painful; parental; particular; passing; patented; paternal; patient; patronizing; peevish; penetrating; pensive; perceptible; permanent; perpetual; perplexed; persistent; persnickety; perturbed; petulant; philosophical; phony; piercing; pinched; pissed-off; pitiful; playful; pointed; ponderous; pop-eyed; portentous; pouting; pouty; pragmatic; predictable; preliminary; preoccupied; pretend; pretty; preventive; previous; prim; private; probing; problematic; prodigious; pronounced; protective; protesting; provoked; puckered; puckering; puckish; pugnacious; purposeful; pursing; put-out; puzzled; puzzling.

Q

quelling; querulous; questioning; quick; quicksilver; quiet; quizzical.

R

raging; rain-slicked; rare; ready; real; rebuking; recriminating; reflected; reflective; regal; regretful; remonstrative; remorseful; repressive; reprimanding;

reproachful; reproving; repulsive; resentful; residual; resigned; responding; restless; returned; righteous; rippling; riveting; rueful.

S

sad; sardonic; satisfied; savage; scalding; scandalized; scared; scathing; schoolmarm; scolding; scornful; scowling; searching; self-conscious; self-deprecating; self-directed; self-impatient; self-recriminating; self-recriminatory; self-reprimanding; self-righteous; semi-permanent; semi-reluctant; serious; several; severe; shadowy; shaken; sharp; shocked; short; shy; sideward; sideways; signature; silencing; silent; silly; single; skeptical; slashing; sleepy; slight; slow; sly; small; smiling; smoldering; smoothed; snapping; snarling; snooty; soap-opera; sober; sobering; soft; solemn; solicitous; somber; sour; sour-apple; spectacular; speculative; stark; startled; stern; stiff; still-not-gone; stoic; stormy; straight; straight-line; straining; strange; stress-packed; stressed; stricken; stubborn; studied; studious; stunned; subsequent; sudden; sulky; sullen; sultry; super-size; superior; suppressed; surly; surprised; surprising; suspicious; sweet; swift; sympathetic; sympathy.

T

taken-aback; taut; teary-eyed; teasing; telling; telltale; temporary; tense; tension; tentative; terrible; terrific; terrifying; terse; theatrical; thick; thin; thin-lipped; thinking; this-is-serious-business; thought; thoughtful; threatening; three-line; thunder-cloud; thunderous; tight; tight-lipped; tiny; tired; tormented; tortured; trademark; tragic; tremendous; troubled; twin; twisted; two-line; typical.

U

ugly; unaccountable; unaccustomed; unbelieving; uncertain; uncharacteristic; uncomfortable; uncomprehending; uncompromising; unconscious; unconvinced; uneasy; unexpected; unguarded; unhappy; unholy; unimpressed; unmistakable; unnoticed; unsatisfied; unsettling; unsympathetic; unusual; unwelcome; unwelcoming; unyielding; upside-down; upward; urgent; usual.

V

V-shaped; vague; vehement; vertical; vexed; vicious; violent.

W

wall-to-wall; warning; wary; watchful; weak; weary; weighty; well-bred; well-marked; where-have-you-been; wide-eyed; wifely; wincing; withering; wonderful; wondering; wordless; worried; worrisome; would-be; wounded; wretched; wrinkle-forming; wrinkled; wry.

1.3 - Noun + Prepositional Phrases

frown of absent concentration; frown of absolute concentration; frown of absorption; frown of acknowledgement; frown of agony; frown of amusement; frown of anger; frown of angry concentration; frown of angry impatience; frown of annoyance; frown of annoyed disapproval; frown of anxiety; frown of apprehension; frown of astonished incomprehension; frown of awareness; frown of bemusement; frown of bewildered amusement; frown of bewilderment; frown of black frustration; frown of bleakness; frown of calculation; frown of censure; frown of compassion; frown of complete concentration; frown of complete exasperation; frown of comprehension; frown of concentration; frown of concern; frown of confusion; frown of constant decision; frown of consternation; frown of contrition; frown of curiosity; frown of curious confusion; frown of deep anxiety; frown of deep concentration; frown of deep concern; frown of deep thought; frown of deep worry; frown of dejection; frown of determination; frown of diabolical concentration; frown of disagreement; frown of disappointment; frown of disapproval; frown of disbelief; frown of discomfort; frown of disconcertion; frown of discontent; frown of discovery; frown of disgust; frown of dislike; frown of dismay; frown of displeasure; frown of disquiet; frown of dissatisfaction; frown of distaste; frown of doctorly concern; frown of doubt; frown of effort; frown of empathetic pain; frown of enquiry/inquiry; frown of exasperation; frown of extreme concentration; frown of extreme severity; frown of false bewilderment; frown of fierce concentration; frown of frustration; frown of genuine concern; frown of grim disapproval; frown of growing disapproval; frown of hard exasperation; frown of haughty enquiry/inquiry; frown of hesitation; frown of hurt bewilderment; frown of impatience; frown of incomprehension; frown of incredulous surprise; frown of indecision; frown of indifference; frown of intense concentration; frown of intense disapproval; frown of intense exasperation; frown of intent; frown of interest; frown of introspection; frown of irritated bewilderment; frown of irritation; frown of mild irritation; frown of misery; frown of mock concentration; frown of mock reproach; frown of murderous wrath; frown of obvious disapproval; frown of outrage; frown of pain; frown of pained displeasure; frown of painful indecision; frown of perplexity; frown of preoccupation; frown of protest; frown of pure irritation; frown of puzzled concern; frown of puzzlement; frown of query; frown of quick anger; frown of raw impatience; frown of recall; frown of recognition; frown of regret; frown of relieved disbelief; frown of reluctant interest; frown of remorse; frown of reproach; frown of resentment; frown of resignation; frown of ruthless determination; frown of sharp distaste; frown of sheer aggravation; frown of sheer perplexity; frown of shocked anger; frown of sincere concern; frown of slight displeasure; frown of sober disapproval; frown of sorrow; frown of sternness; frown of strain; frown of surprise; frown of surprised concentration; frown of surprised disbelief; frown of sympathetic concern; frown of sympathy; frown of tension; frown of tiredness; frown of uncertainty; frown of unconscious dissatisfaction; frown of utter confusion; frown of utter incredulity; frown of wondering incredulity; frown of worry.

1.4 - Noun Phrases

a bit of a frown; a brief glimpse of her frown; a/the brief hint of a frown; a dark wedge of a frown; a facsimile of a frown; a/the flicker of a frown; a forlorn sort of frown; a fraction of a frown; a/the ghost of a frown; a grin instead of a frown; (just/only) a/the hint of a frown; a hint of frown lines; a less intense version of her frown; a little pleat of a frown; a little squiggle of a frown; a little suggestion of a frown; a mock glower of a frown; a multitude of frown lines; a network of frown lines; a pinch of a frown; a puzzled kind of frown; a/the shadow of a frown; a small hint of a frown; a small trace of a frown; a smile instead of a frown; a smudge of a frown; a/the suggestion of a frown; a thread of a frown; a thundercloud of a frown; a tiny pucker of a frown; a trace of a frown; a twitch of a frown; a very intense sort of frown; a wave of a frown; a weary map of frown lines; a wisp of a frown; (absolutely) no trace of a frown; all traces of her frown; an easing of her frown; an odd sort of frown; the almost brooding quality of her frown; the appearance of a frown; the beginning(s) of a frown; the black thundercloud of a frown; the blackest of frowns; the briefest of frowns; the cause of her frown; the cleft of a frown; the corner of her frown; the crease of a frown; the crinkle of a frown; the dark shadow of a frown; the darkness of her frown; the deep crease of a frown; the deep gully of a frown; the deep pinch of a frown; the deepening of her frown; the deepest of frowns; the faintest glimmer of a frown; the faintest hint of a frown; the faintest of frowns; the faintest suggestion of a frown; the ferocity of her frown; the fierceness of her frown; the first hint of a frown; the first suggestion of a frown; the fissure of a frown; the flash of a frown; the form of a frown; the frostiness of a frown; the full effect of her frown; the full force of her frown; the furrow of her frown; the glowering fury of her frown; the irritated slice of her frown; the kind of frown; the line(s) of her frown; the little tuck of a frown; the merest flicker of a frown; the merest hint of a frown; the merest suggestion of a frown; the merest suspicion of a frown; the pair of frowns; the quality of her frown; the quick crease of a frown; the remnants of a frown; the semblance of a frown; the severity of her frown; the sight of her frown; the size of her frown; the slight deepening of her frown; the slight pucker of a frown; the slight trace of a frown; the slightest flick of a frown; the slightest hint of a frown; the slightest of frowns; the slightest shadow of a frown; the slightest trace of a frown; the smallest hint of a frown; the smallest of frowns; the sort of frown; the start of a frown; the strain of her frown; the strength of a frown; the suspicion of a frown; the tension of her frown; the threat of a frown; the thunderous warning of the frown; the tiniest flicker of a frown; the tiniest hint of a frown; the tiniest of frowns; the tiny pucker of a frown; the trench of the frown; the tug of a frown; the twin creases of a frown; the twisted angle of her frown; the vaguest hint of a frown; the very faintest suspicion of a frown; the vestige of a frown; the violence of her frown; the whisper of a frown; the wrinkles of a frown.

1.5 - Verbs: Frown as Subject

Standalone Verbs

appear; blacken; clear; come and go; come (back); darken; decrease; deepen; disappear; disperse; dissipate; dissolve; double; ease; evaporate; even out; fade; flatten out; flee; form; go; grow (more intense)*; harden; increase; intensify; lessen; lift; lighten; melt; melt away; narrow; pass; reinstate (itself)*; relax; remain; return; settle; shift; smooth; smooth out; soften; spread; tighten; vanish; weaken; widen; worsen.

Brow as Object

appear beneath (brow); appear on (brow); become fixed upon (brow); beetle (brow); begin darkening (brow); begin to furrow (brow); begin to mar (brow); begin to wrinkle (brow); bisect (brow); bite deep(ly) into (brow); bite into (brow); bring (back) to (brow); bring to (brow); bunch (brow) together; carve (deep lines) into (brow); carve (deeply) into (brow); carve (twin vertical grooves) in (brow); catch (brow); cause (a crease) on (brow); cause (a deeply drawn cleft) in (brow); cause (deep creases) to appear on (brow); cause (little worry lines) on (brow); cause (little wrinkles) to surface on (brow); clear from (brow); cloud (brow); collect on (brow); come (unexpectedly) to (brow); contort (brow); corrugate (brow); crash down on (brow); crease (brow); crease the center of (brow); crinkle (brow); cross (brow); curl (brow); darken (brow); dart across (brow); deepen on (brow); deepen until (brow) pulled together; dent (brow); descend over (brow); descend upon (brow); develop on (brow); dig (deep furrows) in/into (brow); dig deep(ly) into (brow); dig into (brow); dimple (brow); disappear from (brow); disturb (brow); draw (deep wrinkles) into (brow); drive (deep grooves) in/into (brow); ease from (brow); etch (creases) across (brow); etch (deep lines) into (brow); etch into (brow); etch (its way) across (brow); etch (itself) along (brow); evaporate from (brow); fade from (brow); flash across (brow); flee from (brow); flicker across (brow); flicker over (brow); flit over (brow); form on (brow); fracture (brow); furrow (brow); furrow across (brow); furrow (deep lines) in (brow); gather above (brow); gather on (brow); go from (brow); gouge (brow); groove (brow); grow on (brow); indent (brow); knit (brow); leap to (brow); leave (brow); lessen on (brow); lie across (brow); lift from (brow); lighten on (brow); line (brow); linger on (brow); mar (briefly) (brow); mark (brow); move across (brow); narrow (brow); pass across (brow); persist on (brow); pinch (brow); plant (itself) in (brow); play over (brow); pleat (brow); pucker (brow); pull at (brow); put (a deep crease) in (brow); ravage (brow); reappear on (brow); remain stamped upon (brow); return to (brow); ruff (brow); score (brow); score (deep creases) on (brow); scrunch up (brow); seem cemented into (brow); settle on (brow); shadow (brow); show on (brow); slant (its way) across (brow); slash (brow); slash (deep furrows) across (brow); slice (brow); slice across (brow); slide off (brow); stay on (brow); sweep across (brow); thunder across (brow); tie (brow); tighten (brow); touch (lightly) (brow); toy with (brow); trace (brow); tug (brow) down over eyes; tug (brow) into (a deep furrow); tug at (brow); vanish from (brow); warp (brow); waver on (brow); worm (itself) across (brow); worry (brow); wrinkle (brow).

Eyebrows / Brows as Object

appear between (eyebrows); arch (eyebrows); bring (eyebrows) (closer) together; bring (eyebrows) down in [emotion]; bring (eyebrows) together (over/across) eyes; buckle (the space/the smooth skin) between (eyebrows); bunch (eyebrows); bunch (eyebrows) together; burrow between (eyebrows); carve (twin lines) between (eyebrows); cause (eyebrows) to draw together; cause (eyebrows) to (meet/twitch); come between (eyebrows); come to (eyebrows); connect (eyebrows); connect (eyebrows) together; contract (eyebrows); crease between (eyebrows); crease (the area/region/skin/space) between (eyebrows); crinkle (eyebrows); deepen between (eyebrows); dent the space between (eyebrows); dig (a furrow/line) between (eyebrows); dip (eyebrows); divide (eyebrows); drag (eyebrows) together; drag (eyebrows) down over eyes; draw (a V/line) between (eyebrows); draw at (eyebrows); draw down (eyebrows); draw (eyebrows) deep over eyes; draw (eyebrows) downward(s); draw (eyebrows) into [an expression]; draw (eyebrows) together; drive between (eyebrows); drive down (eyebrows); drive together (eyebrows); drop (eyebrows); drop (eyebrows) low over eyes; emerge between (eyebrows); etch between (eyebrows); etch (its way) between (eyebrows); etch (lines/creases) between (eyebrows); flash between (eyebrows); flick between (eyebrows); flicker over (one eyebrow); flit between (eyebrows); form between (eyebrows); gather (eyebrows) together; gather between (eyebrows); gouge (deep lines) between (eyebrows); grow between (eyebrows); hitch between (eyebrows); hover between (eyebrows); hover over (eyebrows); jam together (eyebrows); jerk together (eyebrows); join (eyebrows); join (eyebrows) together; knit (eyebrows); knit (eyebrows) together; leap between (eyebrows); leave (a crease) between (eyebrows); linger between (eyebrows); lodge between (eyebrows); lower (eyebrows); make (two lines) between (eyebrows); mark (a crease/the space) between (eyebrows); narrow (the distance) between (eyebrows); notch (twin lines) between (eyebrows); nudge together (eyebrows); peak (eyebrows); peek out between (eyebrows); persist between (eyebrows); pinch (skin) between (eyebrows); pinch (eyebrows) together; play between (eyebrows); play over (eyebrows); pleat (eyebrows); pleat (the skin/two lines) between (eyebrows); plough (a furrow) between (eyebrows); pluck at (the space) between (eyebrows); press (eyebrows) into [an expression]; pucker (eyebrows); pucker (the space) between (eyebrows); pull (eyebrows) into [an expression]; pull (eyebrows) together; pull at (eyebrows); pull between (eyebrows); pull down (eyebrows); pull (the space) between (eyebrows) together; push (eyebrows) together; push down (eyebrows); put (a deep crease) between (eyebrows); reappear between (eyebrows); remain stamped between (eyebrows); ridge (eyebrows); score between (eyebrows); score (deep lines) between (eyebrows); seem (permanently etched) between

41

(eyebrows); settle between (eyebrows); show between (eyebrows); slant (eyebrows); slash (a furrow/twin grooves) between (eyebrows); slice (down) between (eyebrows); snap (eyebrows) together; stay between (eyebrows); stay hitched to (eyebrows); stitch (eyebrows); stitch (eyebrows) together; take up residence between (eyebrows); tease (the space) between (eyebrows); tie (eyebrows) together; till (eyebrows); trace (a furrow) between (eyebrows); tug (eyebrows) down into [an expression]; tug (eyebrows) together; tug (a line) between (eyebrows); tug at (eyebrows); twist (eyebrows); twitch (eyebrows) together; vanish from between (eyebrows); vee (eyebrows); waver between (eyebrows); wedge (itself) between (eyebrows); work (its way) between (eyebrows); worm (itself) between (eyebrows); wrinkle (the skin) between (eyebrows).

Eyes as Object

appear above/around (eyes); appear between (eyes); bracket (eyes); cloud (eyes); come (back) into/to (eyes); cut down between (eyes); darken (eyes); deepen between (eyes); ease from between (eyes); enter (eyes); etch (itself) between (eyes); fill (eyes); flicker in (eyes); fold down between (eyes); form about (eyes); form between (eyes); gather above (eyes); gather between (eyes); gather in (eyes); go from between (eyes); groove between (eyes); grow in (eyes); leave (eyes); move into (eyes); narrow (eyes); persist in (eyes); pucker between (eyes); remain between (eyes); return to (eyes); settle between (eyes); shadow (eyes); slice down between (eyes); spring (back) into (eyes); touch (eyes); vanish from between (eyes).

Face as Object

appear on (face); break out on (face); bunch (face); clear from (face); cloud (face); come (back) across (face); come (back) onto/to (face); come down over (face); contort (face); cover (face); crease (face); crinkle (face); criss-cross (face); cross (face); dance across (face); darken (face); deepen on (face); disappear from (face); disfigure (face); ease from (face); elongate (face); engrave (face); etch (face); etch on (face); fill (face); flash across (face); flicker across (face); flicker over (face); flit across (face); flitter across (face); form on (face); furrow (face); gather on (face); gather over (face); go from (face); jump (back) onto (face); leave (face); line (face); linger on (face); lower over (face); make (face) (...); mar (face); mark (face); overtake (face); pass over (face); play about (face); pucker (face); pull at (face); remain on (face); return to (face); ride across (face); set on (face); settle on/onto (face); settle over (face); slice down over (face); slide off (face); slip from (face); slip over (face); slip up (face); snap across (face); stamp on (face); stay on (face); steal across (face); stretch across (face); touch (face); tug at (face); vanish from (face); wash over (face).

Features as Object

appear on (features); brush (features); carve into (features); cloud (features); contract (features); crease (features); creep over (features); cross (features); darken (features); descend over (features); distort (features); etch into (features);

flit across (features); harden (features); inch across (features); interrupt (features); make (features) look (...); mar (features); mat (features); pinch (features); play across (features); remain on (features); score (features); settle on/onto (features); settle over (features); shadow (features); touch (features); worry (features); wrinkle (features).

Forehead as Object

add to (the lines) on (forehead); appear across (forehead); appear on (forehead); bisect (forehead); bite into (forehead); brush (forehead); buckle (forehead); bunch (forehead); burrow across (forehead); burrow into (forehead); carve (a deep trench/itself) into (forehead); carve (forehead); clamp (forehead); clear from (forehead); cloud (forehead); come to (forehead); contract (forehead); corrugate (forehead); cover (forehead); crease (forehead); crinkle (forehead); cross (forehead); cut (deep) into (forehead); darken (forehead); dent (forehead); descend onto (forehead); dig (deep) into (forehead); disappear from (forehead); disturb (forehead); divide (forehead); draw (lines) in (forehead); draw together (forehead); dress (forehead); ease from (forehead); etch (forehead); etch (forehead) with (heavy lines); etch (heavy lines) into (forehead); flick across (forehead); flicker across (forehead); flit across (forehead); flit over (forehead); form on (forehead); furrow (forehead); gather on (forehead); gouge (forehead); groove (forehead); hover on (forehead); incise (lines) into (forehead); indent (forehead); knit (creases) in (forehead); knit (forehead); lift from (forehead); line (forehead); make (faint lines) on (forehead); mark (forehead); mar (forehead); nag at (forehead); pass across (forehead); pattern (forehead); pinch (forehead); play over (forehead); pleat (forehead); pucker (forehead); pull (hard) at (forehead); pull on (forehead); quilt (forehead); reappear on (forehead); reinstate (itself) on (forehead); remain implanted on (forehead); return to (forehead); ruffle (forehead); score (forehead); scour (forehead); scrunch up (forehead); settle on/onto (forehead); slash (forehead); slice (deep) into (forehead); smooth from (forehead); snake across (forehead); spread across (forehead); spread over (forehead); spring to (forehead); stay on (forehead); sweep (fleetingly) across (forehead); tighten (forehead); tighten (the muscles in) (forehead); torment (forehead); touch (forehead); trace (creases) across (forehead); trace (forehead); trace (lines) in (forehead); tug at (forehead); twitch (forehead); worry (forehead); wrinkle (forehead); wrinkle across (forehead).

Lips as Object

[something] bring (frown) to (lips); crease (lips); curve (lips); edge away (smile) on (lips); etch (deep grooves) on either side of (lips); mar (lips); niggle (lips); press (lips) into (a thin line); pucker (lips); pull (lips) down/downward(s); pull at (lips); ruin (lips); shape (lips) into (a thin line); thin (lips); tighten (lips); touch (lips); trace (lips); tug at/on (lips); turn (lips) downward(s); twist (lips).

Mouth as Object

bracket (mouth); build around (mouth); bunch (mouth); pull at (mouth); take over (mouth); thin (mouth); tighten (mouth); transform (mouth) (to stone); tug (mouth) downward(s); tug at (mouth); tug down (mouth); turn (mouth) into (a thin line).

Skin as Object

buckle (skin) between (eyebrows); catch (skin) between (eyebrows); corrugate (skin) between (eyebrows); crease (skin) above (eyebrows/eyes); crease (skin) between (eyebrows); crease (skin) of (brow/face/forehead); crinkle (skin) around (eyes); crinkle (skin) of (brow/face/forehead); furrow (skin) between (eyebrows); furrow (skin) of (brow/face/forehead); mar (skin); mar (skin) of (brow/face/forehead); pinch (skin) between (eyebrows); pleat (skin) between (eyebrows); pucker (skin) across (brow); pucker (skin) between (eyebrows); pucker (skin) of (brow/face/forehead); pull (skin) together between/over (eyebrows); pull at (skin); tug at (skin) between (eyebrows); wrinkle (skin); wrinkle (skin) between (eyebrows).

1.6 - Verbs: Frown as Object

Brow as Subject

beetle into (a frown); bunch in (a frown); clear of (its frown); clench in (a frown); come down in (a frown); contract in (a frown); crease (again) with (a frown); crease in/into (a frown); crimp into (a frown); crinkle in/into (a frown); crumple in/into (a frown); darken with (a frown); deepen into (a frown); dent in (a frown); descend into (a frown); develop (a frown); dip (downward(s)) in (a frown); draw (down) in/into (a frown); draw together in (a frown); edge into (a frown); fix in (a frown); flicker into (a frown); fold into (a frown); form (a frown); furrow in/into (a frown); gather in/into (a frown); hint at (a frown); hold (a frown); indent with (a frown); knit in/into (a frown); knit with (a frown); knot in/into (a frown); knot with (a frown); lift in/into (a frown); line with (a frown); lose (its frown); lower in/into (a frown); mar in/into (a frown); mar with (a frown); meet in (a frown); narrow into (a frown); pinch in/into (a frown); pleat in/into (a frown); pucker in/into (a frown); pucker with (a frown); pull into (a frown); ridge in (a frown); scrunch into (a frown); settle into (a frown); show (a frown); slam down in (a frown); snap (down) into (a frown); squiggle into (a frown); stay indented in (a frown); tense into (a frown); tighten with (a frown); tuck into (a frown); twist into (a frown); twitch into (a frown); twitch with (a frown); wrinkle in/into (a frown); wrinkle with (a frown).

Character (I / He / She) as Subject

aim (a frown) at (him); battle against (a frown); beetle (a frown) at (him); cast (a frown) (in his direction); cast (him) (a frown); conjure up (a frown); couldn't hide (a frown); couldn't prevent (a frown); direct (a frown) across (room/table); direct (a frown) at (him); fake (a frown); feign (a frown); fight (a frown); fight against (a frown); fight back (a frown); fight off (a frown); fix (a frown) on (him); flash (a frown) (in his direction); flashed (a frown) at (him); force (a frown); give (a frown); give (a frown) to (him); give (him) (a frown); level (a

frown) at (him); manage (a frown); offer (a frown); present (a frown) (that ...);
produce (a frown); pull (a frown); receive (a frown) (from him); see (a frown)
(on his face); send (a frown) (his way); shoot (a frown) at (him); shoot (a frown)
up at (him); shoot (him) (a frown); silence (him) with (a frown); slant (a frown)
at (him); slice (a frown) over to (him); smother (a frown); spare (a frown) for
(him); sport (a frown); squelch (a frown); squint (a frown) (in his direction);
struggle with (a frown); suppress (a frown); throw (a frown) at (him); toss (a
frown) (his way); toss (a frown) over to (him); trade (a frown) with (him); turn
(a frown) on (him); wear (a frown).

Eyebrows / Brows as Subject

angle down in (a frown); arch in (a frown); arrow down in (a frown); arrow in (a
frown); arrow together in (a frown); beetle down into (a frown); beetle in/into (a
frown); bend (again) in (a frown); buckle in/into (a frown); bunch into (a
frown); bunch together in (a frown); bunch with (a frown); clamp in (a frown);
clash in (a frown); cleft by (a frown)*; clench in (a frown); clump together in (a
frown); cock in (a frown); collect in (a frown); come (close) together in (a
frown); come down in (a frown); compress in/into (a frown); compress together
in (a frown); connect in (a frown); constrict in (a frown); contract in/into (a
frown); converge in (a frown); cram together in (a frown); crash down in (a
frown); crease in/into (a frown); crease together in (a frown); crease with (a
frown); creep down in/into (a frown); creep together in (a frown); crinkle into (a
frown); crumple in (a frown); crunch together in (a frown); crush together in (a
frown); dance together in (a frown); dart downward(s) in (a frown); dart
upward(s) in (a frown); deepen with (a frown); descend in (a frown); dip down
in (a frown); dip in/into (a frown); dip low in (a frown); dip together in (a
frown); drag together in (a frown); draw close(r) in (a frown); draw down in/into
(a frown); draw downward(s) in/into (a frown); draw in/into (a frown); draw
together in (a frown); drop in/into (a frown); drop to (a frown); fix in (a frown);
fix together in (a frown); flatten in/into (a frown); flex in (a frown); flick (him)
(a frown); flick together in (a frown); flicker into (a frown); fly together in (a
frown); fold down into (a frown); fold into (a frown); form (a frown); form into
(a frown); frown at (him); frown; furrow in/into (a frown); furrow together in (a
frown); gather in/into (a frown); gather together in (a frown); go together in (a
frown); grow closer in (a frown); grow together in (a frown); hook in (a frown);
jag in (a frown); jerk down in (a frown); jerk in/into (a frown); jerk together in
(a frown); join in (a frown); join together in (a frown); knit in/into (a frown);
knit together in (a frown); knit with (a frown); knot in (a frown); knot together
in (a frown); lift in (a frown); link in (a frown); lock in/into (a frown); lock
together in (a frown); lower in/into (a frown); manage (a frown); meet in (a
frown); merge in (a frown); mesh in (a frown); move together in (a frown);
narrow into (a frown); nudge together in (a frown); peak into (a frown); pinch
in/into (a frown); pinch together in (a frown); pleat in/into (a frown); plummet
in/into (a frown); plunge down in (a frown); pucker (faintly) in (a frown); pull
down in (a frown); pull in/into (a frown); pull together in (a frown); push
together in (a frown); quirk downward(s) in (a frown); quirk in (a frown);

rumple into (a frown); rush together (a frown); sag in (a frown); screw together in (a frown); scrunch down in (a frown); scrunch in/into (a frown); scrunch together in (a frown); set in/into (a frown); settle (themselves) into (a frown); shift into (a frown); shoot down into (a frown); shoot together in (a frown); sink into (a frown); slam together in (a frown); slant into (a frown); slant together in (a frown); slash downward(s) in (a frown); slash into (a frown); slash together in (a frown); slide into (a frown); slide together in (a frown); snap down in (a frown); snap into (a frown); snap together in (a frown); stiffen into (a frown); swing down in (a frown); swoop together in (a frown); thicken with (a frown); tilt downward(s) in (a frown); tilt into (a frown); tilt together in (a frown); tip in/into (a frown); tug together in (a frown); twist in (a frown); twitch in/into (a frown); twitch together in (a frown); wrinkle in/into (a frown).

Eyes as Subject

belie (her frown); contain (a frown); crease in/into (a frown); crinkle into (a frown); darken in (a frown); deepen with (a frown); draw into (a frown); draw together in (a frown); frown; jerk together in (a frown); meet (his) with (a frown); narrow in/into (a frown); narrow with (a frown); scrunch in (a frown); seek (his) with (a frown); snap in (a frown); squint into (a frown).

Face as Subject

assume (a frown); become (a frown); border on (a frown); broaden with (a frown); bunch into (a frown); close in (a frown); cloud in (a frown); collapse into (a frown); contort in/into (a frown); contort with (a frown); crack into (a frown); crease in/into (a frown); crease with (a frown); crinkle in/into (a frown); crinkle up in/into (a frown); crumple in/into (a frown); crunch into (a frown); darken in/into (a frown); darken with (a frown); deepen into (a frown); deepen with (a frown); dip into (a frown); display (a frown); draw in/into (a frown); fade into/to (a frown); fall into (a frown); firm into (a frown); flicker in (a frown); fold in/into (a frown); fold up into (a frown); form (a frown); freeze in (a frown); frown; furrow into (a frown); gather into (a frown); go from (a frown) to (...); hold (a frown); make (a frown); mold into (a frown); morph into (a frown); move between (a frown) and (...); move from (a frown) to (...); move to (a frown); narrow into (a frown); pinch in/into (a frown); press into (a frown); pucker in/into (a frown); pucker up in (a frown); pull downward(s) into (a frown); pull into (a frown); pull together in (a frown); relapse into (a frown); reveal (a frown); sag into (a frown); screw into (a frown); screw up in/into (a frown); scrunch in/into (a frown); scrunch up in (a frown); scrunch up with (a frown); scrunch with (a frown); set in (a frown); settle into (a frown); shift to (a frown); sober into (a frown); split into (a frown); squinch into (a frown); tauten in (a frown); tense in/into (a frown); tighten into (a frown); tilt into (a frown); tug into (a frown); twist into (a frown); twist with (a frown); wear (a frown); work into (a frown); wrinkle in/into (a frown); wrinkle up in (a frown).

Features as Subject

arrange in (a frown); clench in (a frown); close in (a frown); collapse into (a frown); compose in/into (a frown); crease in/into (a frown); crease with (a frown); crinkle in/into (a frown); crumple in/into (a frown); darken in (a frown); draw in/into (a frown); edge into (a frown); fold in (a frown); frown; pinch into (a frown); pucker in (a frown); pucker with (a frown); pull into (a frown); screw into (a frown); screw up in (a frown); scrunch in/into (a frown); seam into (a frown); set in/into (a frown); settle into (a frown); shift into (a frown); slip into (a frown); tighten into (a frown); transform into (a frown); twist into (a frown); twist up into (a frown); wear (a frown); wither into (a frown); wrinkle into (a frown).

Forehead as Subject

become (a frown); buckle in (a frown); carve into (a frown); collect (a frown); contract in (a frown); corrugate in (a frown); crease in/into (a frown); crease with (a frown); crimp into (a frown); crinkle in/into (a frown); crinkle under (a frown); crinkle up in (a frown); crumple down into (a frown); crumple in/into (a frown); crunch into (a frown); deepen in (a frown); dig into (a frown); draw in/into (a frown); draw together in/into (a frown); frown; furrow in/into (a frown); furrow with (a frown); hold (a frown); knit in/into (a frown); knit together in (a frown); knot in (a frown); pinch in (a frown); pinch together in (a frown); pleat in/into (a frown); produce (a frown); pucker in/into (a frown); pucker with (a frown); pull into (a frown); scrunch into (a frown); settle into (a frown); show (a frown); tie into (a frown); tighten into (a frown); tighten with (a frown); wrinkle from (a frown); wrinkle in/into (a frown); wrinkle with (a frown).

Lips as Subject

bend into (a frown); bow in (a frown); clamp in (a frown); close (tightly) in (a frown); close together in (a frown); come down in (a frown); come together in (a frown); (tightly) compress in/into (a frown); curl down in (a frown); curve down in (a frown); curve downward(s) in (a frown); curve in (a frown); decline into (a frown); descend into (a frown); dip down into (a frown); draw down in (a frown); draw downward(s) into (a frown); draw into (a frown); draw together in (a frown); droop into (a frown); fall into (a frown); firm in (a frown); form (a frown); form into (a frown); frown; narrow into (a frown); pinch together in (a frown); press (tightly) together (a frown); press down into (a frown); press into (a frown); pucker in/into (a frown); pull down in/into (a frown); pull into (a frown); purse in (a frown); quirk into (a frown); set in (a frown); settle into (a frown); thin to (a frown); tighten in/into (a frown); tilt down in (a frown); tilt downward(s) into (a frown); tilt into (a frown); turn down in/into (a frown); twist in/into (a frown).

Mouth as Subject

clamp in (a frown); compress in/into (a frown); crease in/into (a frown); curl down into (a frown); curl into (a frown); curve downward(s) into (a frown);

curve in/into (a frown); dip down in (a frown); dip into (a frown); downturn into (a frown); draw down in (a frown); draw into (a frown); droop into (a frown); drop into (a frown); edge into (a frown); firm in/into (a frown); fix in (a frown); fold into (a frown); form (a frown); frown; hover into (a frown); lift from (a frown) into (...); pinch into (a frown); press into (a frown); pucker in/into (a frown); pull down in/into (a frown); pull into (a frown); quirk down in (a frown); quirk in/into (a frown); set in (a frown); settle into (a frown); shape into (a frown); shift into (a frown); show (a frown); shut in (a frown); slant in (a frown); slide into (a frown); slip into (a frown); thin in (a frown); tighten into/to (a frown); tilt down in (a frown); turn downward(s) in/into (a frown); twist downward(s) in (a frown); twist in/into (a frown).

NOUN USAGE EXAMPLES

He stared at her, a pained frown on his face.

A frown of puzzlement briefly marred her smooth brow.

The grave frown deepened into a scowl.

With a frown, she watched as both of them disappeared up the stairs.

When he entered the room, Kate's frown of confusion was suddenly replaced by a wry smile.

2. Verb Form

2.1 - Verb Synonyms

corrugate; crease; crimp; crinkle; crumple (up); furrow; pleat; rumple; scrunch (up); wrinkle (up).

2.2 - Adverbs

A
abruptly; absently; absentmindedly; abstractedly; accusingly; admonishingly; angrily; anxiously; apologetically; archly; assertively; attentively; automatically.

B
bemusedly; bewilderedly; blackly; blankly; bleakly; briefly; broodingly.

C

charmingly; chidingly; coldly; combatively; comically; concentratedly; concernedly; confusedly; consideringly; contemplatively; coolly; critically; crossly; curiously.

D

dangerously; darkly; dazedly; deeply; delicately; determinedly; directly at; disapprovingly; discouragingly; disgruntledly; disgustedly; dismissively; disparagingly; distastefully; distractedly; distressedly; doubtfully; dubiously.

E

earnestly; easily; elaborately; enquiringly; exaggeratedly; extremely haughtily.

F

faintly; ferociously; fiercely; fleetingly; forbiddingly; fractionally; furiously.

G

gently; gloomily; grimly.

H

harshly; haughtily; heavily; helplessly; horribly; humorously.

I

immediately afterwards; impatiently; indecisively; indignantly; indulgently; inhospitably; inquiringly; instinctively; intensely; intently; introspectively; inwardly; irritably.

K

knowingly.

L

lightly; loftily; lopsidedly.

M

madly; meaningfully; meaningly; menacingly; mentally; mightily; momentarily; moodily; morosely.

N

narrowly; nervously; noticeably.

O

occasionally; oddly; officiously; ominously; only briefly; only slightly; overly much; owlishly.

P

passingly; peculiarly; pensively; perplexedly; petulantly; playfully; pointedly (at); presently; prettily; professionally.

Q

queryingly; questioningly; quickly; quizzically.

R

repressively; reproachfully; reprovingly; resentfully; resolutely; ruefully.

S

sadly; sassily; savagely; scoldingly; seriously; severely; sharply; shyly; sightlessly; silently; simultaneously; skeptically; sleepily; slightly; slowly; softly; solemnly; solidly; speculatively; steadfastly; steadily; sternly; stiffly; strangely; stubbornly; suddenly; sulkily; suspiciously; swiftly; sympathetically.

T

thoughtfully; threateningly; thunderously; tightly; tiredly.

U

uncertainly; uncomfortably; uncomprehendingly; unconsciously; uneasily; unexpectedly; unhappily; unseeingly.

V

vaguely; violently.

W

warily; warningly; wearily; worriedly; wryly.

2.3 - Adverbials of Emotion, Feeling, Mental State, and Response

in a combination of confusion and an inexplicable sense of disappointment; in a contemplative, gentle way; in a disapproving way; in a distracted way; in a faint, quizzical manner; in a huff; in a new way; in a perplexity which couldn't be genuine; in a preoccupied fashion; in a pretence of concentration; in a puzzled manner; in a puzzled sort of way; in a puzzled way; in a rather pained sort of way; in a repressive fashion; in a short-sighted way; in a strangely preoccupied way; in a sudden realization; in a thoughtful manner; in a troubled fashion; in a troubled way; in a very different way; in a way which alarmed her; in absolute concentration; in absolute confusion; in abstraction; in acknowledgment of that truth; in acute distaste; in aggravation; in agreement; in alarm; in alarmed bewilderment; in amazement; in amusement; in an abstract way; in an effort of concentration; in an effort of memory; in an effort to concentrate; in an effort to drag her thoughts back from (...); in an effort to focus; in an effort to recall (...); in an effort to remember; in anger; in angry confusion; in angry puzzlement; in annoyance; in annoyance as much as confusion; in apology; in apparent astonishment; in apparent bemusement; in apparent concentration; in apparent concern; in apparent shock; in astonishment; in awful concentration; in baffled exasperation; in bafflement; in bemusement; in bewildered astonishment; in bewildered confusion; in bewilderment; in blank incomprehension; in brief uncertainty; in brooding disapproval; in clear confusion; in cold fury; in commiseration; in complete bewilderment; in complete confusion; in complete surprise; in concentration; in concern; in confusion; in confusion and puzzlement; in consideration; in consternation; in contemplation; in curiosity; in deep concentration; in deep concern; in deep reflection; in denial; in desperate concentration; in disagreement; in disappointment; in disapproval; in disbelief; in disgust; in dismay; in dismayed confusion; in displeasure; in dissatisfaction; in distaste; in distress; in disturbed uncertainty; in drowsy puzzlement; in earnest; in earnest concentration; in empathy; in equal bemusement; in evident bewilderment; in evident consternation; in exasperation; in faint bewilderment; in faint disbelief; in faint enquiry; in fierce concentration; in frank bewilderment; in frank dismissal; in frustration; in genuine concern; in genuine confusion; in genuine puzzlement; in grand fashion; in grim irritation; in groggy confusion; in growing bewilderment; in growing concern; in gruff disapproval; in her attempt to remember; in her concentration to find the right words; in her delirium; in her effort to think straight; in her efforts to be coherent; in her efforts to understand what he was saying in her usual fashion; in hesitant concern; in his ignorance; in honest surprise; in horror; in immediate recognition; in impatience; in incomprehension; in incredulous disbelief; in indecision; in indignation; in inquiry; in intense anger; in intense concentration; in irritated confusion; in irritation; in memory; in mild dislike; in mild reproof; in mild surprise; in mock affront; in mock anger; in mock annoyance; in mock concentration; in mock confusion; in mock consternation; in mock despair; in mock disapproval; in mock disgruntlement; in mock disgust; in mock dismay; in mock displeasure; in mock exasperation; in mock outrage; in mock pensiveness; in mock reproof; in mock seriousness; in mock severity; in mock sternness; in mock thoughtfulness; in mocking concern; in momentary concern; in momentary confusion; in momentary perplexity; in mystification; in obvious concern; in obvious confusion; in obvious disapproval; in obvious dismay; in obvious distaste; in obvious frustration; in obvious puzzlement; in obvious thought; in offense; in open confusion; in pain; in pained question; in perplexity; in pleased bewilderment; in polite concern; in preoccupation; in pretend irritation; in pretend preoccupation; in protest; in puzzled bewilderment; in puzzlement; in puzzlement and curiosity; in query; in question; in questioning denial; in quick comprehension; in quick concern; in ready concern; in real bewilderment; in real puzzlement; in rebuke; in recall; in receipt of the subtle criticism; in recognition; in recollection; in remembrance; in reproach; in reproof; in resentment; in resignation; in response; in response to (...); in return; in self-annoyance; in self-condemnation; in self-disapproval; in self-disgust; in sharp question; in sheer annoyance; in shock; in shocked confusion; in silence; in silent disbelief; in simulated consideration; in sincere contrition; in sincere incomprehension; in skepticism; in sleepy disorientation; in sleepy petulance; in sleepy protest; in slight annoyance; in slight bafflement; in some dismay; in some puzzlement; in speculation; in spite of (...); in startled anger; in stunned doubt; in sudden bewilderment; in sudden concern; in sudden consternation; in sudden dismay; in sudden indecision; in sudden mingled dismay and amusement; in sudden suspicion; in sudden uncertainty; in supposed puzzlement; in surprise; in surprise and puzzlement; in surprised confusion; in suspicion; in swift anger; in swift concern; in sympathetic consideration; in sympathy; in thought; in thoughtful concentration; in total concentration; in trepidation; in unaccustomed displeasure; in unaccustomed thought; in unappreciative response; in understanding; in utter bemusement; in utter bewilderment; in utter frustration; in utter perplexity; in vague disapproval; in vague dismay; in vexation; in visible surprise; in wariness; in warning; in what appeared to be genuine confusion; in what could have been confusion; in worry; in youthful concentration; with a fierce mask of concentration; with a hint of bewilderment; with a mixture of apprehension and bewilderment; with a mixture of concern and comprehension; with a mixture of surprise and query; with a sinking feeling; with a sinking heart; with a touch of petulance; with absorption; with academic concentration; with admiration; with adolescent ferocity; with amazement; with amused confusion; with amusement; with an affectionate fierceness; with an effort; with an immediate frisson of impatience; with an unpleasant suspicion; with anger; with angry irritation; with animosity; with annoyance; with anxiety; with anxious concentration; with apparent concern; with assumed concentration; with barely contained annoyance; with bewilderment; with chagrin; with clear disapproval; with comical emphasis; with concentration; with concern; with confused concentration; with confusion; with consternation; with curiosity; with deep irritation; with disappointment; with disapproval; with disbelief; with discomfort; with disconcertion; with discontent; with disgust; with dismay; with displeasure; with dissatisfaction; with distaste; with distrust; with doubt; with effort; with embarrassment; with evident displeasure; with exasperation; with faint concern; with feigned concern; with feigned puzzlement; with foreboding; with frustration; with frustration tempered by a feeling of awe; with genuine puzzlement; with grand dismay; with gratifying concentration; with great ferocity; with great seriousness; with heavy disapproval; with his own preoccupations; with hostility; with immediate sympathy; with impatience; with impatient exasperation; with incomprehension; with increased concern; with incredulity; with inner satisfaction; with intense concentration; with inward glee; with irritation; with maternal pique; with mild concern; with misery in her heart; with mock concern; with mock distaste; with mock ferocity; with mock indignation.; with mock seriousness; with mock severity; with mock sternness; with narrowed curiosity; with perplexity; with pleasure; with pretended concentration; with puzzlement; with quick impatience;

with real concern; with regret; with self-disgust; with sharp scrutiny; with sheer disbelief; with simulated concern; with sincerity; with some surprise; with sudden anxiety; with sudden apprehension; with sudden concern; with sudden fierceness; with sudden uncertainty; with surprise; with surprising seriousness; with suspicion; with that deliberate calm of his; with the effort concentration took; with the effort of concentrating on (...); with the effort of concentration; with the effort of explaining; with the effort of remembering; with the effort of trying to deal with (...); with the effort of trying to remember; with the effort to concentrate; with the effort to find words; with the effort to focus; with the effort to maintain control; with the effort to recall; with the knowledge that (...); with the memory; with the struggle to find the right words; with the tension of her thoughts; with thinly-veiled irritation; with thought; with uncertainty; with unease; with uneasiness; with unmistakable disapproval; with vexation; with worry; with youthful concentration.

VERB USAGE EXAMPLES

Hearing the words, he frowned with sudden concern.

Karen frowned pointedly at him for even suggesting such a thing.

She stared up at him, frowning in a puzzled sort of way.

Frowning at the chattering partygoers as the passed by, Jay knocked back his glass of champagne with a single gulp.

She frowned absently, gazing off into the distance at the rock-strewn landscape.

4
GAPE

1. Noun Form

1.1 - Noun Synonyms

dropped jaw; goggle eyes; look of astonishment; look of awe; look of surprise; look of wonder; mouth agape; mouth wide open; open mouth; saucered eyes.

1.2 - Adjectives

D
dark; disbelieving; dumbfounded.

E
enormous.

F
foolish; full-blown.

G
greedy.

H
half; hollow.

I
involuntary.

L
little; loose.

O
open-mouthed.

P
prodigious.

R
regrettable; round-eyed.

S
slack-jawed; slight; small; staring; stunned.

T
tiny; toothless.

W
whopper-jawed; wide-eyed.

1.3 - Noun + Prepositional Phrases

gape of astonishment; gape of awe; gape of disbelief; gape of horror; gape of indignation; gape of outrage; gape of shock; gape of surprise; gape of wonder.

1.4 - Verbs: Gape as Object

Character (I / He / She) as Subject
form (a gape); give (him) (a gape); have (a gape); have (a gape) at (him).

Facial Constituents as Subject
(I) feel (mouth) (gape) open*; (I) feel (mouth) (gape)*; (jaw) drop in (a gape); (lips) form (a gape); (lips) freeze in/into (a gape); (mouth) drop open in (a gape); (mouth) fall open in (a gape); (mouth) fly open in (a gape); (mouth) form (a gape); (mouth) open in (a gape).

NOUN USAGE EXAMPLES

He couldn't help but give a gape of astonishment at his sister's words.

Helen's mouth dropped open in a gape.

He smirked at her round-eyed gape.

As he entered the room, her lips formed a dumbfounded gape.

Wilma struggled to refrain from laughing at John's gape of indignation.

2. Verb Form

2.1 - Verb Synonyms

gawk; goggle; look saucer-eyed; ogle; peer; regard with awe; rubberneck; show astonishment; stare; stare at goggle-eyed; stare in astonishment; stare open-mouthed; wonder.

2.2 - Adverbs

A
actually*; almost*; angrily; awkwardly.

B
badly; bemusedly; blackly; blatantly; bleakly; breathlessly; briefly.

C
curiously.

D
dangerously; darkly; definitely; disbelievingly; disturbingly.

F
faintly; finally*; foolishly; fractionally; frankly*; fully.

G
gradually.

H
happily; helplessly; horribly; hugely; hungrily.

I
incredulously; indignantly; inelegantly.

L
literally*.

M
merely*; momentarily; mutely.

N
nearly*; nervously.

O
obviously; ominously; only slightly; only*; openly; owlishly.

P
partially; partly*; permanently; positively*; practically*; probably*; promptly*.

R
really*; rudely.

S
silently; similarly; simply*; slightly; speechlessly; stupidly; suddenly.

U
unbelievingly; undisguisedly; usually*.

W
widely; wildly; wordlessly.

2.3 - Adverbials of Emotion, Feeling, Mental State, and Response

in a kind of horror; in a most intriguing fashion; in a most unladylike manner; in a perfect, shocked O; in a tired yawn*; in a very distracting manner; in a very unladylike fashion; in admiration; in amazement; in an approving manner; in an unexpected yawn*; in astonished delight; in astonishment; in astonishment and disappointment; in awe; in bewilderment; in blank confusion; in blank incomprehension; in clear surprise; in confusion; in dawning horror; in disbelief; in dismay; in disorientated surprise; in exaggerated shock; in horrified fascination; in horror; in indignation; in obvious outrage; in open admiration; in open curiosity; in open disbelief; in outrage; in recognition and astonishment; in sheer amazement; in sheer astonishment.; in shock; in silence; in silent disbelief; in spontaneous surprise; in startled surprise; in startled wonder; in stunned amazement; in stunned disbelief; in stunned silence; in stunned surprise; in stupefied silence; in sudden shock; in surprise; in wide-eyed astonishment; in wonder; with admiration; with amazement; with astonishment; with astonishment and indignation; with awe; with disbelief; with embarrassment; with glassy-eyed wonder; with horror; with indignation; with recognition; with satisfying incredulity; with surprise; with undisguised fascination.

VERB USAGE EXAMPLES

In shock, she gaped at the phone.

Sarah's eyes brightened and her mouth gaped.

Horrified, Lucy gaped as the wild animal trotted away.

He gaped at her in silent disbelief.

Brian felt his mouth gape widely.

5
GLARE

1. Noun Form

1.1 - Noun Synonyms

a dark look; a dirty look; a menacing look; a nasty look; a piercing stare; an angry look; evil eye; fixing gaze; frown; glower; lower; scowl; scrutinization.

1.2 - Adjectives

A
abbreviated; abrupt; accompanying; accusative; accusatory; accusing; acerbic; acid; acidic; acrimonious; adamant; admiring; admonishing; admonitory; adversarial; affectionate; affronted; aggravated; aggressive; aggrieved; agitated; agonizing; all-encompassing; amused; angry; annihilating; annoyed; annoying; another; answering; antagonistic; apprehensive; arctic; arrogant; assessing; astonished; astute; austere; authoritarian; authoritative; autocratic.

B
back-off; bad-tempered; baffled; baleful; barbed; basilisk-like; beady; beady-eyed; beleaguered; belligerent; best; betrayed; better; bewildered; big; bitter; black; black-belt-trained; black-eyed; blatant; blazing; bleak; bleak-eyed; blinding; blistering; bloodshot; bloodthirsty; blue-eyed; bold; boyish; brassy; brazen; brief; bristling; brittle; brooding; brotherly; brown-eyed; brutal; burning; burning-eyed.

C
calculating; cast-iron; castigating; caustic; cautionary; cautioning; censorious; censuring; chagrined; challenging; chastising; chiding; chilling; chilly; clinical; cobalt; cold; cold-eyed; collective; combative; commanding; compelling; concentrated; concerned; condemnatory; condemning; condescending; confident; confrontational; confused; consistent; constant; contemptuous; continued; continuing; controlled; cool; corresponding; corrosive; covert; cranky; crazed; crippling; critical; crotchety; crucifying; crude; cruel; crushing; curious; cursory; curt; customary; cutting; cynical.

D

dagger-eyed; dagger-like; dagger-sharp; dagger-worthy; daggered; damp; dampening; dangerous; dare-to-pity-me; daring; dark; dark-browed; dark-eyed; daunting; deadly; deadpan; death; death-adder; death-eye; death-ray; debilitating; decent; deep; defensive; defiant; definite; deliberate; demanding; demeaning; demonic; departing; derisive; desperate; determined; devastating; devilish; dignified; direct; direful; dirty; disappointed; disapproving; disbelieving; discomfited; discouraging; disdainful; disgruntled; disguised; disgusted; disinterested; dismissing; dismissive; disparaging; displeased; distasteful; distrustful; disturbing; dog-with-a-bone; dogged; doleful; don't-argue-with-me; don't-count-me-out; don't-even-go-there; don't-get-any-ideas; don't-mess-with-me; don't-push-me; don't-touch-me; don't-you-dare; double-barreled; double-dare-you; doubtful; down-boy; down-the-nose; downright; droll; drop-dead; drunken; dry; dubious; dueling; dull; dumbfounded; dusky-cheeked.

E

eagle-eyed; eerie; emasculating; embarrassed; embittered; emerald-eyed; emphasizing; emphatic; endearing; endless; enigmatic; enraged; envious; equal; even; evil; evil-eyed; exaggerated; exasperated; expectant; expected; explosive; expressive; extra-resentful; eye-blinking.

F

faint; familiar; famous; fanatical; fearsome; feigned; feisty; feminine; feral; ferocious; fever-glazed; fierce; fierce-eyed; fiery; filthy; final; fire-laden; firm; first-rate; fish-eyed; fishy-eyed; fix-this; fixed; flaming; flat; fleeting; flinty; flinty-eyed; flushed; forbidding; forceful; formidable; forthright; fractious; frank; frazzled; freezing; friendly; frightened; frightening; frigid; frosty; frowning; frozen; frustrated; full; full-blooded; full-fledged; full-on; fulminating; fulsome; fuming; furious; further; furtive.

G

galled; garish; ghastly; gibing; gimlet-eyed; glacial; glassy-eyed; glazed; gleeful; glimmering; glittering; gloating; glowering; go-to-hell; goaded; good; good-natured; green-eyed; grim; grim-eyed; gunslinger.

H

habitual; half-hearted; half-rueful; harassed; hard; hard-as-nails; hard-edged; hard-eyed; hardened; hardening; harsh; hate-filled; hateful; hating; haughty; hawkish; head-on; heartfelt; hearty; heated; heavy; hellish; helpless; high-intensity; homicidal; honey-eyed; horrified; hostile; hot; hot-cheeked; hot-poker; how-could-you; huffy; huge; hundred-volt; hungry; hurt; hypnotic.

I

I-can-handle-this; I-don't-believe-you; I-told-you-so; ice-blue; ice-cold; ice-cool; ice-gray; icy; icy-blue; icy-hot; identical; if-looks-could-kill; immovable; impassioned; impatient; impenetrable; imperious; implicit; imploring; imposing; impotent; incendiary; incensed; incinerating; incisive; incredible; incredulous; indifferent; indignant; indulgent; ineffectual; inevitable; infamous; infuriated; inimical; initial; insane; insolent; instant; insulting; intended; intense; interrogative; intimidating; intolerable; intrusive; irate; irked; irritable; irritated; irritating.

J

jaundiced; jealous; joy-killing; judgmental; just.

K

keep-quiet; kick-butt; killer; knock-me-over; knowing.

L

ladylike; lancing; laser-hot; laser-like; last; lazy; lengthy; less-than-maternal; less-than-pleased; lethal; liberated; lightning-sharp; little; livid; loathing; locked; long; lord-of-the-range; loving; lowering.

M

mad; maddened; magnificent; malevolent; malicious; malignant; manic; masculine; matching; maternal; mean; mean-eyed; mean-girl; meaningful; measured; measuring; menacing; merciless; mere; mesmerizing; mighty; mild; militant; minatory; mischievous; mock; mock-angry; mock-disparaging; mock-exasperated; mock-ferocious; mock-indignant; mock-suspicious; mocking; molten; momentary; moody; most-heated; mulish; murderous; mute; muted; mutinous.

N

naked; narrow; narrow-eyed; narrowed; nasty; nettled; no-excuses; no-nonsense; nonstop; not-buying-it; not-in-this-lifetime; nudging; numbing.

O

obsidian; obstinate; obvious; occasional; off-putting; offended; offensive; ominous; one-eyed; open; out-and-out; outraged; outright; over-the-shoulder; overconfident; overwhelming; owlish; own.

P

pained; painful; paint-stripping; panicked; parental; parting; patented; paternal; peeved; penetrating; peremptory; perpetual; petulant; philistine; piercing; pinched; pitiless; plausible; play-along-with-me; playful; please-don't-talk-anymore; pleased; pointed, poison-tainted; poison-tipped; poisonous; positive; possessive; potent; powerful; practiced; predatory; pretend; princess-tocowhand; private; probing; proprietary; protective; proud; psyche-out; punishing; punitive; puritanical; pursed-lip; put-out; puzzled.

Q

quarrelsome; quavery; quelling; questioning; quick; quizzical.

R

rabbit-caught-in-headlights; raw; razor-eyed; razor-like; razor-sharp; rebellious; recriminating; red-faced; red-hot; regal; relentless; remorseless; remote; renewed; renowned; repressive; reprimanding; reproachful; reproving; repulsed; resentful; respectful; responding; resulting; retina-searing; revealing; revolted; rheumy-eyed; riotous; rock-hard; rolling-eyed; rude; rueful; ruthless.

S

same; sarcastic; sardonic; satirical; saturnine; saucy; savage; scalding; scalpel-like; scandalized; scary; scathing; scolding; scorching; scornful; scowling; screw-you; scrunchy-nosed; scything; searching; searing; secret; seething; self-righteous; semi-irritated; serious; several; severe; shark-like; sharp; sharp-edged; sharp-eyed; she-isn't-available; shocked; shocking; shoot-to-kill; short; short-lived; shrewd; shriveling; sidelong; sideward; sideways; signature; significant; silencing; silent; silly-looking; simmering; simple; simultaneous; single; singular; sinister; sizzling; skeptical; skin-melting; slanting; slashing; slate-eyed; slate-gray; sleepy; sleepy-eyed; slight; slit-eyed; slitted; slitted-eye; slivered; smiling; smoky; smoldering; smug; sneery; sober; solid; somber; soul-crushing; sour; sparkly-eyed; speculative; spiteful; squinty; squinty-eyed; stabbing; stark; startled; startling; stay-where-you-are; steady; steel; steel-eyed; steel-like; steely; steely-eyed; stern; stinging; stolid; stone-cold; stone-eyed; stony; stormy; strident; strong; stubborn; studied; stun-gun; stunning; subzero; sudden; suffocating; sulfuric; sulky; sullen; supercilious; superior; surly; suspicious; sweeping; swift.

T

take-charge; take-no-prisoners; tawny-eyed; tearful; teary-eyed; teasing; teenage; telling; telltale; ten-kilowatt; ten-second; tense; terrible; terrific; territorial; testy; therapist-to-patient; thin-lidded; thin-lipped; this-is-your-fault; threatening; thunderous; thunderstruck; thundery; tigerish; tight; tight-lipped; tolerant; torrid; touch-me-not; tough; toughest; towering; trademark; triumphant; truculent; turbulent; twin.

U

unaccustomed; unamused; unbearable; unblinking; unbreakable; uncomfortable; uncompromising; uncontrolled; unconvinced; underbrowed; uneasy; unexpected; unfair; unfamiliar; unfeminine; unflinching; unforgiving; unfriendly; unholy; unkind; unmistakable; unrelenting; unrepentant; unsmiling; unsmitten; unsparing; unwavering; unyielding; urgent; usual.

V

vehement; vengeful; venomous; vexed; vicious; vile; vindictive; violent; viperous; virulent; vitriolic; vivid; volatile; vulnerable.

W

warning; waspish; watchful; watery; watery-eyed; weak; well-chosen; well-deserved; well-placed; wet; what's-your-problem; white-hot; white-lipped; wicked; wide-eyed; wild; wild-eyed; wildman; wilting; wintry; wish-you-were-dead; withering; wordless; world-class; worried; wounded; wrathful; wry.

Y

you're-not-helping; you-are-dead-meat.

1.3 - Noun + Prepositional Phrases

glare of a serial killer; glare of a wild animal that (...); glare of a woman who (...); glare of a woman wild with jealousy; glare of abhorrence; glare of accusation and betrayal; glare of affront and fury; glare of an approaching juggernaut; glare of an offended man; glare of an ornery bull; glare of anger; glare of angry defiance; glare of animosity; glare of annoyance; glare of antagonism; glare of arctic intensity; glare of azure blue anger; glare of barely masked dislike; glare of biting derision; glare of blank amazement; glare of censure; glare of challenge (in her eyes); glare of condemnation; glare of contempt; glare of death; glare of defiance (in her eyes); glare of disapproval; glare of disbelief; glare of disdain; glare of disgust; glare of dislike; glare of frank irritation; glare of frustration; glare of fulminating loathing; glare of furious contempt; glare of furious reproach; glare of fury; glare of goaded anger; glare of gray eyes; glare of hatred; glare of her anger; glare of his attacking eyes; glare of her own; glare of her scrutiny; glare of her shocked horror; glare of hers/his; glare of his angry eyes; glare of his angry gaze; glare of his bright golden eyes; glare of his disapproval; glare of his (dark) eyes; glare of his fierce scrutiny; glare of his gaze; glare of his look; glare of his panther eyes; glare of his scrutiny; glare of hostility (in her eyes); glare of impatience; glare of indignation; glare of infuriation; glare of injured dignity; glare of instant death; glare of intense dislike; glare of intense scrutiny; glare of intent (in his gaze); glare of loathing; glare of love (in his eyes); glare of moral outrage; glare of outrage; glare of promised retribution; glare of pure hatred; glare of pure loathing; glare of rebellion; glare of recrimination; glare of reproach; glare of reproof; glare of resentment; glare of seething dislike; glare of sorts; glare of such bitter fury; glare of such cold distaste; glare of such intense hatred; glare of such loathing; glare of such murderous rage; glare of such revulsion and hostility; glare of such total contempt; glare of suspicion and dislike; glare of suspicion and hostility; glare of tears; glare of thinly disguised loathing; glare of those cold blue eyes; glare of those dangerous gray eyes; glare of those deep gray eyes; glare of those fierce black eyes; glare of those golden eyes; glare of those luminous eyes; glare of triumph; glare of undisguised dislike; glare of warning.

1.4 - Noun Phrases

a bit of a glare; a couple of glares; a deepening of his glare; a/the hint of a glare; a wallop of a glare; just shy of a glare; one heck of a glare; several long moments of his glare; something just short of a glare; something of a glare; the beam of his angry glare; the brunt of his angry glare; the burn of his glare; the cold burn of his glare; the cold fire of his glare; the combined weight of the glare; the condemnation of his glare; the cruel burn of his furious glare; the crystalline intensity of his glare; the direction of his offended glare; the effect of his contemptuous glare; the ferocity of his glare; the fierceness of his glare; the filthiest of glares; the force of his angry glare; the force of his glare; the force of his killer glare; the frightening force of his glare; the full benefit of his angriest glare; the full benefit of his censuring glare; the full benefit of his contemptuous glare; the full blast of his outraged glare; the full blaze of his furious glare; the full brunt of his displeased glare; the full brunt of his glare; the full force of his burning glare; the full force of his glare; the full force of one of his glares; the full icy force of his baleful glare; the full impact of his warning glare; the full power of his glare; the full splendor of his glare; the full wattage of his heated glare; the full weight of his glare; the heat of his glare; the hot anger of his glare; the hot sulfur of his glare; the ice of his glare; the icy blaze of his glare; the impact of his glare; the increased ferocity of his smoldering glare; the intensity of his glare; the intensity of his predatory glare; the kind of glare; the savagery of his glare; the savagest of glares; the severity of his glare; the sort of glare; the steadiness of his glare; the strength of his glare; the violence of his glare; the worst of his glare(s); those dark eyes of his glare.

1.5 - Verbs: Glare as Subject

Standalone Verbs
compound; cut (deep); darken; deepen; die; disappear; fade; falter; intensify; lighten; return; sharpen; soften; subside; wither; wither away.

Miscellaneous as Object
accompany [something]; amuse (him); answer (him); arrow (his way); assert [something]; become (ferocious / menacing / more intense / tinged with wariness); belie (other emotion/thumping heart); bore into (him); bounce off (him / his impervious profile / the back of his head); break up (into little pieces); brim with (resentment); burn (him); burn (with smoldering resentment); burn into (him); burn through (him); carry (exasperation); catch (him) off guard; catch and hold (him) transfixed; challenge (him); chill (him) (to the marrow / to the bone); clash with (his); come (fierce and instant / his way); confirm

[something]; convey (her disagreement / a silent warning); convict (him); cut (him) off (in midsentence); cut across (crowd); cut off (his words); cut through (air / him / his astonishment); dare (him) to (...); darken (face / features); dazzle (him); defy (his claim); die (from her eyes); die out of (eyes); differ from (the glares she'd given him in the past); discourage (him); distort (features); douse (his ardor); draw (brows together); drift from (him) to (her); drill into (him / his back); drive deeper into (him); drop (temperature in the room by ten degrees); effect (him); elicit [something]; emanate from (her); emit (danger signals) from (him); emphasize [something]; end (debate); exclude (any agreement); fade from (face / eyes); fix on (him); flick over (him); focus on (him); follow (him); freeze (him); gain in (intensity); get (meaner / worse); give (him pause / no quarter); glaze over into (something far more hostile); grow (even darker / even more ferocious / harder); hit (him); impale (him); increase (tenfold); indicate [something]; indicate that (...); insinuate [something]; inspire (fear); interrupt (him); jump to (him); keep (him silent); knife through (him); lance through (him); land on (him); laser holes through (him); last (seconds); leave (him); leave (its mark); level on (him / face); lock on (him / his / face); lose (a little power / all of its power / its force / some of its fierceness); make (him) (angry / blink); match (her own / his); meet (his); melt (his certainty / resolve); move over (him); nail (him); narrow into (slits); narrow on (him); pause on (him); penetrate (him); pierce (him); ping-pong between (him) and (her); pour over (him); proclaim [something]; promise (retribution); prove (he wasn't intimidated); provoke (immediate response); push (him back a step or two); radiate (darts in his direction / disapproval); rake (him); return in (full force); sail (in his direction); sap (him of energy); savage (him); say (more than enough / what words failed to); scare (him) off; scorch (him); sear (him); sear into (his flesh); sear over (him); search (his); send (him packing); shift between (him) and (her); shoot (daggers); shoot out of (eyes); show [something]; silence (him); singe (emotions / heart); sizzle over (him); slant (in his direction); slide away; slide away from (him); slow (him) down; smolder with (barely leashed anger); speak (for her / volumes); spin (him) back to (conversation); stab through (him); stay (in place); stay on (him); stop (him) (cold / in midsentence); stop (him) from (asking any more questions); strike (him); suggest [something]; surprise (him); sweep around (crowd); sweep over (him); swing (back) to (him); switch (back) to (him); swivel to (him); take (him) by surprise; target (him); tell (him) [something]; threaten to (melt him); transfer itself to (him); transfix (him); travel from (him) to (her); turn (calculating / lethal / mutinous / thoughtful / uglier); turn to (acid); unnerve (him); warn (him); warn (him) off; wither (him) (where he stood).

1.6 - Verbs: Glare as Object

Character (I / He / She) as Subject
aim (a glare) (in his direction); aim (a glare) at (him); avoid (a glare) from (him); blast (him) with (a glare); bounce (a glare) off (mirror); can't resist

throwing (a glare) at (him); cast (a glare); cast (a glare) at (him); cast (him) (a glare); content (myself) with (a glare) at (him); cut (him) off with (a glare); deal (him) (a glare); deliver (a glare) (that ...); direct (a glare) (his way); direct (a glare) at (him); divide (a glare) between (both of them); draw (a glare) from (him); drill (him) with (a glare); earn (a glare); earn (a glare) from (him); encounter (a glare) from (him); face (him) with (a glare); favor (him) with (a glare); fire (a glare) at (him); fire (him) (a glare); fire back (a glare) (of my own); fix (a glare) on (him); fix (him) with (a glare); flash (a glare) (his way); flash (him) (a glare); flick (a glare) at (him); flick (him) (a glare); fling (a glare) at (him); force (a glare) at (him); get (a glare) for (my trouble); get (a glare) from (him); gift (him) with (a glare); give (a glare); give (a glare) to (him); give (him) (a glare); hurl (a glare) at (him); impale (him) with (a glare); lance (a glare) at (him); laser (a glare) at (him); laser (him) with (a glare); level (a glare) (in his direction); level (a glare) at (him); level (a glare) on (him); lower (a glare) at (him); manage (a glare); meet (his glare) with (my own); muster up (a glare); nail (him) with (a glare); net (a glare) from (him); offer up (a glare); parry (his glare); pause for (a glare) at (him); pin (him) with (a glare); produce (a glare) from (him); receive (a glare) for (something); receive (a glare) from (him); return (a glare) (of my own); risk (a glare); risk (a glare) at (him); send (a glare) (his way); send (a glare) toward(s) (him); shift (a glare) (back) to (something); shoot (a glare) around (room); shoot (a glare) at (him); shoot (a glare) from (across room); shoot (a glare) toward(s) (him); shoot (a glare) up at (him); shoot (him) (a glare); sizzle (a glare) (in his direction); skewer (him) with (a glare); slam (him) with (a glare); slant (a glare) at (him); slash (him) with (a glare); slice (a glare) at (him); slide (him) (a glare); snap (a glare) at (him); spare (a glare) for (him); spear (him) with (a glare); stop (him) short with (a glare); subject (him) to (a glare); summon up (a glare); supply (him) with (a glare); surprise (him) with (a glare) (instead of ...); swing (a glare) at (him); swivel (a glare) (his way); throw (a glare) at (him); throw (him) (a glare); throw back (a glare) (of my own); thrust (a glare) toward(s) (him); toss (a glare) (his way); transfix (him) with (a glare); treat (him) to (a glare); try (a glare) at (him); turn (a glare) on (him); turn on (him) (a glare); warrant (a glare) from (him); was given (a glare)*; was silenced by (a glare) from (him)*; wither under (a glare) from (him); won (myself) (a glare) from (him).

Eyes as Subject

attack (him) with (a glare); cast (him) (a glare); drill (him) with (a glare); fix (him) with (a glare); flash (him) (a glare); give (him) (a glare); level (a glare) at (him); manage (a glare); nail (him) with (a glare); narrow in/into/to (a glare); pin (him) with (a glare); return (his glare); shoot (him) with (a glare); skewer (him) with (a glare); slant (a glare) at (him); spear (him) with (a glare); transfix (him) with (a glare); turn (a glare) on (him).

NOUN USAGE EXAMPLES

As Ashley strode toward the unkempt man, she speared him with an unholy glare.

Her eyes narrowed into a glare of suspicion.

Trent shot a menacing glare his brother's way for failing to heed his words.

Not even his fiercest glare would deter her from voicing her outrage to the ship's captain.

The condemnation of his glare had Jennifer reeling, the retort dying on her lips.

2. Verb Form

2.1 - Verb Synonyms

bore into; come under scrutiny; fix on/upon; frown; glare down; glower; look angry; look menacingly at; lower; menace; mope; scowl; scrutinize; stare angrily; stare down; stare piercingly; sulk.

2.2 - Adverbs

A
accusingly; aggressively; angrily; antagonistically.

B
balefully; belligerently; bitterly; blackly; blankly; blearily; bluntly; briefly; broodingly.

C
challengingly; coldly; contemptuously; covetously; crossly.

D
dangerously; darkly; defeatedly; defensively; defiantly; dementedly; derisively; desperately; determinedly; directly (at/up at); disagreeably; disapprovingly; disbelievingly; disdainfully; disgustedly; disparagingly; distractedly; dubiously; dyspeptically.

E

emptily; enviously; evilly; exasperatedly; expectantly.

F

ferociously; fiercely; fixedly; forbiddingly; forcefully; formidably; frantically; frostily; frustratedly; furiously.

G

glacially; glaring; grimly; groggily.

H

harshly; hatefully; haughtily; hazily; heatedly; helplessly; hostilely; hotly; hungrily.

I

icily; immediately; immovably; impatiently; impotently; incredulously; indignantly; ineffectively; inimically; insolently; intently; interrogatingly; irritably.

J

jealously.

L

levelly.

M

madly; malevolently; maliciously; meaningfully; meaningly; menacingly; merely; mildly; miserably; mockingly; momentarily; moodily; morosely; mournfully; mulishly; murderously; mutely; mutinously.

O

ominously; only slightly; openly.

P

painfully; playfully; pointedly; profoundly; proudly; pugilistically; pugnaciously.

R

rebelliously; relentlessly; repressively; reproachfully; reprovingly; resentfully; revengefully; rigidly; ruefully.

S

savagely; scornfully; searchingly; severely; sharply; sightlessly; silently; sleepily; speechlessly; spitefully; steadily; sternly; stonily; stormily; stubbornly; suddenly; sulkily; sullenly; suspiciously; swiftly.

T

tearfully; thoughtfully; threateningly; triumphantly.

U

unblinkingly; uncertainly; unhappily; unrelentingly; unrepentantly; unwelcomingly.

V

vehemently; venomously; viciously; vindictively.

W

warily; warningly; wildly; witheringly; wordlessly; wrathfully.

2.3 - Adverbials of Emotion, Feeling, Mental State, and Response

in a decidedly unwelcoming manner; in a frankly murderous fashion; in a frustrated fury; in a hostile fashion; in a manner that spoke volumes; in a way that/which (...); in accusing disbelief; in admonishment; in affront; in an agony of frustration; in an uncompromising fashion; in anger; in angry frustration; in angry pride; in angry resentment; in anguish; in annoyance; in appalled revulsion; in bad temper; in baffled anger; in bitter anger; in blame or censure; in blank dismay; in brooding irritation; in challenge; in cold fury; in confusion; in dawning dismay; in deathly fury; in deep and mounting frustration; in defiance; in defiant challenge; in determined outrage; in disbelief; in disgust; in dislike; in displeasure; in distaste; in exasperation; in frank disgust; in frustrated defiance; in frustration; in furious bafflement; in furious reproof; in fury; in futile resentment; in growing fury; in hatred and frustration; in helpless anger; in helpless frustration; in helpless fury; in helpless pain and fury; in helpless rage; in helpless, impotent rage; in his uncompromising manner; in horror; in hostile silence*; in icy anger; in impotent fury; in impotent rage; in impotent silence*; in incredulous scorn; in indignation; in irritation; in mild exasperation; in mock anger; in mock annoyance; in mock concern; in mock disgust; in mock dismay; in mock exasperation; in mock indignation; in mock irritation; in mock outrage; in mock reproach; in mock severity; in mocking silence*; in mounting frustration; in mute exasperation; in mute frustration; in mute resentment; in obvious aggravation; in obvious anger; in obvious frustration; in obvious outrage; in open affront; in open amazement; in open challenge; in open defiance; in open dislike; in outrage; in pure frustration; in pure rage; in rebellious defiance; in reply; in response; in return; in righteous wrath; in savage triumph; in seething outrage; in self-defense; in self-disgust; in sheer disgruntlement; in shifty-eyed malevolence; in shock; in silence*; in silent defiance; in silent loathing; in silent rage; in simmering distaste; in speechless contempt; in speechless indignation; in stony silence*; in stubborn silence*; in such anger; in sudden anger; in sudden fury; in sudden temper; in surly defiance; in surprise; in terrible anger; in that implacable way; in tight silence*; in total exasperation; in total frustration; in towering fury; in undisguised fury; in undisguised resentment; in utter disgust; in utter frustration; in utter rage; in warning; in wordless reproach; with a hate-filled condemnation; with a kind of pained intensity; with a kind of unholy rage; with a mix of frustration and fascination; with a mixture of accusation and bewilderment; with a mixture of defiance and confusion; with a mixture of disbelief and slowly gathering rage; with a mixture of fury and disbelief; with a mixture of fury and regret; with a mixture of scorn and downright anger; with a rage almost equal to his own; with a rising sense of mutiny; with a warning look; with accusation and disdain; with acute dislike; with all her might; with all the fury she could muster; with all the fury of a caged animal; with amused accusation; with an all-consuming rage; with an icy intensity; with anger and disapproval; with anger and suspicion; with angry belligerence; with angry disbelief; with animosity; with apparent annoyance; with baffled exasperation; with barely concealed amazement; with barely suppressed hostility; with bitter contempt; with black rage; with black resentment; with bristling hatred and fury; with cold contempt; with cold fury; with contempt; with deep hatred; with deep resentment; with defiance; with defiant fury; with determination; with disappointment; with disbelief; with disgruntlement; with disgust; with dislike; with distaste; with distrust and dislike; with dogged dislike; with every ounce of anger she could dredge up; with every ounce of loathing that she felt; with exaggerated distaste; with fervent concern; with fierce concern; with fierce dislike; with fright; with frustrated anger; with frustration and desire; with furious contempt; with fury; with glacial indifference; with grim intent; with hard defiance; with hatred; with heartfelt malice; with hostile dislike; with hostile unwelcome; with hostility; with hurt and accusation; with ill-concealed exasperation; with impotent anger; with impotent fury; with impotent hostility; with impotent rage; with incredulity; with indignation; with intense dislike; with irritation; with jealousy; with loathing; with malice; with malicious intent; with menacing hate; with mock censure; with mock ferocity; with mock fierceness; with more fury than (she had thought herself capable of); with more malevolence than (she had ever seen); with neon intensity; with no small amount of envy; with obvious impatience; with open contempt and hostility; with open disapproval; with open dislike; with open hostility; with open venom; with outrage; with outrage and dislike; with patent venom; with pure dislike; with quiet stubbornness; with rage; with raw frustration; with real loathing; with red-eyed intensity; with renewed venom; with resentful anger; with resentful dislike; with resentment; with resentment and frustration; with rising anger; with savage resentment; with scornful dislike; with seething frustration; with simmering resentment; with smoldering disapproval; with so much fury (that ...); with so much hatred (that ...); with somber resentment; with some of his characteristic suspicion; with something akin to dislike; with subdued fury; with such concentrated fury (that ...); with such dislike (that ...); with such ferocity (that ...); with such fierceness (that ...); with such force (that ...); with such furious resolve that (...); with such fury; with such hatred (that ...); with such heated fury (that ...); with such hostility; with such intensity (that ...); with such intensity; with such loathing; with such menace (that ...); with such ominous intensity (that ...); with sudden fierceness; with sudden malevolence; with suspicion; with suspicion and menace; with the fierceness of an adversary; with the full force of her feelings; with the same fury (as before); with the same intensity as (he'd shown her); with the same undisguised enmity (as before); with thinly veiled hurt; with tight-lipped fury; with unconscious malevolence; with undiluted hatred; with undisguised hatred; with undisguised menace; with unexpected anger; with unexpected ruthlessness; with unguarded resentment; with unvoiced accusation; with venom; with venom and fury; with venomous dislike; with withering scorn; with wounded dislike.

VERB USAGE EXAMPLES

Kate glared at him with all the fury of a caged animal ready to pounce.

Glaring intently at Jake from across the room, she couldn't shake the growing resentment that bubbled inside her.

He glared down at the helpless boy, his icy blue eyes sparkling with malicious intent.

Fed up with waiting a second longer, Jason glared his impatience at his sister through the window of the BMW.

His boss glared at him with such dislike that Michael almost took a step back.

6
GLOWER

1. Noun Form

1.1 - Noun Synonyms

dirty look; fierce look; frown; glare; nasty look; scowl; threatening look.

1.2 - Adjectives

A

accusatory; accusing; adolescent; angry; another; answering; arched.

B

belligerent; best; blue-eyed; brief.

C

challenging; chastising; cold-eyed; condescending; contemptuous; cross.

D

daggered; damning; dark; darkest; defiant; disapproving; disgusted; displeasure-radiating.

E

exaggerated; exasperated.

F

faint; fake; familiar; ferocious; fierce; fiery; final; fleeting; forbidding; foreboding; formidable; frustrated; full-blown; full-fledged; full-on; fulminating; furious.

G

giant.

H

half; hazel-eyed; hostile; hypnotic.

I

I'm-not-amused; identical; imperial; instinctive; intent; intimidating; involuntary; irate; irritated.

L

last.

M

meaningful; menacing; mighty; mock; mock-stern; mocking.

N

narrow-eyed; normal.

O

officious; old-fashioned; over-the-shoulder.

P

part; patented; perpetual; positive; practiced; preoccupied; pretend; pretty.

Q

quick.

R

remote; reproachful.

S

savage; scornful; seductive; silent; skeptical; smoky; stern; sulky; sullen; suspicion-filled; suspicious.

T

threatening; thunderous; tigerish; tight-lipped.

U

unblinking; unhappy; usual.

V

venomous.

W

warning; well-deserved; wrathful.

1.3 - Noun + Prepositional Phrases

glower of a fierce predator; glower of a frown; glower of angry derision; glower of disapproval; glower of discontent; glower of epic proportions; glower of expectancy; glower of (his/her) own; glower of rage; glower of satisfaction.

1.4 - Noun Phrases

a bit of a glower; a weary imitation of his usual glower; a/the hint of a glower; (it was) more of a glower; something of a glower; the full impact of his glower; the open defiance of his glower.

1.5 - Verbs: Glower as Subject

Standalone Verbs
crumble; darken; deepen; grow; intensify; lessen; return; soften.

Eyes as Object
leave (eyes).

Face as Object
appear on (face); come over (face); furrow (face); leave (face); scud across (face).

Features as Object
crease (features); mar (features); transform (features).

1.6 - Verbs: Glower as Object

Character (I / He / She) as Subject
arrow (a glower) in (his direction); attempt (a glower) at (him); cut (him) (a glower); dagger (a glower) at (him); exchange (glowers); fix (him) with (a glower); flick (a glower) at (him); get (a glower) from (him)*; get (a glower) in; give (a glower); give (him) (a glower); have (a glower); ignore (a glower)*; level (a glower) in (his direction); nail (him) in (a glower); receive (a glower)*; send (a glower) (his way); send (a glower) in (his direction); send (him) (a glower); shoot (a glower) at (him); shoot (him) (a glower); throw (a glower) at (him); try (a glower).

Eyebrows / Brows as Subject
draw together in (a glower); draw together over (nose) in (a glower); join in (a glower); lower in (a glower).

Face or Character as Subject
(I) paste (a glower) on (face)*; (I) put (a glower) on (face)*; (I) rearrange (face) (back) into (a glower)*; collapse into (a glower); darken to (a glower); fold into (a glower); screw up in (a glower); turn into (a glower).

Facial Constituents as Subject
(expression) change to (a glower); (expression) shift into (a glower); (expression) turn into/to (a glower); (eyes) impale (him) with (a glower); (eyes) narrow into (a glower); (lips) twist into (a glower); (mouth) twist into (a glower).

NOUN USAGE EXAMPLES

Yasmine gave him an irritated glower.

He stood there, the hint of a glower on his face.

Her bright blue eyes impaled him with an unblinking glower.

She arrowed a glower in Michael's direction.

His face collapsed into an imperial glower.

2. Verb Form

2.1 - Verb Synonyms

frown; give a dirty look; glare; gloom; look black; look daggers; look fierce; lower; scorch with one's eyes; scowl; shoot a dirty look; stare; stare blackly; sulk.

2.2 - Adverbs

A
accusingly; actually*; affectionately; alternately*; alternatively*; angrily; antagonistically.

B
balefully; belligerently; blackly; briefly.

C
challengingly.

D
dangerously; darkly; defiantly; determinedly; disapprovingly; disbelievingly; disdainfully; distractingly.

E
evilly.

F
fairly; ferociously; fiercely; firmly; furiously.

G
gloomily; grimly.

H
harshly; haughtily; helplessly; humorously.

I
immediately; impatiently; imperiously; impotently; impressively; inadvertently; increasingly; indignantly; instantly.

L
literally.

M
meanly; menacingly; merely*; momentarily; moodily; morosely; mostly; mutinously.

N
normally*.

O
obviously; ominously; only*.

P
petulantly; pointedly; positively*; practically*; probably*; protestingly.

R
resentfully.

S

silently; simply*; simultaneously; slightly; sourly; sternly; suddenly; sulkily; sullenly; suspiciously.

T

tearfully; threateningly; thunderously.

U

unmistakably; usually*.

V

vaguely.

W

warningly; witheringly; wrathfully.

2.3 - Adverbials of Emotion, Feeling, Mental State, and Response

in disgust; in exasperation; in mutinous challenge; in protest; in reply; in response; in return; in silence; in silent warning; in warning; in what (he/she) hoped was a threatening manner; with anger; with dark and bitter purpose; with disapproval; with discontent; with disdain; with disgust; with distrust; with ferocity; with fierce intent; with frustration; with fury; with hostility; with rage; with rage and confusion; with so much anger; with suspicion.

VERB USAGE EXAMPLES

He glowered at her, his black brows lowered.

Still glowering, Simone marched into the auditorium.

She glowered with disapproval as he trotted through the door.

Quinn stuck out his lower lip and glowered at them both.

He glowered warningly across the table.

7
GRIMACE

1. Noun Form

1.1 - Noun Synonyms

contortion; frown; glare; look of distaste; moue; pained expression; scowl; sneer; twisted face; wry face.

1.2 - Adjectives

A

abashed; accompanying; acid; acknowledging; affectionate; agonized; amused; angry; anguished; annoyed; another; answering; apologetic; appalling; appealing; attractive; awful; awkward.

B

bad-tempered; baffled; bare-teethed; bemused; bitter; bleak; borderline; breathless; brief.

C

caustic; censorious; characteristic; charming; cheesy; childish; childlike; clownish; cold; comic; comical; commiserating; complicated; compulsive; concealed; confused; conspiratorial; contemptuous; contrite; cool; coy; cringing; crooked; cruel; curious; cutting; cynical.

D

dark; deadly; death-row; deep; defensive; deflated; delicate; deplorable; deprecating; deprecatory; deranged; derisive; derisory; derogatory; despairing; despondent; determined; direful; disappointed; disapproving; discreet; disdainful; disgruntled; disguised; disgusted; dismayed; dismissive; disoriented; disparaging; dispirited; displeased; disproving; dissatisfied; distasteful; distinct; distorted; distracted; disturbing; dour; downward; dramatic; dreadful; dry; dubious; dutiful.

E

earnest; ecstatic; eloquent; embarrassed; empathic; endearing; ensuing; envious; exaggerated; exasperated; excited; explicit; expressive.

F

faint; faintest; false; familiar; fastidious; fatherly; fearful; fearsome; fed-up; feigned; feral; ferocious; fierce; final; first; fixed; flat-line; fleeting; forbidding; forced; foul-looking; frequent; friendly; frightened; frightening; frightful; frowning; frustrated; full; full-face; funny; furious; furtive.

G

gap-toothed; ghastly; gibing; good-humored; good-natured; gorgeous; grotesque; guilty.

H

half; half-amused; half-bitter; half-comical; half-defiant; half-miserable; half-pained; half-smiling; half-wry; handsome; hard; heartfelt; helpless; hidden; hideous; hopeful; hopeless; horrible; horrified; horrifying; hostile; humorless; humorous.

I

I-hate-posing; identical; immediate; impatient; imploring; inconvenienced; indulgent; infinitesimal; inner; instant; instinctive; internal; involuntary; inward; ironic; irritable; irritated.

J

jealous; jutting.

K

knowing.

L

lame; last; laughing; lazy; lift-of-the-lip; light; likeable; little; long-suffering; lopsided.

M

mad; malevolent; manly; masculine; maternal; meaningful; meaningless; menacing; mental; mild; mirthless; mock; mock-doleful; mocking; momentary; mortified; mournful; mouth; musing; mutinous.

N

nasty; nauseated; near; nervous; next; noncommittal; now-or-never.

O

obdurate; obvious; odd; one-cornered; own.

P

pain-filled; pained; painful; painted-on; pale; part; partial; parting; passing; pathetic; peculiar; perpetual; playful; pointed; polite; posed; possessive; practiced; pretty; private; professional; proper; protesting; pseudo-comical; puckish.

Q

quelling; questioning; quick; quivering; quizzical.

R

rare; red-faced; regretful; rejecting; relieved; reluctant; reminiscent; remorseful; reproachful; reproving; resentful; resigned; respectful; responding; resulting; rictus-hard; ridiculous; rigid; rude; rueful.

S

sad; same; sarcastic; sardonic; satisfactory; savage; scary; scathing; scoffing; scornful; scowling; secret; self-chiding; self-condemnatory; self-conscious; self-contemptuous; self-denigrating; self-deprecating; self-deprecatory; self-deriding; self-derisive; self-derisory; self-disgusted; self-effacing; self-mocking; self-recriminatory; self-satisfied; serious; severe; shaky; shamed; shamefaced; shared; sheepish; shrewd; shuddering; sick; sickly; sighing; significant; silent; simple; single; sinister; skeptical; slight; slightest; sly; small; smiling; smoldering; sour; spiteful; startled; steely-eyed; stiff; strong; stubborn; subsequent; sudden; sullen; suppressed; surprised; swift; sympathetic.

T

taut; teasing; teeth-baring; telling; telltale; tender; tense; terrible; theatrical; thin; thin-lipped; thoughtful; threatening; tight; tight-lipped; tiny; tired; toothy; tormented; tortured; trademark; triumphant; troubled; twisted.

U

ugly; unaccepting; unattractive; uncertain; uncomfortable; uncompromising; unconscious; understanding; uneasy; unhappy; unimpressed; unladylike; unlovely; unmistakable; unnatural; unpleasant; unseen; unwilling; up-to-no-good; usual.

V

veiled; vexed; vicious; violent; vulpine.

W

warning; wary; watery; wavering; weak; weary; weird; whimsical; wide; wise; wobbly; woeful; world-weary; worried; worrisome; wrinkled-nose; wry.

Y

yellow-toothed.

1.3 - Noun + Prepositional Phrases

grimace of acceptance; grimace of agony; grimace of agreement; grimace of amazement; grimace of amused protest; grimace of amusement; grimace of anger; grimace of angry distaste; grimace of angry horror; grimace of anguish; grimace of annoyance; grimace of anticipation; grimace of anxiety; grimace of apology; grimace of appalled disgust; grimace of appreciation; grimace of assumed fear; grimace of astonished panic; grimace of aversion; grimace of bearlike rage; grimace of bemusement; grimace of bitter self-disgust; grimace of casual concern; grimace of complete comprehension; grimace of concentration; grimace of contempt; grimace of curiosity; grimace of cynicism; grimace of death; grimace of defeat; grimace of derision; grimace of desperation; grimace of determination; grimace of disagreement; grimace of disappointment; grimace of disapproval; grimace of disbelief; grimace of discomfiture; grimace of discomfort; grimace of discontent; grimace of discouragement; grimace of disdain; grimace of disgust; grimace of dislike; grimace of dismay; grimace of displeasure; grimace of distaste; grimace of distress; grimace of doubt; grimace of dread; grimace of ecstasy; grimace of embarrassment; grimace of exaggerated horror; grimace of exasperation; grimace of excruciating pain; grimace of extreme annoyance; grimace of false delight; grimace of fastidious distaste; grimace of fear; grimace of frustrated fury; grimace of frustration; grimace of frustration and rage; grimace of fury; grimace of genuine confusion; grimace of grief; grimace of guilt; grimace of hatred; grimace of helplessness; grimace of her lips*; grimace of hesitation; grimace of his mouth*; grimace of hurt; grimace of hurt surprise; grimace of impatience; grimace of inflicted pain; grimace of intense ecstasy; grimace of intense frustration; grimace of irony; grimace of irritation; grimace of love and pain; grimace of masculine commiseration; grimace of memory; grimace of misery; grimace of mock pain; grimace of mock horror; grimace of nauseated derision; grimace of need; grimace of pain; grimace of pain and anger; grimace of pained pleasure; grimace of pained regret; grimace of painful distaste; grimace of passion; grimace of personal repugnance; grimace of pleasurable pain; grimace of pleasure; grimace of protest; grimace of pseudo exasperation; grimace of pure anguish; grimace of pure disgust; grimace of pure hatred; grimace of pure masculine embarrassment; grimace of pure pain; grimace of pure pleasure; grimace of pure relief; grimace of quick distress; grimace of rage; grimace of recollection; grimace of refusal; grimace of regret; grimace of relief; grimace of reluctance; grimace of reluctant compassion; grimace of remembrance; grimace of remorse; grimace of reproach; grimace of resentment; grimace of resignation; grimace of restraint; grimace of revulsion; grimace of sadness; grimace of sardonic amusement; grimace of satisfaction; grimace of scorn; grimace of scornful distaste; grimace of self pity and remorse; grimace of self-disgust; grimace of self-pity; grimace of shock; grimace of shock and restraint; grimace of shocked disbelief; grimace of somber understanding; grimace of sorrow; grimace of sorts; grimace of stress; grimace of such concentrated fury; grimace of such utter desolation; grimace of surprise; grimace of surprise and affection; grimace of sympathy; grimace of tenderness; grimace of tension; grimace of terror; grimace of the loose lips*; grimace of the utmost distaste; grimace of torment; grimace of triumph; grimace of uncertainty; grimace of understanding; grimace of vexation; grimace of violent distaste; grimace of woe; grimace of wry disgust; grimace of wry humor; grimace of wry resentment.

1.4 - Noun Phrases

a bit of a grimace; a couple of grimaces; a dry twist of a grimace; a grotesque kind of grimace; a hard sort of grimace; a/the kind of grimace; a mocking kind of grimace; a semblance of a grimace; a series of grimaces; a/the sort of grimace; a stern sort of grimace; a strange kind of grimace; an incredible repertoire of grimaces; just a hint of a grimace; (it was) more of a pained grimace*; one of his grimaces; one of his shrewd grimaces; the ghost of a grimace; the look of a grimace; the most subtle of grimaces; the slight hint of a grimace; the tail end of his grimace.

1.5 - Verbs: Grimace as Subject

Standalone Verbs
appear; come and go; deepen; ease; fade; harden; intensify; sink; soften; tighten; vanish.

Face as Object
add (lines) to (face); appear on (face); bite into (face); break out on (face); carve (lines) in (face); chase across (face); come over (face); contort (face); crease (face); creep over (face); cross (face); dart across (face); dash across (face); distort (face); draw (face); fill (face); flash across (face); flick across (face); flicker across (face); flicker over (face); flit across (face); form on (face); light up (face); mar (face); move across (face); pass across (face); plaster on (face); roll over (face); run across (face); slant (face); slash (face); spread across (face); streak across (face); stretch across (face); sweep across (face); tighten (face); touch (face); twist (face); wrinkle (face).

Features as Object
break out on (features); cloud (features); crease (features); creep over (features); cross (features); darken (features); etch (features); firm (features); flash across (features); flicker across (features); flit (momentarily) across (features); make (appearance) on (features); mar (features); pass (fleetingly) across (features);

pass over (features); shadow (features); skitter over (features); slash (features); spread across (features); steal over (features); tighten (features); touch (features); transform (features); twist (features).

Lips as Object
curl (lips); curve (lips); flatten (lips) to (a thin line); move across (lips); press (lips) into (a crooked line); pull at (lips); purse (lips); stretch (lips); tighten (the corners) of (lips); tighten (lips); tug (lips); twist (lips); work (its way) across (lips).

Mouth as Object
chase across (mouth); contort (mouth); cross (mouth); curl (mouth); curve (mouth); distort (mouth); grip (mouth); lift (one corner) of mouth); make (a tortured line) of (mouth); play across (mouth); pull (the edges) of (mouth) down; pull at (the corners) of (mouth); pull down (the corners) of (mouth); pull up (one corner) of (mouth); touch (mouth); tug (the corner / the edge) of (mouth); tug at (the corners) of (mouth); twist (mouth); twist (one corner / the edge) of (mouth); work (its way) across (mouth).

1.6 - Verbs: Grimace as Object

Character (I / He / She) as Subject
allow (herself) (a grimace); answer with (a grimace); attempt (a grimace); avoid (a grimace); bite back (a grimace); camouflage (her grimace); catch (his grimace)*; chance (a grimace); conceal (a grimace); concede with (a grimace); control (a grimace); curb (a grimace); decipher (his grimace)*; disguise (a grimace); exchange (a grimace) for [something]*; exchange (grimaces); feel (her grimace) against (chest)*; feign (a grimace); fight (a grimace); fight back (a grimace); flash (a grimace); flash (him) (a grimace); flick out (a grimace); force (a grimace); give (a grimace); give (him) (a grimace); hide (her grimace); hold back (a grimace); ignore (his grimace)*; make (a grimace); make out (his grimace)*; manage (a grimace); mask (her grimace); miss (his grimace)*; mistake (his grimace) for [something]*; note (his grimace)*; notice (his grimace)*; observe (his grimace)*; offer up (a grimace); pretend (a grimace); prevent (a grimace); pull (a grimace); recognize (a grimace)*; repress (a grimace); see (his grimace)*; settle for (a grimace); share (a grimace); shoot (him) (a grimace); smother (a grimace); squelch (a grimace); stifle (a grimace); suppress (a grimace); swallow back (a grimace); throw (him) (a grimace); watch (his grimace)*; wipe (the grimace) off (face)*.

Face or Character as Subject
(I) compose (face) into (a grimace)*; (I) contort (face) into (a grimace)*; (I) fight (the grimace) from (face)*, (I) force (face) into (a grimace)*, (I) pull (face) into (a grimace)*; (I) screw (face) into (a grimace)*; (I) screw (face) up in/into

(a grimace)*; (I) screw up (face) into (a grimace)*; (I) stitch (a grimace) on (face)*; (I) try to keep (a grimace) off (face)*; (I) try to keep (the grimace) from (face)*; (I) twist (face) into (a grimace)*; break into (a grimace); contort in/into (a grimace); contort with (a grimace); crack into (a grimace); crease in/into (a grimace); crunch into (a grimace); distort into (a grimace); draw into (a grimace); etch in (a grimace); flatten out into (a grimace); form (a grimace); freeze into (a grimace); harden in (a grimace); is (a grimace); lock in (a grimace); lock in/into (a grimace); pinch in/into (a grimace); pinch with (a grimace); pull (itself) into (a grimace); pull into (a grimace); screw into (a grimace); screw up in/into (a grimace); scrunch in (a grimace); set into (a grimace); settle into (a grimace); shift to (a grimace); strain in (a grimace); stretch into (a grimace); tighten in/into (a grimace); twist in/into (a grimace); wear (a grimace).

Features or Character as Subject

(I) arrange (features) into (a grimace)*; (I) contort (features) into (a grimace)*; (I) distort (features) into (a grimace)*; (I) pull (features) into (a grimace)*; (I) twist (features) into (a grimace)*; break into (a grimace); close in (a grimace); contort in/into (a grimace); crease in (a grimace); draw into (a grimace); form (a grimace); freeze in (a grimace); harden into (a grimace); lock into (a grimace); pucker in (a grimace); pull (a grimace); screw up in (a grimace); tighten with (a grimace); twist in/into (a grimace).

Lips or Character as Subject

(I) clamp (lips) together in (a grimace)*; (I) compress (lips) in (a grimace)*; (I) draw back (lips) in (a grimace)*; (I) flatten (lips) into (a grimace)*; (I) fold (lips) in (a grimace)*; (I) pinch (lips) together in (a grimace)*; (I) press (lips) together in (a grimace)*; (I) purse (lips) in/into (a grimace)*; (I) screw (lips) into (a grimace)*; (I) thin (lips) in (a grimace)*; (I) twist (lips) into (a grimace)*; (I) wipe (a grimace) from (lips)*; compress into (a grimace); curl back in (a grimace); curl in/into (a grimace); curve back from (teeth) in (a grimace); curve in/into (a grimace); draw back into (a grimace); draw back over (teeth) in (a grimace); flatten against (teeth) in (a grimace); flatten with (a grimace); form (a grimace); freeze in (a grimace); hitch in (a grimace); move in (a grimace); part in (a grimace); pinch together in (a grimace); pull back (a grimace); pull into (a grimace); pull taut in (a grimace); pull tight into (a grimace); purse in (a grimace); quirk up (at the corners) in (a grimace); scrunch up in (a grimace); set in (a grimace); sew into (a grimace); shape into (a grimace); slip sideways in (a grimace); straighten into (a grimace); stretch in/into (a grimace); thin in/into (a grimace); tighten in (a grimace); turn downward(s) in (a grimace); turn up in (a grimace); twist in (a grimace); twist in/into (a grimace); twist to form (a grimace); twist with (a grimace); twitch in (a grimace).

Mouth or Character as Subject

(I) cover (mouth) to hide (a grimace)*; (I) draw (mouth) into (a grimace)*; (I) elongate (mouth) into (a grimace)*; (I) pull (mouth) down (at the corners) into (a grimace)*; (I) pull (mouth) into (a grimace)*; (I) shape (mouth) into (a grimace)*; (I) stretch (mouth) in (a grimace)*; (I) turn (mouth) down (at the corners) in (a grimace)*; (I) twist (mouth) in/into (a grimace)*; (one corner of mouth) lift in (a grimace); assume (a grimace); close into (a grimace); contort into (a grimace); crease into (a grimace); curl in/into (a grimace); curve in/into (a grimace); deepen in (a grimace); draw back in (a grimace); ease into (a grimace); flick out (a grimace); form (a grimace); give (a grimace); lift in (a grimace); make (a grimace); move in/into/on (a grimace); part in (a grimace); pinch in (a grimace); pinch up in (a grimace); pout in (a grimace); pull down into (a grimace); pull in/into (a grimace); purse in (a grimace); quirk into (a grimace); screw up in (a grimace); set in/into (a grimace); shape (a grimace); shape into (a grimace); shift into (a grimace); sketch (a grimace); slant in (a grimace); slash in (a grimace); stretch in/into (a grimace); stretch tight in (a grimace); take on (a grimace); thin into (a grimace); tighten in/into/on (a grimace); tilt in (a grimace); tremble in (a grimace); tug into (a grimace); turn back in (a grimace); turn down in (a grimace); turn downward(s) in (a grimace); turn into (a grimace); twist in/into; twist out (a grimace); twist up in (a grimace); twist with (a grimace); twitch into (a grimace); writhe in (a grimace).

Facial Constituents or Character as Subject

(eyebrows) draw together in (a grimace); (eyebrows) raise on (a grimace); (eyebrows) snap down in (a grimace); (I) bare (teeth) in (a grimace)*; (I) bring (teeth) together in (a grimace)*; (I) clench (teeth) in (a grimace)*; (I) flex (jaw) with (a grimace)*; (I) grind (teeth) in (a grimace)*; (I) grit (teeth) in (a grimace)*; (I) set (teeth) in (a grimace)*; (I) wrinkle (nose) in (a grimace)*; (jaw) clench in (a grimace); (jaw) harden in (a grimace); (jaw) lock in/into (a grimace); (jaw) set in (a grimace); (jaw) tighten into (a grimace); (nose) wrinkle in (a grimace); (teeth) clamp down on (bottom lip) to suppress (a grimace); (teeth) come together in (a grimace); (teeth) grind together in (a grimace); (teeth) show in (a grimace).

NOUN USAGE EXAMPLES

His smile morphed into a grimace.

A grimace wrinkled his face.

With each revelation, her father's grimace deepened.

Jessica flashed a weary grimace.

He groaned, his features contorting in an anguished grimace.

2. Verb Form

2.1 - Verb Synonyms

contort; deform; distort; frown; glare; glower; make a face; make a wry face; mug; scowl; screw up one's face; sneer.

2.2 - Adverbs

A
abruptly; actually*; angrily; apologetically; apprehensively; approvingly; awkwardly.

B
bitterly; blindly; briefly.

C
cautiously; charmingly; comically; critically; crossly.

D
deliberately; delicately; derisively; despairingly; disappointedly; disapprovingly; disdainfully; disgustedly; distastefully; doubtfully; drowsily.

E
eloquently; explicitly; expressively.

F
faintly; fastidiously; finally; firmly.

G
guiltily.

H
helplessly; hilariously; humorously.

I
immediately*; impatiently; impressively; instantly*; involuntarily; inwardly; irritably.

K
knowingly.

L
laughingly; lightly.

M
mentally; merely*; mirthlessly; mockingly; momentarily.

N
nearly*; nervously; normally*.

O
only*; only slightly; openly.

P
painfully; partly*; playfully; prettily; promptly*.

R
reassuringly; reproachfully; ruefully; ruefully*.

S
sardonically; savagely; secretly; self-consciously; shakily; significantly; silently; silently*; simply*; slightly; slowly; sourly; suddenly; sympathetically.

T
tauntingly; tightly.

U
uncomfortably; unconsciously; unwillingly; usually*.

V
violently.

W
warily; waspishly; weakly; wryly.

2.3 - Adverbials of Emotion, Feeling, Mental State, Movement, Sound, and Response

in a boyish fashion; in a fake smile*; in a fashion that made her look (...)*; in a half-smile*; in a mixture of agony and ecstasy; in a silent scream*; in acknowledgement; in aggravation; in agony; in agreement; in an effort to still his raging body*; in angry impatience; in annoyance; in answer; in anticipation; in apology; in appalled distaste; in apparent commiseration; in commiseration; in concentration; in concern; in confusion; in defeat; in disappointment; in disbelief; in discomfort; in disgust; in dismay; in distaste; in distress; in doleful anticipation; in embarrassment; in empathy; in eternal frustration; in evident embarrassment; in exasperation; in faint distaste; in frustration; in guilt; in his chin*; in his direction*; in his expression*; in his sleep*; in his voice*; in horrified embarrassment; in horror; in impatience; in irritation; in lieu of a smile*; in memory; in mild displeasure; in mild exasperation; in mock alarm; in mock complaint; in mock disappointment; in mock disgust; in mock dismay; in mock pain; in mock reproval; in mock resignation; in obvious disappointment; in obvious frustration; in obvious pain; in pain; in pleasure; in protest; in pure self-disgust; in real regret; in realization; in recognition; in recollection; in regret; in remembered exasperation; in remembrance; in remorse; in resignation; in resistance to (words)*; in response; in retrospect*; in return; in rueful acknowledgement; in rueful dismay; in rueful self-mockery; in self-deprecation; in self-derision; in self-disdain; in self-disgust; in self-disgust and apology; in self-mockery; in self-rebuke; in self-reproach; in silence*; in silent apology; in silent disapproval; in sudden exasperation; in surrender*; in sympathy; in unhappy acknowledgement; in vexation; in what might have been apology; in wry acknowledgement; in wry self-mockery; with a gesture of self-disgust*; with a rather sardonic inflection*; with a slight element of distaste; with a small hiss*; with a small smile*; with a sort of caustic despondency; with a wry amusement; with a wry twist of his lips*; with amusement; with anger and disgust; with annoyance; with anxiety; with apprehension; with consternation; with denial; with disappointment; with disapproval; with dismay; with displeasure; with distaste; with distaste and dislike; with dry humor; with each movement*; with effort*; with envy; with every jarring landing*; with every movement of the hot, swollen ankle*; with every movement*; with every step*; with feeling; with frustration; with high impatience; with his mouth*; with hollow humor; with impatience; with lingering mortification; with loathing and distaste; with mocking ruefulness; with multiple sensations*; with pain; with relief; with remembered distaste; with remembered frustration; with remembered pain; with resignation; with retrospect; with sad satisfaction; with scorn; with self-disgust; with shock; with something akin to self-disgust; with something close to panic; with sorrow; with strain; with sudden dejection; with sudden pain; with supreme satisfaction; with the effort to control himself*; with the knowledge that (...); with the memory that (...); with the movement*; with the pain; with the semi-pain; with thin tolerance; with unaccustomed bitterness; with what actually might have been concern; with what looked like self-deprecation; with wry amusement.

VERB USAGE EXAMPLES

She grimaced slightly to herself.

He rubbed his eyes and grimaced.

He pulled off his helmet, grimacing.

Grimacing with remembered pain, she walked toward the swimming pool.

He looked at himself in the mirror and grimaced with something close to panic.

8
GRIN / SMILE

1. Noun Form

1.1 - Noun Synonyms

a beaming expression; a delighted look; a happy expression; a laughing expression; a look of amusement; a look of happiness; a pleased look; grin lines; simper; smile lines; smirk.

1.2 - Adjectives

A

A-plus; abashed; abrupt; abstracted; acceptable; accepting; accompanying; accusing; acerbic; acid; acknowledging; actual; admiring; admonishing; adolescent; adorable; adoring; affable; affectionate; aggravating; aggressive; agonized; ain't-I-clever; ain't-I-irresistible; airy; all; all-American; all-encompassing; all-inclusive; all-knowing; all-male; all-masculine; all-out; all-star; all-too-beguiling; all-too-brief; all-too-familiar; all-too-human; all-too-knowing; all-too-sexy; all-too-sloppy; alligator; almost; already-familiar; amazed; amazing; amiable; amused; anarchic; Andalusian-like; angelic; annoying; another; answering; anticipatory; apologetic; appealing; appeasing; appraising; appreciative; apprehensive; approving; arcane; arch; aroused; arresting; arrogant; artful; artificial; artless; ashamed; asinine; assessing; assumed; assured; assuring; astonished; attempted; attractive; audacious; audible; autocratic; automatic; avaricious; avid; aw-shucks; aw-shucks-ma'am; award-winning; awkward.

B

baby; baby-toothed; backward; bad; bad-boy; bad-girl; badass; baddest; baffled; banana; bantering; barbecue-eating; bare; bare-toothed; bashful; battered; beach-boy; beaming; bearish; beat-cha; beatific; beautiful; beckoning; becoming; bedimpled; beginning; begrudging; beguiling; belated; beleaguered; believable; belly-twisting; bemused; benevolent; benign; beseeching; besotted; best; betraying; better; bewitching; beyond-adorable; big; big-as-the-desert; big-as-the-outback; big-ass; big-bad-wolf; big-brother; big-headed; big-kid; big-toothed; bigger; biggest; bighearted; bitter; bittersweet; black; black-eyed; bland; blazing; bleach-toothed; bleached; bleak; bleary; blinding; blissed-out;

blissful; blithe; bloody; blossoming; blushing; blustery; boisterous; bold; bolstering; bone-melting; bone-wilting; boozy; boy-next-door; boyish; bracing; brain-dismantling; brash; brave; brazen; break-your-heart; breath-defying; breath-stealing; breathless; breathtaking; breezy; brief; bright; bright-eyed; bright-toothed; brighter; brightest; brilliant; bring-it-on; brittle; broad; broad-bowed; broadening; broader; broadest; broken-toothed; brotherly; brown-eyed; brown-toothed; bruised; bubbly; buck-toothed; budding; buoyant; burgeoning.

C

cagey; cajoling; calculated; calculating; calendar-girl; callous; campaign; can-do-anything; canary-eating; candid; candy-eating; canine; captivating; carefree; careless; carnal; Casanova; casual; cat-ate-the-canary; cat-got-the-canary; cat-in-the-cream; cat-in-the-creamery; cat-lapping-cream; cat-like; catching; catlike; cats; caustic; cautious; cavalier; ceaseless; celebrity; cereal-box; chafing; challenging; characteristic; charismatic; charm-laden; charm-touched; charmed; charming; checkmate; cheek-splitting; cheek-to-cheek; cheekiest; cheeky; cheerful; cheery; cheesiest; cheesy; cherubic; Cheshire; Cheshire-cat; Cheshire-cat-like; chicken-eating; chiding; childish; child-like; chilling; chimp; chinless; chipmunk-like; chipped-tooth; chipper; chocolate-covered; choirboy; chubby; chummy; civil; clamped-teeth; clever; clock-stopping; closed-lip; closed-mouthed; clown; clownish; coaxing; cock-eyed; cockiest; cocksure; cocky; cocky-as-hell; cold; cold-stiffened; collective; come-and-get-me; come-hither; come-join-the-fun; come-play-with-me; comfortable; comforting; comic; comical; commiserating; companionable; compelling; competitors; complacent; complicit; comprehending; comradely; concealed; conceding; conceited; conciliating; conciliatory; condescending; confident; confidential; confiding; confrontational; confused; confused-little-boy; congenial; congratulatory; conniving; conquering; conquering-hero; consoling; conspiratorial; conspiratory; conspiring; constant; contagious; contemplative; contemptuous; content; contented; continual; contrary; contrite; controlled; convincing; cool; coquettish; cordial; corner-of-the-lip; counterfeit; cousinly; covered; covert; coy; crafty; crazy; crazy-assed; crinkled; crinkly; crinkly-eyed; crocodile; crooked; crooked-tooth; cruel; cryptic; cunning; curious; curly; curved; curving; curvy; customary; cute; cynical.

D

daft; dagger; damn; damn-the-torpedoes; damnable; damned; dangerous; dangerous-looking; daredevil; daring; dark; dark-eyed; darling; dashing; dastardly; dawning; dazed; dazzling; dead-sexy; deadly; deadpan; death; deathlike; debauched; debonair; decadent; decided; deep; deep-dimpled; deep-seated; deepening; defiant; definite; deliberate; delicious; delighted; delightful; delirious; demonic; demure; dentist-perfect; denture-white; departing; deprecating; deprecatory; derisive; derisory; determined; devastating; devil; devil-may-care; devilish; devils; devious; devouring; diabolical; diamond-watt; dimple-cheeked; dimple-popping; dimpled; dimpling; dirt-eating; dirt-smeared; dirty; dirty-minded; disapproving; disarming; disbelieving; discomfited;

dismissive; dispassionate; disreputable; distinct; distracted; disturbing; dizzy; do-or-die; dog-happy; dogged; doggy; don't-give-a-shit; don't-worry-about-it; don't-worry-about-me; doofus; dopey; double-chinned; double-dare; double-dare-you; double-dimple; double-wattage; doubtful; doubtless; dour; Dracula; drawing; drawn; dreamy; droll; drooling; droolly; drop-dead; drowsy; drunk; drunken; dry; dubious; dumb; dumb-ass; dutiful; dynamite.

E

each; eager; ear-splitting; ear-to-ear; earlier; earnest; earsplitting; earthy; easy; easy-going; ecstatic; edgy; eerie; effusive; ego-feeding; egotistical; elated; elect-me; electric; elfin; elfish; elliptical; eloquent; elusive; elvish; embarrassed; embryo; emerging; empathetic; empathic; enchanting; encouraging; endearing; engaging; enigmatic; enlightened; enormous; enquiring; enthusiastic; enticing; entrancing; envious; erotic; errant; ever-loving; ever-present; every-mother-loves-him; evil; evil-looking; evocative; exact; exaggerated; exalted; exasperated; exasperating; excited; exhausted; expanding; expansive; expectant; expected; expressive; exuberant; exultant; eye-lighting; eye-reaching; eye-rolling; eye-twinkling; eyebrow-waggling.

F

fabulous; face-splitting; facetious; fading; faint; faintest; fake; fake-innocent; fallen-angel; false; faltering; familiar; famous; fanged; fantastic; farewell; fascinating; fast; fat; fatalistic; fatherly; fatuous; faux; fearless; feeble; feminine; feral; ferocious; few; fidgety; fiendish; fierce; fighting; filthy; final; firm; first; five-alarm; five-hundred-watt; five-toothed; fixed; flamboyant; flashing; flashy; fledged; fledgling; fleeting; flinty; flippant; flirtatious; flirting; flirty; flustered; foamy; fond; foolhardy; foolish; foolish-looking; fools; football-hero; footloose; forced; forgiving; foul; four-toothed; fox; fox-like; fragile; frank; frayed; freckled; fresh; friendliest; friendly; friends; from-the-heart; frozen; frustrated; full; full-blooded; full-bloomed; full-blown; full-faced; full-fledged; full-hearted; full-mouthed; full-of-herself; full-of-mischief; full-on; full-out; full-points; full-power; full-sized; full-throttle; full-tooth; full-wattage; fully-fledged; fun-loving; funhouse; funny; furtive.

G

gamin; gamine; gamine-like; gap-tooth; gap-toothed; gaping; gapped; gappiest; gappy; gaunt; gay; generous; genial; gentle; genuine; ghastly; ghostly; ghoulish; giant; giddy; gigantic; gimlet; girl-next-door; girlish; giveaway; glad-this-is-over; glad-to-see-him; glassy; glazed; glazed-eyed; gleaming; gleeful; glib; glinting; glinty; glittering; glittery; gloating; glorious; glowing; glued-on; goading; gold-capped; gold-plated; gold-toothed; golden; golden-boy; good-humored; good-natured; good-ol'-boy; good-old-boy; good-tempered; good-time; good-to-see-you; goofiest; goofy; goofy-looking; gorgeous; gotcha; gotta-love-me; graceless; grandfatherly; grandmotherly; grateful; gratified; great; greedy; gregarious; grimy; grisly; grizzled; grotesque; growing; grudging;

grumpy; guaranteed-to-work; guarded; guess-what; guileless; guilty; gum; gum-cracking; gummy; gut-gripping; guy-in-love; guy-next-door; guy-to-guy.

H

habitual; half; half-apologetic; half-assed; half-awake; half-cocked; half-cocky; half-concealed; half-embarrassed; half-formed; half-guilty; half-hearted; half-hidden; half-mast; half-mocking; half-moon; half-reluctant; half-rogue; half-secret; half-sheepish; half-toothed; half-twisted; half-witted; halfway; Halloween-mask; handsome; haphazard; hapless; happy; happy-dizzy; happy-go-lucky; happy-kid; happy-to-see-him; harassed; hard; hard-edged; harmless; harmonious; harried; harsh; hasty; hateful; haughty; He-man; headlight-bright; healthy; heart-breaking; heart-fluttering; heart-knocking; heart-melting; heart-palpitating; heart-pounding; heart-rocking; heart-spinning; heart-stirring; heart-stopping; heart-strumming; heart-stuttering; heart-thudding; heart-thumping; heart-tripping; heart-tugging; heart-turning; heart-warming; heart-wrenching; heartbreaker; heartless; hearty; hello; helpful; helpless; hesitant; hey-baby; hey-good-lookin'; hey-there-gorgeous; hidden; hideous; high-potency; high-powered; high-voltage; high-wattage; hilarious; Hollywood; homecoming-queen; homely; honest; honest-to-god; honest-to-goodness; hopeful; hopeless; horny; horrible; horse; horse-toothed; horsy; hospitable; hot; hotshot; hovering; how's-it-going; Howdy-Doody; however-did-you-guess; huge; hugest; human; humble; humble-pie; humoring; humorless; humorous; hundred-megawatt; hundred-watt; hungry; hunky; hurt.

I

I'm-a-good-guy; I'm-available; I'm-in-heaven; I'm-Jack-the-Ripper; I'm-onto-you; I'm-so-in-love; I'm-so-sexy; I've-got-you; I've-got-you-now; I-can-conquer-anything; I-dare-you; I-dare-you-to; I-love-you; I-told-you-so; identical; idiotic; idle; ill-at-ease; ill-concealed; ill-suppressed; imbecilic; immediate; immense; immodest; impatient; impenitent; impertinent; impetuous; impish; impossible; impressed; improved; impudent; impulsive; inane; inappropriate; incomprehensible; inconsequential; incorrigible; incredible; incredulous; indefatigable; indistinct; indolent; indulgent; inebriated; inevitable; inexplicable; infamous; infantile; infatuated; infectious; infernal; infrequent; infuriating; ingenuous; ingratiating; inimitable; inner; innocent; innocent-looking; inquiring; inquisitive; insane; insincere; insinuating; insipid; insolent; insouciant; inspired; instant; insufferable; insulting; internal; internal-organ-melting; intimate; intoxicating; intrigued; inviting; involuntary; inward; ironic; ironical; irrational; irrepressible; irresistible; irreverent; irritated; irritating; it's-all-good.

J

jack-o'-lantern; jaded; jaunty; jaw-dropping; jaw-locked; jeering; jesters; jokers; jovial; jowly; joyful; joyous; jubilant; just-between-the-boys; just-between-us; just-between-us-guys; just-crooked.

K

ketchup-stained; killer; kind; king-size; kittenish; kitty; knee-dissolving; knee-trembling; knee-weakening; knock-me-out; knock-your-socks-off; knockout; know-all; know-it-all; knowing; knowledgeable.

L

laconic; lady-killer; lady-slaying; laid-back; lame; lancing; languid; lantern; large; lascivious; laser-sharp; last; laugh-filled; laughing; lawyer-like; laziest; lazy; lazy-eyed; lazy-looking; lean; lecherous; leering; leery; legendary; leisurely; leprechaun; less-than-assured; let's-get-it-on; let's-make-a-deal; lethal; level; lewd; life-enhancing; light; light-bulb; light-hearted; lightening; lightning; lightning-charged; lightning-quick; like-what-you-see; likeable; likely; lingering; lip-splitting; lip-tilted; lipless; liquid; little; little-boy; little-boy-helpless; lively; loaded; lolling; long; long-suffering; long-tongued; looking-for-trouble; loopy; loose; loose-mouthed; lopsided; lost-puppy; lovable; love-god; love-struck; lovely; lovesick; loving; low; luminous; lupine; lurching; lurid; lurking; lustful; lusty.

M

macabre; Machiavellian; macho; mad; maddening; magnanimous; magnetic; magnificent; major; make-his-eyes-sparkle; makeshift; male-to-male; malevolent; malicious; man-to-man; maniacal; manic; manly; marvelous; masculine; masking; masochistic; massive; matching; maudlin; mean; meaningful; meaningless; megawatt; melon-like; melt-her-bones; meltdown; melting; memorable; menacing; mental; merciless; mere; merry; mesmerizing; messy; mild; mile-wide; milky; million-dollar; million-watt; mind-stealing; mindless; mini-pirate; mirthful; mirthless; mischief-filled; mischief-riddled; mischievous; mischievous-little-boy; misty; misty-eyed; mock; mock-lascivious; mock-lurid; mock-pitying; mock-salacious; mock-tender; mocking; modest; moist-lipped; momentary; monkey; monkey-like; monkeyish; monstrous; mood-switching; moon-eyed; moon-wide; moonlit; morbid; moronic; motherly; mouse-eating; mouth-splitting; mouthwatering; movie-star; murderous; musing; mutual; mysterious.

N

narrow; narrow-eyed; nascent; nasty; natural; naughtiest; naughty; naughty-boy; naughty-girl; near; near-normal; needling; negligent; neighborly; neon; nerve-needling; nerve-skating; nervous; nervous-looking; never-fail; new; nice; nicotine-stained; no-big-deal; no-good; no-holds-barred; no-nonsense; no-problem; non-committal; non-repentant; nonchalant; none-too-enthusiastic; nonstop; normal; not-provocative; not-quite-contrite; not-quite-focused; not-very-amused; now-familiar; now-I'm-having-fun; nuclear.

O

obliging; oblique; obnoxious; obscene; obvious; odd; off-center; offending; offhand; offside; often-photographed; oh-boy; oh-so-attractive; oh-so-innocent; oh-so-sexy; oily; okay-you-caught-me; old; one; one-cornered; one-dimple; one-dimpled; one-of-the-guys; one-sided; one-toothed; only; onstage; open; open-mouthed; out-and-out; out-of-control; outrageous; outright; outsized; outward; over-the-shoulder; overdone; oversized; overwhelming; owlish; own.

P

pageant; pained; painful; painted-on; pale; panting; parental; part; partial; parting; pasted-on; patented; paternal; patronizing; peace-offering; peanut-butter; pearly; peculiar; penitent; perceptive; perfect; perky; permanent; perpetual; persuasive; pert; perverse; phony; photo; pie-eating; piece-of-cake; pink; pint-size; pious; pirate; piratical; pity; pixie; pixie-like; placating; placid; plaintive; plastered-on; plastic; platonic; play-with-me; playboy; playful; pleading; pleasant; please-notice-me; pleased; pleased-as-punch; pleased-with-himself; plucky; pointed; polite; politicians; positive; possessive; possible; possum-eating; potent; pouty; power-packed; powerful; practical; practiced; predators; predatory; predictable; preoccupied; pretty; previous; pride-filled; prideful; private; promising; proper; proud; proud-papa; proud-parent; proudest; provocative; provoking; prurient; puckered; puckish; pulse-racing; pumpkin; punch-to-the-heart; punishing; puppy; puppy-dog; puppy-like; pure-female; puzzle-headed; puzzled.

Q

quavery; questioning; quick; quick-spreading; quick-witted; quicksilver; quiet; quirking; quirky; quivering; quizzical.

R

radiant; raffish; ragged; rakehell; rakish; randy; rapscallion; raptors; rare; rascally; rascals; raunchy; ravening; ravishing; ready; real; reassuring; rebel; rebellious; reciprocal; reciprocating; reckless; reflective; reflexive; regretful; relaxed; relieved; reluctant; remembering; reminiscent; remorseful; reoccurring; repentant; replete; repressed; reproving; resigned; respectful; responding; responsive; restless; restrained; resulting; resurrected; return; returning; revealing; revolting; ribald; rictus; ridiculous; right-back-at-you; rigid; ripe; rising; rogues; roguish; romantic; rosy-cheeked; rotten; rueful; rugged; ruthless.

S

saber-toothed; saccharine; saccharine-sweet; sad; saddest; salacious; salesman-like; salivary; salty; same; sappiest; sappy; sappy-sweet; sarcastic; sardonic; sassy; satanic; satiated; satiric; satirical; satisfactory; satisfied; satisfied-looking; satisfying; saturnine; satyr-like; satyrs; sauciest; saucy; savage; scalawags; scary, schoolboyish; schoolgirl-like; schoolgirlish; scolding; scornful; screwy; scruffy; second; secret; secretive; seductive; seedy; self-amused; self-assured;

self-confident; self-congratulatory; self-conscious; self-deprecating; self-deprecatory; self-deriding; self-derisive; self-derisory; self-disparaging; self-effacing; self-indulgent; self-mocking; self-satisfied; self-serving; semi-apologetic; senators; sensual; sensuous; seraphic; serene; serviceable; sexier; sexiest; sexual; sexy; sexy-as-hell; sexy-as-sin; sexy-cowboy; shadowy; shaky; shame-faced; shamefaced; shameful; shameless; shared; shark-faced; shark-like; sharkish; sharky; sharp; sharp-toothed; she-devil; sheep-eating; sheepish; sheer; shiny; shit-eater; shit-eating; shocked; short; shrewd; shrimp-eating; shudders-down-the-spine; shy; sick; sickening; sickly; side-slant; side-swipe; sidelong; sideways; sigh-worthy; signature; significant; silent; sillier; silliest; silly; silly-ass; silly-looking; silver-capped; silver-plated; similar; simmering; simple; sincere; sinful; single-man-about-town; sinister; sinners; sisterly; sizzling; skeptical; skewed; slack; slack-jawed; slanted; slanting; slashing; sleazy; sleepy; sleepy-eyed; slight; slightest; slim; slimy; slippery; slit-eyed; slobbering; slobbery; sloping; sloppiest; sloppy; slow; slow-burner; slow-rising; slow-spreading; slow-widening; slumberous; slutty; sly; slyest; small; smarmy; smart-aleck; smart-ass; smashing; smeared; smirking; smirky; smitten; smoking-hot; smoldering; smooth; smothered; smothering; smug; smug-looking; snaggle-tooth; snaggle-toothed; snarky; sneak-attack; sneaky; sneering; snide; soft; softer; softest; solemn; solicitous; solid-gold; somersaulting; soppy; sorrowful; sorry; soul-wrenching; sour; spacy-toothed; sparkling; sparkling-eyed; special; spectacular; speculative; spider-to-the-fly; spirited; spit-slick; spiteful; split; spontaneous; spreading; spunky; standard; starstruck; startled; startling; steadfast; steady; steamy; stellar; stiff; stifled; stomach-flipping; stomach-tickling; straight-toothed; strained; strange; stretched; stretchy; struggling; stubborn; stunned; stunning; stupid; stupid-fool; subdued; sublime; subsequent; subtle; sudden; sugar-white; suggestive; sultry; summer; sunny; sunshine-big; super-sexy; superb; supercharged; supercilious; superior; superior-brother; supersexy; supersize; suppressed; sure; surly; surprised; surprising; surrendering; surreptitious; suspicious; swaggering; swallowed-the-canary; swashbuckling; sweet; sweetest; swift; sympathetic; syrupy.

T

take-no-prisoners; tantalizing; taunting; taut; teasing; teeth-baring; telling; telltale; tempting; tender; tense; tentative; terrible; terrific; testing; Texas-size; Texas-style; thank-you; thankful; theatrical; thick; thigh-melting; thirteen-year-old; thoughtful; thousand-watt; threatening; three-alarm; three-sided; three-toothed; thrilled; throwaway; tigerish; tight; tight-lipped; tilted; time-of-his-life; time-tested; timely; timid; tiny; tiny-toothed; tipped-down; tipsy; tired; to-die-for; tobacco-stained; toe-curling; token; told-you-so; tolerant; tomcats; tongue-in-cheek; tongue-lolling; too-bright; too-handsome; too-hot; too-innocent; too-knowing; too-sexy; tooth-flashing; toothless; toothpaste; toothpaste-ad; toothpaste-white; toothsome; toothy; tormenting; total; tough-street-kid; trademark; traitorous; treacherous; trembling; tremendous; tremulous; tricksters; triumphant; troublemaking; truce; true; truncated; trust-inspiring; trusting; trustworthy; trying-hard-to-hide; TV-cop; twin; twin-dimpled; twinkling;

twinkly; twisted; twisted-looking; twisty; twitching; two; two-against-one; two-mile-wide; two-toothed; typical.

U

ubiquitous; ugly; unabashed; unaccustomed; unaffected; unamused; unanticipated; unapologetic; unashamed; unassuming; unbelieving; unbothered; uncertain; uncharacteristic; uncivilized; uncomfortable; uncomplicated; unconcealed; unconcerned; unconscious; uncontrollable; uncontrolled; unconvinced; unconvincing; unctuous; undaunted; undermining; understanding; undignified; undiluted; undisturbed; uneasy; uneven; unexpected; unfailing; unfriendly; ungainly; ungovernable; unguarded; unholy; unladylike; unmaterialized; unmirthful; unmistakable; unnerving; unnoticed; unoffended; unpleasant; unprofessional; unquenchable; unregretful; unrepentant; unreserved; unrestrained; unruffled; unselfconscious; unsorry; unsteady; unstoppable; unsure; unsympathetic; untamable; untroubled; unwilling; unwise; unworried; unyielding; up-to-no-good; upside-down; upturned; upward; urchin; usual.

V

vacant; vacuous; valedictory; vapid; vast; vengeful; vibrant; vicious; victorious; victors; victory; vile; visible; vivacious; vivid; vixenish; vulpine.

W

waggish; wan; warm; warning; warped; wary; watermelon; watery; wavering; way-too-charming; way-too-sexy; wayward; weak; weary; weaselly; weather-beaten; weepy; welcoming; well-deserved; well-known; well-loved; well-pleased; well-practiced; wet; what-the-hell; whimsical; whistling-in-the-dark; white; white-toothed; whole-face; whole-hearted; wicked; wickedest; wide; wide-angle; wide-eyed; wide-mouthed; wide-open; wide-spread; wide-tooth; wide-toothed; wide-white; widening; wider; widest; wiggly; wild; wild-west; willing; willpower-melting; wily; winner-take-all; winning; winsome; wiped-off; wise; wise-ass; wiseacre; wish-me-luck; wishy-washy; wistful; withering; witty; wizened; wobbling; wobbly; wolf-in-training; wolf-like; wolfish; woman-killer; woman-to-woman; womanly; won't-happen; won-over; wonderful; wondrous; wonky; world-class; world-famous; world-rocking; worldly; worried; wrinkled; wry.

Y

yard-wide; yellow; yellow-toothed; yellowed; you'll-regret-this; you-asked-for-it; you-slay-me; youthful.

Z

zany; zealous.

1.3 - Noun + Prepositional Phrases

grin of a besotted man; grin of a boy; grin of a buffoon; grin of a cartoon chipmunk; grin of a centerfold; grin of a child; grin of a conspirator; grin of a crocodile; grin of a fat cat toying with its prey; grin of a heartbreaker; grin of a lady charmer; grin of a lawyer; grin of a lioness; grin of a lioness about to pounce; grin of a lovesick loon; grin of a man totally at ease; grin of a man used to getting (...); grin of a man well satisfied by (...); grin of a man who (...); grin of a marauding wolf; grin of a mocking devil; grin of a naughty boy; grin of a nervous boy; grin of a sated man; grin of a shark; grin of a siren; grin of a small child; grin of a thoroughly contented man; grin of a ventriloquist; grin of a wolf; grin of a wolf on the hunt; grin of a woman with (...); grin of absolute delight; grin of acceptance; grin of acknowledgement; grin of admiration; grin of affection; grin of agreement; grin of almost boyish delight; grin of amused satisfaction; grin of amusement; grin of an elderly gnome; grin of an old friend; grin of an unrepentant rogue; grin of an unrepentant sinner; grin of answering amusement; grin of anticipation; grin of anticipatory relish; grin of apology; grin of appeal; grin of appraisal; grin of appreciation; grin of appreciative recognition; grin of approval; grin of calculating triumph; grin of candor; grin of challenge; grin of childlike wonder; grin of clear delight; grin of complete and utter satisfaction; grin of complicity; grin of comprehension; grin of comprehension and appreciation; grin of concession; grin of confidence; grin of conquest; grin of contentment; grin of dazzling proportions; grin of dazzling whiteness; grin of delight; grin of delight and happiness; grin of delight and triumph; grin of derision; grin of devilish enjoyment; grin of devilry; grin of devious proportions; grin of disappointment and resignation; grin of disbelief; grin of distaste; grin of ecstasy; grin of elation; grin of embarrassment; grin of encouragement; grin of enjoyment; grin of enlightenment; grin of evil proportions; grin of excited happiness; grin of excitement; grin of exhaustion; grin of exhilaration; grin of expectancy; grin of expectation; grin of experienced charm; grin of exultation; grin of fear; grin of fiendish satisfaction; grin of fierce relief; grin of flashing white teeth*; grin of fond amusement; grin of forced amusement; grin of genuine amusement; grin of genuine appreciation; grin of genuine masculine amusement; grin of genuine pleasure; grin of glee; grin of gloating triumph; grin of gratitude; grin of great charm; grin of greeting; grin of happiness; grin of happy anticipation; grin of happy memory; grin of happy relief; grin of his/her lips*; grin of his/her own*; grin of his/hers/yours*; grin of honest amusement; grin of horror; grin of immense charm; grin of impudence; grin of impudent assurance; grin of incandescent delight; grin of indulgent amusement; grin of infinite amusement; grin of intense happiness; grin of irony; grin of joy; grin of joy and gratitude; grin of joy, gratitude and trust; grin of lazy amusement; grin of male satisfaction; grin of mammoth proportions; grin of masculine appreciation; grin of masculine approval; grin of masculine fellowship; grin of masculine satisfaction; grin of mirth; grin of mischief; grin of mockery; grin of mournfulness; grin of old; grin of pleased surprise; grin of pleasure; grin of practiced charm; grin of predatory satisfaction; grin of pride;

grin of proffered conspiracy; grin of promise; grin of puckish affection; grin of pure amusement; grin of pure anticipation; grin of pure appreciation; grin of pure delight; grin of pure devilment; grin of pure enchantment; grin of pure enjoyment; grin of pure evil; grin of pure glee; grin of pure happiness; grin of pure hope; grin of pure male satisfaction; grin of pure masculine anticipation; grin of pure masculine pride; grin of pure mischief; grin of pure pleasure; grin of pure relief; grin of pure relish; grin of pure satisfaction; grin of pure sibling affection; grin of pure triumph; grin of purely male satisfaction; grin of rare pleasure; grin of real humor; grin of real pleasure; grin of realization; grin of reassurance; grin of reciprocal interest; grin of recognition; grin of recollection; grin of regret; grin of relief; grin of reluctant admiration; grin of remembrance; grin of resignation; grin of sardonic amusement; grin of satisfaction; grin of savage male triumph; grin of secret triumph; grin of self-consciousness; grin of self-deprecation; grin of sexual anticipation; grin of sheer amusement; grin of sheer bravado; grin of sheer delight; grin of sheer enthusiasm; grin of sheer gratitude; grin of sheer happiness; grin of sheer joy and relief; grin of sheer masculine delight; grin of sheer pleasure; grin of simple appreciation; grin of sincere affection; grin of sly stupidity; grin of some charm; grin of sorts; grin of speculation; grin of success; grin of such charm and warmth; grin of such devastation; grin of such epic proportions; grin of such pure happiness; grin of such pure happiness and contentment; grin of such sensuous pleasure; grin of such triumph; grin of such understanding and approval; grin of such unexpected charm; grin of such wickedness; grin of surprise; grin of surprise and pleasure; grin of sympathy; grin of taunting devilry; grin of thanks; grin of the ocean's most feared predator; grin of the painfully attractive variety; grin of total male satisfaction; grin of total satisfaction; grin of total understanding; grin of triumph; grin of triumphant amusement; grin of unbounded delight; grin of uncharitable delight; grin of understanding; grin of undisguised delight; grin of unholy amusement; grin of unholy anticipation; grin of unholy triumph; grin of unspoken relief; grin of utter delight; grin of utter enjoyment; grin of utter relief; grin of victory; grin of welcome; grin of what looked like rueful admiration; grin of womanly power; grin of wry amusement; grin of wry appreciation.

1.4 - Noun Phrases

a bad boy sort of grin; a bit of a grin; a boyish sort of grin; a brief flash of a grin; a circus of grins; a confiding sort of grin; a crooked kind of grin; a deprecating sort of grin; a devastating image of his smooth grin; a different kind of grin; a dry shadow of his grin; a faint echo of his grin; a faint mockery of his usual grin; a faint trace of a grin; a faint version of his characteristic grin; a few molars short of a full grin; a flash of a grin; a fleeting glimpse of a cheeky grin; a fleeting remnant of a grin; a flicker of a grin; a fraction of a grin; a fuzzy sort of grin; a ghost of her gamin grin; a ghost of her old grin; a ghost of his usual grin; a ghost of a grin; a ghost of a wry grin; a glimmer of a grin; a glimpse of his devilish grin; a glimpse of a grin; a goofy sort of grin; a hint of her old grin; a hint of his crooked grin; a hint of a familiar grin; a hint of a genuine grin; a hint of a grin; a hint of a mischievous grin; a/the kind of grin; a knife blade of a grin; a knowing kind of grin; a leering sort of grin; a little sliver of a grin; a lopsided kind of grin; a lopsided tug of a grin; a lopsided version of his famous grin; a lot of grins; a mere ghost of his usual grin; a mockery of a grin; (it was) more of a grin; a number of grins; a pair of grins; a pale kind of grin; a pale shadow of a rueful grin; a pale version of her usual grin; a parody of a grin; a particularly piratical kind of grin; a quarter of a grin; a quick flash of a devilish grin; a quick flash of a grin; a rascal of a grin; a rough resemblance of a grin; a sardonic version of his famous grin; a semblance of his trademark grin; a semblance of a grin; a semblance of a slow grin; a shadow of her normal grin; a shadow of her old grin; a shadow of his former grin; a shadow of a grin; a shining beacon of a grin; a shy sort of grin; a slash of a grin; a sliver of a grin; a snarling kind of grin; a sneaky type of grin; a/the sort of grin; a strained sort of grin; a stunner of a grin; a/the suggestion of a grin; a tired version of his killer grin; a Tom Sawyer kind of grin; a trace of his lopsided grin; a trace of a sardonic grin; a trail of grins; a travesty of his grin; a travesty of a grin; a trio of grins; a twinge of a grin; a twinkle of a grin; a twisted kind of a grin; a twisted sort of grin; a twitch of a contrite grin; a twitch of a grin; a type of grin; a vestige of his old grin; a warm friendly sort of grin; a weak semblance of a boyish grin; a weak sort of grin; a weak version of his sexy grin; a weary version of his famous grin; a whisper of a grin; a whole series of grins; a whopper of a grin; a wicked kind of grin; a wicked tilt of his grin; a wisp of a grin; a wolfish kind of grin; a wry kind of grin; a wry suggestion of a grin; an abbreviation of his usual grin; an animalistic parody of a grin; an approximation of a cheerful grin; an exchange of grins; an image of his grin; an infuriating hint of a grin; an unsettling ghost of a grin; another of his sunny grins; half of a grin; just a touch of a grin; just a/the hint of a grin; no hint of a grin; no sign of a grin; no suggestion of a grin; one hell of a grin; one of her best grins; one of her cheerful grins; one of her familiar grins; one of her wide grins; one of his big grins; one of his broad grins; one of his devilish grins; one of his elfish grins; one of his engaging grins; one of his half grins; one of his lazy grins; one of his lighthearted grins; one of his quick grins; one of his rare grins; one of his sparkling grins; one of his wicked grins; plenty of grins; some semblance of a grin; something of his old grin; something of a grin; the appeal of his crooked grin; the arrival of his lethal grin; the arrogant challenge of his smug grin; the audacity of his grin; the barest flicker of a grin; the barest hint of a grin; the beginning of a crooked grin; the beginning of a surprised grin; the beginning(s) of a grin; the beginnings of a goofy grin; the beginnings of a playful grin; the beginnings of a wolfish grin; the benefit of his disarming grin; the best imitation of a casual grin; the biggest of grins; the blazing heat of his grin; the briefest of grins; the cheekiest of grins; the cheekiness of his grin; the cheeky upturn of his grin; the cheesiest of grins; the cockiest of grins; the confident curve of her grin; the corner of her widening grin; the crooked charm of his grin; the crooked side of his grin; the curve of his grin; the dazzle of her grin; the drollness of her grin; the edge of his cynical grin; the edge of his easy grin; the edge of a grin; the effect of his dazzling grin; the enemy type of grin; the entrancing slant of his grin; the faint blur of his grin; the faintest crook of a grin; the faintest hint of a rakish grin; the faintest hint of a wolfish grin; the faintest of grins; the faintest shadow of a rueful grin; the faintest suspicion of a grin; the falseness of his grin; the familiar curve of his grin; the first hint of a grin; the first signs of his crooked grin; the flash of his grin; the flash of his lopsided grin; the flash of his white grin; the flash of a knowing grin; the flicker of a grin; the force of her impish grin; the full power of his mischievous grin; the ghost of his old grin; the ghost of a grin; the gleam of his grin; the glimmer of a hard grin; the glimmerings of a grin; the glint of his grin; the hint of a confident grin; the hint of a grin; the hint of a quicksilver grin; the hint of a reluctant grin; the hint of a smug grin; the humor of his grin; the image of his mocking grin; the impact of the grin; the impishness of his grin; the impudence of his grin; the incomparable beauty of her grin; the inevitable exchange of grins; the intensity of his stunning grin; the last bit of a grin; the last of his fading grin; the lazy curve of his grin; the lines of a wicked grin; the luxury of a grin; the makings of a grin; the memory of his lopsided grin; the memory of his sly grin; the merest hint of a grin; the merest trace of a grin; the momentary slip of his trademark grin; the most lascivious of grins; the most reluctant of grins; the most wicked of grins; the open kind of grin; the potency of his boyish grin; the power and appeal of his grin; the power of her beaming grin; the quick flash of a grin; the quick widening of the grin; the rare sighting of a grin; (on) the receiving end of a huge grin; the reckless slash of a grin; the remnants of a grin; the return of his arrogant grin; the reward of his grin; the same slash of a grin; the same sort of grin; the satisfaction of a grin; the shameless magic of his grin; the sheer bravado of his grin; the sight of her delighted grin; the sight of his grin; the sight of his potent grin; the silliness of her grin; the simple joy of his wide grin; the size of her grin; the slash of a grin; the slightest hint of a grin; the slightest of grins; the slow spread of his grin; the smallest of grins; the softening effect of his grin; the spontaneity of his grin; the spread of a slow grin; the sudden brief flash of a grin; the surprise appearance of a devilish grin; the suspicion of a grin; the suspicion of a wicked grin; the swift flash of his grin; the tail end of a grin; the teasing hint of a grin; the teasing style of grin; the teasing tilt of his sideways grin; the telltale suggestion of a grin; the tightest of grins; the tilt of his grin; the tiniest of grins; the tiny curve of a grin; the trademark suggestion of a grin; the tug of a grin; the tug of a lazy grin; the ugliness of his grin; the unmistakable hint of a real grin; the unpleasant semblance of a grin; the vaguest hint of a grin; the very faintest of grins; the very faintest suspicion of a grin; the very tiniest edge of a grin; the warmth of his grin; the wattage of her grin; the whisper of a sardonic grin; the white flash of his grin; the white flash of a canine grin; the white gleam of his grin; the white slash of his grin; the white teeth of a grin; the whiteness of a grin; the wicked challenge of his answering grin; the wickedest of grins; the wickedness of his grin; the wide ebullience of her grin; the widening of his grin; the widest of grins; the width of his predatory grin; the width of his smug grin; the wobbliest of grins; the wry twist of a grin; the wryest of grins.

1.5 - Verbs: Grin as Subject

Standalone Verbs

appear; arrive; blaze; blaze out; bleed away; bloom; blossom; bounce back; break free; break loose; break out; break through; break up; brighten; broaden; build; change; come; come and go; come (back); come out; creep (back); creep in; creep out; crook; deepen; die; dim; diminish; disappear; dissolve; droop; drop; drop away; ease; ebb; emerge; escape; evaporate; expand; fade; fade off; fail; fall; fall away; falter; flare; flash; flash out; flatline; flatten; flee; flick back; flicker; flower; follow; form; freeze; get (bigger)*; get (wider)*; glint; glisten; go; grow; grow (bigger)*; grow (broader)*; grow (wider)*; help; hold steady; hover; hurt; ignite; inch back; increase; intensify; leak out; linger; lurk; mellow; melt away; mock; open; peek out; peep through; persist; peter out; pop in; quirk; quiver; reappear; recede; refresh (itself)*; relax; remain; remain intact; resurface; return; sharpen; shift; show; slant more; slide away; slide wider; slip; slip out; sober; soften; sparkle; spread; spread wider; sprout; stand out; steady; step out; stiffen; stop; stretch wider; struggle through; surface; sweep back; switch on; take over; threaten; tighten; tilt; tilt sideways; tip upward(s); tug; twist; unfurl; vanish; wane; waver; widen; wilt; win out; wink out; work magic*.

Cheeks as Object

add (crinkles) to (cheeks); appear in (cheeks); bring (deep creases) to (cheeks); carve (deep grooves) in (cheeks); cause (creases) in (the sides) of (cheeks); cleft (cheeks); climb (cheeks); climb up (cheeks); crawl up (cheeks); crease (cheeks); creep up (cheeks); crinkle (cheeks); cut (deep creases / grooves) in/into (cheeks); deepen (the lines) in (cheeks); dent (cheeks); drive (deep creases) down (cheeks); etch (deep grooves / creases) in/into (cheeks); flirt with (cheeks); give (cheeks) a lift; groove (cheeks); grow so wide, it hurt (cheeks); indent (cheeks); lift (cheeks); line (cheeks); make (cheeks) hurt; make (cheeks) puff out; make (creases) in (cheeks); make (deep creases) down (cheeks); pleat (cheeks); plump (cheeks); pull at (cheeks); pull on (cheeks); put (creases) down (cheeks); shove at (cheeks); show off (dent / grooves) in (cheeks); slash (cheeks); (grin lines) slash (cheeks); slash (lines) in (cheeks); slash (the skin) of (cheeks); split (cheeks); spread across (cheeks); stretch (cheeks); stretch from (cheek to cheek); tug at (cheeks).

Dimples as Object

activate (dimples); bring (dimples) into prominence; bring (dimples) into view; bring (dimples) to life; bring out (dimples) (in cheeks); call (dimples) into action; carve (dimples) down cheeks; cause (dimples) to wink; cement (dimples) in cheeks/chin; crease (dimples) in cheeks; create (dimples) in cheeks; deepen (dimples); dent (dimples) in cheeks; emphasize (dimples); expose (dimples); indent cheeks with (dimples); press (dimples) into cheeks; pull deeply at (dimples) in cheeks; pull into (dimples); pull out (dimples); punch (dimples) deep (into cheeks); put (dimples) in/into (both) cheeks; reveal (dimples); send (dimples) into cheeks; set out (dimples); shoot (dimples) into cheeks; show (dimples); show off (dimples); show up (dimples) in cheeks; showcase (dimples); slash (dimples) in cheeks; strike (dimples) into cheeks.

Expression as Object

alleviate (expression); alter (expression); banish (expression); break across (expression); break through (expression); change (expression); crack (expression); erase (expression); lighten (expression); melt (expression); overtake (expression); relieve (expression); replace (expression); soften (expression); take the edge off (expression); transform (expression).

Eyes as Object

add (a sparkle) to (eyes); add (little crinkles) around (eyes); appear at (the back) of (eyes); begin in (eyes); belie (the fire) in (eyes); bloom in (eyes); bounce from (eyes); brighten (eyes); bring (a twinkle) to (eyes); burst (like a flash) in (eyes); cause (the corners) of (eyes) to crease; cause (the creases) to deepen about (eyes); cause (tiny lines) to crinkle around (eyes); combine with (a glint) in (eyes); come into (eyes); crease (the corners) of (eyes); crease (the sunfolds) at (the outer corners) of (eyes); create (fine crinkle lines) around (eyes); crinkle (eyes); crinkle (the corners) of (eyes); crinkle (the skin) around (eyes); crinkle up (eyes); dance in (eyes); deepen (the laugh lines) at (the corners) of (eyes); deepen (the laugh lines) fanning from (the corners) of (eyes); deepen (the lines) radiating from (eyes); doesn't (quite) reach (eyes); doesn't come close to reaching (eyes); doesn't extend to (eyes); doesn't meet (eyes); doesn't reach (the hardness) in (eyes); doesn't seem to reach (eyes); draw (lines) at (the corners) of (eyes); drop from (eyes); enter (eyes); extend to (eyes); feather (the corners) of (eyes); fill (eyes) (with joy); flash in (eyes); flicker in (eyes); glint in (eyes); go (directly) to (eyes); go from (eyes); illuminate (eyes); is in (eyes); is reflected in (eyes)*; is still in (eyes); kindle in (eyes); leave (eyes); lift to (eyes); light (eyes); light (eyes) with (...); light up (eyes); look out from (eyes); lurk in (eyes); magnify (eyes); make (eyes) crinkle; make (eyes) crinkle (in/at the corners); make (eyes) dance; make (eyes) dance (with humor); make (eyes) dilate; make (eyes) gleam; make (eyes) glint; make (eyes) narrow; make (eyes) shine; make (eyes) twinkle; make (the corners) of (eyes) crinkle; move to (eyes); play around (the edges) of (eyes); put (a sparkle) in (eyes); put a sparkle in (eyes); reach (eyes); send (shards of light) glinting in (eyes); set off (a glimmer) in (eyes); smolder in (eyes); sparkle in (eyes); spread to (eyes); spread to(eyes); start in (eyes) and spread (slowly); start in (the depths) of (eyes); steal up to (eyes); touch (eyes); travel to (eyes); twinkle in (eyes); warm (eyes); work (its way) into (eyes); wrinkle (the corners) of (eyes).

Face as Object

alter (face); alter (the expression) on (face); animate (face); appear (from ear to ear) on (face); appear fixed on (face); appear on (face); banish (the solemnity) from (face); beam from (face); begin to chase (the shadows) from (face); begin to edge across (face); begin to spread across (face); begin to spread on (face); begin to spread over (face); bloom across (face); bloom all over (face); bloom on (face); bloom over (face); blossom on (face); break (face) (in two); break (like sunshine) over (face); break (the tension) in (face); break across (face); break on (face); break onto (face); break out across (face); break out all over (face); break out on (face); break out over (face); break over (face); break through (the hard lines) of (face); brighten (face); burst across (face); burst out on (face); burst over (face); change (face) (once more); chase (the last lingering shadows) from (face); chase away (the last shadows that lingered) on (face); climb (face); come (back) to (face); come across (face); come and go on (face); come into (face); come out on (face); come over (face); come to (face); commandeer (face); continue to blossom on (face); continue to light up (face); cover (about ninety percent) of (face); cover (face); cover (whole) (face); crack (face); crack (face) (from ear to ear); crack (face) (in two); crack (face) (into two halves); crack (the weathered surface) of (face); crack across (face); crawl across (face); crease (face); crease (face) (endearingly); crease (face) (with a myriad of lines); creep (back) onto (face); creep (slowly) onto (face); creep across (face); creep onto (face); creep over (face); creep up (face); crinkle (face); crinkle (the crease) of (face); cross (face); curve (crookedly) across (face); curve (face); curve (wickedly) on (face); curve across (face); curve up (face); cut (a white slash) across (face); cut across (face); dance (a web of fine lines) across (face); dance across (face); dance over (face); dart across (face); dazzle in (face); decorate (face); develop on (face); die on (face); disappear from (face); disturb (face); divide (face); dominate (whole) (face); drain from (face); drift across (face); drop from (face); ease (some of the tension) in (face); ease (the lines) of (face); ease (the tension) stamped on (face); ease across (face); ease over (face); eat up (face); edge (its way) across (face); edge across (face); encompass (face); enhance (face); erupt on (face); etch (face); etch (its way) across (face); etch (itself) across (face); etch across (face); explode across (face); explode on (face); fade from (face); fall (right) off (face); fall from (face); fill (face); find (its way) to (face); fix (itself) on (face); flash (bold and brilliant) in (face); flash (brilliantly) across (face); flash (white) in (face); flash across (face); flash in (face); flash on (face); flash over (face); flee (face); flick (briefly) across (face); flicker across (face); flicker over (face); flit across (face); flit over (face); flood (face); form on (face); freeze on (face); give (charm) to (face); gleam (whitely) in (face); gleam on (face); go across (face); go from one side of (face) to the other; grace (face); grow (wide) across (face); grow on (face); hijack (face); hook up (one side) of (face); illuminate (face); imbue (face) with (energy); inch over (face); infiltrate (face); is (back) on (face); is all over (face); is fixed on (face)*; is on (face); is painted on (face)*; is pasted on (face)*; is pinned to (face)*; is planted on (face)*; is plastered across (face)*; is plastered all over (face)*; is plastered over (face)*; is plastered to (face)*; is smeared over (face)*; is still lighting (face)*; is still lurking on (face)*; is still on (face); lace (face); leave (face); lift (face); lift (one side) of (face); light (face); light up (face); lighten (face); line (face); lurk on (face); make (face) (look boyish); make (face) (more boyish); make (its way) across (face); move across (face); move over (face); part (face); pass over (face); paste (itself) on (face); play across (face); play on (face); quirk across (face); quirk up (one side) of (face); rake across (face); reappear on (face); relieve (some of the tension) in (face); remain on (face); return to (face); settle across (face); settle on (face); settle over (face); shine (white) in (face); shine from (face); shoot across (face); show (briefly) on (face); show on (face); sketch across (face); skip across (face); slant across (face); slash (face); slash across (face); slice (face); slide (slowly) over (face); slide across (face); slide away from (face); slide from (face); slide off (face); slide onto (face); slide over (face); slide up (face); slip across (face); slip from (face); slip up (one side) of (face); slit (face); slow-dance across (face); sneak across (face); soften (face); soften (the contours) of (face); soften (the grim expression) on (face); soften (the hard planes) of (face); soften (the wrinkles) on (face); sparkle across (face); spill onto (face); spill over (face); splash across (face); splash on (face); splay across (face); split (face); split (face) (almost in two); split (face) (from ear to ear); split (face) (in half); split (face) (in two); split across (face); spread (all) over (face); spread (gradually) across (face); spread (like molasses) across (face); spread (prettily) over (face); spread (right) across (face); spread (slowly) across (face); spread (wide) across (face); spread across (face); spread on (face); spread onto (face); spread out across (face); spread out on (face); spread out over (face); spread over (face); spread until it covers (face); start on (face); start slow and spread across (face); start to spread across (face); start to steal across (face); stay on (face); steal across (face); steal onto (face); steal over (face); stole across (face); stomp all over (face); stretch (face); stretch (face) (so hard it hurt); stretch across (face); stretch on (face); stretch so wide (face) hurt; stretch wide across (face); suffuse (face); surface on (face); sweep across (face); swing across (face); take (years) off (face); take center stage on (face); take over (face); take up (entire) (face); tease (face); threaten to break across (face); threaten to break out across (face); threaten to break out all over (face); threaten to expand on (face); threaten to overtake (face); threaten to split (face); threaten to split (face) in half; threaten to split open (face); threaten to spread across (face); threaten to swallow (face); threaten to take over (face); tip (one side) of (face); touch (face); transfigure (face); transform (face); tug at (face); twist (face); unfurl across (face); vanish from (face); warm (face); whip across (face); whisper across (face); widen (until it nearly split) (face); widen on (face); work (its way) to (face); wreathe (face).

Features as Object

appear on (features); begin to spread across (features); break out on (features); break over (features); break through (features); break up (features); brighten (features); burnish (features) with (enthusiasm); chase (the serious aspect) from (features); claim (features); come back to (features); come over (features); crack (features); crease (features); creep across (features); creep over (features); crinkle (features); cross (features); cut (a line) across (features); dance across (features); dance over (features); die away from (features); dispel (the taut anger) of (features); distort (features); ease (the strain) from (features); enliven (features); etch (features); etch (its way) across (features); flash across (features); flicker across (features); flit over (features); form on (features); give (charm) to (features); give (features) (a rakish quality); hijack (features); leap across (features); lend (boyish quality) to (features); lift (features); light (features); light up (features); lighten (features); lighten (the tension) from (features); make (features) (totally irresistible); move across (features); move over (features); overtake (features); play on (features); relax (features); slash (features); slash across (features); slice across (features); soften (features); splash over (features); (nearly) split (features) in two; split (features); spread across (features); spread out over (features); spread over (features); steal across (features); steal over (features); stretch across (features); take (years) off (features); tease (features); transform (features); work (its way) across (features).

Lips as Object

angle across (lips); appear on (lips); begin to chase (its way) across (lips); begin to curl (lips); begin to ease across (lips); begin to form on (lips); begin to tug at (lips); bend (the corners) of (lips); bloom on (lips); blossom on (lips); blossom over (lips); break from (lips); break on (lips); break out on (lips); brush (lips); cant (lips); catch (lips); catch at (lips); catch hold of (lips); chase across (lips); claim (lips); cock (lips); come and go on (lips); come to (lips); crease (lips); creep across (lips); creep over (lips); crook (lips); cross (lips); curl (lips); curl (one side) of (lips); curl (the corners) of (lips); curl across (lips); curl around (lips); curl at (the edges) of (lips); curl up (one corner) of (lips); curve (lips); curve (one side) of (lips); curve (the corner(s)) of (lips); curve at (the corners) of (lips); curve on (lips); curve up (lips); curve up (the corners) of (lips); dance about (lips); dare to tug at (the tight line) of (lips); disappear from (lips); drift over (lips); drop away from (lips); ease across (lips); edge (its way) onto (lips); edge (lips); emerge on (lips); fade from (lips); flash across (lips); flick (lips); flick over (lips); flicker across (lips); flirt with (lips); flit across (lips); flit around (lips); flit over (lips); force (lips) wide; form on (lips); freeze on (lips); ghost (lips); grace (lips); grow on (lips); hover around (lips); hover around (the edges) of (lips); hover on (lips); hover over (lips); leak through (tightly) set (lips); leap to (lips); leave (lips); lift (lips); lift (lips) into (smile / grin); lift (one corner) of (lips); lift (the corner(s)) of (lips); lift (the edges) of (lips); light (lips); linger on (lips); linger upon (lips); lurk behind (lips); mold (lips); move (lips); move (one side) of (lips); move over (lips); nicker on (the edges) of (lips); nip at (lips); part (lips); pass over (lips); play (again) on (lips); play about (lips); play across (lips); play along (lips); play around (lips); play at (lips); play at (the corners) of (lips); play on (lips); play over (lips); play with (lips); pull at (lips); push at (lips); quirk (lips); quirk on (lips); quirk up (the corners) of (lips); quiver across (lips); reach (lips); recede from (lips); return to (lips); ride (lips); rise to (lips); roll across (lips); roll around (lips); saunter across (lips); seize (lips); separate (lips); settle into (a smile / a grin) on (lips); settle on (lips); shape (lips); shoot to (lips); show off (lips); slant (lips); slide across (lips); slide from (lips); slide over (lips); slip to (lips); sneak across (lips); split (lips); spread (lips); spread across (lips); spread along (lips); spread on (lips); spread out over (lips); spread over (lips); spread to (lips); spring to (lips); start to etch (its way) across (lips); start to tug at (lips); stay on (lips); steal over (lips); still cling to (lips); stretch (lips); stretch (lips) wide; stretch across (lips); struggle to take over (lips); sweep over (lips); take control of (lips); take hold of (lips); taunt (lips); tease (a smile / a grin) to (lips); tease (lips); tease at (lips); threaten to curve (lips); tickle (lips); tickle (the corners) of (lips); tilt (lips); tilt (lips) upward(s); tilt (one corner) of (lips); tilt (the corner(s)) of (lips); tilt (the corner(s)) of (lips) up; tip (lips); tip up (the corners) of (lips); touch (lips); touch (the corners) of (lips); toy with (lips); tremble on (lips); try to steal over (lips); tug (lips); tug (lips) upward(s); tug (the corners) of (lips); tug at (lips); tug at (one corner) of (lips); tug at (one side) of (lips); tug at (the corners) of (lips); turn (lips) up at (the corners); turn (lips) upward(s); turn (the corners) of (lips) upward(s); turn up (the corners) of (lips); tweak (lips); twist (lips); twist up (one corner) of (lips); twitch (lips); twitch at (lips); twitch at (the corners) of (lips); twitch on (lips); unfold across (lips); unfold on (lips); upturn (the edges) of (lips); widen (lips); work (its way) across (lips); work (lips); work at (lips).

Mouth as Object

activate (a matching pair of dimples on either side) of (mouth); add (little crinkles) around (mouth); angle across (mouth); appear about (mouth); appear at (one corner / the corner) of (mouth); appear on (mouth); begin to appear on (mouth); begin to curl (mouth); begin to curl at (the corners) of (mouth); begin to play about (the corners) of (mouth); begin to pull at (mouth); blossom in (the corner) of (mouth); bracket (mouth); bracket (one corner) of (mouth); break across (mouth); break on (mouth); break out on (mouth); bring about (a curving) of (mouth); bring up (both corners) of (mouth); build across (mouth); cant (mouth); cant (mouth) (to one side); capture (the corner) of (mouth); carve (deep grooves) beside (mouth); carve (mouth); catch (the corner(s)) of (mouth); catch at (mouth); catch at (the corner) of (mouth); chase (the strain) from (mouth); chase (the tension) from (mouth); chip (one corner) of (mouth); chip at (one corner) of (mouth); claim (mouth); cock (mouth); cock (the corner) of (mouth); come (quickly) to (mouth); come and go on (mouth); come to (mouth); commandeer (mouth); crack (mouth); crawl across (mouth); crawl up (one side) of (mouth); crease (mouth); crease (the corners) of (mouth); crease (the sides) of (mouth); creep (slowly) across (mouth); creep across (mouth); creep from (one side) of (mouth) to (the other); creep over (mouth); creep up (mouth); creep up (to curve) (mouth); crook (mouth); crook (one corner / one side) of (mouth); crook (the corner(s) / the side) of (mouth); crook (the corners) of (mouth); crook up (a corner) of (mouth); cross (mouth); curl (a corner) of (mouth); curl (mouth); curl (one corner) of (mouth); curl (the corner(s)) of (mouth); curl across (mouth); curve (a corner) of (mouth); curve (mouth); curve (one side) of (mouth); curve (the corner(s)) of (mouth); curve (the edges) of (mouth); curve across (mouth); curve back (mouth); curve up (the corners) of (mouth); cut (one corner) of (mouth); cut (the edge) of (mouth); cut across (mouth); dance across (mouth); dance on (mouth); dance on (the edge) of (mouth); deepen (the brackets) beside (mouth); deepen (the lines of fatigue) bracketing (mouth); deepen (the lines) bracketing (mouth); didn't (quite) make it to (mouth); disturb (mouth); draw (a crease) down (one side) of (mouth); drift across (mouth); ease (the corners) of (mouth) upward(s); ease (the deep lines) around (mouth) up;

ease (the lines) bracketing (mouth) upward(s); ease (the stiffness) around (mouth); ease across (mouth); ease up (the corners) of (mouth); edge (mouth); edge (the corners) of (mouth); edge (the corners) of (mouth) upward(s); edge at (mouth); edge upward(s) (at the corners) of (mouth); enhance (the line) of (mouth); (briefly) erase (the strain) from (mouth); etch (the hard line) of (mouth); fade from (mouth); flash across (mouth); flex (one side) of (mouth); flick at (the corner) of (mouth); flick at (the corners) of (mouth); flicker about (mouth); flicker across (mouth); flicker at (the corner) of (mouth); flirt around (the edge) of (mouth); flirt at (the corners) of (mouth); flirt with (mouth); flirt with (the corners) of (mouth); float over (mouth); form on (mouth); grace (mouth); groove (the sides) of (mouth); hijack (mouth); hitch up (a corner) of (mouth); hook (mouth); hook (one corner / one side) of (mouth); hook (the corner(s)) of (mouth); hook up (one side) of (mouth); hover about (mouth); hover around (mouth); hover around (the corners) of (mouth); hover at (one corner) of (mouth); hover at (the corner(s)) of (mouth); hover at (the corners) of (mouth); hover over (mouth); illuminate (mouth); jump about (mouth); kick (mouth) up at (the sides); kick up (a corner / one corner) of (mouth); kick up (one side) of (mouth); kick up (the corner(s)) of (mouth); lap at (the corners) of (mouth); leave (mouth); lift (a corner / one corner) of (mouth); lift (both corners) of (mouth); lift (mouth); lift (one corner) of (mouth); lift (one side) of (mouth); lift (the corner(s)) of (mouth); lift (the edges) of (mouth); light (mouth); linger around (mouth); linger at (the edges) of (mouth); lure (mouth) into (a smile / a grin); lurk around (the corners) of (mouth); lurk at (the corners) of (mouth); lurk in (the corner) of (mouth); make (its way) across (mouth); make (one side) of (mouth) hike up; mold (the corners) of (mouth); never leave (mouth); nip (one corner) of (mouth); nudge at (one corner) of (mouth); open (mouth); overtake (mouth); parenthesize (mouth); perch on (one side) of (mouth); plant (firmly) on (mouth)*; play about (mouth); play across (mouth); play around (mouth); play around (the corners) of (mouth); play around (the edges) of (mouth); play at (mouth); play at (the corner(s)) of (mouth); play over (mouth); ply (the gullies) at (the corners) of (mouth); pull at (mouth); pull at (one corner) of (mouth); pull at (one side) of (mouth); pull at (the corner(s)) of (mouth); pull at (the corners) of (mouth); pull up (one corner) of (mouth); pull up (the corner(s)) of (mouth); pull up (the corners) of (mouth); push (its way) onto (mouth); push (the corners) of (mouth) upward(s); push at (the corners) of (mouth); quirk (mouth); quirk (one corner / the corner) of (mouth); quirk (one end) of (mouth); quirk (the deep grooves) around (mouth); quirk (the edges) of (mouth); quirk around (the corners) of (mouth); quirk at (mouth); quirk at (the corner(s)) of (mouth); quirk at (the corners) of (mouth); quirk up (one corner / the corner) of (mouth); quirk up (one side) of (mouth); raise (one corner) of (mouth); raise (the corner(s)) of (mouth); recapture (one corner) of (mouth); relax (mouth); return to (mouth); return to play at (the corners) of (mouth); reveal (a dimple to the right) of (mouth); ruffle (mouth); settle on (mouth); shade (mouth); shadow (mouth); shape (mouth); slant (mouth); slash (mouth); slash across (mouth); slate (mouth); slice across (mouth); slide across (mouth); slide onto (mouth); slide over (mouth); slip across (mouth); slow-dance across (mouth); snag (mouth);

snap back onto (mouth); sneak across (mouth); sneak onto (mouth); sneak out around (the corners) of (mouth); soften (mouth); soften (the harshness) of (mouth); soften (the lines of tension) around (mouth); split (mouth); split (the weathered lines) around (mouth); split open (mouth); spread across (mouth); spread from (mouth) to (eyes); spread from (the corners) of (mouth); spread over (mouth); start across (mouth); start to tilt at (mouth); steal across (mouth); steal over (mouth); stretch (mouth); stretch (mouth) (nearly ear to ear); stretch across (mouth); swipe (mouth); take command of (mouth); take hold of (mouth); take over (mouth); take possession of (mouth); tease (mouth); tease (the corner(s)) of (mouth); tease at (mouth); tease up (one side) of (mouth); teeter at (the corners) of (mouth); threaten (the tight line) of (mouth); threaten to ruffle (mouth); threaten to soften (mouth); threaten to turn up (the corners) of (mouth); tick at (the corner) of (mouth); tickle (mouth); tilt (mouth); tilt (mouth) crookedly; tilt (one corner) of (mouth); tilt (one side) of (mouth); tilt (the corner(s)) of (mouth); tilt (the edges) of (mouth); tilt (the ends) of (mouth); tilt across (mouth); tilt up (one corner) (mouth); tilt up (the corner(s)) of (mouth); tip (mouth); tip (one corner) of (mouth); tip (the corner(s)) of (mouth); tip up (one corner) of (mouth); tip up (the corner(s)) of (mouth); touch (mouth); touch (one corner) of (mouth); touch (the corner(s)) of (mouth); touch (the edge(s)) of (mouth); try to hijack (mouth); try to pull at (the side) of (mouth); tug (mouth); tug (one corner) of (mouth); tug (the corner(s)) of (mouth); tug (the edge) of (mouth); tug at (mouth); tug at (one corner) of (mouth); tug at (one side) of (mouth); tug at (the corner(s)) of (mouth); tug at (the corners) of (mouth); tug on (mouth); turn (mouth) into (a seductive masterpiece); turn up (the corners) of (mouth); turn up (the edges) of (mouth); tweak (mouth); tweak (one side) of (mouth); tweak (the corner(s)) of (mouth); twist (mouth); twist (one side) of (mouth); twist (the corner(s)) of (mouth); twist (the corners) of (mouth) upward(s); twitch (mouth); twitch (mouth) into (a crooked line); twitch (the corners) of (mouth); twitch across (mouth); twitch around (mouth); twitch at (mouth); twitch at (one corner) of (mouth); twitch at (the corner(s)) of (mouth); twitch in (the corner) of (mouth); vanish from (mouth); widen (mouth); wiggle across (mouth); work (its way) across (mouth); work (its way) to (mouth); work at (mouth); work at (the corners) of (mouth); work over (mouth).

Teeth as Object
display (teeth); expose (teeth); reveal (teeth); show (teeth); show off (teeth); showcase (teeth).

1.6 - Verbs: Grin as Object

Character (I / He / She) as Subject
achieve (a grin); acquire (a grin); adapt (a grin); add (a grin); adopt (a grin); afford (him) (a grin); aim (a grin) at (him); allow (a grin); allow (herself) (a grin); angle (a grin); angle (a grin) at (him); angle (a grin) over (shoulder); angle (him) (a grin); assemble (a grin); assume (a grin); attempt (a grin); attempt (a

grin) at (him); attempt (a grin) back; award (him) (a grin); banish (a grin); battle (a grin); beam (a grin); beam (a grin) at (him); beam (a grin) up at (him); beam (him) (a grin); bestow (a grin) on/upon (him); bestow on (him) (a grin); bite back (a grin); block (a grin) with (hand)*; brave (a grin); bring (a grin) back; bury (a grin); call up (a grin); can't stop (a grin) from breaking out; cast (a grin) at (him); cast (a grin) in (his direction); cast (a grin) over (shoulder); cast (a grin) toward(s) (him); cast (him) (a grin); catch (a grin) from (him)*; catch (herself) fighting (a grin); check (a grin); coax (a grin) from (him)*; coax (a grin) out of (him)*; cock (a grin); cock (a grin) at (him); cock (him) (a grin); combat (a grin); conceal (a grin); conceal (a grin) with (hand)*; concede (a grin); conjure (a grin); conjure up (a grin); conquer (a grin); (barely) contain (a grin); contain (a grin); control (a grin); counter with (a grin); cover (a grin); cover (a grin) with (hand)*; crack (a grin); crook (a grin); crook (a grin) at (him); cultivate (a grin); curb (a grin); curve (a grin); cut (a grin) at (him); cut (him) (a grin); dare (a grin); dart (a grin) (his way); dart (a grin) at (him); dart (him) (a grin); dash (him) (a grin); deal (him) (a grin); deliver (a grin); detect (a grin) in (his voice)*; direct (a grin) (his way); direct (a grin) at (him); direct (a grin) over (shoulder); direct (a grin) toward(s) (him); direct (him) (a grin); discipline (a grin); dispense with (a grin); display (a grin); don (a grin); downplay (a grin); draw (a grin) from (him)*; drop (a grin) (his way); earn (a grin) from (him)*; ease (him) (a grin); elicit (a grin); elicit (a grin) from (him)*; essay (a grin); evoke (a grin) from (him)*; exchange (a grin); exchange (a grin) with (him); expect (a grin) from (him)*; extract (a grin) from (him)*; fake (a grin); fashion (a grin); feed (him) (a grin); feel (a grin) form; fight (a grin); fight back (a grin); find (a grin) (breaking through); find (a grin) from (somewhere); find (herself) fighting (a grin); fire (a grin) at (him); flash (a grin); flash (a grin) (his way); flash (a grin) across (table); flash (a grin) at (him); flash (a grin) from across (room); flash (a grin) in (his direction); flash (a grin) over (shoulder) at (him); flash (a grin) toward(s) (him); flash (a grin) up at (him); flash (him) (a grin); flex (a grin); flick (a grin) at (him); flick (him) (a grin); flicker (a grin); flicker (a grin) at (him); fling (a grin) at (him); fling (a grin) over (shoulder); fling (him) (a grin); flip (a grin) (his way); flip (him) (a grin); force (a grin); force (a grin) at (his comment)*; force (a grin) from (him)*; garner (a grin) from (him)*; get (a grin) back*; get (a grin) from (him)*; get (a grin) out; gift (him) (a grin); give (a grin); give (him) (a grin); give in to (a grin); glint (a grin) across (shoulder) at (him); grace (him) with (a grin); grant (him) (a grin); grin (a grin); grin (a grin) at (him); have (a grin); have (a grin) ready for (him); hear (a grin) in (his voice)*; hide (a grin); hide (a grin) behind (hand)*; hide (a grin) with (hand)*; hold (a grin); hold back (a grin); hope (a grin) will not form; incur (a grin); intercept (a grin)*; issue (a grin); jerk (a grin); keep (a grin) contained; keep (a grin) from appearing; keep (a grin) in check; lay (a grin) on (him); leak (a grin); level (a grin) at (him); level (a grin) back at (him); level (him) (a grin); lob (a grin) (his way); lob (a grin) at (him); lob (him) (a grin); lure (a grin) from (him)*; lure (a grin) out of (him)*; make (a grin); manage (a grin); manage (a grin) for (him); manage (a grin) of (her own); manage to find (a grin) for (him); manufacture (a grin); manufacture (a grin) for (him); mask (a grin); meet (a grin) with (one of her own); muster (a grin); offer (a grin); offer (a grin) across (room); offer (a grin) of (her own); offer (a grin) to (him); offer (him) (a grin); pass (him) (a grin); pin (him) with (a grin); possess (a grin); present (a grin); present (him) with (a grin); prevent (a grin); prevent (a grin) from breaking out; produce (a grin); produce (a grin) from (him)*; proffer (a grin); provoke (a grin) from (him)*; pull (a grin); pull (a grin) from (somewhere); push (a grin) over to (him); put on (a grin); quash (a grin); quell (a grin); quirk (a grin); quirk (a grin) (his way); quirk (a grin) at (him); quirk (a grin) up at (him); raise (a grin); raise (a grin) from (him)*; receive (a grin) back*; receive (a grin) from (him)*; receive (a grin) in (return)*; release (a grin); repress (a grin); reserve (a grin) for (him); resist (a grin); resist (a grin) at (him); restrain (a grin); return (a grin); reveal (a grin); reward (him) with (a grin); risk (a grin); risk (a grin) over (shoulder); send (a grin) (his way); send (a grin) across (room); send (a grin) in (his direction); send (a grin) over to (him); send (a grin) to (him); send (a grin) toward(s) (him); send (a grin) up to (him); send (him) (a grin); shape (a grin); share (a grin); share (a grin) over (table); share (a grin) with (him); shine (a grin) at (him); shoot (a grin) (his way); shoot (a grin) at (him); shoot (a grin) back at (him); shoot (a grin) down at (him); shoot (a grin) in (his direction); shoot (a grin) over (shoulder); shoot (a grin) toward(s) (him); shoot (him) (a grin); show (him) (a grin); simulate (a grin); sketch (a grin); slant (a grin) (his way); slant (a grin) at (him); slant (a grin) in (his direction); slant (a grin) to (him); slant (a grin) toward(s) (him); slant (a grin) up at (him); slant (him) (a grin); slash (a grin); slash (a grin) at (him); slash (him) (a grin); slide (a grin) (his way); slide (a grin) at (him); slide (a grin) in (his direction); slide (a grin) over (shoulder); slide (a grin) toward(s) (him); slide (him) (a grin); sling (a grin) in (his direction); sling (him) (a grin); slip (him) (a grin); slope (a grin); slope (him) (a grin); smile (a grin); smile (a grin) at (him); smother (a grin); smother (a grin) behind (palm)*; spare (him) (a grin); sport (a grin); spread (a grin) around; squash (a grin); squelch (a grin); stall (a grin); startle (a grin) from (him)*; startle (a grin) out of (him)*; stifle (a grin); stifle (a grin) at (him); stifle (a grin) with (hand)*; stop (a grin) (from) spreading; study (him) with (a grin); subdue (a grin); summon (a grin); summon (a grin) for (him); summon up (a grin); suppress (a grin); surprise (him) with (a grin); surrender (a grin); swallow (a grin); swap (a grin) with (him); swing (a grin) at (him); tease (a grin) from (him)*; tease (a grin) out of (him)*; temper (a grin); throw (a grin) at (him); throw (a grin) back at (him); throw (a grin) in (his direction); throw (a grin) over (shoulder); throw (him) (a grin); thrust (a grin) up at (him); tilt (a grin) at (him); tip (him) (a grin); toss (a grin) at (him); toss (a grin) back at (him); toss (a grin) in (his direction); toss (a grin) over (shoulder); toss (a grin) right at (him); toss (a grin) to (him); toss (him) (a grin); treat (him) to (a grin); try (a grin); tug (a grin) from (him)*; tug (a grin) out of (him)*; turn (a grin) in (his direction); turn (a grin) toward(s) (him); twitch (a grin); unleash (a grin); venture (a grin); venture (a grin) at (him); wear (a grin); will (a grin) to appear; wrench (a grin) out of (him)*.

Cheeks or Character as Subject
(I) bite (cheek) to hide (a grin)*; (I) bite (cheek) to hold back (a grin)*; (I) bite down on the inside of (cheek) to prevent (a grin)*; (I) bite the inside of (cheek) to contain (a grin); crease in/into (a grin); crease with (a grin); dimple with (a grin); puff in (a grin); raise up into (a grin); round in (a grin); stretch in (a grin); stretch out in (a grin); twitch in (a grin)*; twitch with the effort to suppress (a grin); widen in/into (a grin).

Dimples or Character as Subject
(I) deepen (dimples) with (a grin)*; (I) expose (dimples) on either side of (grin)*; appear in (cheeks); appear on either side of (a grin); bracket (the corners/sides of mouth); cut deeper into (cheeks) (as grin expands); dent (cheeks) (as grin widens); dig deep in (cheeks); dig holes in (cheeks); flash in (a grin); flash with (a grin); flicker at (the corners/sides of mouth); flicker in (cheeks); form in (cheeks); pierce (cheeks).

Expression or Character as Subject
(I) replace (expression) with (a grin)*; become (a grin); bloom into (a grin); break apart into (a grin); break into (a grin); break up in (a grin); change into/to (a grin); continue to be split by (a grin); deteriorate into (a grin); dissolve into (a grin); ease back into (a grin); fade into (a grin); give place to (a grin); give way to (a grin); is (a grin); lighten into (a grin); melt into (a grin); morph into (a grin); open in/into (a grin); relax into (a grin); replace by/with (a grin)*; shift into (a grin); soften into (a grin); soften with (a grin)*; transform into/to (a grin); transform with (a grin)*; turn into/to (a grin); vanish in/into (a grin); vanish with (a grin)*.

Eyes or Character as Subject
(I) crinkle (eyes) in (a grin)*; (I) meet (his eyes) with (a grin)*; brighten with (a grin); crease in (a grin); crinkle (at the corners) into (a grin); crinkle in (prelude to) (a grin); crinkle in (the beginnings of) (a grin); crinkle in/into (a grin); crinkle with (a grin); glitter with (a grin); hold (a grin); light up with (a grin); light with (a grin); lighten with (a grin); narrow in (a grin); spark with (a grin); sparkle with (a grin).

Face or Character as Subject
(I) bring (a grin) to (face)*; (I) catch (a grin) on (his face)*; (I) discover (a grin) on (his face)*; (I) find (a grin) on (his face)*; (I) find (a grin) spreading across (his face)*; (I) fix (a grin) on (face)*; (I) force (a grin) onto (face)*; (I) force (face) to relax into (a grin)*; (I) keep (a grin) fixed on (face)*; (I) keep (a grin) off (face)*; (I) keep (a grin) on (face)*; (I) paint (a grin) on (face)*; (I) paste (a grin) on (face)*; (I) pin (a grin) on (face)*; (I) plant (a grin) on (face)*; (I) plaster (a grin) on/onto (face)*; (I) pull (face) into (a grin)*; (I) put (a grin) on (his face)*; (I) raise (hand) to (face) to hide (a grin)*; (I) run (hand) down (face) to smother (a grin)*; (I) slap (a grin) on (face)*; (I) sport (a grin) on (face)*; (I)

spot (a grin) lurking on (his face)*; (I) spread (a grin) across (face)*; (I) stick (a grin) on (face)*; (I) tip up (face) with (a grin)*; (I) turn (face) to hide (a grin)*; (I) twist up (face) into (a grin)*; (I) wipe (a grin) off (his face)*; (I) wrinkle (face) in (a grin)*; (nearly) split with (a grin); ache with the effort of maintaining (a grin); beam with (a grin); bear (a grin); begin to crease into (a grin); bloom in (a grin); break apart in/into (a grin); break in/into (a grin); break out in/into (a grin); break out with (a grin); break with (a grin); brighten to (a grin); brighten with (a grin); broaden in (a grin); burst into (a grin); clear into/to (a grin); collapse into (a grin); contort with the effort of swallowing (a grin); cover in (a grin); crack into (a grin); crease in/into (a grin); crease with (a grin); crease with (the lines) of (a grin); crinkle in/into (a grin); crinkle up in (a grin); crumple in (a grin); display (a grin); dissolve into (a grin); ease into (a grin); erupt in/into (a grin); explode into (a grin); fall into (a grin); fight (a grin); fold into (a grin); form into (a grin); harden with (a grin); lift in (a grin); light up in (a grin); light up with (a grin); lighten with (a grin); melt (without warning) into (a grin); melt into (a grin); open in (a grin); part in (a grin); pleat in (a grin); pull into (a grin); relax into (a grin); scrunch up in (a grin); settle into (a grin); slide into (a grin); smooth into (a grin); soften into (a grin); soften with (a grin); spark with (a grin); splinter into (a grin); split (from ear to ear) in (a grin); split in/into (a grin); split wide in (a grin); split with (a grin); spread in/into (a grin); stretch into (a grin); tighten into (a grin); twist in/into (a grin); twitch in (a grin); wear (a grin); wrinkle in/into (a grin).

Features or Character as Subject
(I) pull (features) into (a grin)*; (I) school (features) to hold back (a grin)*; assume (a grin); become split with (a grin); break into (a grin); broaden into (a grin); crease in/into (a grin); dissolve into (a grin); drop into (a grin); melt into (a grin); pucker in (a grin); pull into (a grin); relax in/into (a grin); slash into (a grin); slip into (a grin); soften in/into (a grin); soften to (a grin); soften with (a grin); split in/into (a grin); transform into (a grin).

Lips or Character as Subject
(I) can't prevent (lips) from curling up in (a grin)*; (I) can't stop (lips) from creasing into (a grin)*; (I) compress (lips) in (a grin)*; (I) curl (lips) in/into (a grin)*; (I) curve (lips) in/into (a grin)*; (I) draw (lips) between (teeth) and press them together to stop (a grin)*; (I) force (a grin) to (lips)*; (I) force (lips) into (a grin)*; (I) force (lips) to curve into (a grin)*; (I) imagine (a grin) lurking on (lips)*; (I) lick (lips) to cover (a grin)*; (I) lift (bottle/glass) to (lips) to hide (a grin)*; (I) lift (lips) in (a grin)*; (I) manage to curl (lips) into (a grin)*; (I) manage to force (lips) into (a grin)*; (I) mold (lips) into (a grin)*; (I) part (lips) in (a grin)*; (I) press (lips) together in (a grin)*; (I) press (lips) together to hold back (a grin)*; (I) press (lips) together to stop them from twisting into (a grin)*; (I) press (lips) together to suppress (a grin)*; (I) pull (lips) into (a grin)*; (I) pull back (lips) in (a grin)*; (I) purse (lips) against (a grin)*; (I) purse (lips) to hide (a grin)*; (I) purse (lips) to keep them from stretching into (a grin)*; (I) purse (lips) to stifle (a grin)*; (I) purse (lips) with (a grin)*; (I) quirk (lips) into (a

grin)*; (I) roll (lips) between (teeth) and bite down to hide (a grin)*; (I) shape (lips) into (a grin)*; (I) tighten (lips) into (a grin)*; (I) twist (lips) in/into (a grin)*; (I) twist (lips) to hide (a grin)*; (were) ready with (a grin); begin to curl into (a grin); begin to twitch into (a grin); bloom into (a grin); blossom into (a grin); bow into (a grin); break into (a grin); broaden in/into (a grin); can't help twitching into (a grin); cock in (a grin); cock upward(s) in (a grin); corkscrew into (a grin); crack in (a grin); crease in/into (a grin); crook in/into (a grin); curl back in (a grin); curl back over (teeth) in (a grin); curl back to display (teeth) in (a grin); curl in/into (a grin); curl up in/into (a grin); curl upward(s) in/into (a grin); curve (at the corners) in (a grin); curve back in (a grin); curve back over (teeth) in (a grin); curve in/into (a grin); curve up (at the corners) in (a grin); curve up in/into (a grin); curve upward(s) in/into (a grin); draw back from (teeth) in (a grin); draw back in/into (a grin); draw back over (teeth) in (a grin); draw down in (a grin); draw up in (a grin); ease into (a grin); flirt with (a grin); form (a grin); form in/into (a grin); grow into (a grin); hitch up in (a grin); inch upward(s) into (a grin); keep twitching into (a grin); kick into (a grin); kick up in (a grin); kick up into (a grin); lift in/into (a grin); lift upward(s) in (a grin); lose (their tight line) and curve in (a grin); move (crookedly) into (a grin); move in/into (a grin); part in/into (a grin); part over (teeth) in (a grin); part with (a grin); play with (a grin); progress into (a grin); pull back from (teeth) in (a grin); pull back in/into (a grin); pull back to reveal (a grin); pull into (a grin); pull up in/into (a grin); purse to subdue (a grin); purse together to suppress (a grin); quirk in/into (a grin); quirk up (at the corners) in (a grin); quirk up in/into (a grin); quirk upward(s) in (a grin); quirk with (a grin); quiver into (a grin); relax into (a grin); rise in/into (a grin); screw off (teeth) in (a grin); shape (themselves) into (a grin); shape into (a grin); shut in (a grin); slant in/into (a grin); slant to (a grin); slide back in (a grin); slide into (a grin); spasm into (a grin); split in/into (a grin); spread in/into (a grin); stretch in/into (a grin); struggle to hold back (a grin); struggle to suppress (a grin); thin into (a grin); threaten to become (a grin); threaten to lift in (a grin); tilt (at the corners) in (a grin); tilt in/into (a grin); tilt to (a grin); tilt up (at the corners) in (a grin); tilt up in (a grin); tilt upward(s) in (a grin); tip in/into (a grin); tip up in (a grin); tip upward(s) into (a grin); tremble into (a grin); tug in/into (a grin); tug up in/into (a grin); turn into (a grin); turn up in/into (a grin); turn upward(s) in/into (a grin); twist in/into (a grin); twist to stave off (a grin); twist together in (a grin); twist up in/into (a grin); twitch (almost) to (a grin); twitch in/into (a grin); twitch with (a grin); widen in/into (a grin).

Mouth or Character as Subject

(I) allow (mouth) to curve in/into (a grin)*; (I) allow (mouth) to lurch into (a grin)*; (I) allow (mouth) to relax into (a grin)*; (I) arrange (mouth) into (a grin)*; (I) bite (the inside) of (mouth) to suppress (a grin)*; (I) can't help (mouth) from lifting into (a grin)*; (I) cock (mouth) into (a grin)*; (I) compress (the corners) of (mouth) to subdue (a grin)*; (I) cover (mouth) to disguise (a grin)*; (I) cover (mouth) to hide (a grin)*; (I) crook (the corners) of (mouth) into (a grin)*; (I) curve (mouth) into (a grin)*; (I) draw (the corners) of (mouth) back in (a grin)*; (I) ease (mouth) into (a grin)*; (I) fight to keep the twitch (at the corners) of (mouth) from giving in to (a grin)*; (I) force (mouth) into (a grin)*; (I) hitch up (a single corner) of (mouth) in (a grin)*; (I) keep (mouth) from breaking into (a grin)*; (I) lift (one side) of (mouth) in (a grin)*; (I) mold (mouth) into (a grin)*; (I) open (mouth) in (a grin)*; (I) place (hand) over (mouth) to cover (a grin)*; (I) pull (mouth) into (a grin)*; (I) push (mouth) up in/into (a grin)*; (I) put (hand) over (mouth) to cover (a grin)*; (I) quirk (mouth) in/into (a grin)*; (I) quirk (mouth) up in (a grin)*; (I) rearrange (mouth) into (a grin)*; (I) rub (mouth) to hide (a grin)*; (I) school (mouth) into (a grin)*; (I) shape (mouth) into (a grin)*; (I) slant (mouth) in/into (a grin)*; (I) slap (hand) over (mouth) to hide (a grin)*; (I) soften (mouth) into (a grin)*; (I) stretch (mouth) in/into (a grin)*; (I) tip (one corner) of (mouth) up in (a half-grin)*; (I) turn (mouth) up in/into (a grin)*; (I) twist (mouth) into (a grin)*; (I) wipe (a grin) from (mouth)*; (I) wipe (hand) across (mouth) to cover (a grin)*; assume (a grin); become (a grin); begin to curve in/into (a grin); begin to pull into (a grin); bend in (a grin); betray (a grin); blossom into (a grin); break into (a grin); broaden into (a grin); budge up in (a grin); burst into (a grin); change into (a grin); change into/to (a grin); cock in (a grin); cock upward(s) into (a grin); contort into (a grin); crack in /into (a grin); crease into (a grin); creep up in (a grin); crimp into (a grin); crinkle in/into (a grin); crook (unwillingly) into (a grin); crook in/into (a grin); crook up in/into (a grin); crook up with (a grin); crook upward(s) in (a grin); crook with (a grin); curl (dangerously) into (a grin); curl in/into (a grin); curl up (at the corner) in (a grin); curl up in/into (a grin); curve in/into (a grin); curve up (at the corners) in (a grin); curve up in/into (a grin); curve upward(s) in (a grin); curve with (a grin); draw back in (a grin); draw into (a grin); draw up in (a grin); drift to (a grin); drop open into (a grin); ease into (a grin); edge into (a grin); edge up in (a grin); edge up to (a grin); fashion (a grin); fight (a grin); find (a grin); firm into (a grin); fix in (a grin); flash (a grin); flatten into (a grin); flex in (a grin); flick up in (a grin); flirt with (a grin); force into (a grin); form (a grin); go up in (a grin); hang open in (a grin); hitch in/into (a grin); hitch up in/into (a grin); hitch upward(s) into (a grin); hook into (a grin); inch back in (a grin); inch upward(s) into (a grin); is (a grin); jerk into (a grin); join in with (a grin); kick into (a grin); kick up (at the corners) in (a grin); kick up in/into (a grin); lift (endearingly) into (a grin); lift in/into (a grin); lift into (a grin); lift up in/into (a grin); lift with (a grin); open in (a grin); part in (a grin); pick up (at the corners) in (a grin); press up in (a grin); pull (slowly) into (a grin); pull back in/into (a grin); pull down in (a grin); pull in/into (a grin); pull tight over (teeth) in (a grin); pull to (one side) in (a grin); pull up into (a grin); pull up on (one side) in (a grin); purse into (a grin); quirk (at the corners) in (a grin); quirk (once more) into (a grin); quirk as if to avoid (a grin); quirk in/into (a grin); quirk outward(s) into (a grin); quirk up (at one corner) in (a grin); quirk up (lopsidedly) into (a grin); quirk up in (a grin); quirk up in/into (a grin); quirk upward(s) in/into (a grin); quirk with (a grin); raise in/into (a grin); relax in/into (a grin); rise (at one corner) into (a grin); rise in/into (a grin); roll up in (a grin); round in (a grin); set in (a grin); shape (a grin); shape into (a grin); shift into (a grin); slant down in (a grin); slant in/into (a grin); slant to (a grin); slant up in (a grin); slant upward(s) in (a grin); slant with (a grin); slide into (a grin); slide up into (a grin); slip (briefly) into (a grin); slip into (a grin); slope into (a grin); snake into (a grin); sneak up in (a grin); soften in/into (a grin); soften with (a grin); split (from ear to ear) in (a grin); split in/into (a grin); split open in (a grin); split wide in (a grin); split with (a grin); sport (a grin); spread in/into (a grin); start to widen into (a grin); stretch (lazily) into (a grin); stretch in/into (a grin); stretch out into (a grin); stretch upward(s) in (a grin); struggle to suppress (a grin); sweep into (a grin); take on (a grin); thin to (a grin); tighten (at the corners) into (a grin); tighten into (a grin); tilt in (a grin); tilt in/into (a grin); tilt to (a grin); tilt up in (a grin); tilt upward(s) in (a grin); tilt with (a grin); tip in/into (a grin); tip up in (a grin); tip up in/into (a grin); tip upward(s) in (a grin); try to maintain (a grin); try to twitch into (a grin); tuck into (a grin); tug (to one side) to disguise (a grin); tug down in (a grin); tug in/into (a grin); tug up in/into (a grin); tug upward(s) in (a grin); turn into (a grin); turn up (at the corners) in/into (a grin); turn up in/into (a grin); turn upward(s) in/into (a grin); tweak into (a grin); twist (briefly) into (a grin); twist (itself) into (a grin); twist as if to hide (a grin); twist in/into (a grin); twist to (a grin); twist up in (a grin); twist with (a grin); twitch in/into (a grin); twitch outward(s) into (a grin); twitch to control (a grin); twitch up in (a grin); twitch with (a grin); wear (a grin); widen in/into (a grin); widen to (a grin); widen with (a grin); work into (a grin).

Teeth or Character as Subject
(I) bare (teeth) in (a grin)*; (I) expose (teeth) in (a grin)*; (I) flash (teeth) in (a grin)*; (I) grit (teeth) in (a grin)*; (I) reveal (teeth) in (a grin)*; (I) show (teeth) in (a grin)*; (I) show off (teeth) in (a grin)*; flash in/into (a grin); gleam in (a grin); glint in (a grin); show in (a grin); sparkle in (a grin).

NOUN USAGE EXAMPLES

Dylan's grin broadened even more.

Felix did his best to stifle a grin.

A devilish grin played at the corners of Patty's lips.

He flashed a lopsided grin.

A grin tugged at the corner of her stern mouth.

2. Verb Form

2.1 - Verb Synonyms

beam; crack a grin/smile; express friendliness; grin/smile from ear to ear; grin/smile like a Cheshire cat; look amused; look delighted; look ecstatic; look happy; look pleased; put on a happy expression; simper; smirk.

2.2 - Adverbs

A
abruptly; absently; abstractedly; absurdly; actually*; admiringly; adoringly; affably; affectionately; aggravatingly; airily; alternately; amiably; amicably; amusedly; angelically; annoyingly; apologetically; apparently; appealingly; appreciatively; approvingly; arrogantly; attractively; automatically; awfully; awkwardly.

B
banteringly; barely*; bashfully; beatifically; beguilingly; belatedly; besottedly; blankly; bleakly; blissfully; boldly; boyishly; brashly; briefly; brightly; brilliantly; broadly.

C
calmly; carelessly; casually; certainly*; challengingly; charmingly; cheekily; cheerfully; cheerily; clearly; cockily; coldly; comfortably; companionably; compassionately; complacently; completely; confidently; conspiratorially; conspiringly; contentedly; crazily; crookedly; curiously; cynically.

D
darkly; deeply; defiantly; definitely*; deliberately; deliciously; delightedly; deliriously; derisively; devastatingly; devilishly; directly; disarmingly; disrespectfully; drunkenly.

E
easily; effectively; encouragingly; endearingly; engagingly; enthusiastically; entirely; equally*; eventually; evilly; exactly; excitedly; expectantly; expressively; extremely smugly; exuberantly; exultantly.

F
faintly; familiarly; fatuously; feebly; fiendishly; fiercely; finally*; firmly; fixedly; fleetingly; flirtatiously; fondly; foolishly; fractionally; frankly; fully; furiously.

G
gaily; gamely; giddily; girlishly; gleefully; goadingly; good-naturedly; goofily; gradually; gratefully; grimly; groggily; guilelessly; gummily.

H

halfheartedly; happily; hardly*; hastily; hatefully; haughtily; helplessly; hideously; hopefully; horribly; hugely; humbly; humorlessly; humorously.

I

idiotically; immediately; impenitently; impishly; impossibly; impudently; inanely; incorrigibly; incredibly; indifferently; indulgently; inexplicably; infectiously; infuriatingly; innocently; innocuously; insolently; instantly; involuntarily; inwardly; ironically; irrepressibly; irrepressively; irreverently; irritatingly.

J

jauntily; joyfully; joyously; jubilantly.

K

knowingly.

L

lamely; lasciviously; lazily; lecherously; leisurely; lewdly; likely*; literally; lopsidedly; lovingly.

M

maddeningly; madly; malevolently; maliciously; maniacally; manically; meaningfully; mercilessly; merely*; merrily; miraculously; mirthlessly; mischievously; mockingly; momentarily; mostly; mushily; mysteriously.

N

narrowly; naughtily; nearly*; nervously; nicely; nonchalantly.

O

obligingly; obliquely; obviously*; ominously; only*; openly; outrageously; owlishly.

P

painfully; peacefully; penitently; perfectly; permanently; perpetually; pertly; placatingly; plainly; playfully; pleasantly; pointedly; politely; positively*; possibly*; practically*; precociously; privately; probably*; promptly*; proudly; provocatively; purely.

Q

quickly; quizzically.

R

rakishly; randomly; rapidly; readily*; really*; reassuringly; recklessly; reluctantly; remarkably; reminiscently; remorselessly; repentantly; reproachfully; ridiculously; roguishly; ruefully.

S

sadistically; salaciously; sarcastically; sardonically; satanically; saucily; savagely; secretly; seductively; seemingly*; self-derisively; seriously; sexily; shakily; shamefacedly; shamefully; shamelessly; sharply; sheepishly; shrewdly; shyly; silently; simply*; skeptically; sleepily; slightly; slightly crookedly; slightly shamefacedly; sloppily; slowly; slyly; smugly; softly; solidly; soppily; sourly; spontaneously; strikingly; stupidly; subtly; suddenly; suggestively; surprisingly; surreptitiously; sweetly; swiftly; sympathetically.

T

tantalizingly; tauntingly; tautly; teasingly; temporarily; tentatively; thoughtfully; threateningly; tightly; tiredly; tolerantly; toothily; toothlessly; totally; triumphantly.

U

unabashedly; unapologetically; unashamedly; unbelievingly; unconcernedly; uncontrollably; understandingly; uneasily; unevenly; unexpectedly; unkindly; unpleasantly; unrepentantly; unreservedly; unsteadily; unwillingly; usually*.

V

vacuously; victoriously; virtuously.

W

wanly; warmly; weakly; wearily; welcomingly; wetly; whimsically; whitely; wickedly; widely; wildly; winningly; winsomely; wisely; wolfishly; wryly.

2.3 - Adverbials of Emotion, Feeling, Mental State, Response, Gesture, and Appearance

in a can't-blame-a-guy-for-trying way; in a certain fashion; in a conspiratorial way; in a crestfallen way; in a curious kind of way; in a fairly condescending way; in a fatherly fashion; in a friendly fashion; in a friendly manner; in a friendly way; in a friendly, disarming sort of way; in a funny sort of way; in a good-natured way; in a half shamed, half confiding way; in a knowing sort of way; in a malevolent way; in a manic kind of way; in a manner of sheer male hubris; in a mocking way; in a most maddening fashion; in a placatory manner; in a rather relieved manner; in a reassuring way; in a satisfied way, in a secretive, knowing way; in a self-deprecating way; in a sexy teasing way; in a shy way; in a silly fashion; in a slightly loopy way; in a sort of gamin way; in a suddenly boyish manner; in a teasing way; in a warm, all-embracing way; in acceptance; in acknowledgment; in admiration; in affectionate memory; in agreement; in amazed delight; in amazement; in amusement; in an easygoing way; in an oddly suggestive way; in answer; in anticipation; in apology; in apparent good humor; in appreciation; in approval; in black amusement; in boyish embarrassment; in boyish triumph; in brief acknowledgment; in childish elation; in clear appreciation; in complete delight; in complicity; in comprehension; in confirmation; in contentment; in delight; in delighted disbelief; in devilish delight; in disbelief; in empathy; in encouragement; in enjoyment; in evidence; in evident disbelief; in excitement; in expectation; in exultation; in fiendish triumph; in fond memory; in frank appreciation; in frantic joy; in full; in genuine amusement; in genuine delight; in gratitude; in greeting; in happy anticipation; in happy triumph; in helpless appreciation; in her mind; in high good spirits; in his characteristic manner; in his cocky, masculine way; in his familiar way; in his good-humored way; in his happy way; in his mock servility; in his most ingratiating way; in his old cheerful way; in his usual easy manner; in his usual friendly manner; in his usual manner; in huge delight; in huge enjoyment; in humorous protest; in immediate understanding; in immense satisfaction; in intrigue; in languorous anticipation; in light mockery at himself; in male pride; in malicious delight; in masculine commiseration; in masculine satisfaction; in memory; in mild self-mockery; in mock dismay; in mock gallantry; in mocking triumph; in obvious agreement; in obvious delight; in obvious pleasure; in perfect comprehension; in perfect harmony; in perfect understanding; in pleasure; in pride; in pure challenge; in pure delight; in pure enjoyment; in pure evil; in pure happiness; in pure relief; in quiet surprise; in recognition; in relief; in reluctant acknowledgment; in remembrance; in reminiscence; in reply; in response; in return; in rueful self-mockery; in satisfaction; in secret satisfaction; in self-mockery; in self-satisfaction; in shameless invitation; in shocked surprise; in silent appreciation; in smug delight; in solidarity; in some surprise; in spite of her anxiety; in spite of her bad mood; in spite of her blue mood; in spite of her irritation; in spite of her misgivings; in spite of her mood; in spite of her worry; in spite of herself; in spite of himself; in spite of his current misery; in spite of the conflicting emotions plaguing him; in spite of the depression; in startled surprise and pleasure; in such a friendly fashion; in such a hateful way; in such a sexy way; in such open delight; in sudden amusement; in sudden relief; in sudden sympathy; in sudden understanding; in sudden, devastating humor; in supreme satisfaction; in surprise; in surprised recognition; in sympathy; in that brief and diabolical way of his; in that carefree way of his; in that delightfully endearing way of his; in that disarming way he had; in that doesn't-bother-me way; in that endearing way of his; in that familiar, unrepentant way; in that indulgent, affectionate way; in that infuriating way of his; in that maddening, teasing way; in that reckless way of his; in that same crooked fashion; in that same taunting way; in that sardonic way; in that seriously weakening way; in that sexy way; in that smug, masculine way; in the disarming way he could; in the familiar, irrepressible fashion; in the most knowing and exasperating way; in total unrepentance; in transparent relief;

in triumph; in unashamed delight; in understanding; in victory; in welcome; in wicked delight and anticipation; in wicked triumph; in wry amusement; in wry humor; with a certain degree of pride; with a conspiratorial wink*; with a devilish glint in his eye*; with a devilish look back over his shoulder*; with a disarming flash of white teeth*; with a dismissive shrug*; with a flash of excellent teeth*; with a flash of his usual good humor; with a flash of white teeth*; with a gleeful triumph; with a good deal of satisfaction; with a knowing wink*; with a leer; with a lifted brow*; with a little of his old arrogance; with a marked lack of repentance; with a most unexpected touch of mischief; with a pointedness that was hard to ignore; with a ridiculous surge of satisfaction; with a rush of affection; with a satisfied gleam in his eyes*; with a savage pleasure; with a sense of triumph; with a sudden change of mood; with a surprising trace of humility; with a tinge of grimness; with a total lack of repentance; with a trace of self-mockery; with a trace of sheepishness; with a wicked insouciance; with a wry self-derision; with affection; with affectionate exasperation; with agreement; with all the confidence of someone in the know; with almost silly delight; with amused exasperation; with amused regret; with amusement; with an aggressive flash of white teeth*; with an appealing boyishness; with an effort; with an enthusiasm he didn't quite feel; with an infuriating smugness; with an unexpected touch of impishness; with anticipation; with appealing wryness; with appreciation; with approval; with arrogant pride; with assumed ruefulness; with bemused admiration; with bitter satisfaction; with both relief and anticipation; with boyish embarrassment and pride; with boyish mischief; with brash confidence; with brazen feminine satisfaction; with chagrin; with closed lips*; with complacent amusement; with complete lack of repentance; with complete male satisfaction; with confidence; with customary self-assurance; with cynical amusement; with deep pleasure; with delight; with derision; with devilish challenge; with devilish delight; with difficulty; with easy confidence; with effort; with embarrassment; with enjoyment; with enjoyment and admiration; with enthralling wickedness; with evident relief; with evil delight; with excitement; with exhilarating triumph; with exhilaration; with faint malice; with familiar masculine assurance; with feline satisfaction; with feral savagery; with gamine charm; with genuine amusement; with genuine delight; with genuine happiness; with genuine warmth; with glee; with gleeful anticipation; with gloating satisfaction; with good humor; with great charm; with great gusto, and enthusiasm; with great pleasure; with great satisfaction; with happiness; with health and happiness; with his usual exasperating amusement; with impish enthusiasm; with impish humor; with inane pride; with incorrigible optimism; with indolent devilry; with infuriating amusement; with insolence; with interest; with involuntary enjoyment; with joy; with lascivious purpose; with lazy amusement; with lazy contentment; with lazy insolence; with loving pride; with maddening confidence; with malevolent; with malice; with malicious enjoyment; with malicious glee; with malicious hardness; with malicious pleasure; with malicious satisfaction; with masculine confidence; with masculine satisfaction; with merriment; with mischief; with mischievous intent; with mock apology; with much more confidence than she actually felt; with much satisfaction; with new confidence; with new hope; with obvious delight; with obvious enjoyment; with obvious interest; with obvious male pride; with obvious pleasure; with obvious pride; with obvious relief; with obvious relish; with open appreciation; with open delight; with open enthusiasm; with overplayed guilelessness; with pleasure; with pride; with pride and happiness; with pure amusement; with pure happiness; with pure male challenge; with pure mischief; with radiant, unchecked joy; with real friendliness; with reckless, flashing charm; with recognition; with relief; with relief and delight; with relish; with reminiscent relish; with rueful humor; with rueful self-mockery; with sardonic amusement; with sardonic appreciation; with satisfaction; with satisfaction and triumph; with savage satisfaction; with self-satisfaction; with sheer appreciation; with sheer delight; with silly male pride; with sinful intent; with sneaky triumph; with some effort; with some satisfaction; with such a boyish air; with such charm; with such enthusiasm; with such good cheer; with such tenderness; with such wicked amusement; with sudden boyishness; with sudden impishness; with sudden mischief; with sudden wickedness; with supreme pleasure; with surprising wickedness; with that irresistible, little-boy charm; with the anticipation of fun; with the ease of an old friend; with the pure delight; with the sheer joy of living; with the thought; with the thrill of victory; with thirteen-year-old exuberance; with thorough male satisfaction; with thoroughly evil satisfaction; with triumph; with typical male appreciation; with unabashed delight; with unabashed enthusiasm; with unabashed relish; with unabashed satisfaction; with unconcealed delight; with understanding; with unholy glee; with unreserved masculine appreciation; with what appeared to be genuine affection; with what he hoped was world-class nonchalance; with what was clearly proud satisfaction; with wicked amusement; with wicked complacency; with wicked confidence; with wicked delight; with wicked enjoyment; with wicked intent; with wicked knowing; with wicked pleasure; with wicked satisfaction; with wry affection; with wry amusement; with wry humor.

VERB USAGE EXAMPLES

Casey grinned reassuringly.

Steve grinned with wicked enjoyment.

He grinned across at her.

Grinning lopsidedly at her comment, he removed his hat and sat down beside her.

She grinned up at him in that endearing way of hers.

9
LEER

1. Noun Form

1.1 - Noun Synonyms

goggle; lascivious look; lecherous look; lustful stare; ogle; once-over; salacious look; sidelong glance; sly look; sneer; stare.

1.2 - Adjectives

A
accompanying; admiring; alcoholic; alcohol-induced; amused; animal-like; another; anticipatory; appreciative; audible; awful.

B
bad-guy; bawdy; best; big; bored; brief; broad; burlesqued.

C
cat-like; collective; come-hither; comic; comical; confident; considering; conspiratorial; contemptuous; creditable; customary.

D
decadent; decided; definite; deliberate; delicious; demonic; devilish; disbelieving; discernible; disgusting; distasteful; distorted; Dracula-like; drunken.

E
earlier; engaging; every; evil; exaggerated; expected; experimental.

F
faint; fake; feigned; ferocious; flame-lit; flirtatious; friendly; full-blown.

G
gawping; gentle; good-natured; grinning; grotesque.

H

half-hearted; happy; hideous; hopeful; horrific; hot-eyed; hungriest; hungry.

I

indefinable; infuriating; ingratiating; irritating.

K

king-sized; knowing.

L

lascivious; last; laughable; laughing; lecherous; little; locker-room; lustful.

M

meaningful; melodramatic; mental; mild; mock; mock-lascivious; mocking.

N

nasty.

O

obvious; occasional; off-putting; ogling; old-man; open; ostentatious; outrageous; outright; overdone; owlish.

P

part; particular; patented; piggy-eyed; playful; positive; predatory; pretend; primitive; provocative.

Q

quick.

R

repugnant; repulsive; roguish.

S

salacious; satisfied; seductive; sexist; sexy; shared; sickening; sickly; sinful; slight; slow; sly; smug; spiteful; stage; strange; stricken; suggestive; supercilious; suspicious.

T

taunting; teasing; theatrical; threatening; tobacco-stained; too-confident; tough-girl; triumphant.

U

ugly; unabashed; unfocused; unmistakable; unpleasant; unsteady; usual.

V

veiled; vicious; villainous; vocal.

W

wicked; wink-wink-nudge-nudge; wolfish; worst.

1.3 - Noun + Prepositional Phrases

leer of a curious man; leer of a melodrama villain; leer of hatred; leer of mock admiration; leer of truly villainous dimensions; leer of white teeth.

1.4 - Noun Phrases

a/the hint of a leer; a/the kind of leer; a ladylike version of a leer; a painful parody of a leer; a pale imitation of a sexy leer; a/the sort of leer; an approximation of a leer; any semblance of a leer; his best imitation of a leer; just short of a leer; nothing short of a leer; something of a leer; the faint trace of a leer; the lack of a leer; the prying indecency of a leer.

1.5 - Verbs: Leer as Subject

Standalone Verbs
deepen; evaporate; increase; intensify; return; stop; vanish.

Eyes as Object
come into (eyes); is in (eyes); slip into (eyes).

Face as Object
distort (face); drape (face); fade from (face); is on (face); is upon (face); spread across (face).

Lips as Object
contort (lips); is on (lips); twist (lips).

Mouth as Object
is on (mouth).

Skin as Object
make (her skin) crawl; make (her skin) sizzle.

Teeth as Object
expose (teeth); reveal (teeth); show (teeth).

1.6 - Verbs: Leer as Object

Character (I / He / She) as Subject
attempt (a leer); cast (a leer) upon (him); direct (a leer) at (him); fake (a leer); flash (him) (a leer); give (a leer); give (a leer) at (him); give (a leer) in (his direction); give (him) (a leer); have (a leer) at (him); improvise (a leer); offer (a leer); receive (a leer) from (him)*; resist (a leer); send (him) (a leer); shoot (him) (a leer); simulate (a leer); throw (him) (a leer); toss (him) (a leer); wear (a leer).

Eyebrows / Brows or Character as Subject
(I) raise (eyebrows) in (a leer)*; (I) waggle (eyebrows) in (a leer)*; (I) wiggle (eyebrows) in (a leer)*; (I) wriggle (eyebrows) in (a leer)*; jump in (a leer); rise in (a leer); rise with (a leer).

Eyes or Character as Subject
(I) rake (eyes) over (her body) with (a leer)*; crinkle in (a leer); focus on (her) with (a leer); look (her) over with (a leer); rest on (her) with (a leer).

Face or Character as Subject
(I) contort (face) into (a leer)*; (I) look down at (her face) with (a leer)*; (I) paste (a leer) on (face)*; (I) twist (face) into (a leer)*; break into (a leer); change to (a leer); contort in/into (a leer); mock (her) with (a leer); spread into (a leer); twist into (a leer).

Lips or Character as Subject
(I) twist (lips) into (a leer)*; twist in (a leer).

Mouth or Character as Subject
(I) cover (mouth) with (hand) to stifle (a leer)*; (I) curve (mouth) into (a leer)*; curve into (a leer); lift in (a leer); stretch in (a leer); twist in/into (a leer); twitch into (a leer).

Teeth or Character as Subject
(I) bare (teeth) in (a leer)*; are exposed in (a leer)*; are revealed in (a leer)*; show in (a leer).

NOUN USAGE EXAMPLES

He loomed over her, a leer distorting his handsome face.

126

Edward's grin turned into an appreciative leer.

Richie's mouth twisted into an ugly leer.

He waggled his eyebrows in a mock leer.

He gave her a meaningful leer.

2. Verb Form

2.1 - Verb Synonyms

check out; eye; eye hungrily; eye lasciviously; eye lecherously; eye lustfully; eye salaciously; eyeball; give a dirty look; give a look to kill; give once-over; give the evil eye; glance at sideways; glower; look askance at; look at longingly; look at out of the corner of one's eye; look at slyly; look sidelong; ogle; smirk; stare; undress with one's eyes; watch.

2.2 - Adverbs

A
actually*; amiably.

C
cheerfully; clowningly; comically.

E
eagerly; evilly.

H
happily; hardly*; hatefully; horribly; hungrily.

I
instantly.

J
jovially.

K
knowingly.

L
lasciviously; lustfully.

M
mentally*; merely*; mischievously.

N
nicely.

O
openly; outrageously.

P
perfectly; positively*; practically*.

S
salaciously; secretly; simply*; sleepily; slightly; suggestively.

T
terribly; theatrically; triumphantly.

U
unconvincingly.

V
vacantly.

W
warmly; wickedly.

2.3 - Adverbials of Emotion, Feeling, Mental State, and Response

in a completely soulless manner; in a dignified sort of way; in a lecherous parody; in a lecherous way; in return; in satisfaction; in some amusement; in that vulgar manner; with an obscene aura of tragedy; with intent; with mock lasciviousness; with outright hunger; with unashamed insolence.

VERB USAGE EXAMPLES

When she finally met his gaze, he leered triumphantly.

He leered suggestively at her.

He winked and leered as he took her in.

He leered down at her with unashamed insolence.

Leering in satisfaction, she pushed the older woman out of her way.

10
POUT

1. Noun Form

1.1 - Noun Synonyms

hangdog look; long face; moue; mow; sullen look; wry face.

1.2 - Adjectives

A

accomplished; accusing; aching; adorable; aggrieved; all-out; alluring; angry; annoyed; another; appealing; appreciative; astonished; attractive; authentic.

B

baby; babyish; bad-boy; bad-tempered; beautiful; bee-stung; begging; beguiling; belligerent; bemused; best; betrayed; boyish; brooding; bulldog; by-now-familiar.

C

cantankerous; champion; charming; childish; childlike; clear; coaxing; collagen-enhanced; come-hither; comical; conscious; considering; contemplative; contemptuous; contrite; contrived; convincing; coy; crazy-cute; creased; crestfallen; crimson; crushed-kiss; curvy; customary; cute; cutest; cynical.

D

damn; dark; decided; deep; defensive; defiant; defined; definite; dejected; delectable; deliberate; delicate; delicious; delighted; delightful; demanding; demure; determined; dewy; dimpled; disappointed; disapproving; disconsolate; discontented; disdainful; displeased; dissatisfied; dissenting; distinct; doubtful; down-and-out; downward; dramatic.

E

eat-your-heart-out; elaborate; eloquent; embarrassed; enchanting; enticing; exaggerated; expected; expressive.

F

faint; fake; familiar; famous; fashionable; feigned; feisty; feminine; femme-fatale; ferocious; fetching; fleshy; flirty; fond; frosty; frowning; frustrated; full; full-blown; full-bottom-lip; full-fledged; full-on; furious.

G

gamin; generous; girlish; girls; glorious; glossy; good; gorgeous; grim; grimacing.

H

habitual; half; hard; haughty; heart-shaped; heart-wrenching; heartfelt; heated; hopeful.

I

identical; impatient; imperceptible; indignant; inevitable; injured; innocent; instinctive; intentional; inviting; irresistible.

J

jealous; just-woke-up.

K

kissable.

L

laughing; less-flattering; light; little; little-boy; little-girl; lovely; luscious; lush; lush-lipped.

M

manly; merest; mesmerizing; mighty; militant; miserable; mock; mock-innocent; mock-sullen; moist; mulish; musing; mutinous.

N

natural; naughty; near-perfect; nervous; normal.

O

obstinate; oh-so-familiar; over-the-top; overdone; overdramatic; overstated; own.

P

painted; parted; peach; peeved; pensive; perfect; permanent; perpetual; perplexed; perturbed; petulant; petulant-looking; photogenic; pierced; pink; playful; pleading; plump; ponderous; pornstar; possible; practiced; precise; pretend; pretty; pronounced; provocative; provoking; prudish; puckered; puppy-dog; puzzled.

Q

questioning; quivering.

R

raspberry; raspberry-tinted; rebellious; recalcitrant; red; reddened; regretful; reproachful; resentful; ridiculing; ripe; rose; rosebud; royal; ruby; rueful.

S

sad; same; satisfied; scarlet; schoolgirl; schoolmarmish; schoolmarms; sculpted; seductive; self-indulgent; self-pitying; self-righteous; selfish; sensual; sensuous; sensuous-looking; severe; sexiest; sexy; short; signature; silky; silly; siren; skeptical; slight; slightest; small; smoldering; smug; sniveling; snotty; soft; softer-than-normal; sorrowful; sour; speculative; spoilt; startled; stellar; stubborn; studied; studious; stupendous; subtle; succulent; sudden; suggestive; suitable; sulking; sulky; sullen; sultry; sweet; swollen; sympathetic.

T

tantalizing; teasing; teenage; tempting; tense; theatrical; thick; thoughtful; threatening; three-year-old; thrusting; tight; tiny; toddler; too-perfect; trademark; treacherous; trembling; tremulous; troubled; trout.

U

ugly; unattractive; uncharacteristic; unconscious; understandable; unexpected; unhappy; usual.

V

vampish; voluptuous; vulnerable.

W

weary; well-kissed; well-known; well-practiced; well-timed; wet; whole; wicked; willful; winning; woe-is-me; wounded; wry.

Y

yearning.

1.3 - Noun + Prepositional Phrases

pout of a spoiled child; pout of anger; pout of annoyance; pout of anxiety; pout of awe; pout of battered pride; pout of concern; pout of copper-colored seduction; pout of defiance; pout of denial; pout of disappointment; pout of disapproval; pout of discontent; pout of dislike; pout of distress; pout of enquiry; pout of envy; pout of frustration; pout of good humor; pout of her bottom lip*; pout of her lips*; pout of her lower lip*; pout of her mouth*; pout of her upper lip*; pout of (his/hers)*; pout of indignation; pout of invitation; pout of pretend disappointment; pout of protest; pout of pure sexuality; pout of reproach; pout of such mock hurt; pout of surprise; pout of the fullness of her mouth.

1.4 - Noun Phrases

a baffled sort of pout; a bit of a haughty pout; a pretence of a pout; a suggestion of a pout; a teeny bit of a pout; a/the hint of a pout; another of his pouts; her version of a pout; just a hint of a pout; just enough of a pout; just short of a pout; just shy of a manly pout; just the faintest of pouts; the beginning(s) of a pout; the effect of her pout; the glossy satin of her pout; the luxury of a childish pout; the princess of pout; the right amount of pout; the sort of pout; the suggestion of a defiant pout; the sultry shape of her natural pout; the tiniest of pouts.

1.5 - Verbs: Pout as Subject

Standalone Verbs
appear; come back; come on; deepen; disappear; fade; go; grow; increase; reappear; return; start; vanish; waver.

Face as Object
appear on (face); change (face) from [something] to [something else]; crease (face); ease from (face); form on (face); make (face) crumple; mar (face); settle onto (face); spread across (face).

Lips as Object
appear on (lips); come to (lips); curve (lips); disappear from (lips); draw (lips) (tightly) together; form on (lips); hover over (lips); pucker (lips); pull (lips) together; pull at (lips); purse (lips); settle on (lips); squeeze (lips) together; touch (lips); tug at (lips); twist (lips); waver on (lips).

Mouth as Object
claim (mouth); come (back) to (mouth); curve (mouth); disappear from (mouth); form on (mouth); give (a twist) to (mouth); linger on (mouth); pucker (mouth); spoil (mouth).

1.6 - Verbs: Pout as Object

Character (I / He / She) as Subject
add (a pout); adopt (a pout); affect (a pout); attempt (a pout); bestow (a pout) on/upon (him); demonstrate (a pout); disguise (a pout); earn (a pout) from (him)*; fake (a pout); feel (a pout) coming on; feign (a pout); feign (a pout) at (him); flash (a pout); flash (him) (a pout); force (a pout); form (a pout); give (a

pout); give (a pout) to (him); give (him) (a pout); have (a pout); make (a pout); manage (a pout); offer (a pout); offer (him) (a pout); practice (a pout); pretend (a pout); produce (a pout); pull (a pout); receive (a pout) from (him)*; receive (a pout)*; send (him) (a pout); shoot (him) (a pout); spare (a pout) for (him); stage (a pout); summon (a pout); tease (him) with (a pout); try (a pout); wear (a pout).

Expression as Subject
is (a pout); shift to (a pout); transform to (a pout); turn to (a pout).

Eyebrows / Brows or Character as Subject
(I) draw (eyebrows) into (a pout)*; draw together in (a pout).

Face or Character as Subject
(I) pull (face) into (a pout)*; (I) school (face) into (a pout)*; (I) screw (face) into (a pout)*; (I) set (face) in (a pout)*; contort in/into (a pout); fall in/into (a pout); form (a pout); pull into (a pout); reveal (a pout); screw up in (a pout); set in (a pout); shift into (a pout); take on (a pout); temper with (a pout); turn into (a pout).

Lips or Character as Subject
(I) allow (lips) to assume (a pout)*; (I) arrange (lips) into (a pout)*; (I) bring (a pout) to (lips)*; (I) compress (lips) into (a pout)*; (I) curve (lips) into (a pout)*; (I) draw (lips) into (a pout)*; (I) extend (bottom lip / lower lip) in (a pout)*; (I) fashion (lips) into (a pout)*; (I) force (lips) into (a pout)*; (I) form (a pout) with (lips)*; (I) form (lips) into (a pout)*; (I) hold (lips) in (a pout)*; (I) let (lips) fall into (a pout)*; (I) make (a pout) with (lips)*; (I) make (lips) into (a pout)*; (I) open (lips) in (a pout)*; (I) part (lips) in/into (a pout)*; (I) poke out (bottom lip / lower lip) in (a pout)*; (I) pouch out (bottom lip / lower lip) in (a pout)*; (I) press (lips) together in (a pout)*; (I) pucker (lips) in/into (a pout)*; (I) puff (lips) in (a pout)*; (I) puff out (bottom lip / lower lip) in (a pout)*; (I) pull (lips) into (a pout)*; (I) pull (lips) together to form (a pout)*; (I) purse (lips) in/into (a pout)*; (I) push (lips) out in/into (a pout)*; (I) push out (bottom lip / lower lip) in (a pout)*; (I) put out (bottom lip / lower lip) in (a pout)*; (I) shape (lips) into (a pout)*; (I) shove out (lips) in (a pout)*; (I) stick out (bottom lip / lower lip) in (a pout)*; (I) thrust forward (lips) in (a pout)*; (I) thrust out (bottom lip / lower lip) in (a pout)*; (I) twist up (lips) in (a pout)*; (I) wear (a pout) on (lips)*; affect (a pout); are (a pout); are in (a pout); arrange (themselves) in (a pout); assume (a pout); bloom into (a pout); bow up in (a pout); change to (a pout); come forward in (a pout); come together in (a pout); compress into (a pout); crush into (a pout); curl in/into (a pout); curve downward(s) in (a pout); curve into (a pout); draw into (a pout); fall into (a pout); fold into (a pout); form (a pout); form into (a pout); go into (a pout); lie (slightly) open in (a pout); make (a pout); metamorphose into (a pout); move into (a pout); open in (a pout); part in/into (a pout); press (hard) together in (a pout); press into (a pout); pucker in/into (a pout); pucker up in (a pout); pucker up into (a pout); puff out in (a pout); pull down in (a pout); pull into (a pout); pull together in (a pout); purse

in/into (a pout); push forward in (a pout); push out in (a pout); round in (a pout); set in (a pout); settle into (a pout); shove out in (a pout); slide into (a pout); slide out in (a pout); soft in (a pout); stick out in (a pout); threaten to drop into (a pout); thrust out in (a pout); tighten in (a pout); tilt in (a pout); turn down in/into (a pout); turn into/to (a pout).

Mouth or Character as Subject

(I) compress (mouth) in (a pout)*; (I) drop (the corners) of (mouth) into (a pout)*; (I) fix (mouth) in (a pout)*; (I) keep (mouth) in (a pout)*; (I) kiss (her mouth) (back) into (a pout)*; (I) mold (mouth) into (a pout)*; (I) move (mouth) into (a pout)*; (I) pucker (mouth) in (a pout)*; (I) pull (mouth) down into (a pout)*; (I) pull (mouth) into (a pout)*; (I) purse (mouth) in/into (a pout)*; (I) push (mouth) out in (a pout)*; (I) shape (mouth) into (a pout)*; (I) thrust (mouth) into (a pout)*; (I) turn (mouth) into (a pout)*; adopt (a pout); become (a pout); buckle into (a pout); close into/to (a pout); come close to (a pout); come out in (a pout); curve downward(s) in (a pout); curve in/into (a pout); draw into (a pout); droop in/into (a pout); drop into (a pout); fall into (a pout); fall open in (a pout); flower into (a pout); form (a pout); form into (a pout); gather into (a pout); go into (a pout); go to (a pout); have (a pout); hold (a pout); hold onto (its pout); is (a pout); jut out in (a pout); lift toward(s) (him) in (a pout); move into (a pout); part in (a pout); perform (a pout); pucker in/into (a pout); puff into/to (a pout); pull into (a pout); purse in/into (a pout); purse with (a pout); push forward in (a pout); push into (a pout); push out in (a pout); quiver in (a pout); remain in (a pout); round into (a pout); screw into (a pout); screw up into (a pout); seem to form (a pout); set in/into (a pout); settle into (a pout); shape (itself) into (a pout); show (a pout); sit (softly) in (a pout); thin into (a pout); tighten into (a pout); tuck up (tidily) into (a pout); turn down (at the corners) in (a pout); turn down in/into (a pout); twist into (a pout); wear (a pout); widen into (a pout).

NOUN USAGE EXAMPLES

Carmen stuck out her lower lip in a little-girl pout.

At her words, a boyish pout appeared on his face.

Her lips assumed a stubborn pout.

Amy's rosy lips pulled into a pout.

She compressed her mouth in a pout of mock hurt.

2. Verb Form

2.1 - Verb Synonyms

be cross; be in bad mood; be moody; be petulant; be sad; be sullen; brood; feel sorry for oneself; frown; grouch; grump; hang the lip; look sullen; make a long face; make a moue; make a sad face; make a wry face; mope; put on a long face; roll out one's lip; sniffle; stick one's lip out; sulk.

2.2 - Adverbs

A

actually*; adorably; alluringly; alternately*; angrily; anxiously; attractively.

B

beautifully; briefly.

C

charmingly; clearly*; consideringly; coquettishly; coyly; creamily; crossly; currently*.

D

defiantly; delectably; deliberately; deliciously; derisively; directly; distinctively; distinctly; dramatically; drowsily.

E

engagingly; enquiringly; enticingly; erotically; especially; exaggeratedly.

F

faintly; firmly; flagrantly; flirtatiously.

G

gently; gorgeously.

H

hardly; hungrily.

I

ill-humoredly; impudently; indefinitely; innocently; invitingly.

L

lusciously; lushly.

M

magically; merely*; mutinously.

N

naturally; nearly*.

O

obviously*; occasionally; only*.

P

petulantly; playfully; practically*; prettily; probably*; protestingly; provocatively.

R

rarely; really*; regretfully; reproachfully; rhythmically; rosily.

S

seductively; sensually; sensuously; sexily; simply*; simultaneously; slightly; softly; suddenly; sulkily; sweetly.

T

teasingly; temptingly.

U

uncertainly; unconsciously; usually*.

W

wantonly.

2.3 - Adverbials of Emotion, Feeling, Mental State, and Response

in a flirty manner; in a little grimace; in a plump moue of disbelief; in a sarcastic moue; in a sulky way; in accusation; in agreement; in an attempt at reprimand; in an eye-catching manner; in annoyance; in challenge; in disappointment; in disapproval; in disbelief; in displeasure; in feigned indignation; in frustration; in genuine confusion; in grave tension; in humiliation; in misery; in mock alarm; in mock disappointment; in mock reproach; in mock sulkiness; in mockery; in momentary reproach; in open sexual awareness; in protest; in provocative invitation; in realization; in reproach; in reproof; in resentment; in sensuous arousal; in silence; in supposed hurt; in that same ridiculous way; in thought; with a childish expression; with a demure femininity; with anger; with annoyance; with assumed disappointment; with blatantly false disappointment;

with calculated nastiness; with desire; with dismay; with displeasure; with expert attractiveness; with expert effect; with false sweetness; with feigned impatience; with indignation; with invitation; with not so feigned jealousy; with passion; with resentment; with self-deprecation; with sexy appeal; with sultry invitation; with suppressed rage.

VERB USAGE EXAMPLES

As he stormed past, she pouted a little.

Pouting in feigned indignation, he casually took her in his arms.

When he refused, she pouted moodily.

She pouted provocatively as she touched Trent's arm.

With her lips pouting, she looked up at him adoringly.

11
SCOWL

1. Noun Form

1.1 - Noun Synonyms

angry look; black look; dirty look; disapproving look; evil eye; frown; furled brow; glare; glower; irritated look; knitted brow; lower / lour; nasty look; scowl line(s); snoot.

1.2 - Adjectives

A
abrupt; absolute; accusatory; accusing; admonishing; adorable; affectionate; affronted; aggravated; aggressive; aggrieved; alert; all-out; all-too-familiar; almighty; angriest; angry; anguished; animated; annoyed; another; answering; anxious; appropriate; assessing; attractive; austere; authoritative.

B
backwards; bad-tempered; baleful; bantering; beetle-browed; belligerent; benign; best; better; bewildered; big; bitter; black; black-browed; blackest; blistering; borderline; boy-size; boyish; brief; broad; brooding; businesslike.

C
champion; characteristic; cheerful; childish; chilling; clueless; cold; coldest; comforting; comical; commanding; concentrated; concerned; concluding; condemning; confused; contemplative; contemptuous; contrary; critical; cruel; crushed; curious; curling; current; customary; cynical.

D
damning; dangerous; dark; dark-eyed; darkening; darkest; darkling; daunting; decided; deep; deep-set; deepening; defensive; defiant; definite; deprecating; determined; devil-dark; dignified; dire; disagreeable; disapproving; disbelieving; discernible; discouraging; disgruntled; disgusted; disheartened; dismissive; disparaging; displeased; disrespectful; distinct; distinctive; distracted; disturbing; diva; dominating; don't-even-go-there; don't-mess-with-me; doubtful; downright; drawn; dubious.

E

earlier; ebony; eloquent; embarrassed; embittered; envious; evil; exaggerated; exasperated; expected; extra-ferocious; extra-fierce.

F

faint; fake; familiar; famous; fearful; fearsome; feigned; ferocious; fierce; fiercest; fiery; final; finely-tuned; first; first-of-the-morning; fleeting; flustered; forbidding; formidable; freckled; frequent; fretful; friendly; frightful; frowning; frustrated; full-blown; full-fledged; furious; furry-faced.

G

gamine; genuine; giant; give-it-a-miss; glacial; glaring; gloomy; glowering; good; good-natured; grim; gritty; growing; grumpy; guilty.

H

habitual; half; half-formed; hard; hard-browed; hard-eyed; harsh; hateful; haughty; heartfelt; heavy; hefty; hideous; high-voltage; hollow-point; hooded; horrible; horrid; horrified; hostile; huffy; huge; humorless; hurting.

I

I'm-in-charge-here; I-mean-business; identical; ill-natured; immediate; impatient; imposing; impressive; incipient; indignant; inevitable; infamous; infuriated; initial; instant; insulted; intense; intent; intermittent; intimidating; intolerant; inward; irate; irritable; irritated.

J

jaundiced; joking; judgmental.

L

large; last; laughing; lazy; legendary; less-than-ladylike; let's-not-go-there; lifelong; light; lingering; little; little-girl; lowering.

M

magnificent; majestic; major; malevolent; mandatory; manufactured; massive; matching; meaningful; menacing; mental; mere; mighty; mild; minute; mistrustful; mock; mock-ferocious; mock-fierce; mock-irritated; mocking; momentary; moody; motherly; murderous; mutinous; mysterious.

N

narrow-eyed; nastiest; nasty; nasty-ass; near; nonstop; normal.

O

occasional; officious; old; ominous; outraged; outright; own.

P

pain-streaked; parting; passing; passionate; patent; patented; paternal; patronizing; peevish; penetrating; perennial; permanent; perpetual; perplexed; pert; pessimistic; petrified; petulant; pinched-brow; playful; pointed; positive; possessive; potent; pouty; practiced; preoccupied; pretend; prolonged; pronounced; proper; protective; protesting; pseudo; puckered; pugnacious; punishing; purposeful; puzzled.

Q

quelling; questioning; quick; quiet.

R

real; rebellious; reflective; reluctant; reprimanding; reproachful; reproving; resentful; responding; resulting; returning.

S

same; sardonic; satisfying; savage; scary; scissor-sharp; scolding; self-mocking; semi-permanent; serious; severe; sexiest; sharp; sidelong; sideways; signature; silent; skeptical; slanting; slight; slouchy; small; sober; soft; solemn; sour; squinty-eyed; stabbing; staged; stern; sternest; stoic; stone-faced; stony; stormy; strained; stubborn; sudden; sulking; sulky; sullen; surly; suspicious; swarthy; sweeping; swift.

T

teacher; teenage; teeth-grinding; tempestuous; terrific; terrifying; tetchy; Texas-size; theatrical; thin; thoughtful; threatening; thundering; thunderous; tight; tight-lipped; tiny; toothless; toothy; tough-guy; trademark; trademarked; troubled; twisted.

U

ugly; unbecoming; uncharacteristic; uncompromising; unconcealed; unconscious; under-the-brows; uneasy; unexpected; unforgiving; unfriendly; unhappy; unibrowed; unlovely; unmistakable; unpleasant; unrelenting; unremitting; unsubtle; unwelcoming; unyielding; usual.

V

vexed; vicious; villainous.

W

warlord; warning; wary; watery; weak; weary; well-defined; well-remembered; withering; wordless; worried; worst; wrinkled.

1.3 - Noun + Prepositional Phrases

scowl of absolute frustration; scowl of accusation; scowl of agreement; scowl of alarm; scowl of anger; scowl of annoyance; scowl of concentration; scowl of confusion; scowl of contempt; scowl of determination; scowl of disappointment; scowl of disapproval; scowl of disbelief; scowl of discontent and disillusionment; scowl of dislike; scowl of displeasure; scowl of dissatisfaction; scowl of distaste; scowl of exasperation; scowl of fierce concentration; scowl of frustration; scowl of fury; scowl of her finely plucked eyebrows*; scowl of his dark brown brows*; scowl of (his/hers)*; scowl of (his/her) face*; scowl of (his/her) own*; scowl of impatience; scowl of incredulity; scowl of irritation; scowl of mingled embarrassment and annoyance; scowl of mock disapproval; scowl of outraged dignity; scowl of pain; scowl of pure frustration; scowl of reproof; scowl of resentment; scowl of self-condemnation; scowl of self-hatred; scowl of self-reproach; scowl of sheer hatred; scowl of such ferocity; scowl of sullen resentment; scowl of temper; scowl of warning; scowl of wrath.

1.4 - Noun Phrases

a couple of scowls; a deepening of his scowl; a lot of scowls; a solid black bar of scowl; a/the hint of a scowl; a/the suggestion of a scowl; just short of a scowl; nothing short of a scowl; one of his better scowls; one of his formidable scowls; one of his infamous scowls; one of his legendary scowls; something of a scowl; the beginnings of a scowl; the benefit of his scowl; the dark cloud of a scowl; the darkness of his brooding scowl; the distinct lack of a scowl; the easing of his scowl; the edges of his scowl; the ferocity of his scowl; the flash of a scowl; the focus of his dark scowl; the force of his scowl; the form of a harsh scowl; the full benefit of a mighty scowl; the full force of his irritated scowl; the full force of his scowl; the grimness of his dark scowl; the lingering remnants of his scowl; the look of his scowl; the memory of his damning scowl; the merest hint of a scowl; (his expression was) more of a scowl*; the ominous threat of his dark scowl; the prick of his scowl; the quality of his scowl; the recipient of his dark scowl; the sight of a/the scowl; the source of his fierce scowl; the threat of a scowl; the trace of a petulant scowl.

1.5 - Verbs: Scowl as Subject

Standalone Verbs

abate; appear; begin to form; blacken; bloom; change; clear; come (back); cut (deeper); darken; decrease; deepen; descend; die; die away; diminish; disappear; drain away; drop in place*; ease; even out; fade; fade away; fall; fall away; fall into place*; falter; flee; follow; form; go; go away; grow; increase; intensify; jerk back; leave; lessen; lift; lighten; loosen; mellow; melt; melt away; pass by unnoticed*; persist; reappear; recede; refuse to stay in place*; relax; remain;

remain (firmly) in place*; resurface; retreat; return; sharpen; show up; smooth; smooth out; snap into place*; soften; stay (firmly) in place*; stick; threaten; vanish; waver; wither away; worsen.

Brow as Object

appear on (brow); blacken (brow); cloud (brow); crease (brow); darken (brow); deepen on (brow); disappear from (brow); drag at (brow); etch (brow); etch in (brow); etch on (brow); flash across (brow); form on (brow); furrow (brow); line (brow); lower (brow); make appearance on (brow); mar (brow); pull at (brow); settle on (brow); tattoo on (brow); work (its way) across (brow); wrinkle (brow).

Expression as Object

alter into (a less forbidding expression)*; change to (a bland expression)*; darken (expression); dissolve from (expression); disturb (expression); fade from (expression); form on (expression); harden (expression); is displaced by (a blank expression)*; is replaced by (an expression of dismay)*; make (his expression) waver*; mar (expression); mark (expression); melt into (expression so tender)*; ravage (expression); replace (expression)*; tighten (expression); wipe (the amusement) from (his expression)*.

Eyebrows / Brows as Object

angle (eyebrows) together; angle (eyebrows) together (a little); appear between (eyebrows); begin to form between (eyebrows); bring (eyebrows) down above (eyes); bring (eyebrows) into (one straight line); bring (eyebrows) together; crease (eyebrows); draw (eyebrows) almost together; draw (eyebrows) closer together; draw (eyebrows) into (a perplexed line); draw (eyebrows) inward(s); draw (eyebrows) together; form between (eyebrows); knit (eyebrows) together; lower (eyebrows); lower (eyebrows) over (eyes); pull (eyebrows) low over (eyes); pull (eyebrows) together; reclaim (eyebrows); seem to hover between (eyebrows); snap (eyebrows) together; touch (eyebrows); tug at (eyebrows); tug down (eyebrows); wedge between (eyebrows); work between (eyebrows).

Eyes as Object

all but close (eyes); appear between (eyes); bring tears to (his eyes)*; can't hide (worry) in (eyes)*; cause (deep furrows) between (eyes); create (indentations) between (eyes); crinkle (eyes); darken (eyes); deepen (creases) at (corners of eyes); deepen between (eyes); draw down (sides of eyes); hood (eyes); leave (eyes); lift from (eyes); make (eyes) all but disappear; narrow (eyes); never seem far from (eyes)*; pinch between (eyes); reappear over (eyes); settle between (eyes).

Face as Object

accentuate (the lines) of (face); appear on (face); blacken (face); bloom across (face); blossom on (face); break out on (face); build on (face); clear from (face); cloud (face); come on/onto (face); come over (face); come to (face); cover (face); cross (face); darken (face); darken (the sharp angles) of (face); decorate (face); deepen (the lines) of (face); deepen (the lines) of/on (face); deepen on (face); descend onto (face); disappear from (face); disfigure (face); dissolve from (face); drop off (face); drop over (the angles) of (face); ease from (face); engrave on (face); engulf (face); erase (tenderness) from (face); etch (tight planes) on (face); etch across (face); etch in/into (face); etch on (face); fade from (face); flash over (face); flee from (face); flicker across (face); form on (face); gather on (face); glue to (face); go from (face); harden (face); (firmly) imprint on (face); infiltrate (face); leave (face); lift from (face); line (face); make (face) (even darker); mar (face); mark (face); mellow on (face); move across (face); move across (face) like (a thundercloud); overtake (face); plant on (face); plaster on (face); plaster to (face); race across (face); remain on (face); return to (face); roll across (face) like (a thundercloud); scrunch up (face); seize (face); settle (swiftly) across (face); settle across (face); settle on (face); settle over (face); settle over (the hard angles) of (face); shadow (face); sharpen (the lines) of (face); sit on (face); slash across (face); slide over (face); slide right off (face); spread across (face); spread over (face); start to dawn across (face); steal across (face); suit (face); sweep (face); take over (face); take up residence on (face); threaten to crease (face); threaten to return to (face); thunder across (face); touch (face); transform (face); transform (face) from [something] to [something else]; transform (face) into [something]; turn (face) into [something]; turn (face) to (thunder); twist (face); twist (face) into [something]; twist across (face); wrinkle (face).

Features as Object

appear on (features); cloud (features); crease (features); cross (features); darken (features); dawn over (features); deepen (the lines) of (features); deepen on (features); descend on (features); descend over (features); (don't) detract from (features); distort (features); emphasize (features); etch (features); fade from (features); flit over (features); form on (features); form over (features); harden (features); line (features); mar (features); mark (features); melt from (features); pinch (features); pull at (features); reveal on (features); set on (features); settle over (features); shadow (features); spread over (features); take hold of (features); tug (features) into (a frown)*; turn (features) into (a harsh mask)*; twist (features); wrinkle (features).

Forehead as Object

appear on (forehead); bite (forehead); bring (the tension lines) back to (forehead); bunch (forehead); crease (forehead); crease (lines) across (forehead); create (deep furrows) in (forehead); cross (forehead); cut into (forehead); deepen (the lines) across (forehead); descend onto (forehead); form on (forehead); lift from (forehead); mar (forehead); melt from (forehead); pucker (forehead); wrinkle (forehead); wrinkle across (forehead).

Lips as Object

fix on (lips); pull (lips) into (a thin line); settle around (lips); strain (lips); temper into (a curve of the lips)*; tug at (the corners) of (lips); twist (lips).

Mouth as Object

begin to form in (mouth); carve (deep brackets) beside (mouth); compress (mouth); cross (mouth); draw (mouth) into (a stiff crinkle); draw down (the sides) of (mouth); pinch (mouth); pull (the corners) of (mouth) down; pull (mouth) down into (a pout); pull (mouth) downward(s); shadow (mouth); tighten (mouth); tug down (the corners) of (mouth); turn (mouth) into (a thin line / a thin slash); turn (mouth) into (a thin line); wreck (the shape) of (mouth).

Skin as Object

crease (skin); engrave (lines) in (skin); etch (lines) in (skin).

1.6 - Verbs: Scowl as Object

Brow or Character as Subject

(I) wither (brow) into (a scowl)*; (I) wrinkle (brow) into (a scowl)*; (wrinkle on brow) become (a scowl); crease in/into (a scowl); deepen (almost) to (a scowl); deepen to (a scowl); draw down in (a scowl); draw into (a scowl); draw together in (a scowl); furrow in/into (a scowl); knit in (a scowl); lower into (a scowl); pleat in (a scowl); pull into (a scowl); tie into (a scowl); wrinkle in (a scowl).

Character (I / He / She) as Subject

add (a scowl); affect (a scowl); aim (a scowl) at (him); aim (a scowl) in (his direction); allow (a scowl) to form; attempt (a scowl); award (him) (a scowl); banish (a scowl); barely escape (a scowl)*; bend (a scowl) on (him); bring (a scowl) from (him)*; cast (a scowl) at (him); cast (a scowl) in (his direction); cast (him) (a scowl); catch (a scowl) from (him)*; cause (a scowl) to form; cut (him) (a scowl); dart (him) (a scowl); direct (a scowl) at (him); draw (a scowl) from (him)*; earn (a scowl) from (him)*; earn (herself) (a scowl)*; elicit (a scowl) from (him)*; expect (a scowl)*; fake (a scowl); fake (a scowl) at (him); fashion (a scowl); feed (him) (a scowl); feel (a scowl) begin to form; feign (a scowl); fight (a scowl); flash (a scowl); flash (a scowl) at (him); flash (a scowl) up at (him); flash (him) (a scowl); flick (a scowl) at (him); force (a scowl); get (a scowl) from (him)*; give (a scowl) at (him); give (a scowl) to (him); give (him) (a scowl); grant (him) (a scowl); hold (a scowl); hurl (him) (a scowl); keep (a scowl) going; lend (him) (a scowl); level (a scowl) at (him); level (a scowl) on (him); make (a scowl); manage (a scowl); manage (a scowl) at (him); manufacture (a scowl); note (a scowl)*; notice (a scowl)*; offer (a scowl); offer (him) (a scowl); pass (a scowl) (his way); present (a scowl); pretend (a scowl); produce (a scowl); pull (a scowl); receive (a scowl) from (him)*; receive (a scowl)*; repress (a scowl); resist (a scowl) at (him); run (a scowl) over (him);

send (a scowl) in (his direction); send (a scowl) to (him); send (him) (a scowl); sense (a scowl) (coming on); shoot (a scowl) (his way); shoot (a scowl) at (him); shoot (a scowl) over at (him); shoot (him) (a scowl); slant (a scowl) at (him); slant (him) (a scowl); sling (him) (a scowl); sport (a scowl); stop (a scowl); summon up (a scowl); suppress (a scowl); swing (a scowl) at (him); throw (a scowl) at (him); throw (him) (a scowl); toss (a scowl) at (him); toss (a scowl) over to (him); toss (him) (a scowl); turn (a scowl) on (him); waste (a scowl) on (him); wear (a scowl); win (a scowl) from (him)*.

Expression as Subject

change to (a scowl); darken (even more) with (his scowl); darken into (a scowl); darken with (a scowl); drop into (a scowl); fold into (a scowl); give way to (a scowl); is (a scowl); melt into (a scowl); seem to be (a scowl); tighten into (a scowl); transform into/to (a scowl); turn down in (a scowl); turn into/to (a scowl).

Eyebrows / Brows or Character as Subject

(I) bring (eyebrows) together in (a scowl)*; (I) draw (eyebrows) down in (a scowl)*; (I) draw (eyebrows) together to fashion (a scowl)*; (I) knit (eyebrows) in (a scowl)*; (I) lower (eyebrows) in (a scowl)*; (I) pull (eyebrows) into (a scowl)*; (I) snap (eyebrows) together in (a scowl)*; arrow in (a scowl); beetle in/into (a scowl); beetle together in (a scowl); bristle together in (a scowl); bunch with (a scowl); clamp together in (a scowl); clash in (a scowl); come down in/into (a scowl); come down over (eyes) in (a scowl); come together in (a scowl); contract into (a scowl); crawl together in (a scowl); crinkle into (a scowl); crumple into (a scowl); descend in (a scowl); dip down in (a scowl); dip into (a scowl); draw down in/into (a scowl); draw in/into (a scowl); draw together in (a scowl); drop into (a scowl); fix in (a scowl); flatten into (a scowl); furrow in (a scowl); gather (themselves) into (a scowl); gather into (a scowl); jerk together in (a scowl); jut low in (a scowl); knit in (a scowl); (nearly) knit together in (a scowl); knit together in (a scowl); knot in (a scowl); lock in (a scowl); lower in/into (a scowl); meet above (nose) in (a scowl); (nearly) meet in (a scowl); meet in (a scowl); move in (a scowl); plummet into (a scowl); point downward(s) in (a scowl); pull low over (eyes) in (a scowl); pull together in (a scowl); rush together in (a scowl); scrunch down in (a scowl); set in (a scowl); shoot together in (a scowl); slam down in (a scowl); slam downward(s) in (a scowl); slam together in (a scowl); slash down in (a scowl); slide together in (a scowl); snap down in (a scowl); snap into (a scowl); swoop down in (a scowl); swoop downward(s) in (a scowl); swoop into (a scowl); tangle in (a scowl); twitch (sharply) together into (a scowl); vee down in (a scowl); zap together in (a scowl).

Eyes or Character as Subject

(I) cut (a scowl) between (eyes)*; (I) etch (a scowl) between (eyes)*; change to (a scowl); darken in (a scowl); narrow to (a scowl).

Face or Character as Subject

(I) bring (a scowl) to (face)*; (I) contort (face) into (a scowl)*; (I) fashion (face) into (a scowl)*; (I) feel (a scowl) settle on (face)*; (I) fix (a scowl) on/upon (face)*; (I) force (a scowl) onto (face)*; (I) keep (a scowl) off (face)*; (I) paint (a scowl) on (face)*; (I) plaster (a scowl) across (face)*; (I) pucker (face) in (a scowl)*; (I) reveal (a scowl) on (face)*; (I) screw up (face) in (a scowl)*; (I) scrunch (face) in (a scowl)*; (I) see (a scowl) bloom on (his face)*; (I) see (a scowl) darken (his face)*; (I) see (a scowl) on (his face)*; (I) set (a scowl) across (face)*; (I) set (face) in (a scowl)*; (I) twist (face) into (a scowl)*; (I) twist (face) up into (a scowl)*; assume (a scowl); become (a scowl); break into (a scowl); catch in (a scowl); concentrate into (a scowl); contort in/into (a scowl); crease into (a scowl); crumple into (a scowl); curl into (a scowl); darken in/into/to (a scowl); darken with (a scowl); deepen into/to (a scowl); develop into (a scowl); dip into (a scowl); distort in (a scowl); draw in/into (a scowl); drop into (a scowl); fall into (a scowl); fix in (a scowl); fold into (a scowl); form (a scowl); form into (a scowl); freeze into (a scowl); furrow in/into (a scowl); hold (a scowl); is (a scowl); mar with (a scowl)*; pinch into (a scowl); pucker into (a scowl); pull into (a scowl); reflect in (a scowl); relapse into (a scowl); revert to (a scowl); screw up in/into (a scowl); scrunch into (a scowl); scrunch up in/into (a scowl); seize up into (a scowl); set in/into (a scowl); settle into (a scowl); spoil with (a scowl)*; tighten in/into (a scowl); transform into (a scowl); turn into/to (a scowl); twist in/into (a scowl); wear (a scowl).

Features or Character as Subject

(I) crumple (features) into (a scowl)*; (I) tug (features) into (a scowl)*; clench into (a scowl); close in (a scowl); contort in (a scowl); cover in (a scowl); crease into (a scowl); crumple into (a scowl); darken into (a scowl); distort in (a scowl); draw into (a scowl); draw together in (a scowl); fix in (a scowl); lapse (back) into (a scowl); pinch into (a scowl); pull into (a scowl); screw into (a scowl); screw up in (a scowl); scrunch into (a scowl); scrunch up in (a scowl); seize up into (a scowl); set in (a scowl); settle into (a scowl); slide into (a scowl); slip into (a scowl); slip right into (a scowl); tighten into (a scowl); twist in/into (a scowl); wear (a scowl).

Forehead or Character as Subject

(I) pull (forehead) into (a scowl)*; come together in (a scowl); contract in (a scowl); crease in/into (a scowl); crumple into (a scowl); draw into (a scowl); form (a scowl); furrow into (a scowl); pucker into (a scowl); scrunch into (a scowl).

Lips or Character as Subject

(I) press (lips) together in (a scowl)*; (I) purse (lips) into (a scowl)*; (I) purse (lips) together in (a scowl)*; (I) twist (lips) in (a scowl)*; clamp together in (a scowl), curl into (a scowl); draw back in (a scowl); flatten into (a scowl); narrow into (a scowl); press into (a scowl); press together in (a scowl); pull into (a scowl); set in (a scowl); thin in (a scowl); tighten into (a scowl); turn down in (a scowl); twist in/into (a scowl).

Mouth or Character as Subject

(I) force (mouth) into (a scowl)*; (I) pull (mouth) into (a scowl)*; (I) screw up (mouth) in (a scowl)*; (I) set (mouth) into (a scowl)*; (I) turn (mouth) into (a scowl)*; (I) twist (mouth) into (a scowl)*; dip down in (a scowl); dip into (a scowl); draw down in (a scowl); draw into (a scowl); is (a scowl); move into (a scowl); pull into (a scowl); pull tight in (a scowl); purse into (a scowl); set in (a scowl); shift into (a scowl); slant in (a scowl); slide into (a scowl); tighten into (a scowl); turn down in/into (a scowl); turn up in (a scowl); twist in/into (a scowl).

Nose as Subject

etch in (a scowl).

NOUN USAGE EXAMPLES

The young woman screwed up her face into an angry scowl.

Pausing, she slanted him a reproachful scowl.

He gave his reflection a reprimanding scowl.

He approach them, a fierce scowl of determination etched on his face.

Kim's smile of cooperation turned into a scowl.

2. Verb Form

2.1 - Verb Synonyms

disapprove; frown; give a dirty look; give evil eye; glare; gloom; glower; look black; look gloomy; look sullen; lower / lour; make a face; menace; shoot an angry look; shoot an irritated look; shoot daggers; threaten.

2.2 - Adverbs

A

accusingly; actively; actually*; adorably; almost*; alternately; always*; angrily; anxiously.

B

balefully; barely; belligerently; blackly; briefly; broodily; broodingly.

C

clearly; coldly; consideringly; constantly; critically; crossly; curiously; currently*.

D

daily; darkly; deeply; defiantly; deliberately; despairingly; determinedly; directly; disagreeably; disapprovingly.

F

faintly; fearsomely; ferociously; fiercely; firmly; frankly; furiously.

G

gradually; grandly; grimly.

H

hardly*; heavily; hideously; horribly.

I

immediately; impatiently; impotently; increasingly; indignantly; instantly; intently; internally; inwardly; irritably.

L

literally*.

M

malevolently; meaningfully; menacingly; mentally*; merely*; mightily; miserably; momentarily; moodily; morosely; mutinously.

N

nearly*; never*.

O

ominously; only*; openly.

P

periodically; plainly; playfully; pointedly; positively*; possibly*; practically*; predictably; presumably; prettily; previously; probably*.

R

really*; rebelliously; reflexively; reprimandingly; resentfully.

S

seriously; severely; silently; simply*; sleepily; slightly; slowly; softly; sourly; stubbornly; suddenly; sullenly; surely; suspiciously.

T

theatrically; thoughtfully; threateningly.

U

uncertainly; unconsciously; undoubtedly; unequivocally; ungratefully; unseeingly; usually*.

W

warily; warningly; weakly; wearily.

2.3 - Adverbials of Emotion, Feeling, Mental State, and Response

in a disgruntled fashion; in a familiar way; in acknowledgment; in anger; in annoyance; in anticipation; in boredom; in cold fury; in concentration; in confusion; in contemplation; in disappointment; in disapproval; in disbelief; in disgust; in displeasure; in distaste; in exasperation; in frustration; in fury; in grudging admission; in impotent fury; in irritation; in mock aggravation; in mock anger; in mock fierceness; in mock indignation; in mock pain; in mutual consternation; in perfectly believable surprise; in reaction; in recrimination; in renewed embarrassment; in reply; in response; in response; in return; in secret embarrassment; in self-contempt; in self-deprecation; in sheer exasperation; in silence; in sudden recognition; in that arrogant manner; in thought; with annoyance; with budding jealousy; with concentration; with concern; with curiosity; with cynicism; with defiance; with determination; with disapproval; with displeasure; with distaste; with feigned ferocity; with furious concentration; with fury; with hard-eyed suspicion; with intense concentration; with irritation; with meaning; with mock ferocity; with mock impatience; with mock seriousness; with obvious dislike; with skepticism; with temper; with the pain; with unfamiliar concern; with vexation.

VERB USAGE EXAMPLES

Scowling with defiance, she stomped from the room.

Andrew stood there and she scowled at him.

They scowled at each other in mutual consternation.

He leaned back, scowling, his eyebrows a black bar across his face.

He scowled darkly at her.

12
SMIRK

1. Noun Form

1.1 - Noun Synonyms

grin; leer; simper; sly smile; smile; smug look; sneer.

1.2 - Adjectives

A

accommodating; accompanying; affection-filled; affectionate; aggravating; all-too-knowing; amused; annoying; another; anticipatory; apologetic; appreciative; approving; arrogant; attractive.

B

bad-boy; bad-girl; bashful; beautiful; bedeviling; bemused; best; big; bitter; boyish; broad.

C

calculating; callous; carefree; casual; cat-with-the-cream; cat-like; certain; challenging; characteristic; charming; cheeky; cheerful; clever; cocky; complacent; concealed; condescending; confident; contained; contemptuous; contented; cool; coy; crooked; cunning; cute; cynical.

D

damn; damned; dangerous; decided; defiant; definite; delicious; delighted; delightful; deprecating; derisive; derogatory; determined; devastating; devil-may-care; devilish; dirty; disbelieving; disdainful; disguised; disgusted; dismissive; disparaging; distinct; distorted; dreadful; dubious.

E

earlier; easy; embarrassed; enduring; enigmatic; ever-present; evil; exaggerated.

F

faint; faintest; familiar; final; firm; first; flattered; fleeting; flirty; foolish; full; full-fledged.

G

genuine; gimlet; gleeful; gloating; gold-digging; gratified; grotesque; growing; guilty.

H

half; half-assed; half-concealed; half-knowing; halfhearted; happy; hateful; haughty; hidden; high; holier-than-thou; horrible; humorless; humorous; hungry-tiger.

I

I've-got-you; I-can-do-everything; I-laugh-at-life; I-told-you-so; identical; if-you-say-so; ill-concealed; impatient; imperious; impish; impressed; incredulous; indulgent; inevitable; infamous; infuriating; ingratiating; initial; insincere; insolent; insufferable; internal; invisible; involuntary; inward; ironic; irritating.

J

joyful.

K

know-it-all; knowing.

L

lackadaisical; large; lascivious; laughing; lazy; lecherous; leering; licentious; light; lingering; little; lopsided.

M

macho; male; malicious; masculine; matching; meaningful; menacing; mental; mercenary; mischievous; mocking; movie-star.

N

nastiest; nasty; naughty; nauseating; near; not-quite-disguised; notable.

O

obvious; occasional; odd; off-kilter; oily; one-sided; only-half-the-story; out-and-out; overt; own.

P

pained; partial; particular; perceptible; permanent; perpetual; pitying; playful; pleased; pointed; polite; positive; possum-like; practiced; previous; private; proprietary; proud; provocative; prurient; puzzled.

Q

quick; quiet.

R

recognizable; reminiscent; returning; roguish; rueful.

S

sad; same; sarcastic; sardonic; sassy; satirical; satisfied; satyric; saucy; scornful; secret; self-assured; self-confident; self-congratulatory; self-conscious; self-deprecating; self-effacing; self-righteous; self-satisfied; sensual; sensuous; sexy; shaky; shark-like; sharp; sheepish; short; sickening; sidelong; sideways; signature; silly; sinful; skeptical; slack-jawed; slanted; slanting; slight; slightest; slow; sly; small; smarmy; smart-ass; smug; snotty; speculative; strange; stupid; subtle; sudden; suggestive; sulky; supercilious; superior; suppressed; swift.

T

taunting; teasing; telltale; terrifying; thin; tiger-like; tight; tiny; told-you-so; tolerant; trademark; triumphant.

U

ugly; un-Christian; unappealing; unconvincing; underlying; undisguised; unforgivable; unmistakable; unpleasant; unprofessional; unseen; upward; usual.

V

vacant; veiled; vengeful; venomous; vicious; victorious; virtuous.

W

well-pleased; wicked; wide; wily; wiseass; withering; wolfish; world-renowned; worthy-of-sonnets; wry.

Y

you'll-pay-for-that.

1.3 - Noun + Prepositional Phrases

smirk of a snake; smirk of amusement; smirk of approval; smirk of bitterness; smirk of challenge; smirk of crimson lips*; smirk of deep self-disgust; smirk of delight; smirk of disapproval; smirk of his face*; smirk of his lips*; smirk of (his/her) own*; smirk of humor; smirk of irony; smirk of irritation; smirk of male satisfaction; smirk of malicious amusement; smirk of masculine ego; smirk of pleasure; smirk of satisfaction; smirk of satisfaction and anticipation; smirk of self-disgust; smirk of tolerance; smirk of triumph; smirk of victory; smirk of weary amusement.

1.4 - Noun Phrases

a bit of a smirk; a faint hint of a smirk; a ghost of a smirk; a hint of a satisfied smirk; a little bit of a smirk; a sad kind of smirk; a trace of a smirk; a victorious sort of smirk; a weak semblance of the smirk; a/the chorus of smirks; a/the hint of a smirk; a/the kind of smirk; a/the sort of smirk; just a hint of a smirk; just short of a smirk; just shy of a smirk; more of a satisfied smirk; no sign of a smirk; one of her nastiest smirks; something of a smirk; the barest hint of a smirk; the barest of smirks; the barest trace of a smirk; the faintest hint of a smirk; the faintest of smirks; the faintest suggestion of a smirk; the form of a smirk; the hint of a victorious smirk; the lingering vestiges of her smirk; the memory of his easy smirk; the reappearance of his smirk; the sight of her half smirk; the slightest hint of a smirk; the smallest of smirks; the tiniest hint of a smirk; the trace of a smirk; the twist of a smirk.

1.5 - Verbs: Smirk as Subject

Standalone Verbs
broaden; come and go; deepen; deteriorate; die; diminish; disappear; fade; flash; go; grow; grow wider; heighten; mock; reappear; return; vanish; wane; wash away; widen.

Cheeks as Object
bring out (the dimples) in (cheeks); crease (cheeks); mar (the planes) of (cheeks).

Eyes as Object
flash in (eyes); gleam in (eyes); light (eyes); lurk in (eyes).

Face as Object
appear on (face); broaden (face); come and go on (face); cover (face); creep across (face); cross (face); curl across (face); dance across (face); disappear from (face); edge up (face); edge up face); fall from (face); fall off (face); form on (face); grow on (face); have on (face); inch over (face); leave (face); light (face); light up (face); mar (face); pass over (face); paste on (face); plaster on (face); pop onto (face); return to (face); settle on (face); slide across (face); slide from (face); spread across (face); spread all over (face); spread wide across (face); take over (face); twist (face); vanish from (face).

Features as Object
cross (features); mar (features); touch (features).

Lips as Object

adorn (lips); appear on (lips); coat (lips); come to (lips); cross (lips); curl (lips); curl at (lips); curve (lips); curve up (lips); form on (lips); form unbidden on (lips); pass (lips); play about (lips); play around (lips); play on (lips); pull at (lips); quirk (lips); quiver on (lips); raise (one side) of (lips); roll around (lips); slip off (lips); slip onto (lips); spread across (lips); take over (lips); tilt (lips); touch (lips); tug (lips); tug (lips) upward(s); tug at (lips); tug at (one corner) of (lips); twist (lips); twitch over (lips).

Mouth as Object

curl (the corners) of (mouth); curl over (mouth); curve (mouth); curve (the right-hand corner) of (mouth) upward(s); dance at (the corners) of (mouth); dart across (mouth); define (the laugh lines) around (mouth); distort (mouth); edge (mouth); flash across (mouth); flicker over (mouth); flirt around (mouth); flirt around (the corners) of (mouth); flirt with (the corners) of (mouth); ghost around (the corners) of (mouth); give (mouth) an upturn; lift (one corner) of (mouth); lift (one side) of (mouth); lift (the corners) of (mouth); mar (mouth); play about (mouth); play around (mouth); play at (the corners) of (mouth); pull at (the corner) of (mouth); pull back (one side) of (mouth); smear across (mouth); spread across (mouth); start on (one corner) of (mouth); tease (the corner) of (mouth); tilt (mouth); tilt (the corner) of (mouth); tilt (the corners) of (mouth); tip up (the corner) of (mouth); tug at (mouth); tweak (mouth); twitch (mouth).

Nose as Object

crinkle (the bridge) of (nose).

1.6 - Verbs: Smirk as Object

Character (I / He / She) as Subject

allow (herself) (a smirk); angle (a smirk) at (him); angle (him) (a smirk); award (him) with (a smirk); birth (a smirk); call up (a smirk); cast (him) (a smirk); catch (a smirk) from (him)*; control (a smirk); cover (a smirk); crack (a smirk); detect (a smirk)*; draw (a smirk) from (him)*; earn (a smirk) from (him)*; enjoy (a smirk); exchange (a smirk); exchange (a smirk) with (him); exhibit (a smirk); fix (a smirk) on (him); flash (a smirk); flash (him) (a smirk); form (a smirk); get (a smirk) from (him)*; give (a smirk); give (him) (a smirk); grant (him) (a smirk); have (a smirk); hazard (a smirk) at (him); hide (a smirk); indulge (a smirk); keep (smirk) in check; keep (smirk) in place; manage (a smirk); offer (him) (a smirk); point (a smirk) at (him); release (a smirk); resist (a smirk); resist (a smirk) at (him); see (a smirk)*; send (him) (a smirk); shoot (a smirk) at (him); shoot (him) (a smirk); slant (him) (a smirk); slide (a smirk) (his way); spare (him) (a smirk); stifle (a smirk); summon (a smirk); suppress (a smirk); swallow (a smirk); throw (a smirk) over (shoulder); throw (him) (a smirk); toss (a smirk) at (him); toss (a smirk) over (shoulder); toss (him) (a smirk); try (a smirk); try (her) best to control (a smirk); try to contain (a smirk); turn (a smirk) toward(s) (him); watch (a smirk)*; wear (a smirk).

Expression as Subject
dissolve into (a smirk); lose its (smirk); slip into (a smirk); turn into (a smirk).

Face or Character as Subject
(I) plant (a smirk) on (face)*; (I) plaster (a smirk) on (face)*; (I) punch (the smirk) off (his face)*; (I) slap (the smirk) off (his face)*; (I) wear (a smirk) on (face)*; (I) wipe (the smirk) off (his face)*; (one side of face) is (a smirk); brighten with (a smirk); crack into (a smirk); draw up in (a smirk); lift into (a smirk); twist in (a smirk); wear (a smirk).

Facial Constituents as Subject
(cheeks) tug in (a smirk); (dimples) flash in (a smirk); (eyebrows) go up with (a smirk).

Lips or Character as Subject
(I) allow (a smirk) to cross (lips)*; (I) arrange (lips) into (a smirk)*; (I) bring (a smirk) to (lips)*; (I) feel (a smirk) roll around (lips)*; (I) let (a smirk) slip onto (lips)*; (I) let (a smirk) spread across (lips)*; (I) lift (lips) in (a smirk)*; (I) press (lips) together in (a smirk)*; (I) spread (lips) in (a smirk)*; (I) turn (lips) up in (a smirk)*; (I) wipe (the smirk) off (his lips)*; crease into (a smirk); curl in/into (a smirk); curve in/into (a smirk); form (a smirk); lift in (a smirk); lift upward(s) in (a smirk); part in (a smirk); prim into (a smirk); pull into (a smirk); purse in (a smirk); quirk in/into (a smirk); quirk upward(s) into (a smirk); slide into (a smirk); tauten in (a smirk); thin to (a smirk); tilt into (a smirk); tip into (a smirk); turn up in (a smirk); twist in/into/to (a smirk); twitch into (a smirk).

Mouth or Character as Subject
(I) draw (mouth) into (a smirk)*; (I) pull (one corner) of (mouth) up in (a smirk)*; (I) shift (mouth) into (a smirk)*; (I) wear (a smirk) on (mouth)*; bear (a smirk); broaden into (a smirk); crease in/into (a smirk); curl in/into (a smirk); curl up in (a smirk); curve in/into (a smirk); develop (a smirk); flex in (a smirk); go into (a smirk); go up with (a smirk); harden into (a smirk); is (a smirk); lift in (a smirk); lift with (a smirk); move into (a smirk); open in (a smirk); pull into (a smirk); raise in (a smirk); relax enough to allow (a smirk); rise in (a smirk); slant in (a smirk); stretch into (a smirk); tighten into (a smirk); tilt into (a smirk); tilt up (at one side) in (a smirk); tip (at the corner) in (a smirk); turn up in (a smirk); turn upward(s) in (a smirk); twist in/into (a smirk); twitch in/into (a smirk).

NOUN USAGE EXAMPLES

He noted her blush with a satisfied smirk.

157

Jay and Kyle exchanged a smirk.

The suggestion brought a smirk to her lips.

Her dimples flashed in a mischievous smirk.

His mouth tilted up at one side in a smirk of malicious amusement.

2. Verb Form

2.1 - Verb Synonyms

grin; leer; make a face; mug; simper; smile; sneer.

2.2 - Adverbs

A
actually*; always*.

B
beautifully; blatantly; briefly.

C
complacently.

D
definitely; deliberately; devilishly.

E
exactly.

F
faintly; finally*.

I
idiotically; inwardly.

K
knowingly.

L
literally; loftily.

M
maliciously; mentally*; merely*.

N
nearly*.

O
obviously*; only*; openly; overtly.

P
particularly; partly*; positively*; practically*; prettily; privately; probably*.

Q
quickly.

R
really*.

S
sarcastically; shockingly; simply*; slightly; slyly; smugly; suddenly; sulkily.

T
tiredly; triumphantly.

V
visibly.

W
wilily.

2.3 - Adverbials of Emotion, Feeling, Mental State, and Response

in a way meant to infuriate; in amusement; in bitchy amusement; in reply; in return; in satisfaction; in self-satisfaction; in triumph; in victory; with delight; with derisive amusement; with due humility; with great amusement; with interest; with male superiority; with quiet satisfaction; with satisfaction; with self-assurance; with self-congratulation; with some sort of hidden meaning; with unconcealed amusement; with venom.

VERB USAGE EXAMPLES

Trisha smirked at Ryan from her folding chair across the room.

She glanced at Chad, who smirked.

He smirked with self-assurance as he approached her position.

She smirked at Bree with some sort of hidden meaning on her way out.

When she caught his gaze he was positively smirking.

13
SNEER

1. Noun Form

1.1 - Noun Synonyms

contempt; derision; dig; disdain; fleer; gibe; half-sneer; insult; jeer; mockery; offense; ridicule; sardonic grin; scorn; slap in the face; slight; smirk; snicker; sniff; snort; taunt; wisecrack.

1.2 - Adjectives

A
accompanying; all-knowing; amused; angry; another; answering; aristocratic; arrogant; austere; autocratic; awful.

B
bad-boy; bad-tempered; barbed; best; biggest; biting; bitter; blatant; borderline; brazen; brief; brutal.

C
calculated; calculating; callous; challenging; cheap; chilling; cocky; cold; cold-eyed; cold-hearted; concealed; condemnatory; condescending; contemptuous; cool; covert; crafty; credible; cruel; crushing; curling; customary; cynical.

D
damned; decided; defiant; definite; deliberate; delicate; derisive; derisory; derogatory; disbelieving; disdainful; disgusted; disinterested; dismissive; disparaging; dissatisfied; distinct; doubting; downward; drawling.

E
eloquent; ever-faithful; evil; expressive; exquisite.

F
faint; faintest; familiar; fastidious; feline; feral; fiery; frightening; full; full-blown; fully-fledged.

G

glaring; gloating; good-riddance; gratuitous; grim.

H

half; half-hearted; hard; harsh; hateful; haughty; heavy; hidden; humorous.

I

icy; ill-concealed; implied; impressive; in-control; indignant; insinuating; insolent; insufferable; intentional; inward; ironic; ironical; irritated.

J

jealous.

K

knowing; knowledgeable.

L

lascivious; last; laughing; lazy; little; lofty; low; lupine.

M

malevolent; malicious; masculine; mean; meanest; menacing; might; mild; mirthless; mocking; modish; momentary.

N

narrow-eyed; nasty; near.

O

obvious; odd; oily; one-sided; open; out-and-out; overconfident; overt; own.

P

pained; painful; part; parting; patrician; patronizing; perceptible; permanent; perpetual; petulant; pronounced; provocative; prune-faced.

Q

quiet.

R

reactionary.

S

same; sarcastic; sardonic; satirical; satisfied; scarcely-concealed; scathing; scoffing; scornful; self-derisive; separate; shadowed; sideways; silent; single; skeptical; slight; slightest; sly; small; smarmy; smart-ass; smirking; smug;

snobbish; soft; spiteful; subtle; sudden; suggestive; suitable; supercilious; superior; surly.

T
taunting; terrible; terrifying; thin; thinly-veiled; threatening; tight; tough-guy; triumphant; twisted.

U
ugly; unattractive; uncharacteristic; underlying; undisguised; unfeeling; unintended; unmistakable; unnatural; unpleasant; unrepentant; uppity; usual.

V
vague; veiled; vicious; vilified; vindictive; virulent.

W
well-bred; world-class.

Y
yellow-toothed.

1.3 - Noun + Prepositional Phrases

sneer of (her) lips*; sneer of amusement; sneer of anger; sneer of bitter self-mockery; sneer of contempt; sneer of derision; sneer of disapproval; sneer of disbelief; sneer of disdain; sneer of disgust; sneer of disgust and resignation; sneer of disillusion; sneer of distaste; sneer of empty laughter*; sneer of (his/hers)*; sneer of laughter*; sneer of mockery; sneer of obvious hostility; sneer of open disbelief; sneer of pleasure; sneer of pure disdain; sneer of pure dislike; sneer of rejection; sneer of resentment; sneer of ridicule; sneer of sarcasm; sneer of satisfaction; sneer of savage, cynical amusement; sneer of scorn; sneer of self-disgust; sneer of self-loathing; sneer of superiority; sneer of triumph; sneer of utter contempt; sneer of youthful triumph.

1.4 - Noun Phrases

a bit of a sneer; a fair imitation of a sneer; a slight suggestion of a sneer; a smug sort of sneer; a touch of a sneer; a/the hint of a sneer; a/the kind of sneer; a/the suggestion of a sneer; a/the trace of a sneer; enough of a sneer; just a hint of a sneer; just a touch of a sneer; just short of a sneer; just shy of a sneer; just this side of a sneer; (it was) more of a sneer*; one of his gratuitous sneers; something of a sneer; the beginning of a sneer; the curve of a sneer; (on) the edge of a sneer; the faint trace of a sneer; the faintest hint of a sneer; the faintest of sneers; the faintest trace of a sneer; (being) the object of sneers*; the slightest of sneers; the slightest suspicion of a sneer; the suspicion of a sneer; the tiniest of sneers; (on) the verge of a sneer.

1.5 - Verbs: Sneer as Subject

Standalone Verbs
appear; come easily; deepen; fail; fall away; falter; go; thicken; vanish.

Brow as Object
form on (brow).

Eyes as Object
fade from (eyes); reflect in (eyes).

Face as Object
appear on (face); come across (face); cross (face); distort (face); drop from (face); fade from (face); flash over (face); flicker over (face); flit over (face); form on (face); leave (face); (fractionally) lift (the muscles) of (face); make (face) (almost ugly); mar (face); mar (the features) of (face); mark (face); run over (face); slide across (face); spread (slowly) over (face); twist (face).

Features as Object
appear on (features); cross (features); emphasize (features); etch on (features); mar (features); twist (features); work at (features).

Lips as Object
appear on (lips); catch (lips); curl (lips); curve (lips); dangle from (lips); hover about (lips); issue from (lips); lift (one corner) of (lips); mar (lips); match (lips); pull at (lips); ride (lips); rise to (lips); seem to come to (lips); spread (lips); touch (lips); tug at (the corners) of (lips); twist (lips).

Mouth as Object
appear on (mouth); catch his (mouth); curl (mouth); curl (the corner / the edges) of (mouth); curve (mouth); curve across (mouth); draw (one corner) of (mouth) upwards; draw down (mouth); go from (mouth); hover on (mouth); increase (the curve) of (mouth); lift (one side) of (mouth); lift (the corners) of (mouth); lurk about (mouth); pull at (mouth); touch (mouth); touch (the corners / the outline) of (mouth); tug at (one corner) of (mouth); twist (mouth); twist (the corner) of (mouth); wipe clear of (mouth); wrestle (one corner) of (mouth) up.

1.6 - Verbs: Sneer as Object

Character (I / He / She) as Subject
affect (a sneer); bestow (a sneer) on (him); call up (a sneer); cast (a sneer) at (him); contain (a sneer); control (a sneer); detect (a sneer); force (a sneer); form (a sneer); get (a sneer) from (him)*; give (a sneer); give (him) (a sneer); have (a sneer) at (him); hold (a sneer); make (a sneer); manage (a sneer); notice (a sneer)*; offer (him) (a sneer); prevent (a sneer); pull (a sneer); resist (a sneer) at (him); see (a sneer)*; send (him) (a sneer); sense (a sneer); show (a sneer); smother (a sneer); summon up (a sneer); suppress (a sneer); suspect (a sneer) in (his voice)*; throw (a sneer) at (him); throw (him) (a sneer); try (a sneer); watch (a sneer)*; wear (a sneer).

Face or Character as Subject
(I) fix (a sneer) on (face)*; (I) keep (a sneer) off (face)*; (I) knock (the sneer) from/off (his face)*; (I) remove (the sneer) from (his face)*; (I) swipe (the sneer) from/off (his face)*; (I) wipe (the sneer) from/off (his face)*; contort in/into (a sneer); crease into (a sneer); curl up in (a sneer); draw into (a sneer); harden into (a sneer); hold (a sneer); is (a sneer); pull into (a sneer); screw into (a sneer); seem closer to (a sneer); show (a sneer); turn into (a sneer); twist in/into (a sneer).

Lips or Character as Subject
(I) bring (a sneer) to (lips)*; (I) curl (lips) into (a sneer)*; (I) lift (lips) in (a sneer)*; (I) push (lips) into (a sneer)*; (I) turn (lips) into (a sneer)*; (I) twist (lips) in/into (a sneer)*; are (a sneer); bend (almost) into (a sneer); change to (a sneer); curl back from (teeth) in (a sneer); curl back in/into (a sneer); curl in/into (a sneer); curl up in (a sneer); curve in/into (a sneer); curve upward in (a sneer); dip down into (a sneer); draw back against (teeth) in (a sneer); draw back in/into (a sneer); draw into (a sneer); form (a sneer); form into (a sneer); hold (a sneer); lift in/into (a sneer); part in (a sneer); produce (a sneer); pull back in (a sneer); pull into (a sneer); set in/into (a sneer); slip over (teeth) in (a sneer); thin into (a sneer); tighten in (a sneer); turn back in (a sneer); turn into (a sneer); twist (almost) to (a sneer); twist in/into (a sneer); twitch into (a sneer).

Mouth or Character as Subject
(I) curl (mouth) down in (a sneer)*; (I) curve (mouth) into (a sneer)*; (I) draw (mouth) into (a sneer)*; (I) lift (the corners) of (mouth) in (a sneer)*; (I) pull (mouth) into (a sneer)*; (I) turn (mouth) into (a sneer)*; (I) twist (mouth) into (a sneer)*; angle into (a sneer); assume (a sneer); crook in (a sneer); curl (at the corners) in (a sneer); curl back in/into (a sneer); curl in/into (a sneer); curl to (a sneer); curl up in (a sneer); curl upwards in (a sneer); curl with (a sneer); curve in/into (a sneer); draw down in/into (a sneer); draw into (a sneer); form (a sneer); harden in/into (a sneer); is (a sneer); kick up in (a sneer); lift in (a sneer); move in (a sneer); move upwards in (a sneer); pull back into (a sneer); pull

165

down into (a sneer); quirk into (a sneer); relax in (a sneer); set in (a sneer); show (a sneer); stretch in/into (a sneer); thin into/to (a sneer); tighten in/into (a sneer); tug down (at one corner) into (a sneer); turn back in/into (a sneer); turn back with (a sneer); turn down in/into (a sneer); turn downward(s) into (a sneer); turn into (a sneer); turn with (a sneer); twist down in (a sneer); twist in/into (a sneer); twist up into (a sneer); wear (a sneer); writhe in (a sneer).

Facial Constituents or Character as Subject

(expression) contort into (a sneer); (expression) settle into (a sneer); (features) twist in (a sneer); (I) bare (teeth) in (a sneer)*; (I) show (teeth) in (a sneer)*.

NOUN USAGE EXAMPLES

The corner of his mouth kicked up in a sneer.

Michelle pulled her mouth into a sneer of ridicule.

Casey's lip curled up in a smug sort of sneer.

Danny faced her with a bad-tempered sneer.

She fixed a superior sneer on her face and turned to face him.

2. Verb Form

2.1 - Verb Synonyms

affront; belittle; condemn; curl one's lip; decry; deride; despise; detract; dig; disparage; dump; fleer; flout; gibe; gird; hold in contempt; hold up to ridicule; hold up to scorn; hoot; insult; jeer; jest; knock; lampoon; laugh at; laugh in someone's face; look askance; look down on; make fun of; mock; put down; quip at; revile; ridicule; scoff; scorn; slam; smile sarcastically; smile with contempt; smirk; sneeze at; snicker; sniff; snort; spit upon; taunt; thumb one's nose at; turn up one's nose at; twit; underrate.

2.2 - Adverbs

A
acidly; actually*; almost*; always*.

B
briefly.

C
coldly; contemptuously; continually; coolly; cryptically.

D
deliberately.

F
faintly; fairly often; finally*; firmly; fractionally.

G
grimly.

H
horribly.

I
immediately; involuntarily; inwardly.

M
mentally*; merely*.

N
nastily; nearly*; never*.

O
only*; openly.

P
perceptibly; perfectly; positively*; practically*; privately; probably*; promptly*; proudly.

Q
quickly.

R
really*.

S
sarcastically; secretly; silently; simultaneously; slightly; softly, superciliously.

T

triumphantly.

U

undoubtedly.

V

vaguely; virtually*.

2.3 - Adverbials of Emotion, Feeling, Mental State, and Response

in (his/her) condescension; in (his/her) superiority; in disbelief; in disgust; in distaste; in icy cynicism; in reply; in response; in retaliation; in return; in the back of his mind; in victory; with a mixture of contempt and self-contempt; with as much scorn as (he/she) could muster; with biting sarcasm; with bitter sarcasm; with bitterness; with blistering anger; with blustering bravado; with contempt; with cutting sarcasm; with deliberately calculated nastiness; with disgust; with exasperation; with icy contempt; with icy disdain; with noted sarcasm; with open contempt; with patent resentment; with such savage enjoyment; with total disgust; with triumph.

VERB USAGE EXAMPLES

Katie looked back over her shoulder and sneered.

She sneered at him with patent resentment.

Sneering nastily, he retrieved the diamond necklace from around her neck.

John sneered openly as he watched them work.

As they turned around to face the others, Derek sneered at them with icy contempt.

14
SQUINT

1. Noun Form

1.1 - Noun Synonyms

brief glance; brief look; crinkled eyes; crinkly squint lines; narrowed eyes; quick glance; quick look; scrunched up eyes; side glance; squint lines.

1.2 - Adjectives

A
accusatory; all-business; angry; another; appraising; are-you-kidding.

B
better.

C
Clint Eastwood; cockeyed; cold; confused; contemplative; crinkly; critical; curious.

D
dangerous; decided; deep; disconcerting.

E
embarrassed; evil; exaggerated; expert.

F
faint; full.

G
gray; grim; groggy.

H
hard.

I

indulgent.

L

little.

M

madder-than-hell; manly; marked; mischievous.

N

narrow; narrow-eyed; narrowing; near; new.

O

one-eyed.

P

pained; pale; partial; penetrating; permanent; perpetual; pondering.

Q

questioning; quick.

S

sexy; sharp; sheepish; shrewd; sideways; sleepy; slight; strange; stubborn; studious; sultry; sunburned.

T

terrible; thoughtful; tight; tiniest; tiny; twinkling.

U

upward; usual.

W

warning; white.

1.3 - Noun + Prepositional Phrases

squint of annoyance; squint of disbelief; squint of (his/her) eyes; squint of mild skepticism; squint of pain; squint of pure focus; squint of suspicion.

1.4 - Noun Phrases

a bit of a squint; a skeptical kind of squint; a funny sort of squint; the briefest of squints; the faintest of squints; (all) the hallmarks of a squint.

1.5 - Verbs: Squint as Subject

Standalone Verbs
deepen; develop; diminish; disappear; ease; narrow; return.

Eyes as Object
(squint lines) fan from (the corners) of (eyes); crinkle (eyes); crinkle (the corners / the edges) of (eyes); line (the corners) of (eyes); narrow (eyes); return to (eyes).

1.6 - Verbs: Squint as Object

Character (I / He / She) as Subject
contain (a squint); develop (a squint); examine [something] with (a squint); eye (him) up and down with (a squint); eye (him) with (a squint); flash (him) (a squint); get (a squint) at (him); give (him) (a squint); glance at (him) with (a squint); greet [something] with (a squint); have (a squint); have (a squint) at (him); look at (him) with (a squint); nail (him) with (a squint); peer at (him) with (a squint); regard (him) with (a squint); return (a squint); sidle (a squint) at (him); slice (him) (cleanly) with (a squint); slide (a squint) over toward(s) (him); slide (him) (a squint); stop (him) with (a squint); study (him) with (a squint); survey (him) with (a squint); take (a squint); take (a squint) at (him); turn (a squint) on (him).

Eyes or Character as Subject
(I) blink open (eyes) to (a squint)*; (I) narrow (eyes) in/to (a squint)*; (I) open (eyes) in (a squint)*; (I) open (eyes) to (a squint)*; compress in/into (a squint); crinkle in (a squint); (almost) disappear in (a squint); evolve into (a squint); examine [something] with (a squint); fly up to study (his face) with (a squint); go into (a squint); narrow in/to (a squint); open in/to (a squint); pull into (a squint); tuck into (a squint); watch (him) with (a squint).

Face or Character as Subject
(I) screw up (face) in (a squint)*; (I) scrunch (face) into (a squint)*; (I) scrunch up (face) in (a squint)*; accomplish (a squint); fold up in (a squint); manage (a squint); screw up in (a squint); scrunch into (a squint); scrunch up in (a squint); tuck up in (a squint).

NOUN USAGE EXAMPLES

She resisted taking a squint at him.

Ashley examined the stone artifact with a squint.

He scrunched up his face in a thoughtful squint.

Gill's eyes almost disappeared in a narrow squint.

A questioning squint crinkled the corners of his eyes.

2. Verb Form

2.1 - Verb Synonyms

focus intently; glance obliquely; look askance; look at narrowly; look out of half-closed eyes; look out of the corner of one's eye; look sidewise; peek; peep; peer; peer at with half-closed eyes; screw up one's eyes; scrunch up eyes to look at; skew; squinch.

2.2 - Adverbs

A
actually*; angrily; anxiously; appreciatively; awkwardly.

B
balefully; bitterly; bleakly; blearily.

C
calmly; certainly*; closely; comically; constantly; coolly; crinkly; critically; curiously.

D
dangerously; definitely*; deliberately; desperately; disapprovingly; disbelievingly; distastefully; dizzily; doubtfully; drowsily.

E
eagerly; evilly.

F
fearfully; ferociously; fondly; frantically; furiously.

G
grimly; groggily.

H
happily; helplessly; hopefully; horribly.

I
immediately; impatiently; innocently; instantly; instinctively; intently; irascibly.

M
meaningfully; meditatively; mentally*; merely*; moodily; myopically.

N
narrowly; nearly*; nervously.

O
obligingly; occasionally; only*; owlishly.

P
painfully; permanently; probably*; professionally.

Q
quickly.

R
really*; ruefully.

S
shortsightedly; shyly; sightlessly; sleepily; slightly; slowly; speculatively; suddenly; sulkily; sullenly; surreptitiously; suspiciously.

T
tearfully; thoughtfully; threateningly; tightly.

U
unflatteringly; unhappily; unnecessarily.

V
vainly.

W

warily; wearily; wildly.

2.3 - Adverbials of Emotion, Feeling, Mental State, Response, and Reaction to Environment

in a puzzled frown; in an attractive manner; in an effort to absorb this new piece of information; in an effort to concentrate; in anger; in annoyance; in anticipation; in concentration; in confusion; in disbelief; in displeasure; in dull-eyed disbelief; in fury; in menace; in mild puzzlement; in pain; in pain and shock; in puzzlement; in question; in recognition; in response; in speculation; in the afternoon sun; in the blinding light of the noonday sun; in the bright afternoon light; in the bright afternoon sunshine; in the bright early morning sun; in the bright flood of sunlight; in the bright light streaming through the window; in the bright light(s); in the bright sun; in the bright sunlight; in the bright sunshine; in the bright, tropical light; in the brightness; in the brilliant afternoon sun; in the brilliant golden light; in the brilliant sunshine; in the candlelight; in the dark; in the darkness; in the dim light from the lamp beside the bed; in the dim light of a bedside lamp; in the dim light; in the dimness of the hotel bar; in the dimness; in the dying light of the sunset; in the dying light; in the early-evening sunlight; in the early-morning light; in the fluorescent light; in the glare of the cameras lights; in the glare; in the glaring sun; in the gloom; in the growing darkness; in the harsh light; in the hazy light; in the headlights; in the illumination from the overhead light; in the intense white sunshine; in the last rays of the sun; in the late afternoon sun; in the late-morning sunlight; in the light from the fire; in the light of a streetlamp; in the light of the early-morning sun streaming in the open window; in the light; in the low light; in the low morning light; in the moonlight; in the near twilight; in the shadows; in the shadowy afternoon light; in the shaft of sunlight piercing the room; in the shuttered moonlight; in the soft light; in the strong light; in the sudden brightness; in the sudden wash of light; in the sun's glare; in thought; in what he interpreted to be a mixture of anger and determination; with amusement; with concentration; with critical interest; with curiosity; with disbelief; with exaggeration; with impatience; with indecision; with interest; with laughter; with pain; with something softer than mischief; with suspicion; with temper; with the light; with weary scorn.

VERB USAGE EXAMPLES

Wiping sleep from his eyes, Mike squinted at the bedside clock.

She squinted in the sudden brightness.

Squinting, he trekked up the hill.

His green eyes squinted suspiciously up at her.

Sam squinted in pain when the ball found its mark.

15
STARE

1. Noun Form

1.1 - Noun Synonyms

a blank look; a fixed look; a piercing look; eyeballing; gaping; gawking; gaze; glare; glower; goggling; ogling.

1.2 - Adjectives

A

absorbed; abstracted; accusative; accusatory; accusing; aching; acquisitive; acute; added; admiring; admonishing; adoring; affronted; aggravated; aggressive; aggrieved; aghast; agitated; agonized; alarmed; alert; all-embracing; all-encompassing; all-examining; all-knowing; all-out; all-over; all-pervasive; all-seeing; all-too-perceptive; alluring; almond-eyed; almost-accusatory; aloof; amazed; amber; amused; analytical; anemic; anger-filled; angled; angry; anguished; animal-like; animalistic; annoyed; another; answering; antagonistic; anxious; appalled; appraising; appreciative; apprehensive; approving; aquamarine; arched; arctic; ardent; are-you-for-real; arrogant; assessing; astonished; astounded; astute; attentive; attracted; attracting; audacious; authoritative; autocratic; avaricious; avid; awed; awestruck; awkward; azure.

B

baby-blue; baby-like; back-off; backward; baffled; baffling; baleful; basilisk; basilisk-like; basilisk-style; battle-fatigued; battle-ready; be-quiet; beady; beady-eyed; beaky; beautiful; beetle-browed; befuddled; belittling; belligerent; bemused; benevolent; benign; beseeching; bewildered; bewitched; bewitching; big-bad-mom; big-brother; big-eyed; big-sister; bitter; black; black-devil; black-diamond; black-eyed; black-ice; black-rimmed; black-Russian; bland; blandest; blank; blank-eyed; blank-faced; blanked-off; blankest; blatant; blazing; blazing-eyed; blazoning; bleaching; bleak; bleak-eyed; bleary; bleary-eyed; blighting; blind; blinking; blinkless; blistering; blood-heating; bloodshot; blue; blue-eyed; blue-gray; blue-green; blunt; bold; bone-chilling; bone-melting; bone-slicing; bone-stripping; boozy; bored; bottomless; brazen; brief; bright; bright-eyed; brilliant; bristling; brooding; broody; brook-no-argument; brow-tipped; brown;

brown-eyed; bruising; bulldog-like; bullet-gray; bullet-like; burning; burnished; business; business-like; butter-him-up; butterscotch.

C

calculated; calculating; callous; calm; candid; caressing; carnal; casual; cat-like; caught-in-the-headlights; caustic; cautioning; cautious; censoring; censorious; censuring; cerulean; challenging; charged; cheeky; Chicago-cop; child-like; childish; chill; chilliest; chilling; chilly; chocoholic; cinnamon; claiming; clamp-jawed; classic; clear; clear-eyed; clear-sighted; clinical; close; coal-black; cobalt; cock-eyed; cocky; coherent; cold; cold-eyed; coldest; collected; collective; combative; combined; combustible; come-get-me; come-hither; come-on-baby; commanding; compassionate; compelling; competitive; competitors; complete; composed; comprehending; comprehensive; concentrated; concerned; concerted; condemnatory; condemning; condescending; confident; confrontational; confused; conservative; considered; considering; constant; consuming; contemplative; contemptuous; continuing; continuous; controlled; cool; cool-eyed; cooling; cop; corporate; courtroom; covert; covetous; cow-like; coy; coyote-like; creepy; critical; cross-eyed; cruel; crushing; cryptic; crystal-blue; crystalline; cuckoo; curious; curious-as-a-baby; cutting; cynical.

D

dagger; dagger-filled; dagger-like; dagger-worthy; dangerous; daring; dark; dark-blue; dark-chocolate; dark-eyed; dark-lashed; dark-pupiled; darkened; darkening; darkest; daunting; dazed; dead; dead-eyed; dead-on; deadlocked; deadly; deadpan; death; death-like; death-ray; deep; deep-set; deer-in-the-headlights; defeated; defensive; defiant; deliberate; delighted; demanding; denigrating; denim-blue; derisive; derisory; desiring; despairing; desperate; detached; determined; devastating; devil-dark; devouring; diabolic; diabolical; diamond-hard; diffident; dilated; direct; dirty; disapproving; disbelieving; discerning; discomfited; disconcerted; disconcerting; discontented; discouraging; discourteous; discreet; disdainful; disgruntled; disgusted; disinterested; dismayed; dismissive; disparaging; dispassionate; disquieting; dissecting; distant; distinct; distracted; distrustful; disturbed; disturbing; do-something-quick; doe-eyed; doe-like; dog-like; doleful; dominating; don't-even-try-it; don't-mess-with-me; doting; double-take; doubtful; doubting; down-the-barrel; down-the-nose; down-your-nose; downward; drawn-out; dreamy; dreamy-eyed; drilling; droll; drop-dead; drowsy; dry; dubious; dull; dull-eyed; dumbstruck.

E

each; eager; eagle; eagle-eyed; earnest; Eastwood-stony; eat-shit-and-die; ebony; electric-blue; embarrassed; embarrassing; emerald; emerald-eyed; emerald-green; emotionless, empathetic; emphatic; empty; empty-eyed; enchanted; encompassing; encouraging; end-of-discussion; enigmatic; enraged; entranced; entrapping; enveloping; envious; evaluating; evil; evil-eyed; evil-mom; exaggerated; examining; exasperated; excited; expectant; explicit; expressionless; eye-popping; eye-to-eye; eyeball-to-eyeball.

F

familiar; far-seeing; far-sighted; fascinated; fatherly; fathomless; fearful; fearless; feed-me-or-die; feline-like; feminine; ferocious; feverish; few; fiction-piercing; fierce; fierce-eyed; fiercest; fiery; filthy; firelit; firm; first; fish-eyed; fixated; fixed; flabbergasted; flagellating; flashing-eyed; flat; flat-eyed; flesh-melting; flickering; flint-eyed; flint-like; flinty; flinty-eyed; flirtatious; flirting; flummoxed; focused; following; forbidding; forceful; forever-accusing; formidable; forthright; forward; frank; frantic; freaky; freezing; frequent; fresh; friendly; frightened; frightening; frigid; frog-eyed; frostiest; frosty; frowning; frozen; frustrated; full; full-on; fulminating; fuming; funny; furious; fuzzy.

G

gaping; gathering; gauche; gawking; gentle; get-over-yourself; get-real; get-to-the-point; gimlet; gimlet-eyed; girlish; glacial; glacier-cold; glacier-gray; glacier-like; glaring; glass-green; glassy; glassy-eyed; glazed; glazed-eyed; gleaming; glinting; glittered; glittering; glittery; gloating; gloomy; glowering; glowing; go-to-hell; Godzilla-like; goggle-eyed; goggling; gold-green; golden; golden-eyed; golden-hot; good; gorgeous; gotcha; grandfatherly; grandmotherly; granite; grave; gray; gray-eyed; gray-green; greatest; greedy; green; green-eyed; green-fire; green-gray; grilling; grim; grim-faced; grim-visaged; grinning; groaning; groggy; grouchy; grudging; guarded; guileless; guilty; gypsy-eyed.

H

half-amused; half-anxious; half-apologetic; half-impatient; half-insolent; half-lidded; half-smiling; hands-off; happy; hard; hard-as-emerald; hard-edge; hard-edged; hard-eyed; hardened; hardening; hardest; harrowing; harsh; harshest; hate; hate-filled; hateful; haughtiest; haughty; haunted; haunting; hawk-like; hawkish; hazel; hazel-eyed; hazel-green; hazy; He-man; head-snapping; head-turning; heady; heady-eyed; heart-melting; heart-stopping; heart-thundering; heartfelt; heated; heavy; heavy-eyed; heavy-lidded; helpless; hesitant; high-nosed; high-powered; hollow; hollow-eyed; honest; hooded; horrid; horrified; hostile; hot; hot-eyed; humiliated; humor-laced; humorless; hungry; hurt-filled; hypnotic; hypnotized.

I

I'll-get-you-yet; I-don't-believe-it; I-told-you-so; ice-blue; ice-chip; ice-gray; ice-green; ice-pick; ice-water; iced-green; iciest; icy; icy-blue; identical; if-looks-could-kill; impartial; impassioned; impassive; impatient; impenetrable; imperative; imperious; impersonal; impertinent; imperturbable; impervious; implacable; imploring; impudent; incendiary; incinerating; incisive; incredible; incredulous; incriminating; incurious; indecipherable; indescribable; indifferent; indignant; indigo; inescapable; inevitable; infant-like; infatuated; inflexible; infringing; infuriated; infuriating; ingenuous; inimical; initial; innocent;

innumerable; inquiring; inquisitive; inscrutable; insightful; insistent; insolent; inspecting; insulting; intelligent; intense; intense-looking; intensive; intent; interested; interfering; interminable; interrogating; interrogative; interrogatory; intimate; intimidating; intoxicated; intrigued; intrusive; invasive; inviting; involuntary; irate; iron; ironic; ironical; irritated.

J

jade-green; jaundiced; jaunty; jealous; jet-black; jet-dark; jewel-bright; judgmental; judicial.

K

keen; keen-eyed; killers; kittenish; knife-edge; knowing.

L

lackluster; lancing; languid; languishing; languorous; large; large-eyed; lascivious; laser; laser-beam; laser-blue; laser-bright; laser-cold; laser-focused; laser-like; laser-sharp; last; law-enforcement; lawyer-like; lawyerly; lazy; leaden; lecherous; leering; leery; legal-eagle; leisurely; lengthy; less-than-impressed; less-than-subtle; less-than-welcoming; lethal; level; level-eyed; leveled; leveling; lewd; licentious; lidded; lifeless; limpid; lingering; lions; liquid-green; little; little-girl-lost; lizard-eyed; loaded; locked; lofty; long; long-distance; long-suffering; longest; longing; lovers; loving; lowering; ludicrous; luminous; lustful; lustrous; lusty.

M

mad; maddening; magma; magnetic; malevolent; malicious; malignant; man-to-man; manic; many; marble; marble-hard; martyred; masculine; masked; matched; matching; mean; meanest; meaningful; measured; measuring; meditative; Medusa-like; memory-filled; menacing; merciless; mesmeric; mesmerized; mesmerizing; metallic; midnight; midnight-blue; mighty; mild; miles-away; militant; mind-melting; mindless; mini; mirthful; misty; misty-eyed; mock-baleful; mock-ferocious; mock-fierce; mock-stern; mocking; molten; mom-knows-all; momentary; moms; monocled; moody; mother-hen; mother-son; motherly; mothers; mournful; mulish; murderous; musing; mute; mutinous; mutual; myopic; mysterious; mystified.

N

naked; narrow; narrow-eyed; narrowed; narrowing; nasty; navy-blue; nearly-black-eyed; needle-sharp; needy; nerve-tingling; nervous; neurotic; neutral; never-ending; nihilistic; ninety-minute; no-negotiation; no-nonsense; noncommittal; nondescript; none-of-your-business; none-too-subtle; nonplussed; nosy; not-so-subtle; notorious; numb.

O

objective; oblique; observant; obsidian; obvious; occasional; odd; oddest; off-putting; offended; official; ogling; old-fashioned; ominous; one; one-eyed; only; onyx; opal; opaque; opaque-eyed; open; open-jawed; open-mouth; open-mouthed; oppressive; out-and-out; out-of-this-world; outraged; outright; outward; overbold; overt; owl-like; owlish; own.

P

pained; paint-stripping; pale-blue; pale-eyed; pale-green; panda; panic-stricken; panicked; pantherish; parents; passion-glazed; passion-hazed; passion-heavy; passionate; passionless; pathetic; patient; patronizing; peculiar; penetrating; pensive; perceptive; peremptory; perfunctory; permanent; perplexed; persistent; pertinent; petrified; piercing; pinning; pinpoint; pit-bull; pitied; pitiless; pitying; plaintive; pleading; pointed; poisonous; pole-axed; polished-jet; pop-eyed; possessive; potent; potential; pouty; powerful; predators; predatory; pregnant; preoccupied; probing; professional; prolonged; protesting; protracted; provocative; psychoanalytic; pugnacious; puissant; punishing; puppy-eyed; purposeful; puzzled.

Q

quailing; queer; quelling; questing; questioning; quick; quiet; quizzical.

R

rabid; raisin-black; raking; rampant; rancorous; rapier-sharp; rapt; razor-blue; razor-sharp; rebellious; rebuking; red-hot; reflected; reflective; regal; regretful; relaxed; relentless; reluctant; remorseful; remorseless; remote; repelling; repressive; reprimanding; reproachful; reproving; reptilian; resentful; resigned; resolute; responsive; restless; restrained; resultant; reticent; return; returned; returning; revealing; rheumy; rigid; riveted; riveting; road-driller; robot-fixed; rock-hard; round; round-eyed; rude; ruffled; ruthless.

S

sad; salacious; same; sanctimonious; sapient; sapphire; sappy; sarcastic; sardonic; satirical; saucer-eyed; saucy; savage; scalding; scalpel-like; scandalized; scathing; scorching; scornful; scowling; scrutinizing; sea-blue; sea-green; searching; searing; seductive; seething; self-assured; senile; sensual; sensuous; serene; serious; several; severe; sexual; sexy; shadowed; shaken; shamed; sharp; sharp-edged; sharp-eyed; sharpened; sheepish; shimmering; shiny; shivery; shocked; shocked-looking; shrewd; shriveling; shut-up; shuttered; shy; sidelong; sideways; sightless; significant; silencing; silent; silver; silver-dollar-sized; silvered; silvery; similar; simmering; simple; sincere; single; sinister; sizzling; skeptical; skewering; sky-blue; slant-eyed; slanted; slanting; sleek; sleepy; sleepy-eyed; slight; slit-eyed; slitted; slitty-eyed; sloe-dark; slow; slumberous; sly; smarmy; smiling; smoke-gray; smoked-glass; smoky; smoky-eyed; smoldering; smug; snake-like; snapping; sneaky; snobby; snooty; snooty-rich-girl; sober; soft; solemn; solemn-eyed; somber; soul-deep; soul-penetrating; soul-piercing; soul-searching; soul-searing; soul-stripping; soulful; soulful-looking; soulless; sour; sour-tempered; spaced-out; sparring; special; speculative; speechless; Sphinx-like; spiteful; squelching; squint-eyed; squinted; squinty; squinty-eyed; stabbing; stand-down; stark; starry-eyed; startled; startling; steadfast; steady; steady-eyed; steamy; steel-blue; steel-bright; steel-cold; steel-like; steel-tipped; steel-trap; steely; steely-eyed; stern; stern-eyed; sternest; stifled; stifling; stink-eye; stoic; stolid; stone-cold; stone-face; stone-faced; stony; stormy; straight; straightforward; strained; strange; strangest; stricken; stubborn; studied; studious; studying; stunned; stupefied; stupid; sub-zero; sudden; suggestive; sulky; sullen; sultry; supercilious; superior; supervising; sure; surgical-steel; surly; surprised; surreptitious; suspicious; sweeping; sweet-little-innocent; swift; swooning; sword-like; sympathetic.

T

take-no-crap; taunting; tawny; tearful; teasing; telling; ten-mile; ten-second; ten-thousand-yard; tenacious; tender; tense; terrified; terrifying; testing; thorough; thoughtful; thousand-mile; thousand-yard; threatening; thunderous; tiger-like; tight; tight-lipped; tired; tolerant; too-direct; too-innocent; too-penetrating; too-perceptive; too-probing; topaz; tormented; tortured; tough-girl; trance-like; tranced; transfixed; trawling; triumphant; troubled; truculent; trusting; truth-seeking; tumultuous; turquoise; twisting.

U

ultramarine; unabashed; unapologetic; unbelieving; unblinking; unbreakable; uncaring; uncertain; unchild-like; uncomfortable; uncomprehending; uncompromising; uncool; underbrowed; understanding; undisguised; unemotional; unfathomable; unfeeling; unflinching; unfocused; unfocusing; unforgiving; unfriendly; unguarded; unhappy; unhelpful; unhesitating; uniform; unimpressed; uninterested; unkind; unmoved; unmoving; unnerving; unnoticed; unpleasant; unreadable; unrelenting; unremitting; unrepentant; unresponsive; unrevealing; unruffled; unseeing; unsettled; unsettling; unsmiling; unsurprised; unswerving; untouchable; untoward; unwavering; unwelcoming; unwinking; unyielding; up-and-down; upward; usual.

V

vacant; vacuous; veiled; velvety; vengeful; venomous; verdant; vexed; vicious; vigilant; vindictive; violet-blue; violet-eyed; vivid.

W

waiting; wanting; warm; warning; warrior-like; wary; watchful; watching; watery; wavering; weak; weighty; white-faced; white-hot; white-lipped; wicked; wide; wide-angle; wide-eyed; wide-open; widened; widening; wild; wild-eyed; winning; wintry; wise; wistful; withering; wolf-like; wolfhound; wondering; wooden; wordless; worldly-wise; worried; worshipful; wounded; wrathful; wry.

X
X-ray.

Y
yearning; you're-an-idiot; you-are-completely-insane; you-need-to-chill.

Z
zombie.

1.3 - Noun + Prepositional Phrases

stare of a bewildered child; stare of a bird of prey; stare of a child who (...); stare of a collector; stare of a falcon; stare of a hawk; stare of a hunter; stare of a jackal; stare of a kitten; stare of a large carnivore; stare of a man in total control; stare of a man who (...); stare of a marble statue; stare of a marksman; stare of a pair of narrowed gray eyes; stare of a predator; stare of a rabbit confronted by a hunter; stare of a raging queen; stare of a Siamese cat; stare of a snake; stare of a streetfighter; stare of a thug; stare of a trapped wild creature; stare of a troubled man; stare of a woman who (...); stare of a young boy; stare of active dislike; stare of adoration; stare of almost hypnotic intensity; stare of aloof enquiry; stare of amazement; stare of amused disbelief; stare of amusement; stare of an accident victim going into shock; stare of an angry cat; stare of an animal; stare of anger; stare of annoyance; stare of appreciation; stare of apprehension; stare of astonishment; stare of astonishment and dismay; stare of beady eyes; stare of bemusement; stare of bewilderment; stare of bitter condemnation; stare of bitter resentment; stare of blank astonishment; stare of blank confrontation; stare of blank disbelief and shock; stare of bleary indignation; stare of bold curiosity; stare of burning intensity; stare of censure; stare of challenge; stare of cold steel; stare of complete incomprehension; stare of complete innocence; stare of condemnation; stare of contempt; stare of curiosity; stare of dark blue eyes; stare of dead certainty; stare of death; stare of deliberate nonchalance; stare of disapproval; stare of disbelief; stare of disgust; stare of disgust and resentment; stare of dislike; stare of dismay; stare of dismissal; stare of displeasure; stare of expectancy; stare of eyes as black as midnight; stare of frustrated incomprehension; stare of gray eyes; stare of green eyes; stare of gunmetal gray; stare of hard green eyes; stare of her alert eyes; stare of her bright blue eyes; stare of her dark brown eyes; stare of her enormous eyes; stare of her gaze; stare of her green eyes; stare of her round eyes; stare of his black eyes; stare of his cold blue eyes; stare of his cool gray eyes; stare of his dangerous gray eyes; stare of his dark brown eyes; stare of his dark eyes; stare of his/her own*; stare of his/hers*; stare of horrified objection; stare of icy dislike; stare of icy rejection; stare of ill-humor; stare of incredulity; stare of indifference; stare of inquiry; stare of intense dislike; stare of interest; stare of intimidation; stare of irritable impatience; stare of laser-like intensity; stare of loathing; stare of madness; stare of many expressionless black eyes; stare of masculine intent;

stare of mild surprise; stare of mystification; stare of open curiosity; stare of open hostility; stare of outraged condemnation; stare of outraged innocence; stare of polite attention; stare of pure amazement; stare of pure dislike; stare of pure stubbornness; stare of puzzlement and interrogation; stare of rather keen interest; stare of rebellion; stare of resignation; stare of savage impatience; stare of sexual assessment; stare of sheer incredulity; stare of shock; stare of sisterly dislike; stare of smoky lenses; stare of smoldering challenge; stare of some predatory hunter; stare of some predatory hunting cat; stare of someone profoundly shaken; stare of someone waiting for a connection; stare of speculation; stare of startling eyes; stare of stern reproach; stare of stomach-churning power; stare of such directness that (...); stare of surprise; stare of surprised inquiry; stare of surprised interrogation; stare of suspicion; stare of tawny eyes; stare of the dark glasses; stare of those amazing eyes; stare of those cold blue eyes; stare of those coldly assessing eyes; stare of those dark blue eyes; stare of those darkened eyes; stare of those eyes; stare of those hypnotic eyes; stare of those wintry gray eyes; stare of unconcealed desire; stare of undisguised astonishment; stare of undisguised interest; stare of undisguised lust; stare of unwavering confidence; stare of utter amazement; stare of utter blankness; stare of wide eyes; stare of wonder; stare of wonderment.

1.4 - Noun Phrases

a charged battle of stares; a couple of stares; a deepening of her stony stare; a distant kind of stare; a fair imitation of her grandmother's stare; a lot of stares; a mirror image of her intimidating stare; a particularly lengthy clash of stares; a roomful of stares; a share of stares; a slew of stares; a victim of stares; a vision of her intense stare; an odd sort of stare; another dose of the stare; another of her icy stares; her approximation of a fierce stare; her most steely of stares; ignoring the remainder of the stares; one of her basilisk stares; one of her cold stares; one of her disdainful stares; one of her gotcha stares; one of her guileless stares; one of her hard stares; one of her haughty stares; one of her intense stares; one of her laser stares; one of her objective stares; one of her penetrating stares; one of her piercing stares; one of her rapier stares; one of her stares; one of her unreadable stares; plenty of stares; some kind of stare; some of the stares; the almost physical force of her stare; the baleful bleakness of her stare; the baleful coldness of her stare; the battery of stares; the beam of her stare; the benefit of her iciest stare; the bitter hardness of her stare; the black ice of her stare; the blankness of her stare; the blaze of her ebony stare; the blaze of her golden stare; the blazing hostility of her stare; the blazing intensity of her brief stare; the bleakness of her stare; the blue steel of her stare; the boldness of her stare; the briefest of stares; the brilliant blue of her stare; the brooding impatience of her stare; the brooding intensity of her stare; the brunt of her stare; the burn of her stare; the burning intensity of her stare; the calculated insolence of her stare; the calm condescension of her stare; the challenge of her stare; the changing quality of her stare; the chill of her stare; the cold blankness of her stare; the cold glare of her stare; the cold intelligence of her stare; the cold menace of her chilling stare; the cold surprise of her stare; the coldest of stares; the coldness of her stare; the collection of stares; the compelling heat of her stare; the concentration of her stare; the contempt of her stare; the cool blueness of her stare; the cool probe of her stare; the cool warning of her stare; the crystalline intensity of the stare; the curiosity of her stare; the cynical amusement of her stare; the dangerous glitter of her stare; the dark intensity of her bold stare; the dark intensity of her stare; the dark unblinking force of her stare; the darkness and intensity of her stare; the deep penetration of her stare; the deliberate intensity of her stare; the devouring hunger of her stare; the direction of her admiring stare; the direction of her bold stare; the direction of her stare; the directness of her blue stare; the directness of her stare; the dread of a cool stare; the dumb incomprehension of her stare; the emerald ice of her stare; the endless blue of her stare; the energy of her stare; the erotic intensity of her stare; the eroticism of her hot stare; the exchange of stares; the explosive quality of her hard stare; the ferocious intensity of her stare; the ferocity of her provocative stare; the ferocity of her stare; the fierce intentness of her dark stare; the fierce sharpness of her stare; the fierceness of her stare; the fixed intensity of her stare; the fixed lance of her stare; the fixity of her stare; the focus of her hot stare; the focus of her stare; the force of her stare; the force of her venomous stare; the full benefit of her contemptuous stare; the full benefit of her disapproving stare; the full blast of her green stare; the full blast of her icy stare; the full blast of her piercing stare; the full brunt of her devastating stare; the full force of her cool stare; the full force of her green stare; the full force of her icy stare; the full force of her laser stare; the full force of her stare; the full force of her wounded stare; the full impact of her hungry stare; the full intensity of her laser stare; the full onslaught of her dark stare; the full power of her magnetic stare; the full weight of her blistering stare; the glacial pierce of her stare; the glaring intensity of her stare; the glittering intensity of her stare; the glittering onslaught of her narrowed stare; the gray pierce of her stare; the hardness of her stare; the harsh burn of her stare; the harshness of her stare; the heat and weight of her stare; the heat of her angry stare; the heat of her hypnotic stare; the heat of her stare; the heated intensity of her stare; the heaviness of her attentive stare; the heaviness of her stare; the heavy force of her stare; the hold of her steady stare; the horrible insolence of her open stare; the hostility of her stare; the hypnotic intensity of her stare; the hypnotism of her intense stare; the icy contempt of her stare; the icy impact of her stare; the icy implacability of her stare; the impact of her accusing stare; the impact of her compassionate stare; the impact of her intense stare; the impact of her level stare; the impact of her piercing stare; the impact of her stare; the impact of her unwavering stare; the impassive scrutiny of her stare; the impenetrable darkness of her black stare; the imprisonment of her stare; the indignity of her stare; the intense heat of her stare; the intense impact of her stare; the intensity of her black stare; the intensity of her blue stare; the intensity of her cobalt stare; the intensity of her dark stare; the intensity of her hot stare; the intensity of her hungry stare; the intensity of her narrowed stare; the intensity of her searching stare; the intensity of her stare; the intentness of her stare; the intimacy of her stare; the intimidating effect of her stare; the jealousy of her stare; the kind of stare; the lance of her angry stare; the leashed hunger of her stare; the lingering intensity of her stare; the magnetic intensity of her stare; the magnetic quality of her stare; the magnetic tug of her unblinking stare; the memory of her burning stare; the memory of her hard stare; the memory of her heated stares; the memory of her simmering stare; the mesmerizing power of her stare; the mesmerizing spotlight of her stare; the mockery of her stare; the mocking challenge of her stare; the narrowed assessment of her stare; the narrowed probe of her stare; the object of her stare; the object of stares; the onslaught of stares; the openness of her stare; the other end of her stare; the penetrating quality of her stare; the penetration of her stare; the piercing blue of her stare; the piercing directness of her stare; the piercing intensity of her stare; the piercing penetration of her stare; the piercing scrutiny of her stare; the power of her dark stare; the power of her demanding stare; the power of her stare; the pressure of her angry stare; The pressure of her stare; the pressure of her unrelenting stare; the probe of her stare; the probing penetration of her stare; the proximity of her stare; the pull of her hypnotic stare; the quality of her stare; the ravaging intensity of her glittering stare; the receiving end of a disbelieving stare; the receiving end of stares; the recipient of a stare; the recipient of stares; the remainder of the stares; the reverse end of a glacial stare; the roam of her stare; the savage brilliance of her stare; the scrutiny of her hard stare; the searing heat of her stare; the searing intensity of her stare; the seduction of her heated stare; the shadowed power of her stare; the sharp glimmer of her stare; the sharp pierce of her stare; the sharp stab of her stare; the sheer black power of her stare; the sheer magnetic force of her dark stare; the sheer power of her stare; the sheer weight of her stare; the shimmering gold of her stare; the shock of her stare; the silent intensity of her stare; the silver magnetism of her stare; the silvery dazzle of her stare; the skyward direction of her stare; the slight hauteur of her stare; the slow deliberate needle of her stare; the slow speculation of her stare; the smoky hue of her stare; the solid punch of her stare; the sort of stare; the stalemate of stares; the steadiness of her stare; the steady glitter of her azure stare; the steeliness of her stare; the steely depths of her stare; the steely needle of her hard stare; the strength of her even stare; the strength of her stare; the subtlety of her stare; the sudden intensity of her stare; the sudden stabbing quality of her stare; the suffocating stranglehold of her stare; the sweep of her disparaging stare; the tawny blaze of her hot stare; the touch of her stare; the type of stare; the unashamed curiosity of stares; the unmasked evil of her stare; the unnerving intensity of her stare; the very force of her stare; the violence of her stare; the warmth of her stare; the watchful hostility of her stare; the watchful intensity of her stare; the weight of her heavy stare; the weight of her reproving stare; the weight of her stare; the wrathful intensity of her stare; those endless kinds of stares.

1.5 - Verbs: Stare as Subject

Standalone Verbs

become (calculating)*; become (intent)*; become (hard)*; blaze; build; chill; clear; come and go; cool; darken; deepen; end; falter; glow; go; grow; grow (bleak)*; grow (harsh)*; grow (inscrutable)*; grow (intense)*; grow (prolonged)*; harden; hold fast; intensify; lengthen; linger; lower; narrow; radiate out; remain (unwavering)*; return; shift; show (shock)*; simmer; sizzle; soften; stop; turn (hard)*; turn (icier)*; vanish; wither.

Character (Me / Him / Her) as Object

accuse (him); answer (him); arrest (him); ask (him) [sth]*; bewitch (him); burn (him); catch (him) off guard; catch (his); challenge (him); chill (him); clash with (his); compel (him); converge with (his); convince (him); cool (him); crush (him); cut into (him); cut through (him); devour (him); direct at (him); disconcert (him); duel with (his); falter on (him); find (him); fix on (him); follow (him); frustrate (him); glance (him); go to (him); graze (him); harden on (him); hit (him); hold (his); humble (him); impale (him); imprison (him); infuriate (him); intensify on (him); is transfixed on (him)*; land on (him); laser (him); level (him); level on (him); linger on (him); lower on (him); meet (his); melt (him); move to (him); narrow on (him); penetrate (his); pierce (him); pin (him); pinion (him); point toward(s) (him); probe (him); provoke (him); question (him); raise on (him); rake over (him); remain fixed on (him); return to (him); rock (him); run over (him); sadden (him); scorch (him); shake (him); shift to (him); shock (him); show (him) [sth]*; silence (him); snag (him); speak [sth] to (him)*; spear (him); stay on (him); stop (him); stop on (him); tell (him) [sth]*; transfix (him); trap (him); travel over (him); unnerve (him); warm (him); wither (him).

Eyes as Object

can't break from (his eyes); capture (his eyes) (and hold them prisoner); come from (eyes); enter (eyes); focus on (his eyes); linger on (his eyes); meet (his eyes); move to (his eyes); penetrate (his eyes); pierce into (his eyes); probe (his eyes); seem to dive down into (his eyes); spear into (his eyes); strike (him) (like a bullet) between (the eyes).

Face as Object

aim (directly) at (his face); cover (his face); dissect (his face); fasten on (his face); fix on (his face); fly to (his face); focus on (his face); home in on (his face); is steady on (his face)*; (does not) leave (his face); (never) leaves (his face); level on (his face); linger on (his face); make a slow sweeping survey from (his feet) to (his face); miss (his face) by a mile; move over (his face); rest on (his face); return to (his face); return to fix on (his face); rip from (his face); roam over (his face); scan (his face); scour (his face); search (his face); settle on (his face); shift to (his face); stay fixed on (his face); stay on (his face); sweep (his face); sweep over (his face); take in (every detail) of (his face); train (directly) on (his face); wander from (his face) to (his hand); (never) waver from (his face).

1.6 - Verbs: Stare as Object

Character (I / He / She) as Subject

add (a stare); adopt (a stare); afford (him) (a stare); aim (a stare) (his way); aim (a stare) at (him); angle (a stare) at (him); angle (a stare) up at (him); answer (him) with (a stare); appreciate (a stare) from (him)*; attract (a stare) from (him)*; bend (a stare) on (him); bestow (a stare) upon (him); bestow on (him) (a stare); blaze (a stare) at (him); blaze (a stare) into (his eyes/face)*; brave (a stare)*; bring (a stare) from (him)*; burn (a stare) through (him); can't prevent (a stare) that darted from (her)*; cast (a stare) at (him); cast (a stare) toward(s) (him); cast (him) (a stare); catch (a stare) from (him)*; challenge (him) with (a stare); confer (a stare) on (him); convey (a stare) at (him); cut (him) (a stare); dart (him) (a stare); deal (him) (a stare); deliver (a stare); direct (a stare) across (room); direct (a stare) at (him); direct (a stare) into (his face); direct (a stare) over (shoulder); direct (a stare) toward(s) (him); direct (a stare) up at (him); direct (him) (a stare); divide (a stare) between (them); draw (a stare) from (him)*; drill (a stare) at (him); drill (a stare) into (him); drill (him) with (a stare); earn (a stare) from (him)*; earn (a stare)*; encounter (a stare) from (him)*; encounter (a stare)*; endure (a stare)*; evoke (a stare) from (him)*; exchange (a stare); exchange (a stare) with (him); eye (a stare) at (him); face (a stare) from (him)*; fasten (a stare) on (him); favor (him) with (a stare); feed (him) (a stare); fix (a stare) at (him); fix (a stare) on (him); fix (a stare) upon (him); fix (him) (a stare); fix (him) with (a stare); flash (a stare) at (him); flash (a stare) on (him); flash (him) (a stare); flick (a stare) at (him); flick (a stare) in (his direction); flick (him) (a stare); focus (a stare) on (him); focus (a stare) right at (him); focus (a stare) upon (him); force (a stare) on (him); garner (a stare) from (him)*; get (a stare) at (him); get (a stare) from (him)*; give (a stare); give (a stare) at (him); give (a stare) in (his direction); give (a stare) to (him); give (him) (a stare); glean (a stare) from (him)*; grace (him) with (a stare); have (a stare); have (a stare) at (him); hazard (a stare); hold (a stare); intercept (a stare) from (him)*; interrupt (him) with (a stare); keep (a stare) on (him); lance (him) with (a stare); land (a stare) right at (him); laser (a stare) on (him); level (a stare) (his way); level (a stare) at (him); level (a stare) in (his direction); level (a stare) on (him); level (him) (a stare); level (him) with (a stare); meet (a stare); muster (a stare); narrow (a stare) at (him); narrow (a stare) on (him); offer (him) (a stare); pass (a stare) over (him); pass (him) (a stare); perfect (a stare); pierce (him) with (a stare); pin (him) with (a stare); plant (a stare) directly on (his face); produce (a stare) in (his direction); raise (him) (a stare); rake (a stare) across (him); rake (a stare) over (him); rake (him) with (a stare); receive (a stare) back*; receive (a stare) from (him)*; receive (a stare)*; regard (him) with (a stare); resume (a stare); return (a stare); return (him) (a stare); reveal (a stare); run (a stare) down (his body); run (a stare) over (him); scrutinize (him) with (a stare); send (a stare) (his way); send (a stare) across (room); send (a stare) at (him); send (a stare) in (his direction); send (him) (a stare); serve (him) (a stare); set (a stare) on (him); share (a stare); shoot (a stare) (his way); shoot (a stare) around (room); shoot (a stare) at (him); shoot (him) (a stare); shoot back (a stare); slant (a stare) at (him); slant (him) (a stare); smother (him) with (a stare); squint (a stare); squint (a stare) at (him); study (him) with (a stare); survey (him) with (a stare); sweep (him) with (a stare); swing (a stare) at (him); swing (a stare) to (him); take (a stare) at (him); take (him) in with (a stare); test (him) with (a stare); throw (a stare) (his way); throw (a stare) after (him); throw (a stare) at (him); throw (a stare) over (shoulder); throw (him) (a stare); throw back (a stare); toss (a stare) at (him); toss (him) (a stare); try to pin (a stare) on (him); turn (a stare) (his way); turn (a stare) at (him); turn (a stare) in (his direction); turn (a stare) on (him); turn (a stare) toward(s) (him); turn (a stare) upon (him); weather (a stare)*; whip (a stare) in (his direction); won (a stare) from (him)*.

Eyes or Character as Subject

(I) capture (his eyes) in (a stare)*; (I) hold (his eyes) in/with (a stare)*; (I) meet (his eyes) in/with (a stare)*; (I) narrow (eyes) in/into (a stare)*; (I) open (eyes) in (a stare)*; (I) widen (eyes) in/into (a stare)*; (they) lock (eyes) in (a stare)*; are caught in (a stare); are dull with (a stare); are fixed in (a stare); are half-closed in (a stare); are set in (a stare); become entangled in (a stare); blast (him) with (a stare); bore into (his) with (a stare); burn into (his) with (a stare); capture (his) with (a stare); caress (him) with (a stare); catch (his) in (a stare); catch and hold (his gaze) in (a stare); clash with (a stare); clash with (his) in (a stare); collide with (his) in (a stare); come up to meet (his) in (a stare); compel (him) to hold (a stare); connect with (his stare)*; continue to hold (his) in (a stare); fall in front of (his stare); fall to avoid (a stare); fasten on (him) in (a stare); fasten on (his) with (a stare); find (him) with (a stare); fix (him) with (a stare); fix (his) in (a stare); fix (his) with (a stare); fix firmly upon (him) in (a stare); fix on (him) in (a stare); fix on (his) in (a stare); fix on (his) with (a stare); flick down (his body) in (a stare); fly wide in (a stare); focus on (him) with (a stare); freeze (his) into (a stare); gaze (him) in (a stare); gaze (up) at (him) with (a stare); give (him) (a stare); glitter with (a stare); have (a stare); hold (his gaze) in (a stare); hold (his) in (a stare); impact with (his stare)*; impale (him) with (a stare); latch on to (him) almost in (a stare); lift and collide with (a stare); linger for (a stare); linger on (him) for (a stare); lock in (a stare); lock with (his) in (a stare); look at (him) with (a stare); meet (his) in (a stare); meet (his) with (a stare); meet in (a stare); mesh with (his stare)*; move over (him) in (a stare); narrow in/into (a stare); observe (him) with (a stare); open in (a stare); open wide in (a stare); pierce (him) with (a stare); pierce (his) in (a stare); pin (him) in (a stare); pin (him) with (a stare); pop open to meet (his stare)*; rake (him) with (a stare); reconnect with (his stare)*; refuse to waver under (his stare)*; regard (him) with (a stare); remain fixed in (a stare); return (his look) with (a stare); rove down over (him) with (a stare); sear (him) with (a stare); seek (him) out with (a stare); shift and sink beneath (his stare)*; shoot open in (a stare); slide sideways to escape (his stare)*; subject (him) to (a stare); survey (him) with (a stare); sweep over (him) in (a stare); track (his) in (a stare); trap (his) in (a stare); treat (him) to (a stare); watch (him) with (a stare); widen in (a stare); widen into (a stare); zero in on (him) in (a stare).

NOUN USAGE EXAMPLES

He narrowed his gray eyes in a stare of sheer incredulity.

Frank drilled the other man with a penetrating stare.

She gave Peter a beady-eyed stare and put her hands on her hips.

Then he turned an accusatory stare toward Sally.

She fixed him with an inquisitive stare.

2. Verb Form

2.1 - Verb Synonyms

bore into; burn holes with one's eyes; eye; eyeball; fix on; fix one's gaze on; focus on; gape; gawk; gaze; glare; goggle; keep an eye on; lay eyes on; look; look fixedly; observe; ogle; peer; pin with one's eyes; regard; rivet; rubberneck; scorch with one's eyes; scrutinize; spear with one's eyes; stare down; stare off in the distance; study; take in; watch.

2.2 - Adverbs

A
abruptly; absently; absentmindedly; absorbedly; abstractedly; absurdly; accusatorily; accusingly; achingly; acrimoniously; actively; actually*; admiringly; admonishingly; adoringly; affectionately; aggressively; agitatedly; agonizingly; aimlessly; airily; alertly; aloofly; alternately; amusedly; angelically; angrily; antagonistically; anxiously; apologetically; apparently; appealingly; appraisingly; appreciatively; apprehensively; approvingly; arrogantly; ashamedly; assessingly; automatically; avidly; awkwardly.

B
balefully; barely*; basically*; beadily; beguilingly; belligerently; bemusedly; benignly; beseechingly; bewilderedly; bitterly; blackly; blandly; blankly;

blatantly; bleakly; blearily; blindly; blissfully; blithely; blurrily; boldly; boyishly; bravely; brazenly; breathlessly; briefly; brightly; broodily; broodingly; busily.

C

calmly; candidly; carefully; carelessly; casually; cautiously; censoriously; certainly*; challengingly; chillily; chillingly; churlishly; clearly*; closely; cluelessly; coldly; collectively; comically; commandingly; commiseratingly; compassionately; compellingly; complacently; completely; compulsively; concentratedly; concernedly; confidently; confidingly; confusedly; consideringly; constantly*; contemplatively; contemptuously; contentedly; continually; continuously; coolly; courageously; covertly; covetously; critically; crossly; crudely; cruelly; curiously; currently*; cynically.

D

darkly; dazedly; deafly; deeply; defeatedly; defiantly; definitely*; dejectedly; deliberately; delicately; delightedly; demonically; demurely; desolately; despairingly; desperately; despondently; desultorily; detachedly; determinedly; devilishly; devouringly; dimly; diplomatically; directly; disagreeably; disappointedly; disapprovingly; disbelievingly; disconcertingly; disconsolately; discontentedly; discreetly; disdainfully; disgustedly; disinterestedly; dismally; dismissively; disparagingly; dispassionately; dispiritedly; distantly; distastefully; distractedly; distractingly; distrustfully; dizzily; doggedly; dolefully; doubtfully; doubtlessly; dramatically; dreamily; drily; drowningly; drowsily; drunkenly; dubiously; dully; dumbfoundedly; dumbly; dutifully.

E

eagerly; earnestly; easily; ecstatically; edgily; embarrassedly; emotionlessly; emptily; endlessly; engagingly; enigmatically; entreatingly; enviously; equally intently; evenly; evidently; exactly*; exaggeratedly; exasperatedly; excitedly; exhaustedly; expectantly; explosively; expressionlessly.

F

fascinatedly; favorably; fearfully; fearlessly; ferociously; fetchingly; feverishly; fiercely; finally*; firmly; fitfully; fixatedly; fixedly; flatly; foggily; fondly; foolishly; forlornly; forthrightly; fractionally; frankly; frantically; frenziedly; frequently; fretfully; frigidly; frostily; frowningly; frozenly; fruitlessly; frustratedly; fully; fulminatingly; furiously; fuzzily.

G

gently; glacially; glassily; glazedly; glintingly; gloomily; gloweringly; glumly; gormlessly; gravely; greedily; grimly; groggily; grumpily; guardedly; guiltily.

H

happily; harmlessly; harshly; hastily; hatefully; haughtily; hauntedly; hazily; heatedly; heavily; heedlessly; helplessly; hesitantly; hopefully; hopelessly; hostilely; hotly; hugely; humiliatedly; hungrily; huntedly; hurriedly; hypnotically.

I

icily; idiotically; idly; immediately; impassively; impatiently; imperiously; imperturbably; implacably; imploringly; impotently; inadvertently; inanely; inappropriately; incomprehensibly; incomprehensively; incredibly; incredulously; incuriously; indecisively; indifferently; indignantly; indolently; ineffectually; inimically; innocently; inordinately; inquiringly; inquisitively; inscrutably; insistently; insolently; instantly; instinctively; insultingly; intensely; intentionally; intently; interestedly; interrogatingly; intimately; intimidatingly; introspectively; invitingly; involuntarily; irately; irresolutely; irritably.

J

jealously; jerkily.

K

keenly; kindly; knowingly.

L

lackadaisically; languidly; lasciviously; laughingly; lazily; leisurely; lethargically; levelly; lifelessly; likely*; limitlessly; limpidly; limply; lingeringly; listlessly; literally*; longingly; lovingly; ludicrously; lustfully; lustily.

M

madly; malevolently; maliciously; malignantly; meaningfully; measuringly; mechanically; meditatively; menacingly; mentally; merely*; merrily; mesmerically; mindlessly; miserably; mistily; mockingly; momentarily; moodily; moonily; morbidly; morosely; mostly; motionlessly; mournfully; mulishly; musingly; mutely; mutinously; myopically.

N

narrowly; nearly*; nearsightedly; negligently; nervelessly; nervously; nonchalantly; normally*; numbly.

O

obdurately; obediently; objectively; obliviously; obsessively; obstinately; obviously*; occasionally; oddly; ominously; only*; openly; openmouthedly; ordinarily; ostensibly; ostentatiously; overtly; owlishly.

P

painfully; palely; particularly*; partly*; passionately; passively; pathetically; patiently; peacefully; penetratingly; pensively; perceptively; permanently; perplexedly; persistently; persuasively; petulantly; piercingly; piteously; pityingly; placidly; plaintively; pleadingly; pleasurably; poignantly; pointedly; pointlessly; politely; ponderously; positively*; possessively; possibly*; poutingly; practically*; presently; presumably; primly; probably*; profoundly; promptly*; proudly; provocatively; provokingly; pugilistically; pugnaciously; purposefully; purposely; puzzledly.

Q

questioningly; quickly; quietly; quizzically.

R

rapidly; raptly; rapturously; really*; rebelliously; recently; recklessly; reflectively; reflexively; regally; regretfully; relentlessly; reluctantly; remorselessly; remotely; repeatedly; reproachfully; resentfully; resignedly; resolutely; respectfully; restlessly; reverently; ridiculously; ridiculously primly; rigidly; romantically; rudely; ruefully; ruminatively; ruthlessly.

S

sadly; sardonically; savagely; scornfully; searchingly; secretively; seductively; seemingly; seemingly fixedly; self-consciously; sensuously; serenely; seriously; severely; shakenly; shamelessly; sharply; sheepishly; shrewdly; shyly; sightlessly; significantly; silently; simply*; skeptically; sleepily; sleeplessly; slightlessly; slightly; slowly; smilingly; smokily; sniffily; soberly; softly; solemnly; somberly; somnolently; soulfully; soundlessly; sourly; speculatively; speechlessly; squarely; stalwartly; starkly; staunchly; steadfastly; steadily; sternly; stiffly; stoically; stolidly; stonily; stormily; straightly; strangely; strickenly; stubbornly; studiously; stupidly; successfully; suddenly; sulkily; sullenly; surlily; surreptitiously; suspiciously; sweetly; swiftly.

T

tautly; tearfully; tearily; telepathically; tellingly; tenderly; tensely; tentatively; tersely; thirstily; thoroughly; thoughtfully; thoughtlessly; threateningly; thunderously; tightly; tiredly; tortuously; totally*; tragically; transfixedly; transparently; tremulously; triumphantly; truculently; trustingly.

U

unabashedly; unaccountably; unapologetically; unashamedly; unbelievably; unbelievingly; unblinkingly; uncertainly; uncomfortably; uncomprehendingly; uncompromisingly; unconcernedly; unconsciously; undecidedly; undoubtedly; uneasily; unemotionally; unenthusiastically; unfalteringly; unflinchingly; unfocusingly; unguardedly; unhappily; uninterestedly; uninvitingly; unkindly; unnervingly; unobtrusively; unreadably; unrepentantly; unreservedly;

unseeingly; unsmilingly; unsuspectingly; unswervingly; unwaveringly; unwillingly; unwinkingly; urbanely; urgently; uselessly; usually*; utterly*.

V

vacantly; vacuously; vaguely; venomously; viciously; visibly.

W

warily; warmly; watchfully; wearily; weepily; wholly unseeingly; wickedly; widely; wildly; winsomely; wisely; wistfully; witlessly; woefully; wonderingly; wondrously; woodenly; wordlessly; worriedly; worshipfully; wrathfully; wretchedly; wryly.

Y

yearningly.

2.3 - Adverbials of Emotion, Feeling, Mental State, Appearance, and Response

in a battle of wills; in a bemused fashion; in a bored stupor; in a daze; in a dazed fashion; in a dazed way; in a defeated fashion; in a distant fascination; in a kind of dazed disbelief; in a kind of dazed horror; in a kind of disbelieving daze; in a kind of eerie transfixion; in a kind of fascination; in a kind of horror; in a kind of trance; in a moment of intense awareness; in a sort of dumb amazement; in a sort of fascination; in a sort of savage despair; in a sort of superstitious dread; in a startled way; in a state of paralysis; in a steady beam; in a trance; in a way that she knew betrayed her nervousness; in abject admiration; in abject fear; in abject mounting horror; in abject terror; in absolute disbelief; in absolute dismay; in absolute horror; in absolute silence; in absorbed fascination; in abstracted amusement; in acute embarrassment; in admiration; in admiration and trepidation; in adoration; in affront; in affronted outrage; in agony; in alarm; in alarmed fascination; in almost ecstatic wonderment; in almost hypnotic fascination; in amazed appreciation; in amazed confusion; in amazed consternation; in amazed excitement; in amazement; in amazement and disbelief; in amazement and incredible, bubbling joy; in amazement and wonder; in amused amazement; in amused dismay; in amusement; in an engrossed manner; in an odd way; in an unfocused manner; in an unmitigated horror; in angry disbelief; in anguish; in annoyance; in answer; in appalled fascination; in appalled horror; in appalled silence; in apparent amazement; in apparent fascination; in appraisal; in appreciation; in apprehension; in astonished amusement; in astonished fury; in astonished recognition; in astonished surprise; in astonished wonder; in astonishment; in astounded disbelief; in astounded silence; in awe; in awe and wonder; in awe and wonderment; in awed adoration; in awed delight; in awed disbelief; in awed fascination; in awestruck wonder; in awkward silence; in bafflement; in bemused awe; in bemused disbelief; in bemused fascination; in bemused pleasure; in bemused shock; in bemused silence; in bemused wonder; in bemusement; in bewilderment; in blank amazement; in blank and stunned disbelief; in blank astonishment; in blank bemusement; in blank bewilderment; in blank bewilderment and confusion; in blank confusion; in blank disbelief; in blank dismay; in blank hopelessness; in blank incomprehension; in blank surprise; in blatant appreciation; in blatant disbelief; in blatant interest; in blatant panic; in blind misery; in blinking disbelief; in blistering horror; in blushing confusion; in both utter disappointment and acute relief; in breathless awe; in breathless silence; in brooding preoccupation; in brooding silence; in brooding, frustrated silence; in challenge; in challenging contempt; in clear disbelief; in complete amazement; in complete and telling silence; in complete bewilderment; in complete non-comprehension; in complete shock; in concentration; in concern; in confusion; in confusion and disbelief; in consternation; in contempt; in curiosity; in curious amusement; in dazed bewilderment; in dazed compulsion; in dazed confusion; in dazed disbelief; in dazed hunger; in dazed surprise; in dazed wonder; in defeat; in defiance; in delight; in delight and disbelief; in delighted disbelief; in despair; in desperation; in disbelief; in disbelief and bemusement; in disbelief and confusion; in disbelief and delight; in disbelief and horror; in disbelieving horror; in disconcertion; in disgust; in dismay; in displeasure; in distaste; in distress; in dread; in dread and fearful fascination; in dreadful fascination; in dry-mouthed horror; in dumb amazement; in dumb astonishment; in dumb silence; in dumbfounded silence; in dumbfounded surprise; in dumbstruck disbelief; in embarrassment; in enchanted silence; in envy; in even greater horror; in exaggerated horror; in exaggerated surprise; in exasperation; in expectant excitement; in expectation; in eye-blinking amazement; in faint shock; in fascinated amazement; in fascinated awe; in fascinated confusion; in fascinated curiosity; in fascinated horror; in fascinated revulsion; in fascinated silence; in fascination; in fear; in forbidden longing; in frank admiration; in frank amazement; in frank astonishment; in frank disbelief; in frank fascination; in frank incredulity; in frantic and mute appeal; in frowning concentration; in frozen amazement; in frozen shock; in frozen silence; in frozen terror; in frustration; in furious disbelief; in fury; in genuine bewilderment; in glazed anticipation; in grateful surprise; in grim silence; in growing consternation; in growing horror; in growing indignation; in growing wonderment; in guilt; in guilty horror; in half dazed surprise; in half-shocked amazement; in heart-lurching shock; in heart-pounding anticipation; in helpless awe; in helpless bewilderment; in helpless fascination; in helpless fury; in helpless horror; in helpless wonderment; in his proud masculine manner; in honest astonishment; in horrible disbelief; in horrid fascination; in horrified amazement; in horrified disbelief; in horrified fascination; in horrified nauseous disbelief; in horrified shock; in horrified silence; in horror; in humiliating silence; in hushed silence; in hypnotized fascination; in ill-concealed surprise; in incomprehension; in incredulity; in incredulous amazement; in incredulous fury; in incredulous unbelief; in indignant surprise; in initial dismay; in interest; in intimate recognition; in intrigued silence; in level challenge; in maddening surprise; in marbled fright; in mesmerized fascination; in mild disbelief; in mild shock; in mingled admiration and astonishment; in misery; in mock disbelief; in momentary curiosity; in momentary surprise; in morbid fascination; in mortification; in mounting exasperation; in mute astonishment; in mute awe; in mute despair; in mute disbelief; in mute disgust; in mute dismay; in mute distress; in mute fascination; in mute fury; in mute protest; in mute shock; in mute silence; in narrow-eyed fury; in near disbelief; in near horror; in near-mesmerized fascination; in numb disbelief; in numb dismay; in numb, horrified disbelief; in obvious astonishment; in obvious disbelief; in obvious enjoyment; in open admiration; in open alarm; in open amazement; in open awe; in open curiosity; in open dismay; in open doubt; in open fascination; in open hunger; in open pleasure; in open stupefaction; in open surprise; in open-eyed astonishment; in open-eyed, open-mouthed shock; in open-mouthed admiration; in open-mouthed amazement; in open-mouthed astonishment; in open-mouthed awe; in open-mouthed bewilderment; in open-mouthed disbelief; in open-mouthed dismay; in open-mouthed horror; in open-mouthed horror and astonishment; in open-mouthed outrage; in open-mouthed pleasure; in open-mouthed protest; in open-mouthed shock; in open-mouthed surprise; in open-mouthed wonderment; in outrage; in outraged disbelief; in outraged indignation; in panic; in paralyzed horror; in paralyzed mortification; in paralyzed terror; in patent disbelief; in perplexed annoyance; in perplexity; in pleasant disbelief; in preoccupation; in pure astonishment; in puzzled delight; in puzzlement; in rabid fascination; in rage; in rapt adoration; in rapt attention; in rapt wonder; in reaction; in real dismay; in recognition; in relief; in reply; in resentful fury; in resignation; in response; in return; in revulsion; in rigid disappointment; in rising horror; in round-eyed astonishment; in round-eyed horror; in searching and slightly incredulous curiosity; in seemingly rapt fascination; in self-condemnatory disbelief; in shaken disbelief; in sheer amazement; in sheer bewilderment; in sheer delight; in shock; in shock and bewilderment; in shock and blank horror; in shock and dismay; in shock and fury; in shock and horror; in shock and outrage; in shocked amazement; in shocked anxiety; in shocked bemusement; in shocked comprehension; in shocked consternation; in shocked disbelief; in shocked dismay; in shocked fascination; in shocked horror; in shocked recognition; in shocked silence; in shocked surprise; in sick disbelief; in sick shock; in sickened horror; in silence; in silent admiration; in silent amazement; in silent astonishment; in silent awe; in silent condemnation; in silent contemplation; in silent desperation; in silent ecstasy; in silent enmity; in silent fascination; in silent frustration; in silent horror; in silent if grim appreciation; in silent shock; in silent trepidation; in silent wonder; in simple disbelief; in simple wonder; in slack-jawed shock; in sleepy bewilderment; in slight wonderment; in some absorption; in some admiration; in some amazement; in some astonishment; in some awe; in some bewilderment; in some confusion; in some consternation; in some disbelief; in some dismay; in some surprise; in something between appreciation and awe; in something like dismay; in speculation; in speechless amazement; in speechless bewilderment; in speechless horror; in speechless shock; in speechless wonder; in star-struck awe;

in stark disbelief; in startled disbelief; in startled fascination; in startled recognition; in startled silence; in startled surprise; in startled wonderment; in stoical silence; in stony silence; in stricken fascination; in stricken horror; in stunned amazement; in stunned astonishment; in stunned awe; in stunned bewilderment; in stunned disbelief; in stunned dismay; in stunned fascination; in stunned horror; in stunned realization; in stunned recognition; in stunned shock; in stunned silence; in stunned surprise; in stunned wonder; in stunned wonderment; in stupefaction; in stupefaction and growing suspicion; in stupefied amazement; in stupefied disbelief; in stupefied silence; in such a blatant way; in such shock; in sudden alarm; in sudden dismay; in sudden, brilliant hope; in sullen silence; in surprise; in surprise and anger; in surprise and pleasure; in sympathy; in terror; in that same dazed, emotionless way; in the utmost surprise; in thoughtful silence; in thoughtful surprise; in thunderstruck silence; in tight-fisted silence; in tormented accusation; in total amazement; in total bemusement; in total bewilderment; in total confusion; in total disbelief; in total fascination; in total incomprehension; in total shock; in total silence; in total surprise; in transfixed amazement; in trepidation; in triumph; in troubled fascination; in unabashed lust; in unbelief; in uncomfortable silence; in uncomprehending disbelief; in undisguised astonishment; in undisguised consternation; in undisguised contempt; in undisguised curiosity; in undisguised disbelief; in unspeakable dismay; in unwilling fascination; in unwinking hostility; in utter amazement; in utter and complete fascination; in utter astonishment; in utter bewilderment; in utter disbelief; in utter dismay; in utter dread; in utter fascination; in utter feminine fascination; in utter horror; in utter silence; in utter stupefaction; in utter surprise; in utter wonder; in varying degrees of horror; in vexation; in voracious hunger; in wary silence; in what could only be delight; in white-faced disbelief; in wide, innocent inquiry; in wide-eyed amazement; in wide-eyed astonishment; in wide-eyed confusion; in wide-eyed embarrassment; in wide-eyed fascination; in wide-eyed shock; in wide-eyed silence; in wide-eyed wonderment; in wild disbelief; in with stunned amazement; in wonder; in wonder and recognition; in wonderment; in wordless horror; in wordless shock; in wordless wonder; with a blank expression; with a bleak expression; with a certain amount of horror; with a child's curiosity; with a cold hauteur; with a complete lack of interest; with a complete lack of self-consciousness; with a critical eye*; with a curious intensity; with a dazed expression; with a desperate kind of pleading; with a dreadful fascination; with a dropped jaw*; with a faint touch of insolence; with a faraway look in his blue eyes*; with a fascinated gaze; with a fixed gaze; with a frown; with a gaze dark and impersonal; with a hint of despair; with a horrified gaze; with a hostile expression; with a look of comical horror; with a look of mute misery; with a look of shock and disappointment in her eyes*; with a look of surprised elation on her face*; with a look she couldn't put a name on; with a melding of astonishment and indignation; with a mix of exasperation and incredulity; with a mixture of bemusement and horror; with a mixture of curiosity and hostility; with a mixture of disbelief and disgust; with a mixture of grief and bewilderment; with a mixture of horror and fascination; with a mixture of mournfulness and love; with a mixture of pleasure and disdain; with a narrowed, angry gaze; with a nervous defiance; with a peculiar expression; with a peculiar kind of hunger; with a peculiar, fierce intensity; with a peculiar, vulnerable intensity; with a perplexed look on his face*; with a puzzled expression; with a puzzled frown; with a puzzled, slightly worried expression; with a raised brow*; with a remote expression; with a scowl; with a softened expression; with a sort of awe; with a sort of fascinated wonderment; with a sort of fascination; with a sort of horrified fascination; with a sort of repulsed fascination; with a sort of sad fascination; with a startled lassitude; with a stony expression; with a sudden frown; with a sudden searching intentness; with a taut smile; with a tense expression; with a tight smile; with a touch of consternation; with a touch of loathing; with a vague sense of annoyance; with a weird look on her face; with a wondering expectation; with abandon; with absent distaste; with absolute faith; with absolute seriousness; with abstracted eyes*; with aching eyes*; with aching green-brown eyes*; with aching, dazzled eyes*; with acute distaste; with adoration; with affection; with affront; with aggravation; with agonized eyes*; with alarm; with alert curiosity; with all her courage; with all the openness and courage she could muster; with amazed fear; with amazement; with amusement; with amusement and a hint of respect; with an absent frown; with an enigmatic hardness that turned pensive; with an expectant, eager face*; with an eyebrow raised in question*; with an indulgent smile*; with an intensity that made her breath catch; with an open mouth*; with an unfocused gaze; with an unnerving stark ferocity; with anger; with angry eyes*; with angry resentment; with angry, unseeing eyes*; with anguished eyes*; with animal lust; with annoyance; with anticipation; with apathetic acceptance; with apparent fascination; with appreciation; with appreciation, anticipation; with apprehension; with apprehensive eyes*; with arctic eyes*; with as much composure as she could summon; with as much equanimity as she could; with assumed concentration; with astonishment; with avid curiosity; with avid interest; with awe; with awe and wonder; with bated breath; with bemused fascination; with bemused frustration; with bemusement; with bewildered eyes*; with bewildered incomprehension; with bewilderment; with big eyes*; with big, solemn dark eyes*; with bitter helplessness; with bland appraisal; with blank contempt; with blank eyes*; with blank innocence; with blank, hypnotized eyes*; with blatant curiosity; with blazing green eyes*; with bleak determination; with blind eyes*; with bloodshot intensity; with blurred intensity; with bored eyes*; with bright eyes*; with bright, stubborn eyes*; with brooding concentration; with brooding eyes*; with brooding intensity; with brooding reflectiveness; with brooding thoughtfulness; with bucolic interest; with bulging eyes of scorn*; with burning eyes*; with burning intensity; with button-eyed indifference; with calm eyes*; with carnal eyes*; with clearly shocked eyes*; with clouded eyes*; with commendable directness; with concentrated hunger; with concentration; with concern; with confusion; with consternation; with contempt; with controlled deliberation; with cool appraisal; with crawling fascination; with curiosity; with curiously vacant eyes*; with dagger-like eyes*; with damp eyes*; with dark dread; with dark eyes*; with dark jealousy and uncertainty; with dark

197

machismo; with dark pain-filled eyes*; with dark, compassionate eyes*; with darkened eyes*; with dawning excitement; with dazed eyes*; with dazed incomprehension; with dazed intensity; with deceptive solemnity; with defiance; with deliberate arrogance; with deliberation; with delight; with delighted disbelief; with delighted eyes*; with delighted surprise; with desolate eyes*; with detached uninterest; with determination; with dilated eyes*; with disbelief; with disbelief and sudden fear; with disbelieving eyes*; with disfavor; with disgust; with dislike; with dismay; with dismay and disgust; with dispassionate interest; with displeasure; with distant eyes*; with distaste; with dread; with drowsy eyes*; with dry, hot eyes*; with dry-eyed misery; with dull hostility; with dumbfounded expressions on their faces*; with effortless ease; with empty eyes*; with enigmatic steadiness; with envy; with equal intensity; with equal parts horror and consternation; with evident appreciation; with exasperation; with eyes and mouth wide*; with eyes both knowing and luminous*; with eyes completely devoid of emotion*; with eyes like hard blue gems*; with eyes that glittered with anger and tears*; with eyes that seemed to him enormous*; with eyes that sparkled*; with eyes wide open*; with eyes wide with admiration*; with fascinated eyes*; with fascinated horror; with fascination; with fatalistic calm; with fear; with feigned fascination; with fierce attention; with fierce concentration; with fiery eyes*; with fixed attention; with fixed concentration; with fixed eyes*; with fixed guilt and shame; with fixed intensity; with fixed, sharp eyes*; with fixity; with flattering fascination; with frank curiosity; with frightened eyes*; with frightening intensity; with frustration; with furious concentration; with furious disbelief; with gape-mouthed wonder; with glass eyes*; with glassy eyes*; with glazed eyes*; with glazed fixity; with glinted amber eyes*; with glittering eyes*; with great blank eyes*; with great concern; with great determination; with great fascination; with great intensity; with great interest; with grim inquiry; with gritted teeth*; with growing horror; with half-closed eyes*; with half-mad eyes*; with hard amber eyes*; with hard challenge; with hard eyes*; with hard implacability; with hatred; with haunted eyes*; with helpless fixation; with helpless longing; with her eyes narrowed*; with her light blue eyes*; with her mouth agape*; with her mouth hanging open; with her mouth hanging open*; with her mouth open*; with her mouth wide open*; with his cool assurance; with his face scrunched up*; with his hot lubricious gaze; with his mouth open*; with his take-no-prisoners blue eyes*; with hope; with horrified eyes*; with horrified fascination; with horrified, incredulous eyes*; with horror; with horror-struck, dazed eyes*; with hostile eyes*; with hostility; with hot eyes*; with hot, furious eyes*; with hot, hungry eyes*; with huge blue eyes*; with huge, stricken eyes*; with hungry eagerness; with hunted eyes*; with hurt, disbelieving eyes*; with hurt, unhappy eyes*; with icy disdain; with ill-concealed curiosity; with immense regret; with impotent hatred; with increasing shock; with incredulous disbelief; with incredulous eyes and wide-open mouth*; with incredulous fury; with indignant misery; with inimical stoniness; with intense acute pleasure; with intense concentration; with intense curiosity; with intense fascination; with intensity; with intent, hard eyes*; with interest; with interested eyes*; with irritation; with keen interest; with kindly sympathy; with lackluster eyes*; with large shocked eyes*; with large worried eyes*; with large, saddened eyes*; with layman's perplexity; with loathing; with longing; with malevolent eyes*; with masculine satisfaction; with measuring, amber eyes*; with mild interest; with mixed feelings; with morbid fascination; with more than a little dismay; with mounting horror; with mouth agape*; with mouth open and eyes stretched wide*; with mouths wide open*; with much fascination; with muted horror; with mutinous, stubborn persistence; with mystified amazement; with mystified intensity; with naked adoration; with narrow, flickering eyes*; with narrowed eyes*; with narrowed, probing eyes*; with near-sighted interest; with new eyes*; with no expression; with no expression on his face*; with nothing to say; with obsessional intent; with obvious curiosity; with open curiosity; with open disbelief; with open eyes*; with open mouth*; with open mouths and wide eyes*; with open rudeness; with open-mouthed astonishment; with open-mouthed wonder; with overt hunger; with owl-eyes*; with owlish eyes*; with pain-filled eyes*; with parted lips*; with patient, incurious eyes*; with penetrating eyes*; with pleasure; with pleasure around; with pouting dissatisfaction; with pretend interest; with pride; with profound interest; with puzzled eyes*; with quickening interest; with quizzical amazement; with rapt appreciation; with rapt attention; with rapt interest; with rapt violet eyes*; with reddened eyes*; with regret; with reluctance; with repugnance; with resentment; with resignation; with resigned eyes*; with revulsion; with rising terror; with riveted attention; with round eyes*; with rounded eyes*; with sad eyes*; with sardonic amusement; with satisfaction; with scandalized eyes*; with scorn; with seeming disbelief; with serious consideration; with serious gray eyes*; with shaded eyes*; with shadowed eyes into space*; with sharp eyes*; with shock; with shock and contempt; with shocked amazement; with shocked disbelief; with shocked gray eyes*; with shocked, suspicious eyes*; with shocked, unfocused eyes*; with sightless eyes*; with silent shock; with skin-peeling intensity; with smiling interest; with smoky eyes*; with so frank a curiosity; with solemn eyes*; with solemn violet eyes*; with somber eyes*; with somber speculation; with some apprehension; with some attention; with some bewilderment; with some confusion; with some desperation; with some disfavor; with some fixity; with some intensity; with some perplexity; with some wonderment; with something close to resentment; with something like fear; with something like horror; with something like longing; with sore eyes*; with sparkling eyes*; with speculation; with stark dismay; with stars in his eyes*; with startled; with startled blue eyes*; with startled eyes and open-mouthed astonishment*; with startled eyes*; with steady defiance; with steady eyes*; with strained intensity; with strange intentness; with stricken eyes*; with stricken incredulity; with stunned amazement; with stunned, disbelieving eyes*; with such an expression of jealous hatred; with such an intent expression; with such blatant appreciation; with such boldness; with such fascination; with such intensity; with such longing, such envy; with such open antagonism; with such profound adoration; with such unswerving intensity; with sudden fascination; with sudden intentness; with suddenly burning eyes*; with surprise; with surprised blue

199

eyes*; with suspicion; with suspicious eyes*; with swift concern; with tear-blinded eyes*; with teenage intensity; with terrible attention; with terrible eyes*; with terrified eyes*; with terrified fascination; with terror; with that same bemused look of happiness on her face*; with the awe of discovery; with the eyes of a wounded animal*; with the same penetrating quality as surgical steel; with the shocked look of a hunted animal; with the utmost attention; with those adoring brown eyes*; with those enigmatic blue eyes*; with those green, green eyes*; with those round dark eyes*; with triumph; with unabashed appreciation; with unabashed curiosity; with unabashed delight; with unabashed fascination; with unabashed interest; with unabashed pleasure; with unapologetic directness; with unashamed interest; with unashamed longing; with unashamed pleasure; with unashamed surprise and curiosity; with unbelieving eyes*; with unblinking solemnity; with uncomfortable intensity; with uncomfortable thoroughness; with uncomprehending, sad, blank eyes*; with uncompromising eyes*; with uncompromising harshness; with unconcealed amazement; with unconcealed curiosity and fairly open dislike; with unconcealed dislike; with undisguised astonishment; with undisguised curiosity; with undisguised fascination; with undisguised interest; with unfocused eyes*; with unnerving directness; with unseeing blue eyes*; with unseeing brown eyes*; with unseeing eyes*; with unseeing weariness; with unseeing, half-closed eyes*; with unusual concentration; with unwarranted rudeness; with unwilling fascination; with utter astonishment; with utter concentration; with utter fascination; with vacant eyes*; with vacant, unseeing eyes*; with varying degrees of disbelief; with weary frustration; with what could only be called interest; with what she felt sure was grim malevolence; with white-faced intensity; with wide and serious eyes*; with wide blue eyes*; with wide blue-gray eyes*; with wide eyes*; with wide wet eyes*; with wide, astonished eyes*; with wide, eager eyes*; with wide, frightened eyes*; with wide, haunted eyes*; with wide, honest eyes*; with wide, interested eyes*; with wide, milk-chocolate eyes*; with wide, panic-stricken eyes*; with wide, petrified eyes*; with wide, stricken eyes*; with wide, tear-filled eyes*; with wide, unseeing eyes*; with wide-eyed amazement; with wide-eyed apprehension; with wide-eyed confusion; with wide-eyed disbelief; with wide-eyed excitement; with wide-eyed exuberance; with wide-eyed fascination; with wide-eyed wonder; with wide-stretched eyes*; with widened eyes*; with widening and wondering eyes*; with wild and beady glass eyes*; with wonder; with wondering eyes*; with wooden fixity; with wounded eyes*; with wrinkled brow*.

VERB USAGE EXAMPLES

Karen stared at him, astonished.

Mark stared into space.

Fran stared at the scene with wide-eyed fascination.

She stared into his slate-gray eyes that seemed to know everything.

Without moving an inch, Cassie stared stubbornly through the screen door at her rival.

16
WINCE

1. Noun Form

1.1 - Noun Synonyms

blink; cringe; flinch; grimace; shiver; shudder.

1.2 - Adjectives

A

accompanying; all-out; annoyed; another; apologetic; appalled; audible; automatic; awkward.

B

betraying; brief.

C

controlled; convincing.

D

definite; delicate; despairing; disguised; dramatic.

E

earlier; elaborate; embarrassed; endearing; every; exaggerated; extravagant.

F

faint; faintest; fake; familiar; fastidious; fleeting.

G

girly; guilty.

H

hard; helpless; hesitant; humiliated; hurt.

I

immediate; impatient; inadvertent; infinitesimal; inner; instinctive; internal; involuntary; inward.

L

light; little.

M

manly; masculine; mental; mighty; mock; mocking; mortified.

N

noticeable.

O

obvious; occasional; one; own.

P

pain-filled; pained; painful; perceptible; pitying; playful; puzzling.

Q

quick.

R

reflexive; regretful; reminiscent; rueful.

S

second; self-conscious; self-disgusted; several; sharp; shuddering; sincere; single; slight; slightest; small; smallest; smiling; smothered; soft; startled; sudden; suggestive; sympathetic.

T

tender; theatrical; tiny.

U

uncharacteristic; uncomfortable; uncontrollable; unspoken.

V

veiled; visible.

1.3 - Noun + Prepositional Phrases

wince of a smile; wince of anguish; wince of bitter pain; wince of contrition; wince of discomfort; wince of dismay; wince of distaste; wince of distress;

wince of dread; wince of embarrassed uneasiness; wince of enjoyment; wince of exasperation; wince of foreboding; wince of frustration; wince of horror; wince of intolerable excitement; wince of jealous hurt; wince of obvious pain; wince of pain; wince of pain and pleasure; wince of pleasure; wince of pure pleasure; wince of regret; wince of rejection; wince of reproach; wince of self-disgust; wince of shame; wince of shocked disgust; wince of sorrow; wince of sympathy; wince of terror; wince of unexpected pain.

1.4 - Noun Phrases

a combination of a wince and a frown; a good imitation of a wince; a slight trace of a wince; a trace of a wince; another series of winces; (the expression was) more of a wince; the faintest hint of a wince; the faintest of winces; the flicker of a wince; the slightest hint of a wince; the smallest of winces; the sound of the wince.

1.5 - Verbs: Wince as Subject

Miscellaneous as Object

break (facade / mask); bring (him) to realization (he was hurting her)*; cause (him) to [do something]; concede (point); contradict (words); crease (features); crinkle (corners of eyes); cross (face / features); dash across (face); deepen; dispel (his) (mirth); draw (mouth) down; flash across (face); flicker over (face); give (warning); go (unnoticed); indicate [something]; mar (brow); match (someone else's); narrow (eyes); pass over (features); pop out; precede [movement]; pull (mouth) down; reveal (pain); show on (face); speak volumes; spread across (features); stir (his) (laugh); stop (him) cold; tell [something]; wipe away (his) (smile).

1.6 - Verbs: Wince as Object

Character (I / He / She) as Subject

(I) acknowledge (his wince)*; battle (a wince); battle back (a wince); bite back (a wince); (I) catch (his wince)*; conceal (a wince); contain (a wince); control (a wince / her wince reflex); counteract (a wince); cover (a wince); cover up (a wince); crush (a wince); (I) don't miss (his wince)*; fake (a wince); (I) feel (him) (wince)*; feign (a wince); fight (a wince); fight back (a wince); fight off (a wince); give (a wince); halt (a wince); (I) hear (his wince)*; hide (a wince); hold back (a wince); hold in (a wince); (I) ignore (his wince)*; (she) is oblivious to (his wince)*; (she) is unprepared for (his wince)*; issue (a wince); (I) listen to (his wince)*; (can only) manage (a wince); mask (a wince); mirror (his wince); (I) misinterpret (his wince)*; (I) miss (his wince)*; (I) note (his wince)*; (I) notice (his wince)*; push back (a wince); (I) relish (his wince)*; (I) remember (his wince)*; repress (a wince); respond with (a wince); restrain (a wince); (I) see (his wince)*; smile to cover (a wince); smother (a wince); stall (a wince); stifle (a wince); struggle to corral (a wince); suppress (a wince); swallow (a wince); try to disguise (a wince); turn to camouflage (a wince); volunteer (a wince); (I) watch (his wince)*; (I) watch for (a wince)*.

Facial Constituents as Subject
(brow) pull together in (a wince); (eyebrows / brows) knit in (a wince); (eyelids / lids) lower in (a wince); (eyelids / lids) squeeze in (a wince); (eyes) close in/with (a wince); (face) pull tight in (a wince); (face) reveal (a wince); (face) scrunch into (a wince); (face) wrinkle in (a wince); (lips) part in (a wince); (nose) crease into (a wince).

NOUN USAGE EXAMPLES

Lisa responded with a self-conscious wince.

A wince of dread flickered over her face.

Upon hearing the question, Michael's brow pulled together in a wince.

He barely managed to stifle a wince.

Looking on, she gave a sympathetic wince.

2. Verb Form

2.1 - Verb Synonyms

blanch; blench; blink; brace oneself; cower; cringe; dodge; draw back; duck; falter; flinch; grimace; make a face; quail; quake; quiver; recoil; shiver; shrink; shudder; shy away; squirm; start; startle; tremble; writhe.

2.2 - Adverbs

A
actually*; alternately*; angrily; apologetically; appealingly; audibly; automatically; awkwardly.

B
barely*; briefly.

C
convincingly; convulsively.

D
definitely*; (didn't) exactly*; dramatically.

E
exaggeratedly; extravagantly.

F
faintly.

G
guiltily.

H
hardly*.

I
immediately; instantly; instinctively; internally; involuntarily; inwardly; irritably.

L
lightly; literally*; loudly.

M
mentally; merely*; minutely; miserably; mockingly; momentarily.

N
naturally*; nearly*; noticeably.

O
occasionally; only*; only a bit; only once; only slightly; openly; outwardly.

P
painfully; perceptibly; physically; playfully; positively*; practically*; probably*; promptly*.

Q
quickly; quietly.

R
regretfully; regrettably; ruefully.

S
scarcely*; sharply; significantly; silently; simultaneously; slightly; soberly; suddenly; sympathetically.

T
theatrically.

U
uncomfortably; unconsciously; uncontrollably; uneasily; unhappily.

V
visibly.

W
wryly.

2.3 - Adverbials of Emotion, Feeling, Mental State, and Response

in a sheepish way; in a mime of compassion; in acknowledgement; in agony; in amused sympathy; in annoyance; in answer; in anticipated pain; in anticipation; in apology; in astonishment; in automatic sympathy; in chagrin; in commiseration; in consternation; in despair; in disbelief; in discomfiture; in discomfort; in dismay; in distaste; in distress; in embarrassment; in empathy; in even greater consternation; in evident embarrassment; in exaggerated pain; in frustration; in guilt; in heartfelt sympathy; in helpless protest; in horror; in instinctive sympathy; in intolerable grief; in memory; in misery; in mock pain; in momentary envy; in mortification; in near-pain; in nervous distress; in obvious agony; in obvious pain; in pain; in pretend regret; in protest; in pure pleasure; in reaction; in realization; in recognition; in regret; in remembered embarrassment; in remembered shame; in remembrance; in response; in retrospect; in return; in rueful remembrance; in sharp distress; in sighing pleasure; in silent pain; in sudden pain; in surprise; in swift distaste; in sympathy; in what could only be pain; with a fresh wave of pain; with a new twinge of pain; with a pain so deep that (...); with a pang of guilt; with a particular kind of pain; with a pleasure that was like pain; with a smile; with a twist of pain; with agony; with an agony which (...); with annoyance; with bittersweet pain; with bone-deep regret; with chagrin; with comic exaggeration; with disappointment; with disgust; with displeasure; with distaste; with dread; with embarrassment; with emotion; with exaggerated pain; with glee; with guilt; with horror; with humiliation; with humiliation and sorrow; with longing; with mirth; with need; with pain; with pain and shame; with physical pain; with pity; with pleasure; with pretend guilt; with regret; with regret and remorse; with sadness; with shame; with shocked pain; with such exaggerated pain; with sudden pain; with surprise; with sympathy; with the pain; with the remembered pain; with theatrical exaggeration; with uneasiness; with unexpected discomfort; with very real pain; with visible regret.

VERB USAGE EXAMPLES

Ruth winced in evident embarrassment at the frankness of his question.

He winced internally as she closed the door on her exit.

Trevor winced with regret at the memory.

She squeezed his forearm so hard, he winced.

Wincing slightly, Martha turned back to her companion.

17
WINK

1. Noun Form

1.1 - Noun Synonyms

bat of the eyes; blink; flutter of eyelids; nictitation.

1.2 - Adjectives

A
A-OK; accompanying; admiring; affable; affectionate; aggravating; alluring; amorous; amused; annoying; another; answering; apologetic; approving; assuring; attagirl; audacious.

B
barest; bawdy; beaming; big; blatant; bold; bolstering; boyish; brazen; brief; bright; broad; brotherly.

C
careless; catty; charming; cheekiest; cheeky; cheerful; cheery; cocky; collusive; come-to-mama; comforting; comprehending; comradely; confident; confidential; confiding; conspiratorial; conspirators; conspiring; contented; covert; coy; crafty.

D
damnable; damned; dashing; definite; deliberate; delicious; delighted; delightful; devastating; devil-may-care; devilish; disarming; discernible; disconcerting; discreet; distracting; dramatic.

E
elaborate; eloquent; emphatic; enchanting; encouraging; engaging; enigmatic; enormous; evil; exaggerated; exchanged; explicit; expressive; extra.

F
faint; faintest; fake; familiar; fast; few; final; fleeting; flirtatious; flirty; fond; foxy; fractional; frequent; friendly; furtive.

G

genial; gentle; get-past-this; giant; girl-to-girl; girlish; glamorous; gleeful; good-humored; good-natured; gotcha; graceless; grateful.

H

half; happy; heart-stopping; hearty; hidden; huge.

I

I'm-on-the-case; imperceptible; impertinent; impish; impudent; incomprehensible; indecorous; indiscreet; indulgent; insider; insinuating; insufferable; invisible; ironic; ironical; irrepressible.

J

jaunty; jovial; just-between-us.

K

kindly; knowing.

L

languid; languorous; large; lascivious; last; lazy; lecherous; leering; leery; let's-take-this-further; lewd; light-hearted; lighthearted; little; lively; long-lashed; lopsided; lovely; lurid; lusty.

M

man-to-man; many; masculine; mean-spirited; meaningful; merest; merry; mischievous; mocking; modest; mysterious.

N

naughty; nonchalant; none-too-subtle; noticeable.

O

obligatory; oblique; obvious; occasional; odd; offhanded; one; ornery; outrageous; over-the-top; oversized.

P

parting; patented; perceptible; playful; please-let's-cooperate-here; ponderous; portentous; possessive; pragmatic; prettiest; private; prodigious; promising; provocative.

Q

quick.

R

rakish; random; reassuring; rebellious; reprehensible; return; returning; ribald; roguish; rueful.

S

salacious; sassy; satisfied; saucy; second; secret; seductive; self-conscious; self-deprecating; sensual; several; sexy; sexy-as-hell; shrewd; sidelong; sideways; signature; significant; simple; sinful; single; sirens; sisterly; slight; slow; sly; small; smiling; smug; sneaky; snide; sober; soft; solemn; speculative; sprightly; studly; subtle; sudden; sugary; suggestive; sultry; sure; surprised; surreptitious; swift; sympathetic.

T

tantalizing; taunting; teasing; telling; tender; theatrical; tiny; trademark; triumphant; two.

U

ugly; ultra-hunky; uncharacteristic; understanding; undignified; unexpected; unmistakable; unrepentant; unseen; unsettling; unsubtle; urgent; usual.

V

vampish; victorious.

W

warning; well-placed; wicked; woman-to-woman; wry.

Y

you'll-be-fine.

1.3 - Noun + Prepositional Phrases

wink of acknowledgment; wink of amusement; wink of an eye; wink of an eyelash; wink of apology; wink of approval; wink of camaraderie; wink of complicity; wink of conspiracy; wink of encouragement; wink of his/her eye; wink of his/her good eye; wink of his/her own; wink of Odin; wink of one crystal blue eye; wink of one eye; wink of one watery blue eye; wink of promise; wink of recognition; wink of sardonic amusement; wink of those baby blues; wink of triumph; wink of warning.

1.4 - Noun Phrases

a couple of winks; a flurry of winks; a rakish kind of wink; a travesty of a wink; a/the flicker of a wink; a/the ghost of a wink; a/the suggestion of a wink; a/the

211

suspicion of a wink; a/the whisker of a wink; another of his cheeky winks; her best version of a lascivious wink; just a hint of a wink; lots of winks; one of her flirtatious winks; one of his blatant winks; one of his patented winks; one of his usual winks; the barest suggestion of a wink; the briefest of winks; the broadest of winks; the earlier exchange of winks; the effect of his wink; the exchange of winks; the faintest suggestion of a wink; the flash of a wink; the ghost of a conspiratorial wink; the merest suggestion of a wink; the playful kind of wink; (on) the receiving end of his wink; the shadow of a wink; the slightest glimpse of a wink; the slightest suggestion of a wink; the slightest suspicion of a wink; the startling impression of a wink; the verbal equivalent of a wink; the very faintest suggestion of a wink; the very slightest suspicion of a wink; the vestige of a wink.

1.5 - Verbs: Wink as Object

Brow or Character as Subject
(I) raise (brow) and attempt (a wink)*; lower to deliver (a wink).

Character (I / He / She) as Subject
add (a wink); aim (a wink) at (him); aim (a wink) in (his direction); aim (a wink) toward(s) (him); attempt (a wink); bestow (a wink) in (his direction); bestow (a wink) on (him); bestow (a wink) over (shoulder) at (him); cast (a wink) at (him); cast (a wink) in (his direction); cast (a wink) over (shoulder); cast (him) (a wink); catch (a wink) from (him)*; chance (a wink); consider (a wink); deliver (a wink) at (him); deliver (a wink) in (his direction); deny (him) (a wink); direct (a wink) at (him); direct (a wink) in (his direction); direct (a wink) toward(s) (him); direct (him) (a wink); draw (a wink) from (him)*; drop (a wink) (his way); drop (a wink) at (him); drop (him) (a wink); earn (a wink) from (him)*; exaggerate (a wink) at (him); exchange (a wink) with (him); favor (him) with (a wink); fire (a wink) at (him); flash (a wink); flash (a wink) (his way); flash (a wink) at (him); flash (a wink) back at (him); flash (him) (a wink); flick (a wink) at (him); flicker (a wink); flicker (a wink) at (him); fling (a wink) at (him); force (a wink) at (him); get (a wink) from (him); get (a wink) from (him)*; give (a wink) to (him); give (him) (a wink); lower (him) (a wink); make (a wink) at (him); manage (a wink); manage (a wink) at (him); manage (a wink) in (his direction); mirror (a wink); offer (a wink); offer (a wink) in (his direction); offer (a wink) to (him); offer (him) (a wink); pass (a wink) at (him); pass (him) (a wink); receive (a wink)*; resist (a wink); send (a wink) (his way); send (a wink) at (him); send (a wink) in (his direction); send (a wink) to (him); send (a wink) toward(s) (him); send (him) (a wink); share (a wink); share (a wink) with (him); shoot (a wink) (his way); shoot (a wink) at (him); shoot (a wink) in (his direction); shoot (a wink) over (shoulder); shoot (him) (a wink); slant (a wink) toward(s) (him); slant (him) (a wink); slice (him) (a wink); slide (him) (a wink); slip (a wink) at (him); slip (a wink) to (him); slip (him) (a wink); sneak (a wink) at (him); spare (him) (a wink); tease (him) with (a wink); throw (a wink) (his

way); throw (a wink) at (him); throw (him) (a wink); tip (him) (a wink); toss (a wink) at (him); toss (a wink) back at (him); toss (a wink) in (his direction); toss (a wink) over (shoulder); toss (him) (a wink); trade (a wink) with (him); wink (a wink) at (him).

Eye or Character as Subject
(I) close (one eye) in (a wink)*; (I) drop (left eye) in (a wink)*; close in (a wink); droop in (a wink); favor (him) with (a wink); give (a wink); narrow in (a wink); open and close in (a wink); shut in (a wink).

Eyelid or Character as Subject
(I) close (left eyelid) in (a wink)*; (I) dip (one eyelid) in (a wink)*; (I) droop (eyelid) at (him) in (a wink)*; (I) drop (one eyelid) in (a wink)*; (I) let (one eyelid) slide closed in (a wink)*; (I) lower (one eyelid) in (a wink)*; (I) press (one eyelid) down in (a wink)*; close with (the suggestion of a wink); descend in (a wink); droop in (a wink); drop toward(s) (him) in (a wink); flick downward(s) in (a wink); flicker in (just the slightest suggestion of a wink); flutter (briefly) in a (a wink); lower (briefly) in (a wink).

NOUN USAGE EXAMPLES

He gave her a conspiratorial wink.

He dropped an eyelid in the slightest suggestion of a wink.

She grinned and sent him a wink.

He shot a wink in Debbie's direction, and her heart flip-flopped.

Derek responded with a wink of promise.

2. Verb Form

2.1 - Verb Synonyms

bat eyelids; blink; close and open eyes; flutter eyelids; give a conspiratorial glance; give a knowing look; hint; nictate; nictitate; sign; signal.

2.2 - Adverbs

A

abruptly; absently; accusingly; actually*; affectionately; alluringly; amenably; appreciatively; audaciously.

B

badly; balefully; barely*; benignly; blankly; blindly; boldly; boyishly; brazenly; briefly; brightly; broadly.

C

cautiously; cheekily; cheerfully; cheerily; cockily; coldly; comically; companionably; complacently; confidentially; conspiratorially; coquettishly; covertly; coyly; crudely.

D

damningly; defiantly; deliberately; derisively; devilishly; discreetly; distinctly.

E

encouragingly; enigmatically; erotically; exaggeratedly.

F

feebly; festively; flirtatiously; fondly.

G

gaily; gallantly; gently; gleefully; gloriously; gradually.

H

happily; hugely.

I

immediately; impishly; impudently; innocently; insolently; intermittently; invariably.

J

jauntily; jovially.

K

kindly; knowingly.

L

lasciviously; lazily; lecherously; lewdly.

M

madly; malevolently; maliciously; meaningfully; merely*; merrily; mischievously; mockingly.

N
naughtily.

O
ominously; only*; openly; outrageously.

P
playfully; ponderously; positively*; promptly*; provocatively.

Q
quickly.

R
rakishly; really*; reassuringly; recently; reflexively; reproachfully; reprovingly.

S
salaciously; saucily; secretly; seductively; sexily; simply*; sleepily; slightly; slowly; slyly; soberly; softly; solemnly; sporadically; steadily; suddenly; suggestively; surreptitiously; sympathetically.

T
tauntingly; teasingly; temptingly; triumphantly.

U
unblushingly; unsympathetically; usually*.

W
wickedly; wryly.

2.3 - Adverbials of Emotion, Feeling, Mental State, and Response

in a friendly fashion; in a provocative way; in a rakish way; in a way that made her flush; in a way that meant only one thing; in an extremely vulgar and provincial manner; in an obvious manner; in answer; in answer to (her reproachful stare); in appreciation; in approval; in exaggerated camaraderie; in his usual good-humored fashion; in open invitation; in passing; in reply; in response; in return; in silent thanks; in some sort of secret agreement; in what he thought of as a charming manner; with a big smile; with a boastful gleam in his eyes; with a knowing nod; with a lightness she was far from feeling; with a sly nod; with a sly smile; with a smile; with bright cheer; with but half the sparkle in his eyes; with devilish satisfaction; with faint suggestiveness; with feigned enthusiasm; with good cheer; with his good eye; with his one good eye; with lightheartedness; with mock lasciviousness; with one eye knowingly.

VERB USAGE EXAMPLES

He folded his arms and winked salaciously down at her.

Winking with devilish satisfaction, George strolled past her and exited the room.

Glancing up, Anne winked at him.

Tucker looked across at Lily and winked in silent thanks.

A faint smile flashed across her lips and she winked knowingly.

18
YAWN

1. Noun Form

1.1 - Noun Synonyms

gape; opened jaw; sign of boredom; sign of drowsiness; sign of fatigue; sign of tiredness; wide-open mouth.

1.2 - Adjectives

A
aching; air-gulping; almighty; another; artificial; audible.

B
backhanded; best; big; biggest; body-shaking; body-stretching; bored; brief; broad.

C
cat-like; cavernous; colossal; complaining; concealed; contented; continuous; contrived; convenient; convincing; convulsive; covered; cracking; creaking.

D
dainty; deep; deliberate; delicate; delicious; discreet; disdainful; doggy; double; drawn-out; drowsy.

E
ear-popping; elaborate; enormous; exaggerated; exhausted; expansive; eye-watering.

F
face-stretching; faint; fake; feigned; feline; few; fierce; final; first; forced; frequent; full-body.

G
gap-toothed; genuine; giant; gigantic; good; good-natured; grand; great; grumbling; guilt-inspiring; guilty.

H

half; half-hearted; half-muffled; half-reproachful; half-stifled; hand-covered; hard-to-suppress; head-splitting; heartfelt; hearty; heavy; helpless; hippopotamus; huge; human; hundredth.

I

ill-contrived; ill-disguised; ill-timed; impressive; incipient; increasing; induced; inelegant; inescapable; insidious; insulting; involuntary; irrepressible.

J

jaded; jaw-breaking; jaw-cracking; jaw-creaking; jaw-popping; jaw-snapping; jaw-splitting; jaw-stretching; jet-lagged.

K

kittenish.

L

ladylike; languid; large; late-afternoon; lavish; lazy; light; little; long; loud; lusty; luxuriant; luxurious.

M

major; make-believe; mammoth; manly; manufactured; many; masculine; massive; mighty; mock; mocking; monotonous; monster; mouth-stretching; mouthed; muffled.

N

near; next; noisy; nonchalant.

O

obvious; occasional; odd; open-mouthed; ostentatious; overdone.

P

petulant; phony; pink-tongued; polite; possible; pretend; prodigious; prolonged; pronounced; protracted.

Q

quite-genuine; quivering.

R

real; realistic; relaxed; rising; rueful; rummy; rustling.

S

sated; satisfied; satisfying; savage; second; serious; several; sexy; shaking; shivering; shuddering; shuddery; silent; simulated; sleepy; slight; small; smiling;

smothered; soft; spurious; squeaky; stifled; sudden; suppressed; surreptitious.

T

teasing; telltale; terrific; theatrical; tiny; tired; tremendous.

U

uncontrollable; unconvincing; undignified; unexpected; unhurried; uninterested; uninterrupted; unladylike.

V

vast.

W

weary; welcome; well-disguised; well-simulated; wholesome; wide; wide-mouthed.

1.3 - Noun + Prepositional Phrases

yawn of a tired woman; yawn of a woman tired out; yawn of boredom; yawn of contentment; yawn of exhaustion; yawn of fatigue; yawn of (his/her) own; yawn of longing; yawn of mammoth proportions; yawn of mental and physical exhaustion; yawn of pure tiredness; yawn of tiredness; yawn of total boredom.

1.4 - Noun Phrases

a couple of yawns; a fit of yawns; a good imitation of a yawn; a series of yawns; a whole series of yawns; full of yawns; (on) the back of a huge yawn; the beginning(s) of a yawn; (on) the brink of a yawn; the hint of a yawn; (in) the middle of a yawn; the onset of a yawn; the pretence of a yawn; the return of the yawns; the sound of a yawn; the stifling of a yawn; the suggestion of a yawn; the tail end of a yawn; (on) the verge of a yawn.

1.5 - Verbs: Yawn as Subject

Standalone Verbs

approach; break through; come and go; come on; cut off; die; disappear; emerge; end; escape; evaporate; follow; rise; slip out; stop; threaten; well up.

Character (Me / Him / Her) as Object

attack (him/her); catch (him/her) by surprise; catch (him/her) unawares; claim (him/her); creep up on (him/her); defeat (him/her); escape (him/her); interrupt (him/her); overcome (him/her); overtake (him/her); overwhelm (him/her); ripple through (him/her); seize (him/her); shake (him/her); sneak up on (him/her); startle (him/her); surprise (him/her); take hold of (him/her).

Face as Object

(nearly) break (face) in two; contort (face); crack (face); overwhelm (face); split (face); stretch (face); stretch (face) wide; stretch and distort (face).

Lips as Object

draw (lips) open; escape (lips); round (lips); shape (lips) into a big O; stretch (lips) wide open.

Mouth as Object

capture (mouth); come to (mouth); ease from (mouth); escape from (mouth); force (mouth) open; pull (mouth) open; seize (mouth); stretch (mouth); stretch (mouth) wide.

1.6 - Verbs: Yawn as Object

Character (I / He / She) as Subject

achieve (a yawn); affect (a yawn); approximate (a yawn); awake with (a yawn); block (a yawn) with (back of hand)*; capture (a yawn) on (back of hand)*; capture (a yawn) with (palm)*; catch (a yawn); catch (herself) stifling (a yawn); conceal (a yawn); contain (a yawn); contrive (a yawn); control (a yawn); counterfeit (a yawn); cover (a yawn); cover (a yawn) with (hand)*; detect (a yawn)*; do (a yawn); emit (a yawn); enjoy (a yawn); exaggerate (a yawn); execute (a yawn); expel (a yawn); fabricate (a yawn); fake (a yawn); favor (him) with (a yawn); feel (a yawn) come on; feel (a yawn) creep up; feel (a yawn) well up; feign (a yawn); fight (a yawn); fight back (a yawn); fight off (a yawn); finish (a yawn); force (a yawn); give (a yawn); give (him) (a yawn); have (a yawn); hear (a yawn)*; heave (a yawn); hide (a yawn) behind (hand)*; hide (a yawn) with (hand)*; issue (a yawn); let out (a yawn); make (a yawn); make no effort to hide (a yawn); manage (a yawn); manufacture (a yawn); mask (a yawn) with (hand)*; mime (a yawn); mimic (a yawn); mirror (a yawn); muffle (a yawn); muffle (a yawn) with (hand)*; pantomime (a yawn); pretend (a yawn); pretend to stifle (a yawn); produce (a yawn); raise (a yawn); release (a yawn); repress (a yawn); restrain (a yawn); screen (a yawn); shield (a yawn) behind (hand)*; shield (a yawn) from (him); shield (a yawn) with (hand)*; sigh (a yawn); simulate (a yawn); smother (a yawn); smother (a yawn) against (back of hand)*; smother (a yawn) behind (hand)*; smother (a yawn) beneath (hand)*; smother (a yawn) into (back of hand)*; smother (a yawn) with (hand)*; stifle (a yawn); stifle (a yawn) against (back of hand)*; stifle (a yawn) behind (hand)*; stifle (a yawn) with (back of hand)*; still (a yawn) with (hand)*; stop (a yawn); struggle to hold back (a yawn); summon (a yawn); suppress (a yawn); suppress (a yawn) behind (hand)*; suppress (a yawn) with (hand)*; swallow (a yawn); try (a yawn); try to disguise (a yawn).

Face as Subject
contort in (a yawn); crack into (a yawn); is (a yawn); split in (a yawn); split with (a yawn).

Jaw or Character as Subject
(I) clamp (jaws) to stop (a yawn)*; (I) clench (jaw) on (a yawn)*; (I) clench (jaws) to stop (a yawn)*; (I) crack (jaw) with (a yawn)*; crack on (a yawn); open in (a yawn); stiffen against (a yawn); tense with (a yawn).

Lips or Character as Subject
(I) press (lips) together to suppress (a yawn)*; part in (a yawn).

Mouth or Character as Subject
(I) clap (hand) over (mouth) to hide (a yawn)*; (I) clap (hand) to (mouth) to disguise (a yawn)*; (I) cover (mouth) for (a yawn)*; (I) cover (mouth) to conceal (a yawn)*; (I) cover (mouth) to hide (a yawn)*; (I) cover (mouth) to stifle (a yawn)*; (I) cover (mouth) with (a yawn)*; (I) cover (mouth) with (both hands) to hide (a yawn)*; (I) cover (mouth) with (hand) to conceal (a yawn)*; (I) cover (mouth) with (hand) to hide (a yawn)*; (I) cover (mouth) with (hand) to stifle (a yawn)*; (I) hold (back of hand) over (mouth) to mask (a yawn)*; (I) lift (hand) to (mouth) to conceal (a yawn)*; (I) lift (hand) to (mouth) to cover (a yawn)*; (I) lift (hand) to (mouth) to hide (a yawn)*; (I) lift (hand) to (mouth) to mask (a yawn)*; (I) lift (hand) to (mouth) to stifle (a yawn)*; (I) open (mouth) in (a yawn)*; (I) open (mouth) to give (a yawn)*; (I) open (mouth) wide with (a yawn)*; (I) place (hand) over (mouth) to smother (a yawn)*; (I) press (back of hand) to (mouth) to stifle (a yawn)*; (I) press (fingers) to (mouth) to smother (a yawn)*; (I) put (hand) over/to (mouth) to smother (a yawn)*; (I) put (hand) over/to (mouth) to stifle (a yawn)*; (I) raise (hand) to (mouth) to smother (a yawn)*; (I) raise (hand) to (mouth) to stifle (a yawn)*; (I) stretch (mouth) wide in (a yawn)*; compress trying to hide (a yawn); curve into (a yawn); gape in (a yawn); indulge in (a yawn); open in (a yawn); open wide in (a yawn); pop open in (a yawn); round into (a yawn); stretch in/into (a yawn); stretch wide in/into (a yawn); widen into (a yawn).

NOUN USAGE EXAMPLES

Wendy lifted a hand to her mouth to conceal a yawn.

Harry flopped back on the sofa with an irrepressible yawn.

She feigned a yawn before excusing herself from the table.

She failed to suppress a yawn of total boredom from overtaking her.

His jaw opened in a wide yawn.

2. Verb Form

2.1 - Verb Synonyms

doze; drowse; feel fatigue; gape; nap; open mouth wide; sleep; snooze.

2.2 - Adverbs

A
actively*; actually*; adorably; alternately; audibly.

B
beautifully; broadly.

C
carefully; convulsively.

D
daintily; deeply; deliberately; delicately; disgustedly; dismissively; dramatically; drowsily.

E
elaborately; elegantly; endlessly; enormously; exaggeratedly; expansively; extravagantly.

F
fastidiously; ferociously; finally*; fitfully; frankly; freely; fretfully.

G
giddily.

H
happily; hugely.

I
immediately; impolitely; impossibly; inadvertently; inappropriately; increasingly; ingloriously; inquiringly; interminably; involuntarily; inwardly.

222

L
languidly; lazily; leisurely; lengthily; loudly; luxuriously.

M
madly; magnificently; menacingly; merely*; mightily.

N
nearly*; noisily.

O
obscenely; occasionally; only*; openly; ostentatiously.

P
patiently; pointedly; practically*; prettily; probably*; prodigiously; promptly*; properly; publically.

Q
quickly.

R
realistically; really*; repeatedly; rudely.

S
sickeningly; simply*; sleepily; slightly; softly; steadily; suddenly; surprisingly; surreptitiously.

T
tiredly.

U
unaffectedly; uncontrollably.

V
visibly.

W
widely.

2.3 - Adverbials of Emotion, Feeling, Mental State, and Response

in a bored sort of way; in a bored, impatient sort of way; in a convulsive way; in a disdainful gesture; in a showy way; in agreement; in an exaggerated manner;

in anguish; in anticipation; in disgust; in her mind; in reply; in sleepy satisfaction; in spite of her anxiety; in spite of her long nap; with a soft groan; with a stretch; with a wide maw; with an unconcealed boredom; with animal enjoyment; with bored indolence; with boredom; with difficulty; with disapproval; with dramatic flair; with effort; with exhaustion; with fatigue; with genuine weariness; with great exaggeration; with happy contentment; with her hand over her mouth*; with her usual daintiness; with just a shade of ostentation; with pretend indifference; with relish; with sheer satisfaction; with slow deliberation; with supreme indifference; with the sheer boredom of it all; with tiredness; with weariness.

VERB USAGE EXAMPLES

He yawned in a bored sort of way, then took his leave.

She yawned widely as she stood.

Joanne blinked her eyes, yawning in sleepy satisfaction.

Then he yawned with one hand over his mouth and rubbed his eyes.

Tina yawned deeply, and Bryan glanced at his watch.

Appendix
FACIAL EXPRESSIONS

1.1 - Adjectives

A

abashed; abject; above-it-all; absent-minded; absorbed; abstract; abstracted; abused; academic; acceptable; accepting; accidental; accommodating; accompanying; accurate; accusative; accusatory; accusing; acerbic; aching; acid; acidulated; acrimonious; actual; acute; adamant; added; additional; addled; adequate; admiring; admonishing; adorable; adoring; adult; adult-like; affable; affected; affectionate; afflicted; affronted; age-old; aggravated; aggressive; aggrieved; aghast; agitated; agog; agonized; agonizing; agreeable; ah-ha; airy; alarmed; alarming; alert; alien; alive; all-at-sea; all-business; all-charm; all-is-forgiven; all-knowing; all-seeing; all-too-familiar; all-too-innocent; all-too-knowing; all-too-serious; all-too-visual; almost-admiring; almost-awed; almost-dazed; almost-pleased; almost-shy; aloof; altered; altering; always-serious; amazed; amazing; ambiguous; ambitious; ambivalent; amenable; amiable; amorous; amused; amusing; analytical; angelic; angry; anguished; animalistic; animated; annoyed; annoying; another; answering; antagonistic; anticipatory; anxiety-ridden; anxious; anxious-looking; apathetic; apologetic; apoplectic; appalled; appalling; apparent; appealing; appraising; appreciable; appreciative; apprehensive; appropriate; approving; apt; arctic; ardent; are-you-kidding; aren't-you-cute; argumentative; aristocratic; armor-plated; army-colonel; aroused; arrested; arrogant; articulate; artificial; artistic; artless; ashen; assertive; assessing; assumed; assuming; assured; assuring; astonished; astounded; astounding; astute; asymmetrical; attentive; attractive; austere; authentic; authoritative; autocratic; avaricious; avid; aw-shucks; aware; awed; awesome; awestruck; awful; awkward.

B

back-off; bad; bad-tempered; badass; badly-done-to; baffled; baffling; baiting; baleful; balky; banished; bantering; basic; battle; battle-ready; baulking; beaming; beaten; beatific; beautiful; beckoning; becoming; bedazzled; bedeviling; befuddled; begging; begrudging; beguiled; beguiling; beleaguered; believable; believing; bellicose; belligerent; bemused; beneficent; benevolent; benign; benumbed; bereaved; bereft; beseeching; besotted; best; betrayed; betraying; better; bewildered; big-city; big-sister; big-sister-type; bitten-down; bitter; bittersweet; bizarre; black; black-as-thunder; black-browed; blackened; blackening; blanched; bland; blandest; blank; blank-eyed; blanked-off; blankest; blasé; blatant; blazing; bleak; bleakest; bleary-eyed; blind; blinded; blinding; blissed-out; blissful; blitzed; blue; blunt; blustery; bold; bone-chilling; bone-clenched; bored; bored-with-it-all; bothered; bovine; boyish; brave; brave-but-not; breath-snagging; breathless; bred-to-be-snooty; breezy; brief; bright; bright-eyed; brightened; brightest; brilliant; brisk; brittle; broken; brokenhearted; brooding; broody; bruised; bruised-looking; bruising; brutal; Buddha-like; budding; bug-eyed; building; bulldog; bullish; buoyant; burdened; burning; business; business-like; businessman; busy; butter-won't-melt; butter-wouldn't-melt; buttoned-up.

C

caged; cagey; cajoling; calculated; calculating; callous; calm; calm-executive; calmest; candid; canny; cantankerous; capable; captain-of-industry; captivated; captive; captured; capturing; carefree; careful; careful-lawyer; careless; careworn; caring; carnal; cartoonish; carved; carved-granite; carved-in-stone; cast-iron; casual; cat-got-the-cream; cat-in-the-cream; cat-in-the-creamery; cat-lapping-cream; cat-like; cat-with-cream; catty; caught-out; caustic; caution-filled; cautionary; cautious; censored; censorious; certain; chafing; chagrined; challenging; changeable; changed; changing; characteristic; charged; charitable; charmed; charming; chaste; chastened; chastised; chastising; cheeky; cheerful; cheerless; cheery; cherubic; Cheshire-cat; chiding; child-like; childish; chill; chilled; chilling; chilly; chiseled; chivalrous; churlish; circumspect; civil; civilized; clash-of-wills; classic; clear; clear-as-glass; clear-eyed; clenched; cliché; clinical; cloaked; closed; closed-down; closed-eyed; closed-in; closed-off; closed-up; closing; clouded; clouding; cloudy; cloudy-eyed; clowning; clueless; coarse; coaxing; cockiest; cocksure; cocky; cold; cold-as-steel; cold-eyed; coldest; collapsing; collective; colorful; combative; combined; come-hither; comforting; comic; comical; commanding; commiserating; commiserative; common; compassionate; compelling; competent; complacent; complete; complex; complicated; composed; comprehensive; compromising; concealed; concealing; conceited; conceivable; concentrated; concerned; concessionary; conciliatory; concrete; condemnatory; condemning; condescending; confident; conflicted; conflicting; confounded; confrontational; confused; confusing; congealing; congenial; congratulatory; conscience-stricken; conscious; considering; conspiratorial; constrained; consummate; contained; contemplative; contemptuous; content; contented; continually-changing; contorted; contrary; contrasting; contrite; controlled; convenient; conventional; convinced; convincing; convulsive; cool; cooling; cordial; cornered; corny; correct; corresponding; couldn't-care-less; courteous; coveting; covetous; coy; coyote-like; crafty; craggy; cranky; crazed; creased; credible; crestfallen; crimson; crinkling; critical; cross; cross-examination; crude; cruel; cruel-to-be-kind; crumpled; crusading; crushed; cryptic; cultivated; cunning; curious; current; cursory; customary; cute; cutest; cynical.

D

daffy; damnable; damsel-in-distress; dangerous; dare-devil; dare-me; daring; dark; dark-eyed; darkened; darkening; darkest; darkling; darling; daunting; dawning; dazed; dazed-looking; dazzled; dead; dead-serious; deadened; deadly;

deadpan; deadpanned; dear; death-like; debauched; decadent; deceptive; decimated; decipherable; decisive; dedicated; deep; deep-concentration; deep-set; deepening; deepest; deeply-troubled; deer-caught-in-headlights; deer-in-headlights; deer-in-the-headlights; deer-staring-into-headlights; default; defeated; defenseless; defensive; defiant; defied; definable; definite; definitive; deflated; dejected; deliberate; delicate; delicious; delighted; delightful; delirious; delusory; demanding; demonic; demoralized; demure; demurest; departing; deprecating; depressed; deriding; derisive; derisory; derogatory; descriptive; desire-filled; desirous; desolate; despairing; desperate; desperate-for-junk-food; despondent; destroyed; detached; determined; devastated; devil-may-care; devilish; devious; devoted; devouring; devout; dewy-eyed; diabolical; different; differing; difficult; diffident; dignified; diplomatic; dire; direct; disagreeable; disappointed; disapproving; disarming; disbelieving; discernible; discerning; disciplinary; disciplined; discomfited; disconcerted; disconcerting; disconsolate; discontented; discouraged; discouraging; disdainful; disenchanted; disgruntled; disguised; disgusted; disgusting; disheartened; dishonest; disillusioned; disingenuous; disinterested; dismal; dismayed; dismissive; disorientated; disoriented; disparaging; disparate; dispassionate; dispirited; displeased; disquieting; dissatisfied; dissipated; distanced; distant; distant-because-I'm-scared; distasteful; distempered; distinct; distinguished; distracted; distraught; distressed; distrustful; disturbed; disturbing; ditzy-blond; do-me; docile; doctor-in-charge; doe-like; dog-like; dogged; doleful; doll-like; dolorous; domestic; dominant; domineering; don't-argue-with-me; don't-blow-it; don't-cross-me; don't-dare-hope; don't-look-at-me; don't-mess-with-me; don't-push-me; doomed; doomsday; dopey; doting; doubt-filled; doubtful; doubting; dour; down; downbent; downcast; downfallen; downtrodden; drained; drawn; drawn-out; dreadful; dream-like; dream-ridden; dreaming; dreamy; dreamy-eyed; droll; drooling; drooly; drooping; drowsy; drunken; dry; dubious; dueling; dull; dulled; dumb; dumb-guy; dumbfounded; dumbstruck; duplicate; dying.

E

each; eager; eager-to-flee; eager-to-please; eagle-like; earlier; earnest; earthy; easily-read; easy; easy-going; ecstatic; edgy; efficiency-mode; efficient; elaborate; elated; elegant; eloquent; elusive; embarrassed; embittered; emotion-filled; emotion-jolting; emotional; emotionless; empathetic; emphatic; empty; enamored; enchanted; enchanting; encountered; encouraging; end-of-story; end-of-the-world; endearing; endorsing; engaged; engaging; engrossed; enigmatic; enigmatical; enraged; enraptured; ensuing; entertained-by-life; enthralled; enthused; enthusiastic; enticing; entire; entranced; entreating; envious; envisioned; envying; equable; equal; equivocal; erotic; essential; etched; euphoric; evasive; ever-changing; ever-disdainful; everything's-hunky-dory; evil; evocative; exact; exaggerated; exasperated; exasperating; excellent; excessive; excited; exciting; excluded; exhausted; exhilarated; existing; exotic; expectant; expectant-yet-anxious; expected; explicit; explosive; exquisite; extraordinary; extravagant; extreme; exuberant; exultant; eye-rolling; eyes-slightly-narrowed.

F

facetious; facial; facing-the-firing-squad; faded; faint; faintest; fake; fake-innocent; fall-back; false; faltering; familiar; famous; fanatical; far-away; far-off; far-seeing; far-too-intrigued; fascinated; fascinating; fastidious; fatalistic; father-knows-best; fatherly; fathomless; fatuous; faux-shocked; faux-tough; favorable; favored; favorite; fawning; fearful; fearless; fearsome; fed-up; feigned; feisty; feline; feminine; feral; ferocious; ferret-faced; fervent; fevered; feverish; few; fiendish; fierce; fierce-looking; fiercest; fiery; fighting; filthy; final; fine; finest; firm; first; fish-mouth; fish-out-of-water; fixed; flabbergasted; flaring; flat; flat-lipped; flattened; flattered; flattering; fleeting; flickering; flinching; flint-edged; flint-hard; flint-like; flinty; flippant; flirtatious; flirty; flitting; floored; florid; flowery; fluctuating; fluid; flummoxed; flushed; flustered; focused; foggy; fond; foolish; foot-in-mouth; forbearing; forbidden; forbidding; forced; forceful; foreboding; foreign; forgiving; forlorn; forlorn-puppy-dog; formal; former; formidable; formless; forthright; foul; foxy; fragile; frank; frantic; fraught; frazzled; free; frenzied; frequent; fretful; friendly; frightened; frightening; frigid; frost-bitten; frosty; frowning; frozen; frustrated; fuddled; fugitive; full; full-bodied; full-face; full-on; fullest; fulminating; fulsome; fun-loving; funereal; funny; furious; furnace-hot; furrowed; furtive; futile; fuzzy.

G

ga-ga; gamin-like; gamine; gape-jawed; gape-mouthed; gaping; gargoyle; gasping; gaunt; gay; general; generic; genial; genial-host; gentle; gentlemanly; genuine; get-serious; ghoulish; giddy; girlish; give-away; give-me-a-break; give-me-some-answers; give-nothing-away; giving; giving-nothing-away; glacial; glacier; glaring; glassy; glazed; glazed-looking; gleaming; gleeful; glinting; glittering; glittery; gloating; gloom-and-doom; gloomy; glorious; glowering; glowing; glowy; glum; gnome-like; go-to-hell; goaded; goading; gobsmacked; goggle-eyed; gone-in-a-heartbeat; good; good-humored; good-natured; gooey; goofiest; goofy; goon; gorgeous; gorgonish; gormless; gotcha; graceful; gracious; granite; granite-eyed; granite-hard; granite-jawed; granite-like; graphic; grateful; gratified; gratifying; grave; graven; great; greedy; green; green-eyed; grief-filled; grief-stricken; grim; grim-faced; grim-looking; grim-mouthed; grimacing; grimmest; grinning; gritted-teeth; gritty; grossed-out; grouchy; grown-up; grudging; gruff; grumbling; grumpiest; grumpy; guard-dog; guarded; guileless; guilt-ridden; guilt-stricken; guiltless; guilty; guilty-as-sin; guppy-like; gushing; gutted.

H

habitual; hackneyed; haggard; half-accusing; half-affectionate; half-afraid; half-amused; half-angry; half-anxious; half-asleep; half-aware; half-bitter; half-concerned; half-crazed; half-cynical; half-dead; half-defiant; half-disturbed; half-exasperated; half-expectant; half-forlorn; half-frightened; half-guilty; half-hopeful; half-humorous; half-inexplicable; half-joking; half-knowing; half-lidded; half-mocking; half-pleading; half-puzzled; half-questioning; half-resigned; half-sad; half-sheepish; half-sick; half-smiling; half-sneering; half-surprised; half-teasing; half-tender; half-uncertain; half-wary; half-witted; half-yearning; halting; hands-off; hands-tied; handsome; hangdog; happiest; happy; happy-go-lucky; harassed; hard; hard-as-nails; hard-ass; hard-bitten; hard-boiled; hard-boned; hard-done-by; hard-edged; hard-eyed; hard-faced; hard-jawed; hard-set; hard-to-read; hardened; hardening; harmless; harried; harrowed; harsh; harsh-faced; harshest; hassled; hastily-assumed; hasty; hateful; haughtiest; haughty; haunted; haunting; hawkish; hawk-like; hazy; he-must-be-crazy; healthy; heart-jerking; heart-rending; heart-stopping; heart-wrenching; heartbreaking; heartbroken; heartfelt; heartless; heartwarming; hearty; heated; heavy; heavy-lidded; hectic; hedonistic; heedless; hell-no; help-me-out; helpful; helpless; hesitant; hidden; hideous; high-born; high-strung; hilarious; hit-and-run; hit-by-a-brick; hoity-toity; holier-than-thou; hollow; honest; hooded; hope-filled; hopeful; hopeless; hormone-free; horrible; horrid; horrified; horrifying; horror-filled; horror-stricken; horror-struck; hospitable; hostile; hot; hound-at-the-pound; hounded; huffy; human; humble; humbled; humiliated; humiliating; humorless; humorous; hung-over; hungry; hungry-wolf; hunted; hurt; hurtful; hurting; hypnotic; hypnotized; hysterical.

I

I'm-a-badass; I'm-in-charge-here; I'm-not-discussing-this; I'm-not-pleased; I've-heard-everything-now; I-am-gravely-offended; I-can't-believe-this; I-dare-you; I-dare-you-lady; I-don't-believe-this; I-don't-believe-you; I-got-this; I-pity-you; I-smell-something-rank; I-solved-the-problem; I-thought-as-much; I-told-you-so; I-warned-you; I-wonder-who's-next; ice-cold; ice-queen; iciest; icy; icy-cold; identical; identifiable; idiotic; idolizing; ill; ill-concealed; ill-humored; ill-used; illuminating; imagined; immediate; immovable; immutable; impartial; impassioned; impassive; impatient; impenetrable; impenitent; imperial; imperious; impermeable; impersonal; impertinent; imperturbable; impervious; impetuous; impish; implacable; implicit; imploring; impossible-to-misread; impossible-to-read; impregnable; impressed; impudent; in-awe; inadequate; inane; inappropriate; incandescent; incensed; incoherent; incomprehensible; incongruous; incredible; incredulous; incurious; indecent; indecipherable; indefinable; indefinite; indelible; indescribable; indifferent; indignant; indirect; indiscernible; indistinguishable; individual; indolent; indomitable; indulged; indulgent; indulging; inebriated; inelegant; inevitable; inexcusable; inexorable; inexplicable; infatuated; infernal; inflexible; infrequent; infuriated; infuriating; ingenuous; ingratiating; inimical; initial; injured; innocent; innocent-little-girl; innocent-of-all-charges; innocuous; inquiring; inquisitive; insane; inscrutable; insecure; insightful; insincere; insipid; insolent; insouciant; instant; instinctive; insulted; insulting; intangible; intelligent; intense; intent; interested; interesting; interminable; interrogating; interrogative; intimate; intimidated; intimidating; intolerant; intractable; intrigued; intriguing; introspective; introverted; intuitive; invigorated; inviting; involuntary; involved; inward; irate; iron; ironic; ironical; irresistible; irritable; irritated; irritating; isn't-she-darling.

J

jaded; jaguar-like; jarring; jaundiced; jaunty; jaw-sagging; jealous; jeering; joking; jovial; joyful; joyless; joyous; jubilant; judging; judgmental; judicial; judicious; just-kissed; just-taken; juvenile.

K

keen; keep-your-distance; kicked-puppy; kidding; kind; kindest; kindly; kindred; kingly; kiss-me; kissable; kissing; kittenish; knocked-out; know-all; know-it-all; knowing.

L

lackluster; lady-like; laid-back; languid; languishing; languorous; lascivious; last; latest; laugh-with-me; laughable; laughing; lazy; leaden; lean; learned; leashed; lecherous; leering; leery; leisurely; lemon; lemon-sucking; less-than-delighted; less-than-enthusiastic; less-than-excited; less-than-impressed; less-than-pleasant; less-than-pleased; less-than-subdued; less-than-welcoming; lethal; level; lewd; lifeless; light; light-hearted; lightened; lightening; limpid; lined; lingering; liquid; listening; listless; little; little-boy; little-boy-lost; little-girl; little-girl-lost; little-lost-girl; lively; livid; loathsome; locked-out; lock-jawed; lofty; lonely; lonesome; long-suffering; longing; loopy; lopsided; lordly; lost; lost-little-boy; lost-little-girl; lost-puppy; love-drenched; love-drugged; love-of-life; love-struck; lovelorn; lovely; lover-like; lovesick; loving; lowered; lowering; lowly; lucid; ludicrous; lugubrious; lukewarm; luminous; lupine; lurking; lust-drunk; lustful; lusty; lying.

M

macho; mad; maddening; madder-than-hell; Madonna-like; magnetic; magnificent; male; malevolent; malicious; malignant; man-to-man; maniacal; manic; manly; many; many-changing; marble; martial; martyred; martyrs; marvelous; masculine; mask-like; masked; masterful; matched; matching; maternal; maternal-guilt; matter-of-fact; mature; mean; mean-looking; meaningful; meaningless; measured; measuring; meditative; meek; melancholic; melancholy; mellow; melodramatic; melting; menacing; mercenary; merciful; merciless; mere; merest; merry; mesmerized; mesmerizing; metallic; mettled; micro; miffed; mild; militant; military; million-dollar; mindless; mingled; minimal; mirroring; mirthful; mischief-filled; mischievous; miserable; misleading; mistrustful; mistrusting; misty; misunderstood; mixed; mobile; mock; mock-bashful; mock-disgusted; mock-grim; mock-humiliated; mock-innocent; mock-offended; mock-penitent; mock-rueful; mock-serious; mock-snooty; mock-solemn; mock-stern; mock-wounded; mocking; modest; molten; momentary; monkish; moody; moon-eyed; moonlit; moonstruck; moony; mopy; mordant; morning-after; morose; morphing; mortified; motherly; mournful; mouse-sees-snake; moving; much-too-anxious; mulish; mulling; murderous; musing; mute; mutinous; mutual; muzzy; mysterious; mystery-woman; mystified; mystifying.

N

naive; naked; nameless; narrow-eyed; narrowed; narrowing; nasty; natural; naughtiest; naughty; nauseating; near-human; near-hysterical; near-tears; necessary; needing; needy; negative; nervous; nervous-fawn; nervy; neutral; new; next; nice; nicest; no-big-deal; no-cracks; no-guts-no-glory; no-holds-barred; no-kidding; no-longer-composed; no-nonsense; noble; non-committal; non-comprehending; non-existent; nonchalant; nonconspiratorial; nondescript; nonjudgmental; nonplussed; nonthreatening; normal; nostalgic; not-ogling; not-quite-masked; not-quite-with-it; not-so-excited; not-too-happy; noticeable; novel; now-familiar; now-stony; now-wary; numb.

O

obdurate; obedient; oblique; oblivious; obscure; obscured; observant; obstinate; obvious; occasional; occasional-fleeting; occupied; odd; oddest; odious; off-guard; off-putting; offended; offensive; offered; official; officious; often-guarded; oh-hell; oh-so-affable; oh-so-clear; oh-so-feminine; oh-so-innocent; oh-so-serious; oh-so-severe; oh-so-sincere; oh-you-poor-thing; okay; old; older-brother; ominous; once-burned-twice-shy; once-guarded; one; only; only-for-you-darling; open; open-eyed; open-looking; open-mouthed; opposed; optimistic; orgasmic; orgiastic; original; ornery; otherworldly; out-of-place; out-of-this-world; outraged; outrageous; outward; over-anxious; over-bright; over-earnest; over-hearty; over-the-top; overall; overconfident; overdone; overrated; overriding; overt; overused; overwhelmed; owl-eyed; owlish; own.

P

pain-filled; pained; painful; painted-on; pale; panic-laced; panic-stricken; panicked; panicking; panicky; paradoxical; paralyzed; pardoning; parental; particular; parting; passing; passion-filled; passion-glazed; passionate; passive; pasty; patented; paternal; pathetic; patient; patrician; patronizing; pay-up; peace-on-earth; peaceful; peculiar; peeved; peevish; penetrating; penetrative; penitent; pensive; pent-up; perceptible; perceptive; perennial; perfect; perfect-lawyer; perfected; perfunctory; permanent; permitted; perpetual; perplexed; persistent; personable; personal; perspicacious; persuasive; perturbed; pessimistic; petrified; pettish; petty; petulant; philosophic; phony; physical; picturesque; piercing; pigheaded; pinched; pinup; pious; piquant; piqued; piratical; pissed-off; pissy; pitbull; piteous; pitiable; pitiful; pitiless; pitying; pixieish; placatory; placid; placid-whatever-the-circumstances; plaintive; platonic; playful; pleading; pleasant; please-help-me; please-take-me-home; pleased; pleased-as-pie; pleased-with-himself; pleasing; pleasured; poignant; pointed; poised; poker; poker-faced; pole-axed; polite; polite-in-company; pompous; pondering; poor-puppy-dog; positive; possessed; possessive; possible; pouting; pouty; powerful; practical; practiced; precise; predatory; predictable; predominant; premature; preoccupied; prepared; prepossessing; present; pretty; previous; priceless; prickly; prideful; prim; prim-and-proper; primal; primitive; primordial; private; probing; problem-solving; professional; profound; profuse; promising; proper; proprietorial; prosaic; protective; protesting; proud; provocative; provoking;

prudish; prune-faced; prune-sucking; pseudo; pseudo-serious; pseudo-stern; public; puckered; puckish; puffed-up; pugilistic; pugnacious; pulled-in; punishing; puppy; puppy-dog; purer-than-driven-snow; puritanical; purposeful; pursed; puzzled; puzzling.

Q

quaint; quasi-serious; queasy; queenly; queer; queerest; quelling; querulous; querying; questing; questioning; quick; quick-changing; quicksilver; quiet; quirky; quivering; quizzical.

R

rabbit-caught-in-headlights; radiant; raffish; rage-filled; ragged; raised-brow; raised-eyebrow; rakish; randy; rapacious; rapt; rapturous; rare; rarely-used; rational; ravaged; ravenous; raw; razor-sharp; reactionary; readable; real; rearranged; reasonable; reassuring; rebellious; rebuffed; rebuking; recalled; receptive; reckless; recognizable; reflected; reflective; refused; regal; regret-filled; regretful; regular; rejected; relaxed; relentless; relieved; reluctant; remembered; reminiscent; remorseful; remote; removed; renewed; repeated; repentant; repressive; reproachful; reproving; repulsed; requisite; resentful; resenting; reserved; resigned; resolute; resolved; respectful; respective; responding; responsible; restless; restrained; resulting; retaliatory; reticent; returning; revealing; reverent; revolted; revolting; rich-man; ridiculing; ridiculous; right; righteous; rigid; rising; riveted; robust; rock-hard; rock-like; rocky; roguish; romantic; rough-and-ready; round-eyed; routine; rubber-faced; ruddy; rude; rueful; ruffled; rugged; ruined; ruthless.

S

sad; saddened; saddest; sagacious; saint-like; saintly; salacious; sallow; same; sanctimonious; sanguine; sappiest; sappy; sarcastic; sardonic; satanic; sated; satiated; satirical; satisfied; saturnine; satyr-like; saucy; savage; scandalized; scandalous; scared; scared-rabbit; scary; scathing; scatterbrained; scheming; scholarly; schooled; schooled-into-stone; schoolmarm; schoolmarmish; schoolmasterish; schoolmistress; schoolmistressy; scorching; scorn-filled; scornful; scowling; scowly; screwed-up; scrunched-up; scrunchy; scrutinizing; seamless; searching; searing; second; secret; secretive; sedate; seductive; seeking; seen-it-all-before; seething; self-amused; self-ashamed; self-assured; self-centered; self-complacent; self-condemning; self-congratulatory; self-conscious; self-contained; self-deprecating; self-derisive; self-effacing; self-important; self-indulgent-princess; self-ironic; self-mocking; self-pitying; self-possessed; self-protective; self-rebuking; self-righteous; self-satisfied; semi-amused; semi-bored; semi-flirtatious; semi-glazed; semi-outraged; semi-serious; semi-sheepish; semi-shocked; sensational; sensible; sensitive; sensual; sensuous; seraphic; serene; serious; serious-dad; serious-looking; servant-like; set; set-in-stone; several; severe; sex-starved; sexiest; sexual; sexy; shadowed; shadowy; shaken; shaky; shame-shaded; shamed; shamefaced; shared; sharp; sharpened; sharpening; shattered; sheepish; shell-shocked; shielded; shifting; shifty; shifty-eyed; shining; shock-frozen; shocked; showing; shrewd; shrewish; shut; shut-down; shut-in; shuttered; shy; sick; sickened; sickly; sidelong; significant; signifying; silent; silky; silliest; silly; silly-looking; similar; simmering; simpering; simple; sincere; sinful; single; singular; sinister; sink-or-swim; sizzling; skeletal; skeptical; skin-deep; skittish; slack-jawed; slant-eyed; slanted; slanting; slashing; sleep-bewildered; sleeping; sleepy; sleepy-eyed; slight; slit-eyed; sloe-eyed; slow; slumberous; sly; small; smarmy; smartass; smiling; smirking; smirky; smitten; smoky; smoky-eyed; smoldering; smooth; smug; snarling; snarly; sneering; snide; snootiest; snooty; sober; sobered; sobering; social; soft; soft-hearted; softened; softening; softest; solemn; solemn-eyed; solicitous; solitary; somber; somnolent; soothing; soppy; sorrowful; sorry; sorry-about-that; sorry-for-himself; soul-deep; soul-searching; soulful; soulless; sour; sour-puss; souring; sourpuss; spacey; spaniel; spaniel-eyed; spaniel-like; sparkling; special; speculative; speechless; spellbinding; sphinx-like; spirited; spiteful; spoilt; spontaneous; spur-of-the-moment; square-jawed; squeamish; staged; staggered; staid; stalwart; standard; star-struck; starched; stark; starlit; starry-eyed; startled; starving; statue-of-a-saint; steadfast; steady; steamy; steeliest; steely; steely-eyed; stern; stern-faced; stern-teacher; sternest; stiff; stiffening; stifled; still-bemused; still-dazed; still-fiery; still-serious; still-stubborn; stilted; stock; stoic; stoical; stolid; stone-carved; stone-cold; stone-faced; stone-hard; stone-like; stone-wall; stonewalling; stony; stony-faced; stormy; straight; straightforward; strained; straining; strait-laced; strange; strangely-aloof; strangest; strangled; stressed; stressed-out; stricken; strong; struck; stubborn; studied; studious; stung; stunned; stunned-fish; stunned-to-his-toes; stupefied; stupid; stymied; suave; subdued; sublime; submissive; submit-and-surrender; subsequent; subservient; subtle; succeeding; sucked-on-a-lemon; sudden; suffering; sugary; suggestive; suitable; sulking; sulky; sullen; sultry; sunniest; sunny; sunshine-bright; sunshiny; super-hot; super-serious; superb; supercilious; superior; superior-looking; superior-to-thou; supportive; suppressed; supreme; surface; surly; surprised; suspicious; sustained; sweet; sweetest; swift; swiftly-changing; swooning; sympathetic; sympathy-filled; syrupy.

T

taciturn; take-charge; take-no-prisoners; taken-aback; tangible; tangled; tantalizing; taunting; taut; tautening; tear-filled; tearful; teary; teary-eyed; teasing; telling; telltale; tempting; tenacious; tender; tenderest; tenderhearted; tense; tensed; tentative; terrible; terrible-terrible; terrified; terrify-the-troops; terrifying; territorial; terror-stricken; terrorized; terse; testy; thank-God; thankful; that'll-be-the-day; thawing; theatrical; thin-lipped; thin-mouthed; thinking; this-is-serious; thoughtful; thoughtless; threatening; thrilled; throw-back-your-head; thundercloud; thundercloud-dark; thundering; thunderous; thunderstruck; thundery; thwarted; ticked-off; tidy; tigerish; tight; tight-assed; tight-faced; tight-jawed; tight-lipped; tight-mouthed; tightened; tightening; timid; tiny; tired; to-hell-with-you; token; tolerant; tongue-in-cheek; too-amused; too-angelic; too-bland; too-bright; too-calm; too-concerned; too-controlled; too-dreamy; too-familiar; too-innocent; too-knowing; too-polite; too-quiet; too-ready; too-serious; too-solemn; too-vulnerable; tormented; tormenting; torn; torpid; torrid; tortured; total; touch-me-not; touching; tough; tough-girl; toxic; trademark; tragic; trance-like; tranquil; transcendent; transfixed; transformed; transient; transparent; trapped; traumatized; travel-weary; tremulous; trite; triumphant; troubled; troubling; truculent; true; trust-me; trustful; trusting; trying-not-to-smile; tsk-tsk; tumultuous; turbulent; turned-on; twisted; tycoon-in-action; typical.

U

ugly; uh-oh; ultimate; ultra-calm; unaffected; unaltered; unamused; unanimous; unapologetic; unapproachable; unassuming; unattractive; unaware; unbelievable; unbelieving; unbending; unblinking; unbridled; uncanny; uncarefree; uncaring; uncertain; unchanged; unchanging; uncharacteristic; unchaste; unchildlike; uncomfortable; uncommunicative; uncomplicated; uncomprehending; uncompromising; unconcealed; unconcerned; unconscious; unconvinced; unconvincing; undecided; undecipherable; undeniable; underlying; understandable; understanding; undersubtle; undesirable; undignified; undisguised; undone; undying; uneasy; unedited; unemotional; unenlightened; unenthusiastic; unexpected; unexpressive; unfamiliar; unfathomable; unfavorable; unfazed; unfeeling; unfestive; unfettered; unflappable; unflattering; unflinching; unflustered; unfocused; unforgettable; unforgiving; unfortunate; unfriendly; ungentle; ungiving; ungovernable; unguarded; unhappy; unhidden; unholy; unidentifiable; uniform; unillusioned; unimpressed; uninhibited; unintelligent; uninterested; uninviting; unique; unladylike; unlawyerlike; unmasked; unmistakable; unmoved; unmoving; unnatural; unnerved; unnerving; unperturbed; unpleasant; unpredictable; unpromising; unreadable; unreasonable; unregretful; unrelenting; unrepentant; unresponsive; unrestrained; unrevealing; unromantic; unruffled; unsatisfied; unschooled; unseeing; unselfconscious; unsettled; unsettling; unshrinking; unsmiling; unsubtle; unsure; untamed; unthreatening; untroubled; unusual; unvarying; unwavering; unwelcome; unwelcoming; unyielding; upbeat; uplifted; upset; uptight; upturned; urbane; urgent; urging; useful; useless; usual.

V

vacant; vacuous; vague; vanilla; varied; variegated; various; varying; vehement; veiled; vengeful; venomous; vexed; vibrant; vicious; victorious; vile; vindicated; vindictive; vinegary; violent; virginal; virile; virtuous; visible; visual; vivacious; vivid; volatile; volcanic; vulgar; vulnerable.

W

waif-in-the-storm; waif-vulnerable; waifish; waiting; waking; wan; want-to-know-everything; wanting; wanton; war-like; warm; warning; warring; warrior-like; wary; wary-feline; wasted; watchdog; watchful; waterlogged; watery; wavering; waxen; waxworks; way-out; weak; wearied-to-death; wearing; weary; weaselly; weathered; weighty; weird; welcome; welcome-home; welcoming;

well-bred; well-known; well-loved; well-pleased; well-satisfied; what's-your-deal; what-did-you-expect; what-in-the-world; whimsical; whipped-puppy; white; white-faced; who-cares; whole; wholehearted; whopper-jawed; why-do-you-care; wicked; wide-eyed; wide-open; widened; wifely; wild; wild-eyed; willful; wincing; winning; winsome; wintry; wiped-out; wise; wise-beyond-his-years; wise-little-owl; wish-this-was-over; wishful; wistful; withdrawn; withered; withering; witless; wizened; woe-begone; woe-is-me; woeful; wolfish; woman-in-control; woman-of-the-world; womanly; wonderful; wondering; wonderstruck; wondrous; wooden; wordless; world-toughened; world-weary; worldly; worldly-wise; worn; worried; worrisome; worrying; worshipful; worshipping; worst; wounded; wracked; wrathful; wrecked; wretched; wrong; wry.

Y
yearning; yielding; youthful.

Z
Zen-like; zoned-out.

1.2 - Noun + Prepositional Phrases

expression of a baby at peace; expression of a barracuda on the prowl; expression of a bored teenager; expression of a boy who (...); expression of a businessman; expression of a cat who had cornered a mouse; expression of a cherub; expression of a child watching a magician; expression of a child who (....); expression of a child with the keys to a candy store; expression of a choir boy; expression of a closed book; expression of a concerned father; expression of a conqueror; expression of a doe; expression of a dog who knows he did something wrong; expression of a dutiful official; expression of a facelift veteran; expression of a faun; expression of a girl deeply in love; expression of a girl who (...); expression of a gladiator; expression of a Greek statue; expression of a horse running a race; expression of a hungry bird; expression of a hungry lion; expression of a hunted rabbit; expression of a hurt child; expression of a keen businessman; expression of a kid in a candy store; expression of a kid on Christmas morning; expression of a lady who (...); expression of a man weighing up his options; expression of a man who (...); expression of a man with no secrets; expression of a medieval saint; expression of a mischievous pixie; expression of a mother who (...); expression of a naughty schoolboy; expression of a person who (...); expression of a recalcitrant teenager; expression of a Renaissance Madonna; expression of a reproachful parent; expression of a robot; expression of a satyr; expression of a scientist absorbed in an experiment; expression of a seasoned performer; expression of a shark; expression of a spectator at the zoo; expression of a startled fawn; expression of a statue; expression of a sulky child; expression of a sullen child; expression of a sympathetic parent; expression of a tender heart; expression of a tiger;

expression of a tiger moving in for the kill; expression of a tight and bursting excitement; expression of a tragedy queen; expression of a warrior; expression of a warrior about to head off to battle; expression of a winner; expression of a woman in love; expression of a woman who (...); expression of a woman with a mission; expression of a wounded animal; expression of a young animal; expression of a zombie; expression of abiding love; expression of abject apology; expression of abject desolation; expression of abject horror; expression of abject misery; expression of abject penitence; expression of absolute arrest; expression of absolute astonishment; expression of absolute awe; expression of absolute bewilderment; expression of absolute concentration; expression of absolute contempt; expression of absolute delight; expression of absolute despair; expression of absolute determination; expression of absolute disbelief; expression of absolute disgust; expression of absolute dread; expression of absolute ecstasy; expression of absolute exasperation; expression of absolute fury; expression of absolute glee; expression of absolute horror; expression of absolute hunger; expression of absolute neutrality; expression of absolute patience; expression of absolute shock; expression of absolute surprise; expression of absolute wonder; expression of absorption; expression of acceptance; expression of accomplishment; expression of accusation; expression of acute agony; expression of acute anger; expression of acute anger and exasperation; expression of acute anticipation; expression of acute anxiety; expression of acute boredom; expression of acute disapproval; expression of acute disdain; expression of acute dislike; expression of acute dismay; expression of acute distaste; expression of acute distress; expression of acute embarrassment; expression of acute horror; expression of acute impatience; expression of acute relief; expression of acute suffering; expression of admiration; expression of admiration and approval; expression of admiration for (...); expression of admonition; expression of adoration; expression of adoring indulgence; expression of adulation; expression of adult exasperation; expression of advanced horror; expression of affection; expression of affection and amusement; expression of affection and fondness; expression of affection and vast admiration; expression of affectionate exasperation; expression of affront; expression of aggression; expression of agitation; expression of agonized betrayal; expression of agonized ecstasy; expression of agonized self-restraint; expression of agonized understanding; expression of agony; expression of agreement; expression of alarm; expression of alarm and disgust; expression of alarmed coyness; expression of alert concentration; expression of alert curiosity; expression of alert intensity; expression of alertness; expression of almost angry anxiety; expression of almost awe; expression of almost blank coolness; expression of almost bored scorn; expression of almost boyish delight; expression of almost boyish eagerness; expression of almost boyish eagerness and interest; expression of almost childlike disappointment; expression of almost classical melancholy; expression of almost clinical interest; expression of almost comical amazement; expression of almost comical discomfiture; expression of almost comical dismay; expression of almost comical shock; expression of almost despair; expression of almost fatuous adoration; expression of almost feline pleasure; expression of almost fiendish satisfaction; expression of almost glazed intentness; expression of almost harsh satisfaction; expression of almost human disgruntlement; expression of almost hungry desire; expression of almost intent puzzlement; expression of almost ludicrous astonishment; expression of almost ludicrous surprise; expression of almost maternal concern; expression of almost pained pleasure; expression of almost painful pleasure; expression of almost painful pride; expression of almost patrician disgust; expression of almost rapt enjoyment; expression of almost savage intensity; expression of almost savage intensity and purpose; expression of almost smug possession; expression of almost unbelievable pleasure; expression of almost vicious anger; expression of almost wondering admiration; expression of aloof detachment; expression of aloof good humor; expression of aloof indifference; expression of aloof tolerance; expression of aloof uninterest; expression of aloof withdrawal; expression of aloofness; expression of aloofness and pride; expression of amazed amusement; expression of amazement; expression of amazement tinged with indignation; expression of amiable surprise; expression of amused admiration; expression of amused and faintly bewildered speculation; expression of amused apprehension; expression of amused benevolence; expression of amused bewilderment; expression of amused comprehension; expression of amused contempt; expression of amused curiosity; expression of amused delight; expression of amused derision; expression of amused disbelief; expression of amused disdain; expression of amused disgust; expression of amused indifference; expression of amused indulgence; expression of amused irony; expression of amused mockery; expression of amused outrage; expression of amused pleasure; expression of amused resignation; expression of amused scorn; expression of amused self-mockery; expression of amused tolerance; expression of amused triumph; expression of amusement; expression of amusement and a faint boredom; expression of amusement and horror; expression of an angel; expression of an embarrassed schoolgirl; expression of an emotion she couldn't name; expression of angelic consideration; expression of angelic innocence; expression of anger; expression of anger and amazement; expression of anger and contempt; expression of anger and disapproval; expression of anger and frustration; expression of anger and pride; expression of anger as well as love; expression of anger mixed with rejection; expression of anger or approval; expression of anger or contempt; expression of anger or contempt or both; expression of angry contempt; expression of angry discomfiture; expression of angry disgust; expression of angry frustration; expression of angry hauteur; expression of angry hunger in; expression of angry incredulity and wariness; expression of angry resentment; expression of anguish; expression of anguished apology; expression of anguished despair; expression of anguished pain; expression of animation; expression of animosity; expression of annoyance; expression of annoyance and surprise; expression of annoyed chagrin; expression of annoyed dismay; expression of antagonism; expression of antagonism and dislike; expression of anticipation; expression of anticipation and secret knowledge; expression of anxiety; expression of anxiety and apprehension; expression of anxiety compounded with fear; expression of anxious disappointment and anger; expression of anxious inquiry; expression of anxious wariness; expression of apologetic adoration; expression of apology; expression of apology and pleading; expression of appalled chagrin; expression of appalled comprehension; expression of appalled guilt; expression of appalled realization; expression of apparent appraisal; expression of appeal; expression of appreciation; expression of appreciation and encouragement; expression of appreciative bliss; expression of apprehension; expression of approval; expression of approval and interest; expression of ardor; expression of arousal; expression of arousal and satisfaction; expression of aroused satisfaction; expression of arrogance; expression of arrogant amusement; expression of arrogant belligerence; expression of arrogant dismissal; expression of assessment; expression of assumed outrage; expression of assured authority; expression of astonished outrage; expression of astonished recognition; expression of astonishment; expression of astonishment and disbelief; expression of astonishment and dismay; expression of astonishment and recognition; expression of astonishment and wounded innocence; expression of astonishment that bordered on fright; expression of astounded disbelief as; expression of attentiveness; expression of austere disdain; expression of authority; expression of avarice; expression of avarice and need; expression of avid fascination; expression of avid interest; expression of awakening desire; expression of awe; expression of awe and anticipation; expression of awe and appreciation; expression of awe and disbelief; expression of awe and faint horror; expression of awe and responsibility; expression of awe and reverence; expression of awe and wonder; expression of awed admiration; expression of awed confusion; expression of awed delight; expression of awed surprise; expression of awed wonder; expression of baffled delight; expression of baffled dislike; expression of baffled frustration; expression of baffled hatred; expression of baffled rage; expression of bafflement; expression of barely concealed impatience; expression of barely controlled fury; expression of barely controlled mirth; expression of barely disguised irritation; expression of barely restrained passion; expression of barely suppressed excitement; expression of barely suppressed savagery; expression of barely veiled cynicism; expression of barely veiled regret; expression of beatific adoration; expression of beatific contentment; expression of beatific pleasure; expression of beauty; expression of befuddlement and outrage; expression of beguiling innocence; expression of being in love; expression of being inwardly focused; expression of being slightly at a loss; expression of bemused confusion; expression of bemused curiosity; expression of bemused delight; expression of bemused incredulity; expression of bemused innocence; expression of bemused shock; expression of bemused tranquility; expression of bemusement; expression of bemusement close to laughter; expression of benevolence; expression of benevolence and friendship; expression of benevolent indulgence; expression of benign approval; expression of benign complacency; expression of benign goodwill; expression of benign hauteur; expression of benign interest; expression of betrayal; expression of bewildered innocence; expression of bewildered longing; expression of bewildered outrage; expression of bewildered panic; expression of bewildered resignation; expression of bewilderment; expression of bewilderment and disbelief; expression of biting scorn; expression of bitter acrimony; expression of bitter anger; expression of bitter darkness; expression of bitter derision; expression of bitter disappointment; expression of bitter disbelief; expression of bitter distaste; expression of bitter humor; expression of bitter hunger; expression of bitter sadness; expression of bitter self-mockery; expression of bitterness; expression of black anger; expression of black fury; expression of black rage; expression of black rage and frustration; expression of blame and impatience; expression of bland curiosity; expression of bland indifference; expression of bland innocence; expression of bland inquiry; expression of bland inscrutability; expression of bland interest; expression of bland smugness; expression of blank amazement; expression of blank astonishment; expression of blank bewilderment; expression of blank defiance; expression of blank disbelief; expression of blank dismay; expression of blank exhaustion; expression of blank incredulity; expression of blank misery; expression of blank outrage; expression of blank rejection; expression of blank shock; expression of blank surprise; expression of blank uninterest; expression of blatant possession; expression of blazing hatred; expression of blazing lust; expression of bleak bitterness; expression of bleak desolation; expression of bleak dissatisfaction; . expression of bleak mercilessness; expression of bleak resignation; expression of bleakness; expression of blind adoration; expression of blind sensuality; expression of bliss; expression of bliss mingling with pain; expression of blissful concentration; expression of blistering contempt; expression of bored derision; expression of bored haughtiness; expression of bored indifference; expression of bored sulkiness; expression of bored superiority; expression of bored unconcern; expression of boredom; expression of boredom and contempt; expression of both embarrassment and suffering; expression of both protest and resignation; expression of both satisfaction and pride; expression of boyish delight; expression of boyish excitement; expression of boyish fear; expression of boyish innocence; expression of boyish mischief; expression of brainless adoration; expression of bravado; expression of breathless excitement; expression of brief puzzlement; expression of bright fear; expression of bright hope; expression of bright interest; expression of bright pleasure; expression of brooding; expression of brooding disappointment; expression of brooding discontent; expression of brooding irritation; expression of bruised hope; expression of buoyant happiness; expression of burgeoning disbelief; expression of burning curiosity; expression of burning hatred; expression of burning intensity; expression of burning scorn; expression of burning triumph; expression of calm; expression of calm assurance; expression of calm composure; expression of calm contentment; expression of calm detachment; expression of calm dismissal; expression of calm friendliness; expression of calm innocence; expression of calm inscrutability; expression of calm intent; expression of calm resignation; expression of candid sincerity; expression of candor; expression of care; expression of careful calm; expression of careful inquiry; expression of careful scrutiny; expression of careful serenity; expression of carefully concealed distress; expression of carefully controlled indifference; expression of careless indifference; expression of careless unconcern; expression of caring concern; expression of casual affection; expression of casual disdain; expression of casual indifference; expression of casual interest; expression of casual intimacy; expression of casual self-assurance; expression of catlike satisfaction; expression of caution; expression of caution and watchfulness; expression of cautious alarm; expression of celebration; expression of censure; expression of censure and reproof; expression of certainty; expression of chagrin; expression of chagrin and laughter; expression of chagrined consternation; expression of challenge; expression of challenge and passion; expression of charm; expression of charmed bemusement; expression of charming appeal; expression of cheer; expression of cheerfulness; expression of cheery brightness; expression of cherubic innocence; expression of childish adoration; expression of childish innocence; expression of childlike alarm; expression of childlike content; expression of chilling hauteur; expression of chilling menace; expression of chilly hauteur; expression of clinical indifference; expression of cold anger; expression of cold arrogance; expression of cold contempt; expression of cold courtesy; expression of cold derision; expression of cold detached contempt; expression of cold detachment; expression of cold determination; expression of cold disapproval; expression of cold disgust; expression of cold distaste; expression of cold hatred; expression of cold hauteur; expression of cold indifference; expression of cold inquiry; expression of cold mockery; expression of cold satisfaction; expression of cold speculation; expression of cold triumph; expression of cold withdrawal; expression of coldness; expression of coldness mingled with stormy anger; expression of combined shock and disbelief; expression of comfort; expression of comical astonishment; expression of comical confusion; expression of comical disillusionment; expression of comical dismay; expression of comical dismay tinged by embarrassment; expression of comical modesty; expression of comical surprise; expression of command; expression of commiseration; expression of commitment; expression of compassion; expression of compassionate respect; expression of compassionate understanding; expression of competent professionalism; expression of complacency; expression of complete adoration; expression of complete amazement; expression of complete and absolute possession; expression of complete and total awe; expression of complete and utter ecstasy; expression of complete astonishment; expression of complete awe; expression of complete bewilderment; expression of complete calm; expression of complete confidence; expression of complete detachment; expression of complete disbelief; expression of complete dislike; expression of complete exasperation; expression of complete horror; expression of complete incomprehension; expression of complete incredulity; expression of complete indifference; expression of complete innocence; expression of complete insecurity; expression of complete love and trust; expression of complete satisfaction; expression of complete seriousness; expression of complete surprise; expression of complete unconcern; expression of completely satisfied desire; expression of composed moderate interest; expression of composure; expression of comprehension; expression of compromise; expression of compunction; expression of concentrated curiosity;

expression of concentrated love; expression of concentrated wonder; expression of concentration; expression of concentration and demand; expression of concern; expression of concern and caring; expression of concern and curiosity; expression of concern and mistrust; expression of concern and regard for (him/her); expression of concern and tenderness; expression of concern for (him/her); expression of concern for (his/her) welfare; expression of concern for (his/her) well-being; expression of condemnation; expression of condolence; expression of confidence; expression of confidence in (him/her); expression of confident assurance; expression of confused alarm; expression of confused innocence; expression of confused relief; expression of confusion; expression of confusion and then disbelief; expression of consideration; expression of conspiratorial guilt; expression of constant amazement; expression of consternation; expression of consternation and horror; expression of consternation and veiled astonishment; expression of contempt; expression of contemptuous appraisal; expression of contemptuous indifference; expression of contemptuous loathing; expression of contentment; expression of contrition; expression of control; expression of controlled ferocity; expression of controlled fury; expression of conviction; expression of cool amazement; expression of cool appraisal; expression of cool authority; expression of cool composure; expression of cool disdain; expression of cool disinterest; expression of cool distaste; expression of cool efficiency; expression of cool indifference; expression of cool politeness; expression of cool remoteness; expression of cool reserve; expression of cool self-satisfaction; expression of cool superiority; expression of cool surprise; expression of cool triumph; expression of coolly confident composure; expression of coolness; expression of courteous interest; expression of courteous politeness; expression of courtesy; expression of creepy interest; expression of cruel dissipation; expression of cruelty; expression of cunning; expression of curiosity; expression of curiosity and bemusement; expression of curious absorption; expression of curious contemplation; expression of curious distaste; expression of curious irony; expression of curious regard; expression of cutting disdain; expression of cynical amusement; expression of cynical awareness; expression of cynical detachment; expression of cynical disbelief; expression of cynical disdain; expression of cynical disinterest; expression of cynical enjoyment; expression of cynical indifference; expression of cynical self-assurance; expression of cynical skepticism; expression of cynicism; expression of cynicism and rough sympathy; expression of dancing mischief; expression of dangerous and stubborn intent; expression of dangerous calm; expression of daring and rapture; expression of dark anger; expression of dark arousal; expression of dark arrogance; expression of dark brooding intensity; expression of dark cynicism; expression of dark despair; expression of dark determination; expression of dark frustration; expression of dark intensity; expression of dark intent; expression of dark satisfaction; expression of dark sensuality; expression of dark triumph; expression of darkest evil; expression of dawning awareness; expression of dawning comprehension; expression of dawning delight; expression of dawning horror; expression of dawning understanding; expression of dazed awe and wonder; expression of dazed bewilderment; expression of dazed disbelief; expression of dazed incredulity; expression of dazed pleasure; expression of dazed terror; expression of deadly intent; expression of deadly seriousness; expression of decision and determination; expression of decisiveness; expression of dedication; expression of deep admiration; expression of deep affront; expression of deep animosity; expression of deep anxiety; expression of deep calculation; expression of deep concentration; expression of deep concern; expression of deep confusion; expression of deep consternation; expression of deep contemplation; expression of deep contentment; expression of deep disappointment; expression of deep disgust; expression of deep distaste; expression of deep emotion; expression of deep feeling; expression of deep foreboding; expression of deep frustration; expression of deep gloom; expression of deep gratitude; expression of deep happiness; expression of deep hostility; expression of deep interest; expression of deep love; expression of deep offence; expression of deep pain; expression of deep pleasure; expression of deep regret; expression of deep relief; expression of deep respect; expression of deep sadness; expression of deep satisfaction; expression of deep self-dismay; expression of deep shock; expression of deep skepticism; expression of deep sorrow; expression of deep suspicion; expression of deep sympathy; expression of deep vulnerability; expression of deep wariness; expression of deepest affection; expression of deepest anxiety; expression of deepest concern; expression of defeat; expression of defiance; expression of defiant unconcern; expression of definite pleasure; expression of deflation; expression of deliberate inscrutability; expression of deliberate insolence; expression of deliberate unconcern; expression of delicious absurdity; expression of delight; expression of delight and desire; expression of delight and relief; expression of delight and wonderment; expression of delighted disbelief; expression of delighted recognition; expression of delighted remembrance; expression of delighted surprise; expression of demonic purpose; expression of depression and resignation; expression of derision; expression of desire; expression of desire and blatant need; expression of desolation; expression of despair; expression of despairing resignation; expression of desperate anxiety; expression of desperate hopelessness; expression of desperate longing; expression of desperate need; expression of desperation; expression of detached intensity; expression of detached scorn; expression of detachment; expression of determination; expression of determination and defiance; expression of determination and interest; expression of determined caution; expression of determined cheerfulness; expression of determined concentration; expression of devastating charm; expression of devotion; expression of dewy youth; expression of diabolical laughter; expression of dignity; expression of disagreeable astonishment; expression of disappointment; expression of disappointment and frustration; expression of disapprobation; expression of disapproval; expression of disbelief; expression of disbelief and bewilderment; expression of disbelief and consternation; expression of disbelief and disapproval; expression of disbelief and distaste; expression of disbelieving awe; expression of discomfiture; expression of discomfort; expression of discontent; expression of discontent and disdain; expression of discontentment; expression of disdain; expression of disdainful contempt; expression of disdainful hauteur; expression of disgruntlement; expression of disguised amusement; expression of disgust; expression of disgust and craving; expression of disgusted incredulity; expression of disillusionment; expression of disinterest; expression of dislike; expression of dislike that bordered on hatred; expression of dismay; expression of dismay and chagrin; expression of dismayed shock; expression of dismissal; expression of dispassionate assessment; expression of displeased surprise; expression of displeasure; expression of disquiet; expression of dissatisfaction; expression of dissension; expression of distaste; expression of distasteful scorn; expression of distinct shock; expression of distress; expression of distrust and maybe even regret; expression of distrust and wariness; expression of doleful suffering; expression of doom; expression of doubt; expression of doubt and determination; expression of doubt and perplexity; expression of doubt and rather tentative hope; expression of dread; expression of dreamy contentment; expression of dreamy desire; expression of dreamy speculation; expression of dreamy want; expression of driven need; expression of driving urgency; expression of drowsy contentment; expression of drowsy innocence; expression of drowsy longing; expression of dry amusement; expression of dry humor; expression of dulled confusion; expression of dumb amazement; expression of dumbfounded horror; expression of eager anticipation; expression of eager curiosity; expression of eager expectancy; expression of eagerness; expression of earnestness; expression of earnestness and responsibility; expression of easy amusement; expression of easy confidence; expression of easy good humor; expression of ecstasy; expression of ecstatic bliss; expression of edgy fascination; expression of efficiency; expression of ego and conceit; expression of either rejection or praise; expression of elegant surprise; expression of elfin mischief; expression of embarrassed astonishment; expression of embarrassed concern; expression of embarrassment; expression of emotion; expression of emotional agony; expression of emotional distance; expression of empathy; expression of empathy and concern; expression of emptiness; expression of encouragement; expression of endearing perplexity; expression of endless patience; expression of enjoyment; expression of envy; expression of equanimity; expression of erotic hunger; expression of eternal good will; expression of even deeper malice; expression of even greater concern; expression of even greater dismay; expression of evil bliss; expression of exaggerated affront; expression of exaggerated amazement; expression of exaggerated awe; expression of exaggerated concentration; expression of exaggerated disgust; expression of exaggerated fear; expression of exaggerated horror; expression of exaggerated innocence; expression of exaggerated pain; expression of exaggerated patience; expression of exaggerated relief; expression of exaggerated suffering; expression of exaggerated sympathy; expression of exaltation; expression of exasperated stubbornness; expression of exasperated tenderness; expression of exasperation; expression of excited anticipation; expression of excited surprise; expression of excitement; expression of excruciating embarrassment; expression of exhausted patience; expression of expectancy; expression of expectant joy; expression of expectation; expression of exquisite desolation; expression of exquisite gentleness; expression of exquisite pleasure; expression of exquisite sexual frustration; expression of exquisite torture; expression of extraordinary anguish; expression of extraordinary gratification; expression of extraordinary tenderness; expression of extreme anticipation; expression of extreme astonishment; expression of extreme bitterness; expression of extreme boredom; expression of extreme curiosity; expression of extreme cynicism; expression of extreme disquiet; expression of extreme distaste; expression of extreme embarrassment; expression of extreme exasperation; expression of extreme forbearance; expression of extreme frustration; expression of extreme harassment; expression of extreme hauteur; expression of extreme hurt; expression of extreme indignation; expression of extreme innocence; expression of extreme mirth; expression of extreme reasonableness; expression of extreme responsibility; expression of extreme revulsion; expression of extreme sadness; expression of extreme satisfaction; expression of extreme self-disgust; expression of extreme severity; expression of extreme shock; expression of extreme solicitousness; expression of extreme suffering; expression of extreme truculence; expression of extreme unhappiness; expression of extreme wariness; expression of exuberance; expression of exultant disbelief; expression of exultation; expression of faint amazement; expression of faint amusement; expression of faint boredom; expression of faint contempt; expression of faint disapproval; expression of faint disgust; expression of faint distaste; expression of faint irritation; expression of faint mystic revelation; expression of faint perplexity; expression of faint surprise; expression of fake surprise; expression of false affability; expression of false compassion; expression of false exasperation; expression of false interest; expression of false vivacity; expression of farewell; expression of fascinated bemusement; expression of fascinated curiosity; expression of fascinated interest; expression of fascinated puzzlement; expression of fascination; expression of fastidious disgust; expression of fastidious distaste; expression of fastidious inquiry; expression of fatherly delight; expression of fathomless suffering; expression of fatuous devotion; expression of fatuous worship; expression of faux shock; expression of fear; expression of fear and concern; expression of fear and desire; expression of fear and distaste; expression of fear and dread; expression of fear and heartache; expression of fear and horror; expression of fear and incredulity; expression of fear and mistrust; expression of fear and panic; expression of fear mixed with longing; expression of fearful anticipation; expression of feeble suffering; expression of feeling; expression of feelings; expression of feelings that went soul deep; expression of feigned adoration; expression of feigned happiness; expression of feigned innocence; expression of feigned terror; expression of feline contentment; expression of feline satisfaction; expression of feline triumph; expression of feral hunger; expression of ferocious anger; expression of ferocious fascination; expression of ferocity; expression of fierce anger; expression of fierce concentration; expression of fierce determination; expression of fierce disdain; expression of fierce distaste; expression of fierce fascination; expression of fierce frustration; expression of fierce pride;

expression of fierce rage; expression of fierce satisfaction; expression of fierce tenderness; expression of fierce triumph; expression of finality; expression of firm determination; expression of firmness and resolution; expression of fixed concentration; expression of fleeting distaste; expression of fleeting torment; expression of flirtatious interest; expression of focused interest; expression of fond amusement; expression of fond remembrance; expression of fondness; expression of forbearance; expression of forbidding anger; expression of formidable will; expression of fragile melancholy; expression of frank appreciation; expression of frank astonishment; expression of frank disbelief; expression of frank hostility; expression of frank surprise; expression of frazzled desperation; expression of freedom; expression of friendly acknowledgment; expression of friendly concern; expression of friendly congratulation; expression of fright; expression of frightened desperation; expression of frowning incredulity; expression of frozen dismay; expression of frozen distaste; expression of frozen horror; expression of frozen resentment and disbelief; expression of frustrated bafflement; expression of frustrated disgust; expression of frustrated incredulity; expression of frustrated irritation; expression of frustration; expression of frustration and unhappiness; expression of furious anger; expression of furious disgust; expression of furious distaste; expression of furious hatred; expression of furious impatience; expression of furious outrage; expression of fury; expression of futility; expression of generosity; expression of gentle amusement; expression of gentle and compassionate forgiveness; expression of gentle coaxing; expression of gentle concern; expression of gentle eagerness; expression of gentle solicitude; expression of gentle sympathy; expression of gentleness; expression of gentleness and patience; expression of genuine astonishment; expression of genuine bewilderment; expression of genuine concern; expression of genuine contrition; expression of genuine dismay; expression of genuine emotion; expression of genuine feeling; expression of genuine glee; expression of genuine horror; expression of genuine loathing; expression of genuine love; expression of genuine pleasure; expression of genuine relief; expression of genuine surprise; expression of genuine sympathy; expression of glacial contempt; expression of glad surprise; expression of gladness or joy; expression of glazed agony; expression of glazed horror; expression of glazed intensity; expression of glazed pleasure; expression of glee; expression of gleeful anticipation; expression of glittery panic; expression of gloating; expression of gloom; expression of glorious anticipation; expression of glorious satisfaction; expression of glowering rage; expression of glowing contentment; expression of glowing contentment and languid radiance; expression of glumness; expression of good cheer; expression of good humor; expression of good wishes; expression of goodwill; expression of goodwill and encouragement; expression of goofy enthusiasm; expression of grace; expression of grandmotherly reproach; expression of gratified pleasure; expression of gratitude; expression of grave detachment; expression of grave disapproval; expression of grave exasperation; expression of grave seriousness; expression of gravity; expression of great concern; expression of great disgust; expression of great distaste; expression of great geniality; expression of great gravity; expression of great happiness; expression of great importance; expression of great interest; expression of great kindness; expression of great patience; expression of great pride; expression of great respect; expression of great satisfaction; expression of great seriousness; expression of great suffering; expression of great superiority; expression of great tenderness; expression of great unhappiness; expression of great virtue; expression of great weariness; expression of great wisdom; expression of greed; expression of greed and desire; expression of greedy wonder; expression of green envy; expression of greeting; expression of grief; expression of grief and loss; expression of grim amusement; expression of grim anger; expression of grim astonishment; expression of grim desperation; expression of grim determination; expression of grim disapproval; expression of grim fury; expression of grim impatience; expression of grim satisfaction; expression of grim suspicion; expression of grim tension; expression of grim thoughtfulness; expression of grim understanding; expression of grimness; expression of gritty determination; expression of growing amusement; expression of growing astonishment; expression of growing bewilderment; expression of growing consternation; expression of growing enlightenment; expression of growing fascination; expression of growing guilt; expression of growing irritation; expression of grudging admiration; expression of grudging patience; expression of guarded amusement; expression of guarded reserve; expression of guarded watchfulness; expression of guilt; expression of guilt and horror; expression of guilt and remorse; expression of habitual pugnacity; expression of haggard distress; expression of half irritation, half fear; expression of half pleasure, half pain; expression of half scared triumph; expression of happiness; expression of happiness and contentment; expression of happiness and delight; expression of happiness and utter contentment; expression of happy adoration; expression of happy anticipation; expression of happy bewilderment; expression of happy satisfaction; expression of happy surprise; expression of harassment; expression of hard cynicism; expression of hard desire; expression of hard incredulity; expression of hard indifference; expression of hard resolve; expression of hardness; expression of harmony; expression of harried impatience; expression of harsh satisfaction; expression of hate; expression of hatred; expression of haughtiness; expression of haughty amusement; expression of haughty arrogance; expression of haughty disbelief; expression of haughty disdain; expression of haughty distaste; expression of haughty indifference; expression of haughty irritation; expression of haughty resignation; expression of haunted agony; expression of haunted regret; expression of haunted sadness; expression of hauteur; expression of heartfelt regret; expression of heartfelt relief; expression of heartrending pity; expression of heartrending struggle; expression of heated desire; expression of heavenly delight; expression of heavenly wonder; expression of heavy sensuality; expression of hedonistic enjoyment; expression of helpless dismay; expression of helpless frustration; expression of helpless impotence; expression of helplessness; expression of helplessness and shock; expression of heroic resolution; expression of hesitancy; expression of hidden amusement; expression of hidden laughter; expression of hidden malice; expression of high hauteur;

expression of highly bred disdain; expression of his/her affection for him/her; expression of his/her affectionate good wishes; expression of his/her core; expression of his/her current unsettled mood; expression of his/her dark eyes*; expression of his/her deepest desire; expression of his/her deepest feelings; expression of his/her emotional torment; expression of his/her emotions at that moment; expression of his/her face*; expression of his/her fears; expression of his/her features*; expression of his/her feelings; expression of his/her inadequacy; expression of his/her inner mind; expression of his/her inner turmoil; expression of his/her innermost feelings; expression of his/her innermost self; expression of his/her intense and nervous energy; expression of his/her intention; expression of his/her lack of any desire; expression of his/her love for him/her; expression of his/her mental fury; expression of his/her mood; expression of his/her mouth*; expression of his/her own loneliness; expression of his/her regard for him/her; expression of his/her spirit; expression of his/her thoughts; expression of holy innocence; expression of honest enthusiasm; expression of hope; expression of hope and despair; expression of hope and pleading; expression of hope mixed with worry; expression of hopeful affection; expression of hopeful curiosity; expression of hopeful encouragement; expression of hopelessness; expression of horrified amazement; expression of horrified concern; expression of horrified disbelief; expression of horrified disgust; expression of horrified fascination; expression of horrified guilt; expression of horrified panic; expression of horrified shock; expression of horrified yet smug disgust; expression of horror; expression of horror and loathing; expression of horror and rejection; expression of hospitality; expression of hostile suspicion; expression of hostility; expression of hostility and bitterness; expression of hot temper; expression of humble admiration; expression of humility; expression of humor; expression of humorous resignation; expression of hunger; expression of hungry anticipation; expression of hungry hope; expression of hungry longing; expression of hunted innocence; expression of hurt; expression of hurt and betrayal; expression of hurt and bewilderment; expression of hurt and disbelief; expression of hurt and loss; expression of hurt bewilderment; expression of hurt confusion; expression of hurt incomprehension; expression of hurt indecision; expression of hurt innocence; expression of hurt surprise; expression of ice; expression of icy arrogance; expression of icy derision; expression of icy dislike; expression of icy distaste; expression of icy loathing; expression of icy resentment; expression of icy withdrawal; expression of idiotic amazement; expression of idle interest; expression of immeasurable surprise; expression of immense relief; expression of immense weariness; expression of impassive professionalism; expression of impatience; expression of impatience rather than dismay; expression of impatient disbelief; expression of impatient disdain; expression of impatient tolerance; expression of impenetrable cynicism; expression of imperiousness; expression of implacability; expression of implacable determination; expression of implacable dislike; expression of implacable resolve; expression of implacable ruthlessness; expression of incomprehension; expression of inconsequence; expression of inconsolable sadness and hurt; expression of incredible hauteur; expression of incredible sadness; expression of incredible tenderness; expression of incredulity; expression of incredulity and awe; expression of incredulity and bewilderment; expression of incredulous admiration; expression of incredulous amazement; expression of incredulous anger; expression of incredulous anger and dismay; expression of incredulous delight; expression of incredulous disbelief; expression of incredulous fury; expression of incredulous joy; expression of incredulous outrage; expression of incredulous pity; expression of incredulousness; expression of indecision; expression of indescribable tenderness; expression of indifference; expression of indignant horror; expression of indignant outrage; expression of indignant reproach; expression of indignation; expression of indignation and anger; expression of indignation and outrage; expression of individuality; expression of indolent amusement; expression of indulgence; expression of indulgent adoration; expression of indulgent amusement; expression of indulgent pity; expression of indulgent solicitude; expression of indulgent tenderness; expression of ineffable sadness; expression of inexplicable sorrow; expression of infinite compassion; expression of infinite despair; expression of infinite sadness; expression of infinite tenderness; expression of infinite tenderness and pleasure; expression of infuriating blankness; expression of infuriating insolence; expression of injured innocence; expression of inner disquiet; expression of inner satisfaction; expression of innocence; expression of innocence and desire; expression of innocent amazement; expression of innocent appreciation; expression of innocent astonishment; expression of innocent inquiry; expression of innocent surprise; expression of inquiry; expression of inquiry and budding uneasiness; expression of inscrutability; expression of insolence and ingratitude; expression of insolent contempt; expression of insolent triumph; expression of insult; expression of insulted outrage; expression of intense anger; expression of intense appreciation; expression of intense boredom; expression of intense concentration; expression of intense concern; expression of intense curiosity; expression of intense delight; expression of intense delight and pride; expression of intense desire; expression of intense desolation; expression of intense focus; expression of intense fury; expression of intense gloom; expression of intense gratitude; expression of intense interest; expression of intense irritation; expression of intense longing; expression of intense misery; expression of intense pain; expression of intense peace; expression of intense pleasure; expression of intense protective care; expression of intense satisfaction; expression of intense scorn; expression of intense self-absorption; expression of intense suffering; expression of intense worry; expression of intensely focused concentration; expression of intensely male satisfaction; expression of intensity; expression of intent; expression of intent awareness; expression of intent menace; expression of intention; expression of interest; expression of interest and amusement; expression of interest and approval; expression of interest and good faith; expression of interested amusement; expression of interested concern; expression of interested surprise; expression of intimacy; expression of intimate bonding; expression of intimate humor; expression of intuitive certainty; expression of iron calm; expression of ironic amusement; expression of ironical amusement; expression of ironical expectancy; expression of irony; expression of irritability; expression of irritated amusement; expression of irritating sobriety; expression of irritation; expression of jealous hatred; expression of jealousy; expression of jollity; expression of joy; expression of joy and complete trust; expression of joy and gratitude; expression of joy and pleasure; expression of joy mingled with ecstatic surprise; expression of joyful awe; expression of joyful incredulity; expression of justifiable aggravation; expression of justifiable curiosity; expression of juvenile repugnance; expression of keen anticipation; expression of kindly sympathy; expression of kindly tolerance; expression of kindly wisdom; expression of kindness; expression of kittenish innocence; expression of knowing male complicity; expression of knowing sympathy; expression of laughing devotion; expression of laughing ease; expression of lazy amusement; expression of lazy appreciation; expression of lazy disinterest; expression of lazy lechery; expression of lazy mockery; expression of lazy satisfaction; expression of lazy victory; expression of lazy warmth; expression of leashed aggression; expression of lecherous interest; expression of lifelong gratitude; expression of light affection; expression of light mockery; expression of lighthearted indifference; expression of limitless patience; expression of lingering bitterness; expression of lingering pain; expression of liquid warmth; expression of lively but uncomprehending interest; expression of lively interest; expression of loathing; expression of loathsome speculation; expression of loneliness and isolation; expression of longing; expression of longing and love; expression of loss; expression of loss and defeat; expression of love; expression of love and caring; expression of love and commitment; expression of love and compassion; expression of love and concern; expression of love and longing; expression of love and need; expression of love and sorrow; expression of love and sorrow and longing; expression of love and sweet sympathy; expression of love and tenderness; expression of love and understanding; expression of loving adoration; expression of loving disbelief; expression of loving exasperation; expression of loving tenderness; expression of ludicrous disbelief; expression of ludicrous dismay; expression of lust; expression of lust and disappointment; expression of lust and greed; expression of lustful insolence; expression of malcontent; expression of male approval; expression of male chauvinism; expression of male outrage; expression of male vanity; expression of malevolence; expression of malevolent determination; expression of malice; expression of malicious satisfaction; expression of marital bliss; expression of martyred stoicism; expression of marveling innocence; expression of masculine admiration; expression of masculine pride; expression of masculine toughness; expression of masculine triumph; expression of masculine understanding; expression of matching solemnity; expression of maternal concern; expression of maternal longing; expression of maternal pride; expression of maternal satisfaction; expression of mature concentration; expression of measured restraint; expression of meek shame; expression of menace; expression of mild amusement; expression of mild complacency; expression of mild concern; expression of mild confusion; expression of mild curiosity; expression of mild distaste; expression of mild indignation; expression of mild inquiry; expression of mild interest; expression of mild irritation; expression of mild irritation and pity; expression of mild puzzlement; expression of mild surprise; expression of mild sympathy; expression of mingled alarm and delight; expression of mingled amusement and affection; expression of mingled amusement and annoyance; expression of mingled anxiety and relief; expression of mingled astonishment and dismay; expression of mingled concern and puzzlement; expression of mingled disgust and disbelief; expression of mingled dismay and astonishment; expression of mingled fury and alarm; expression of mingled guilt and anger; expression of mingled hurt and anger; expression of mingled panic and dismay; expression of mingled regret and resignation; expression of mingled regret and speculation; expression of mingled shock and amusement; expression of mirth; expression of mischief; expression of mischief mixed with anticipation; expression of misery; expression of mixed awe and horror; expression of mixed exasperation and tenderness; expression of mixed surprise and annoyance; expression of mixed surprise and distaste; expression of mixed surprise and triumph; expression of mock affront; expression of mock amazement; expression of mock amusement; expression of mock awe; expression of mock concern; expression of mock confusion; expression of mock consternation; expression of mock disappointment; expression of mock disbelief; expression of mock disgust; expression of mock dismay; expression of mock distress; expression of mock fear; expression of mock gravity; expression of mock horror; expression of mock indignation; expression of mock innocence; expression of mock offense; expression of mock outrage; expression of mock pain; expression of mock regret; expression of mock repentance; expression of mock seriousness; expression of mock severity; expression of mock shock; expression of mock solemnity; expression of mock surprise; expression of mock sympathy; expression of mockery; expression of mocking amusement; expression of mocking contempt; expression of mocking disbelief; expression of mocking indolence; expression of mocking inquiry; expression of mocking triumph; expression of moderate pleasure; expression of molten rage; expression of morose resignation; expression of mortified horror; expression of motherly solicitude; expression of mounting frustration; expression of mournful reproach; expression of mulish obstinacy; expression of mulish rebellion; expression of murder; expression of murderous rage; expression of musing mockery; expression of mute appeal; expression of mute apprehension; expression of mute hostility; expression of mutiny; expression of mutual agreement; expression of mutual joy; expression of mutual love; expression of mutual love and tenderness and; expression of mutual respect; expression of mystification; expression of naked and passionate sincerity; expression of naked desire; expression of naked hunger; expression of naked loneliness; expression of naked longing; expression of naked pain; expression of naked pleading; expression of naked regret; expression of nasty delight; expression of near anger; expression of near ecstasy; expression of near horror; expression of near joy; expression of near panic; expression of near reverence; expression of need and relief; expression of need and urgency; expression of need and want; expression of need and want and longing; expression of negation; expression of neither gladness nor amusement; expression of nervous kindliness; expression of nervous uncertainty; expression of nervousness; expression of nervousness and fear; expression of neutrality; expression of newfound love; expression of noble suffering; expression of nonchalance; expression of noncommittal blandness; expression of nostalgia; expression of nostalgic sentiments; expression of nothingness; expression of obvious dislike; expression of obvious distaste; expression of obvious relief; expression of offense; expression of omniscience; expression of open admiration; expression of open adoration; expression of open affection; expression of open challenge; expression of open disbelief; expression of open excitement; expression of open skepticism; expression of open wonder; expression of openness; expression of outrage; expression of outrage and fury; expression of outrage and indignation; expression of outrage and shock; expression of outraged astonishment; expression of outraged dignity; expression of outraged disbelief; expression of outraged horror; expression of outraged incredulity; expression of outraged innocence; expression of overbearing smugness; expression of overt suspicion; expression of overwhelming frustration; expression of pain; expression of pain and anger; expression of pain and bitterness; expression of pain and disgust; expression of pain and distaste; expression of pain and frustration; expression of pain and grief; expression of pain and hopelessness; expression of pain and passion; expression of pain and sadness; expression of pained comprehension; expression of pained contempt; expression of pained ecstasy; expression of pained exasperation; expression of pained exhaustion; expression of pained innocence; expression of pained intensity; expression of pained reproach; expression of pained surprise; expression of painful conviction; expression of pale hauteur; expression of panic; expression of panic and expectancy; expression of parental wrath; expression of passion; expression of passionate abandon; expression of passionate desire; expression of passionate surrender; expression of passionate tenderness; expression of patent surprise; expression of patently forced indifference; expression of patience; expression of patient encouragement; expression of patient indulgence; expression of patient resignation; expression of patient virtue; expression of peace; expression of penitence; expression of pent-up rage; expression of perfect joy; expression of perfect serenity; expression of permanent amusement; expression of permanent dissatisfaction; expression of permanent pleasure; expression of perpetual arrogance; expression of perpetual concentration; expression of perpetual mild anxiety; expression of perplexity; expression of personal interest; expression of petulant impatience; expression of physical affection; expression of physical desire; expression of physical lust; expression of physical need; expression of pitiless arrogance; expression of pity; expression of pity mingled with contempt; expression of pity mingled with disbelief; expression of pitying affection; expression of placid good humor; expression of playful affection; expression of pleading; expression of pleasant anticipation; expression of pleasant surprise; expression of pleased anticipation; expression of pleased satisfaction; expression of pleased surprise; expression of pleasurable excitement; expression of pleasure; expression of pleasure and absorption; expression of pleasure and excitement; expression of pleasure and expectancy; expression of pleasure and interest; expression of pleasure and pride; expression of poignant sorrow; expression of poise; expression of polite bewilderment; expression of polite boredom; expression of polite but indifferent interest; expression of polite curiosity; expression of polite disbelief; expression of polite disinterest; expression of polite distance; expression of polite indifference; expression of polite indulgence; expression of polite inquiry; expression of polite interest; expression of polite neutrality; expression of polite patience; expression of polite regret; expression of polite surprise; expression of polite yet clear distaste; expression of pompous superiority; expression of positive emotions; expression of possession; expression of possessive instincts; expression of pouting dissatisfaction; expression of power; expression of powerful love; expression of practiced innocence; expression of predatory intent; expression of predatory satisfaction; expression of pretend shock; expression of pride; expression of pride and awe; expression of pride and disdain; expression of pride and excitement; expression of pride and love; expression of pride and possession; expression of pride and rapture; expression of pride and tenderness; expression of prim disapproval; expression of prim efficiency; expression of primal fear; expression of primal need and hunger; expression of primal possessiveness; expression of primitive male desire; expression of primitive possession; expression of professional blandness; expression of professional concern; expression of professional detachment; expression of profound dismay; expression of profound gravity; expression of profound impatience; expression of profound interest; expression of profound irritation; expression of profound love; expression of profound regret; expression of profound relief; expression of profound sadness; expression of profound shock; expression of profound tenderness; expression of promise; expression of promised retaliation; expression of propriety; expression of protest; expression of protesting disbelief; expression of pure adoration; expression of pure agony; expression of pure alarm; expression of pure anguish; expression of pure befuddlement; expression of pure bliss; expression of pure contempt; expression of pure contentment; expression of pure cynicism; expression of pure delight; expression of pure disgust; expression of pure dislike; expression of pure ecstasy; expression of pure exasperation; expression of pure frustration; expression of pure fury; expression of pure glee; expression of pure happiness; expression of pure hatred; expression of pure hedonistic delight; expression of pure hope; expression of pure horror; expression of pure indulgence; expression of pure innocence; expression of pure jealousy; expression of pure joy; expression of pure loathing; expression of pure love; expression of pure love and longing; expression of pure male bafflement; expression of pure male satisfaction; expression of pure malevolence; expression of pure malice; expression of pure mischief; expression of pure mockery; expression of pure need; expression of pure parental reprimand; expression of pure pleasure; expression of pure pleasure and delight; expression of pure rage; expression of pure rapture; expression of pure scorn; expression of pure sensual delight; expression of pure shock; expression of pure steel;

expression of pure triumph; expression of pure wonder; expression of purest rage; expression of purest relief; expression of purpose; expression of purposefulness; expression of puzzled amusement; expression of puzzled curiosity; expression of puzzled disbelief; expression of puzzled inquiry; expression of puzzled politeness; expression of puzzled tenderness; expression of puzzlement; expression of puzzlement and confusion; expression of puzzling uncertainty; expression of queenly disdain; expression of query; expression of quick distaste; expression of quick tenderness; expression of quiet amusement; expression of quiet happiness; expression of quiet rage; expression of quiet speculation; expression of quiet triumph; expression of quiet understanding; expression of quite extraordinary cupidity; expression of quizzical but very male interest; expression of quizzical detachment; expression of quizzical puzzlement; expression of radiant elation; expression of radiant expectancy; expression of radiant welcome; expression of rage; expression of rampant exasperation; expression of rampant skepticism; expression of rank condemnation; expression of rapt attention; expression of rapt concentration; expression of rapt concern; expression of rapt delight; expression of rapt fascination; expression of rapt intensity; expression of rapt interest; expression of rapt preoccupation; expression of rapture; expression of rare tenderness; expression of rather pitying amusement; expression of rather wicked glee; expression of raw agony; expression of raw desire; expression of raw frustration; expression of raw grief; expression of raw incredulity; expression of raw pain; expression of raw shock; expression of real caring; expression of real futility; expression of real interest; expression of real pain; expression of realization; expression of reasonableness; expression of rebellion; expression of recrimination; expression of refusal; expression of regret; expression of rejection; expression of relief; expression of relief and gratitude; expression of relieved surprise; expression of reluctance; expression of reluctant admiration; expression of reluctant confrontation; expression of reluctant entreaty; expression of reluctant fascination; expression of remembered pain; expression of reminiscence; expression of remorse; expression of remorse and regret; expression of remote efficiency; expression of remoteness; expression of renewed determination; expression of repentance; expression of repose; expression of repressed pain; expression of reproach; expression of reproof; expression of repudiation; expression of repugnance; expression of repulsion; expression of resentment; expression of resentment and pouting depression; expression of reserve; expression of resignation; expression of resigned acceptance; expression of resigned determination; expression of resigned disapproval; expression of resigned impatience; expression of resigned patience; expression of resigned sorrow; expression of resigned tolerance; expression of resolution; expression of respect; expression of respect and care; expression of respectful gravity; expression of restrained violence; expression of reverence; expression of revulsion; expression of revulsion and rejection; expression of ridicule; expression of righteous distaste; expression of rigid control; expression of rigid control and ferocious focus; expression of rigid distaste; expression of rueful amusement; expression of rueful appeal; expression of rueful indulgence;

expression of rueful resignation; expression of ruthless resolve; expression of sad indulgence; expression of sad resignation; expression of sadness; expression of sadness and caring; expression of sage perplexity; expression of saintly patience; expression of sarcastic amusement; expression of sardonic amusement; expression of sardonic expectancy; expression of sardonic inquiry; expression of sardonic satisfaction; expression of sardonic triumph; expression of satirical inquiry; expression of satirical unrest; expression of satisfaction; expression of savage anger; expression of savage concern; expression of savage contempt; expression of savage rage; expression of savagery; expression of scorn; expression of scorn and anger; expression of scornful contempt; expression of scornful disbelief; expression of scowling bewilderment; expression of scowling discomfort; expression of scowling impatience; expression of scowling indifference; expression of searing inscrutability; expression of seething frustration; expression of self-contempt; expression of self-conscious guilt; expression of self-reproach; expression of sensual anticipation; expression of sensual appreciation; expression of sensual concentration; expression of sensual contentment; expression of sensual delight; expression of sensual hunger; expression of sensual pleasure; expression of sensual satisfaction; expression of sensuous tenderness; expression of serene interest; expression of serenity; expression of serious concentration; expression of serious distaste; expression of serious intent; expression of seriousness; expression of settled contentment; expression of severe disapproval; expression of severity; expression of severity and disapproval; expression of sexual desire; expression of sexual need; expression of sexual pleasure; expression of sexuality; expression of shaken fascination; expression of shame; expression of shared feelings; expression of shared joy; expression of shared laughter; expression of shared love; expression of shattered disbelief; expression of sheepishness; expression of sheer alarm; expression of sheer anger; expression of sheer astonishment; expression of sheer awe; expression of sheer bewilderment; expression of sheer bliss; expression of sheer confusion; expression of sheer delight; expression of sheer despair; expression of sheer disbelief; expression of sheer disgust; expression of sheer dread; expression of sheer exasperation; expression of sheer frustration; expression of sheer happiness; expression of sheer hatred; expression of sheer horror; expression of sheer incredulity; expression of sheer joy; expression of sheer joy and contentment; expression of sheer longing; expression of sheer lust; expression of sheer pain; expression of sheer panic; expression of sheer pleasure; expression of sheer relief; expression of sheer terror; expression of sheer vitriol; expression of sheer wicked amusement; expression of sheer wonder; expression of shining pleasure; expression of shock; expression of shock and amazement; expression of shock and anger; expression of shock and anguish; expression of shock and bewilderment; expression of shock and confusion; expression of shock and dismay; expression of shock and horror; expression of shock and hurt; expression of shock and incredulity; expression of shock and injury; expression of shock and regret; expression of shock and stunned disbelief; expression of shock and then annoyance; expression of shock and wonder; expression of shocked amazement; expression of shocked and mischievous delight; expression of shocked comprehension; expression of shocked disbelief; expression of shocked dismay; expression of shocked excitement; expression of shocked fascination; expression of shocked horror; expression of shocked incredulity; expression of shocked indignation; expression of shocked innocence; expression of shocked joy; expression of shocked outrage; expression of shocked recognition; expression of shocked surprise; expression of shocked understanding; expression of shuttered indifference; expression of shy delight; expression of shy modesty; expression of sick hungry yearning; expression of silent pleading; expression of silent torment; expression of simmering excitement; expression of simmering fury; expression of simmering impatience; expression of simpering stupidity; expression of sincere concern; expression of sincere happiness; expression of sincere regret; expression of skepticism; expression of skepticism and disapproval; expression of slavish adoration; expression of sleepy amazement; expression of sleepy amusement; expression of slight boredom; expression of slight distaste; expression of slight puzzlement; expression of slightly cynical skepticism; expression of slightly sardonic amusement; expression of slowly dawning comprehension; expression of slumberous speculation; expression of sly triumph; expression of smiling enjoyment; expression of smiling good humor; expression of smiling inconsequence; expression of smiling interest; expression of smiling tenderness; expression of smoldering dislike; expression of smoldering hatred; expression of smoldering relish; expression of smoldering resentment; expression of smug awareness; expression of smug bliss; expression of smug male arrogance; expression of smug satisfaction; expression of smug self-vindication; expression of smug superiority; expression of smugness; expression of sneering triumph; expression of so much horror; expression of so much shock; expression of sober fury bordering on fear; expression of sober grimness; expression of soft contentment; expression of soft indulgence; expression of softness; expression of solemn curiosity; expression of solemn reserve; expression of solemn shock; expression of solemnity; expression of solicitude; expression of some emotion she couldn't name; expression of some sort of affection; expression of some sort of sympathy; expression of some surprise; expression of someone about to (...); expression of someone anxious to (...); expression of someone carried away by (...); expression of someone deeply preoccupied; expression of someone doing a few mental calculations; expression of someone doing something against his will; expression of someone in shock; expression of someone looking forward to (...); expression of someone lost in their work; expression of someone not fully awake; expression of someone not quite sure of (...); expression of someone posing for the camera; expression of someone staring defeat in the face; expression of someone unaccustomed to (...); expression of someone wanting to (...); expression of someone who (...); expression of something akin to horror; expression of something akin to regret; expression of something approaching desperation; expression of something approaching disgust; expression of something approaching sorrow; expression of something intangible; expression of something like fury; expression of something like guilt; expression of something like pain; expression of something she couldn't name; expression of something very like pain; expression of somewhat sardonic amusement; expression of soothing seriousness; expression of sorely tried patience; expression of sorrow; expression of sorrow and pity; expression of sorrow and regret; expression of soulful understanding; expression of speechless amazement; expression of speechless horror; expression of spontaneous tenderness; expression of spurious interest; expression of stark concentration; expression of stark curiosity; expression of stark disbelief; expression of stark fear; expression of stark horror; expression of stark incredulity; expression of stark loneliness; expression of stark misery; expression of stark pain; expression of stark pain and horror; expression of stark tenderness; expression of stark vulnerability; expression of startled amazement; expression of startled anxiety; expression of startled desire; expression of startled disapproval; expression of startled disbelief; expression of startled dismay; expression of startled distress; expression of startled embarrassment; expression of startled hurt; expression of startled relief; expression of startled surprise; expression of steely determination; expression of stern concentration; expression of stern determination; expression of stern disapproval; expression of stern displeasure; expression of stern superiority; expression of sternness; expression of stiffness; expression of stoicism; expression of stone; expression of stony anger; expression of strain; expression of strain and discontent; expression of strain and uncertainty; expression of strained expectancy; expression of strained patience; expression of strange intensity; expression of strange surprise; expression of strength; expression of strong disapproval; expression of stubborn anger; expression of stubborn determination; expression of stubbornness; expression of studied blankness; expression of studied casualness; expression of studied disinterest; expression of studied indifference; expression of studied patience; expression of stunned amazement; expression of stunned anxiety; expression of stunned astonishment; expression of stunned despair; expression of stunned disbelief; expression of stunned ecstasy; expression of stunned incredulity; expression of stunned indignation; expression of stunned panic; expression of stunned pleasure; expression of stunned shock; expression of stunned surprise; expression of stupefaction; expression of stupefied surprise; expression of subdued admiration; expression of subdued apology; expression of sublime contentment; expression of sublime pleasure; expression of such adoration; expression of such anger; expression of such anguished love; expression of such anxiety; expression of such astonished admiration; expression of such awe and devotion; expression of such bitter cynicism; expression of such bitter devastation; expression of such bland innocence; expression of such bleak anguish; expression of such bleak despair; expression of such bold admiration; expression of such bored resignation; expression of such caring; expression of such casual intimacy; expression of such cold disdain; expression of such comical indignation; expression of such concentrated authority; expression of such confusion; expression of such cutting contempt; expression of such dark malevolence; expression of such deep appreciation; expression of such deep suspicion; expression of such deep suspicion and dislike; expression of such demonic ruthlessness; expression of such desolation; expression of such despair; expression of such desperation; expression of such desperation and pain; expression of such devouring intensity; expression of such disgust; expression of such dismay; expression of such fear; expression of such fear and pain; expression of such feral need; expression of such fierce determination; expression of such friendly reason; expression of such furious hunger; expression of such haunting sadness; expression of such horror; expression of such idiotic bliss; expression of such immeasurable longing; expression of such infectious excitement; expression of such innocent gravity; expression of such innocent surprise; expression of such intense disgust; expression of such intense emotions; expression of such intense fascination; expression of such intense hunger; expression of such intense yearning; expression of such joy; expression of such joy and happiness; expression of such longing; expression of such loss; expression of such love; expression of such love and concern; expression of such love and devotion; expression of such malevolence; expression of such melancholy; expression of such misery; expression of such mortified horror; expression of such murderous rage; expression of such naked and incredulous outrage; expression of such outraged indignation; expression of such pain; expression of such pain and longing; expression of such pain and regret; expression of such pleasure; expression of such profound affection; expression of such questioning tenderness; expression of such relief; expression of such savagery; expression of such scornful resentment; expression of such sensual contentment; expression of such sick disgust; expression of such soft passion; expression of such suffering; expression of such surprise; expression of such surprise and relief; expression of such sweetness; expression of such tender amusement; expression of such tender amusement and affection; expression of such tender compassion; expression of such tenderness; expression of such torment; expression of such total adoration; expression of such total astonishment; expression of such total contempt; expression of such unguarded love; expression of such unguarded tenderness; expression of such unholy malice; expression of such utter indifference; expression of such utter intensity; expression of such vulnerability; expression of such want; expression of such warmth and happiness; expression of such wistfulness; expression of such wonder; expression of sudden interest; expression of sudden relief; expression of suitable gravity; expression of sulky defiance; expression of sultry invitation; expression of sultry warning; expression of sunny contentment; expression of superb confidence; expression of supercilious outrage; expression of superiority; expression of superstitious fear; expression of supplication; expression of support; expression of suppressed amusement; expression of suppressed curiosity; expression of suppressed excitement; expression of suppressed fury; expression of suppressed rage; expression of supreme annoyance; expression of supreme complacency; expression of supreme happiness; expression of supreme irritation; expression of supreme male confidence; expression of supreme satisfaction; expression of supreme self-confidence; expression of supreme tolerance; expression of surliness; expression of surprise; expression of surprise and chagrin; expression of surprise and confusion; expression of surprise and consternation; expression of surprise and curiosity; expression of surprise and disappointment; expression of surprise and grudging respect; expression of surprise and irritation; expression of surprise and longing; expression of surprise and pleasure; expression of surprise and then disquiet; expression of surprise and understanding; expression of surprise and vague recognition; expression of surprised confusion; expression of surprised interest; expression of surrender; expression of suspicion; expression of suspicious curiosity; expression of suspicious disapproval; expression of sweet adoration; expression of sweet anguish; expression of sweet innocence; expression of sweet longing; expression of sweetness and gentleness; expression of sweetness and obstinacy; expression of sympathetic mortification; expression of sympathetic understanding; expression of sympathy; expression of taunting derision; expression of tautness and purpose; expression of teary gratitude; expression of teasing devilment; expression of temper; expression of tender amusement; expression of tender anguish; expression of tender apology; expression of tender love; expression of tender lust; expression of tender mockery; expression of tenderness; expression of tenderness and concern; expression of tenderness and desire; expression of tenderness and longing; expression of tenderness and thanksgiving; expression of tenderness mingled with exasperation; expression of tense determination; expression of tense preoccupation; expression of tense reserve; expression of tense resignation; expression of tension; expression of tentative joy; expression of terrible sadness; expression of terror; expression of thankfulness; expression of thanks; expression of thanks and joy; expression of the emotions which swirled through (him/her); expression of the fire burning within; expression of the greatest happiness; expression of the hatred boiling up inside; expression of the hurt inside; expression of the inner turmoil raging inside (him/her); expression of the intense frustration coursing through (him/her); expression of the joy (he/she) felt inside; expression of the joyous feeling within (him/her); expression of the most open admiration; expression of the most primitive human need; expression of the most unutterable sorrow; expression of the overwhelming love she felt; expression of the purest joy; expression of the rage and frustration that boiled inside (him/her); expression of the stinging current of need coursing through (him/her); expression of the turmoil going on inside (him/her); expression of the utmost concern; expression of the utmost contempt; expression of the utmost disdain for (him/her); expression of the utmost gravity; expression of the utmost irritation; expression of the utmost maternal tenderness; expression of thought; expression of thoughtful concern; expression of thoughtful consideration; expression of thoughtful contemplation; expression of thoughtful occupation; expression of tigerish desire; expression of tight anger; expression of tight concentration; expression of tight disapproval; expression of tiredness; expression of tolerance; expression of tolerant amusement; expression of tolerant inquiry; expression of torment; expression of tormented anguish; expression of tortured love; expression of total absorption; expression of total adoration; expression of total amazement; expression of total and bitter grimness; expression of total appreciation; expression of total astonishment; expression of total bewilderment; expression of total bliss; expression of total comprehension; expression of total concentration; expression of total confidence; expression of total devotion; expression of total disbelief; expression of total disdain; expression of total disgust; expression of total displeasure; expression of total distaste; expression of total failure; expression of total hostility; expression of total impassivity; expression of total imperviousness; expression of total incredulity; expression of total innocence; expression of total inscrutability; expression of total intractability; expression of total relaxation; expression of total seriousness; expression of total shock; expression of total surprise; expression of totally unexpected and inappropriate longing; expression of tragic pain; expression of tranquility; expression of transparent relief; expression of trepidation; expression of triumph; expression of triumph and avarice; expression of triumph and happiness; expression of triumphant amusement; expression of triumphant delight; expression of triumphant satisfaction; expression of troubled gravity; expression of true affection; expression of true love; expression of trust; expression of trust and understanding; expression of ultimate hope; expression of unadulterated fascination; expression of unadulterated shock; expression of unbearable sorrow; expression of unbearable torment; expression of unbelievable calm; expression of unbelievable tenderness; expression of unbridled desire; expression of uncertainty; expression of uncommon intensity; expression of uncompromising severity; expression of unconcealed delight; expression of unconcealed disdain; expression of unconcealed disfavor; expression of unconcealed dismay; expression of unconcealed satisfaction; expression of unconcealed surprise; expression of unconcealed surprise and disapproval; expression of unconcern; expression of unconscious and very feminine cunning; expression of unconscious arrogance; expression of unconscious wistfulness; expression of unconscious yearning; expression of uncontrollable lust; expression of uncontrolled rage; expression of unconvincing confusion; expression of undeniable yearning; expression of understanding; expression of undiluted fury; expression of undiluted pleasure; expression of undisguised astonishment; expression of undisguised concern; expression of undisguised contempt; expression of undisguised delight; expression of undisguised dislike; expression of undisguised hostility; expression of undisguised impatience; expression of undisguised interest; expression of undisguised love; expression of undisguised relief; expression of undisguised suspicion; expression of undisguised triumph; expression of undisguised victory; expression of uneasiness; expression of uneasy concern; expression of uneasy curiosity; expression of unfaltering confidence; expression of unguarded delight; expression of unhappiness; expression of unhappy appeal; expression of unhidden distaste; expression of unholy delight; expression of unholy disbelief; expression of unholy fascination; expression of unholy glee; expression of uninterest; expression of unmistakable dislike; expression of unmistakable pride; expression of unmistakable puppy love; expression of unmistakable relief; expression of unmistakable surprise; expression of unmistakable tenderness; expression of unmitigated anger; expression of unqualified approval; expression of unrelenting defiance; expression of unrest; expression of unrestrained fury; expression of unsettling knowing; expression of unspeakable fright; expression of unspeakable sorrow; expression of unutterable sadness; expression of unwilling admiration; expression of unwilling compassion; expression of urbane attention; expression of urgency; expression of urgency and need; expression of urgent excitement; expression of utmost gentleness; expression of utmost gravity; expression of utmost misery; expression of utmost seriousness; expression of utter amazement; expression of utter astonishment; expression of utter bewilderment; expression of utter bliss; expression of utter concentration; expression of utter confidence; expression of utter confusion; expression of utter contempt; expression of utter contentment; expression of utter conviction; expression of utter defeat; expression of utter dejection; expression of utter delight; expression of utter despair; expression of utter detachment; expression of utter devotion; expression of utter disbelief; expression of utter disgust; expression of utter dismay; expression of utter distaste; expression of utter fatalism; expression of utter fear; expression of utter fear and desolation; expression of utter helplessness; expression of utter horror; expression of utter incredulity; expression of utter indifference; expression of utter innocence; expression of utter joy; expression of utter loathing; expression of utter longing; expression of utter love; expression of utter love and devotion; expression of utter misery; expression of utter mortification; expression of utter need; expression of utter numbness; expression of utter outrage; expression of utter pain; expression of utter rage; expression of utter relief; expression of utter satisfaction; expression of utter scorn; expression of utter self-loathing; expression of utter seriousness; expression of utter shock; expression of utter shock and bewilderment; expression of utter shock and disbelief; expression of utter shock and incredulity; expression of utter sincerity; expression of utter surprise; expression of utter tedium; expression of utter terror; expression of utter torment; expression of utter tranquility; expression of utter trust; expression of utter vulnerability; expression of utter weariness; expression of utter withdrawal; expression of utter woe; expression of utter wonder; expression of vacant idiocy; expression of vague amusement; expression of vague confusion; expression of vague interest; expression of vague regret; expression of vagueness; expression of vast amusement; expression of vast relief; expression of veiled amusement; expression of veiled exasperation; expression of veiled surprise; expression of very slight distaste; expression of viciousness; expression of Victorian affront; expression of victory; expression of violence; expression of violent rage; expression of vulnerability; expression of vulnerability and hurt; expression of wanting; expression of wanton dismay; expression of wanton sensuality; expression of wariness; expression of warm admiration; expression of warm anticipation; expression of warm approval; expression of warm concern; expression of warm delight; expression of warm friendliness; expression of warm satisfaction; expression of warm tenderness; expression of warmth; expression of warmth and appreciation; expression of warmth and interest; expression of warmth and understanding; expression of wary alarm; expression of wary alertness; expression of wary amusement; expression of wary confusion; expression of wary curiosity; expression of wary disbelief; expression of wary incredulity; expression of wary interest; expression of watchful distance; expression of watchful reserve; expression of watchful waiting; expression of weariness; expression of weariness and strain; expression of weary amusement; expression of weary curiosity; expression of weary cynicism; expression of weary displeasure; expression of weary exasperation; expression of weary exhaustion; expression of weary pain; expression of weary persistence; expression of weary resignation; expression of welcome; expression of welcoming warmth; expression of what might have been disappointment; expression of what might have been pleasure; expression of what seemed to be genuine surprise; expression of whimsical surprise; expression of wholehearted approval; expression of wicked amusement; expression of wild hope; expression of wild relief; expression of winsome appeal; expression of wistful amusement; expression of wistful envy; expression of wistful yearning; expression of wistfulness; expression of withdrawal; expression of withering scorn; expression of woe; expression of wonder; expression of wonder and caution; expression of wonder and disappointment; expression of wonder and ecstasy; expression of wondering tenderness; expression of wonderment; expression of worry; expression of worry and guilt; expression of wounded dignity; expression of wounded disappointment; expression of wounded innocence; expression of wounded pride; expression of wrath; expression of wretched despair; expression of wry admiration; expression of wry amusement; expression of wry amusement mixed with cynicism; expression of wry annoyance; expression of wry defeat; expression of wry disbelief; expression of wry emotion; expression of wry frustration; expression of wry resignation; expression of wry self-mockery; expression of wry surprise; expression of wry surrender; expression of wry understanding; expression of yearning; expression of youthful innocence; expression of youthful passion.

1.3 - Noun Phrases

a bewildering range of expressions; a bland hardness of expression; a bland lack of expression; a brooding sort of expression; a careful lack of expression; a certain gravity of expression; a certain sadness of expression; a certain solemnity of expression; a change of expression; a childlike innocence of expression; a chilling lack of expression; a cold lack of expression; a complete absence of expression; a complete blankness of expression; a complete change of expression; a complete lack of expression; a complicated series of expressions; a cool lack of expression; a curious lack of expression; a curious softening of his expression; a curious sort of expression; a cutting lack of expression; a darkening of his expression; a decided lack of expression; a detached sort of expression; a distinct change of expression; a dreadful bitterness of expression; a dry lack of expression; a faint change of expression; a faint hardening of her expression; a flat lack of expression; a fleeting change of expression; a fleeting range of expressions; a flicker of expression; a flickering change of expression; a frigid lack of expression; a funny kind of expression; a gamut of expressions; a lack of expression; a lightning change of expression; a magnificent lack of expression; a marked change of expression; a marked lack of expression; a minute change of expression; a mirror of his own expression; a mixture of expressions; a momentary change of expression; a momentary relaxing of his somber expression; a muted facsimile of her usual expression; a myriad of expressions; a new sort of expression; a noticeable hardening of his expression; a noticeable lack of expression; a perceptible brightening of expression; a perceptible lack of expression; a quick change of expression; a quick flitter of expressions; a quicksilver series of expressions; a range of expressions; a rapid change of expressions; a rapid succession of expressions; a remarkable lack of expression; a riot of expressions; a ripple of expression; a series of expressions; a slight change of expression; a slight flicker of expression; a slight lessening of his stony expression; a slight lightening of her expression; a slight softening of his expression; a slow change of expression; a smiling tightness of his expression; a soft sort of expression; a softened version of the expression; a stony lack of expression; a strange flicker of expression; a strange lack of expression; a strange mixture of expressions; a stricken sort of expression; a studied blankness of expression; a subtle change of expression; a subtle shift of expression; a sudden change of expression; a swift change of expression; a terrible lack of expression; a terrible mixture of expressions; a tiny change of expression; a total draining of expression; a total lack of expression; a variety of expressions; a whole gamut of expressions; a whole host of expressions; a whole range of expressions; a wide range of expressions; a wild confusion of expressions; a wild spectrum of expressions; a wistful sort of expression; a wooden lack of expression; a wry sort of expression; the abrupt shift of his expression; the absolute coldness of his expression; the absolute implacability of his expression; the absolute inscrutability of his expression; the absolute seriousness of his expression; the absorbed interest of her expression; the accusing fury of his expression; the agony of his expression; the amused tolerance of his expression; the appeal of his expression; the arctic frost of his expression; the arrogance of his expression; the arrogant maleness of his cold expression; the black fury of his expression; the black violence of his expression; the bland innocence of his expression; the bland neutrality of his expression; the blandness of his expression; the blank incredulity of his expression; the blankness of his expression; the bleak ferocity of his expression; the bleak formality of his expression; the bleakness of his expression; the boyishness of his expression; the brave determination of her expression; the brief glimpse of his expression; the briefest glimpse of her expression; the brittle calm of her expression; the brooding darkness of his expression; the brooding menace of his expression; the brooding shift of his expression; the burning intensity of his expression; the burning urgency of his expression; the calm mask of his usual expression; the calm resolution of his expression; the calm serenity of her expression; the careful blandness of her expression; the careful blankness of his expression; the careful composure of her expression; the careful emptiness of expression; the casual unconcern of his expression; the change of expression; the childlike longing of her expression; the chilling indifference of his expression; the cold anger of his expression; the cold bitterness of his expression; the cold distaste of her expression; the cold haughtiness of her expression; the cold impassivity of his expression; the cold remoteness of his expression; the cold set of his expression; the coldness of his expression; the compelling determination of his expression; the complete absence of expression; the complete absorption of his expression; the complete implacability of his expression; the complete indifference of his expression; the complete lack of expression; the contentment of her expression; the continued grimness of his expression; the controlled impassivity of his expression; the controlled set of his expression; the controlled tautness of his conscious expression; the controlled tranquility of her expression; the cool arrogance of his expression; the cool deliberation of his expression; the cool derision of his expression; the cool gravity of his expression; the cool grimness of his expression; the cool mask of his expression; the cool neutrality of his expression; the cooling of his expression; the coolness of her expression; the crucifying blandness of his expression; the cynical contempt of his expression; the cynicism of his expression; the dangerous blankness of his expression; the dangerous darkening of his expression; the dark cloud of his expression; the dark intensity of his expression; the dark mask of his expression; the dark menace of his expression; the dark mockery of his expression; the dark nuances of his expression; the dark solemnity of his expression; the dark venom of her expression; the darkening anger of his expression; the darkening of his expression; the deadly seriousness of his expression; the deceptive demureness of her expression; the deliberate blandness of his expression; the deliberate lack of expression; the determined set of her expression; the devilish charm of his expression; the discipline of his expression; the drawn quality of his expression; the dreamy edges of her expression; the dreamy seriousness of his expression; the dreamy sweetness of her own expression; the dullness of her expression; the eagerness of her expression; the entire lack of expression; the extraordinary peacefulness of his expression; the extreme gravity of his expression; the extreme hardness of his expression; the faint altering of his expression; the faint austerity of her expression; the faint clouding of his expression; the faint easing of his expression; the faint hardness of her expression; the faint nuances of her expression; the faint severity of her expression; the ferocity of his expression; the fierce anger of his expression; the fierce concentration of his expression; the fierce intensity of his expression; the fierce urgency of his expression; the fierceness of his expression; the fine nuances of her expression; the first blaze of expression; the first change of expression; the first glimpse of his expression; the first lightening of his expression; the fixed rigidity of his expression; the fixity of his expression; the flash of a mischievous expression; the flawless serenity of her expression; the flushed wildness of his expression; the forbidding grimness of his expression; the fresh alertness of her expression; the frosty set of her expression; the frowning strain of his expression; the full force of his expression; the gentle tenderness of her expression; the gentleness of his expression; the genuine hauteur of his expression; the genuine warmth of his expression; the genuineness of his expression; the gradual rearrangement of his expression; the gravity of his expression; the grayness of his expression; the grim bleakness of his expression; the grim cynicism of his expression; the grim determination of his expression; the grim hardness of his expression; the grim intensity of the expression; the grim lines of his expression; the grim seriousness of his expression; the grim set of his expression; the grimness of his expression; the habitual hauteur of his expression; the handsome acceptance of her expression; the handsome severity of his expression; the hard anger of his expression; the hard authority of his expression; the hard cast of his expression; the hard command of his expression; the hard contours of her expression; the hard determination of his expression; the hard edges of her expression; the hard impatience of his expression; the hard implacability of his expression; the hard intensity of his expression; the hard set of his expression; the hard shell of his habitual expression; the hardness of his expression; the harsh aloofness of his expression; the harsh carnality of his expression; the harsh displeasure of his expression; the harsh inflexibility of his expression; the harsh set of his expression; the harsh unhappiness of his expression; the harshness of his expression; the hauntedness of his expression; the haunting appeal of her expression; the hawklike intensity of his expression; the hazy vulnerability of her expression; the healthy brightening of her expression; the heat of her rapt expression; the helpless openness of his expression; the honest clarity of her expression; the hot possession of her expression; the iciness of his expression; the icy disdain of his expression; the icy fury of his expression; the image of his stunned expression; the immediate darkening of his expression; the immobility of his expression; the implacable anger of his expression; the indifference of his expression; the ingenuousness of her expression; the innate confidence of his expression; the innocence of his expression; the inscrutability of his expression; the inscrutable mask of his expression; the intense seriousness of his expression; the intensity of his expression; the intensity of his guarded expression; the intentness of her expression; the interplay of expressions; the intimacy of his expression; the kind of expression; the lack of expression; the Latin mobility of his expression; the leashed passion of his expression; the lethal ice of his expression; the lightening of his expression; the marble facade of her expression; the mask of his expression; the meekness of his expression; the memory of her crushed expression; the memory of his aghast expression; the memory of his expression; the memory of his implacable expression; the memory of his puzzled expression; the memory of his smug expression; the memory of his stunned expression; the mental picture of his resolute expression; the mercurial shift of her expression; the mild serenity of his expression; the mildness of her expression; the mixture of expressions; the mock sternness of his expression; the molten ferocity of the expression; the momentary flash of a revealing expression; the most benign of expressions; the most curious of expressions; the most gentle of expressions; the most sincere of expressions; the mournful mobility of her expression; the mulish obstinacy of her expression; the myriad of expressions; the naked intensity of his expression; the naked malevolence of his expression; the natural aloofness of her expression; the natural gravity of his expression; the normal charm of her expression; the nuances of his expressions; the ominous darkening of his expression; the open vulnerability of his expression; the openness of her expression; the peculiar intensity of his expression; the perpetual sleepiness of his expression; the poignancy of his expression; the polite facade of his expression; the protesting plea of her expression; the quality of her expression; the quelling darkness of his expression; the questioning speculation of his expression; the quick closing of his expression; the quiet satisfaction of his expression; the radiance of his expression; the rapid change of his expression; the raw intensity of his expression; the rawness of his entire expression; the ready intelligence of his expression; the remote calmness of his expression; the remoteness of his expression; the rest of his expression; the right kind of expression; the rigid coldness of her expression; the rigid distaste of his expression; the rigidity of her expression; the ruthlessness of his expression; the sadness of her expression; the same arrogance of expression; the same intensity of expression; the same kind of expression; the same lack of expression; the same mixture of expressions; the same sincerity of expression; the same sort of expression; the sarcastic imperiousness of his expression; the savage derision of his expression; the sensuous appreciation of his expression; the serene radiance of her expression; the seriousness of his expression; the settled gravity of his expression; the severe displeasure of her expression; the severity of his expression; the sheer arrogance of his expression; the sheer beauty of the expression; the sheer confidence of his expression; the sheer haughtiness of his expression; the sheer intensity of his expression; the sheer magnetism of his expression; the shocked astonishment of his expression; the shocked incredulity of his expression; the shuttered bleakness of his expression; the sight of her cheerful expression; the sight of his intent expression; the sight of his set expression; the sincerity of the expression; the sizzling impact of his sensual expression; the slight change of his expression; the slight gravity of his expression; the slight grimness of his expression; the slight hardening of his expression; the slight moodiness of his expression; the slight softening of her expression; the slight wistfulness of her expression; the sly triumph of his expression; the smooth serenity of her expression; the smooth surface of his expression; the smugness of her expression; the sobriety of his expression; the softened warmth of her rueful expression; the softening of his expression; the softness of her expression; the solemnity of his expression; the somber cast of his expression; the somber quality of his expression; the somberness of his expression; the sort of expression; the sparkling change of her expression; the sparkling eagerness of her expression; the speculative arrogance of his expression; the stark gravity of his expression; the steadiness of his expression; the steady coolness of his expression; the steely remoteness of his expression; the stern composure of his expression; the stern cut of his expression; the sternness of his expression; the stillness of her expression; the stony detachment of his expression; the stony inflexibility of her expression; the strain of his expression; the strained uncertainty of her expression; the strained whiteness of her expression; the strange intensity of his expression; the strangest mixture of expressions; the studied detachment of his expression; the studied lack of expression; the subtle rearrangement of his expression; the subtle shifting of expressions; the sudden beauty of her expression; the sudden blandness of his expression; the sudden blanking of his expression; the sudden darkening of his expression; the sudden dimming of her expression; the sudden fierceness of his expression; the sudden freezing of expression; the sudden gauntness of his expression; the sudden gentling of his expression; the sudden intensity of his expression; the sudden keenness of his expression; the sudden lightening of his expression; the sudden luminosity of her expression; the sudden radiance of her expression; the sudden rigidity of his expression; the sudden seriousness of his expression; the sudden sobering of his expression; the sudden softening of his expression; the sudden somberness of his expression; the sudden sternness of his expression; the sudden tautening of his expression; the sudden tightening of his expression; the surprising grimness of his expression; the sweet innocence of his expression; the sweet intensity of his expression; the sweet serenity of her expression; the sweet seriousness of her expression; the sweetness of her expression; the swift change of expression; the swift flicker of expression; the swift succession of expressions; the swift tightening of his expression; the tail end of her guarded expression; the taunting bitterness of his expression; the taut inquiry of his expression; the taut mask of his expression; the taut wariness of his expression; the tautening of his expression; the tautness of his expression; the teasing humor of her expression; the teasing quality of his expression; the telling lack of expression; the tenderness of his expression; the tenseness of his expression; the tight set of her expression; the tiny nuances of his expression; the total blankness of his expression; the total lack of expression; the tough inflexibility of his expression; the tough precision of his handsome expression; the tranquility of his expression; the trembling vulnerability of her expressions; the tremulous uncertainty of her expression; the troubled cast of her expression; the true nature of the expression; the unbearable flash of expressions; the uncertainty of her expression; the uncomfortableness of his expression; the uncompromising hardness of his expression; the uncompromising harshness of his expression; the unconscious stiffening of her expression; the underlying grimness of his expression; the unexpected gentleness of his expression; the unfamiliar intensity of his expression; the unforgiving hardness of his expression; the unyielding hardness of his expression; the usual impassivity of his expression; the utter contentment of his expression; the utter genuineness of the expression; the utter ruthlessness of his expression; the utter selfishness of her expression; the utter seriousness of his expression; the utter sweetness of her expression; the varied range of expressions; the variety of his expressions; the very blandness of his expression; the very lack of expression; the vivid mobility of his expression; the vulnerability of his expression; the waiting quality of his expression; the wariness of his expression; the warmth of his expression; the wistfulness of his expression; the woodenness of her expression; the youthful earnestness of his expression.

1.4 - Verbs: Expression as Subject

Standalone Verbs

alter; answer; become (grim)*; become (impassive)*; become (intense)*; become (speculative)*; blacken; brighten; calm; cave in; change; clear; cloud over; collapse; contort; cool; crack; crumble; crumple; curdle; darken; deepen; deflate; die; dim; diminish; disappear; dissipate; dissolve; distort; drain away; droop; drop; drop away; dry up; ease; ebb away; evaporate; even out; fade; fall; fall away; falter; firm; flare; flash; flatten; flee; flicker; flinch; fold; form; fracture; freeze; frost over; frown; furrow; give (nothing away)*; glaze over; glow; go (dark)*; go away; grow; grow (darker)*; grow (dull)*; grow (harder)*; grow (more serious)*; grow (soft)*; grow (tight)*; halt; harden; ice over; ignite; increase; intensify; leave; lengthen; lessen; lift; lighten; linger; liquefy; liven up; loosen; lurk; mellow; melt away; mist over; morph; move; narrow; open; pale; pass; perk up; persist; recede; relax; remain; remain (remote)*; reply; resume; return; sharpen; shatter; shift; shudder; sizzle; slide away; slip away; slump; smile; smolder; smooth out; smooth over; sober; soften; sour; speak (volumes)*; splinter; stay; steady; stiffen; still; stir; subside; tense; thaw; tighten; transform; turn (hard)*; turn (sad)*; turn (serious)*; turn (somber)*; turn to (ice)*; turn to (stone)*; twist; unfreeze; vanish; wane; warm; waver; wilt; wither; wither away; wobble.

Brow as Object

arch (brow); crease (brow); cross (brow); flit across (brow); furrow (brow); knit (brow); lift (brow); line (brow); lower (brow); mar (brow); pucker (brow); tug at (brow); wrinkle (brow).

Eyebrows / Brows as Object

create (a tiny line) between (eyebrows); crinkle (the skin) between (eyebrows); drag down (eyebrows); draw (eyebrows) together; knit (eyebrows); lower (eyebrows); make (eyebrows) arch; make (eyebrows) lift; pull (eyebrows) together; raise (eyebrows); vee (eyebrows).

Eyes as Object

appear in (eyes); begin in (eyes); belie (eyes); blaze from (eyes); blaze in (eyes); bring (tears) to (eyes); build in (eyes); burn in (eyes); change in (eyes); charge (eyes); cloud (eyes); come (back) into (eyes); creep into (eyes); crinkle (the corners) of (eyes); cross (eyes); darken (eyes); die from (eyes); dilate (eyes); dim (the glow) in (eyes); disappear from (eyes); do not leave (eyes); do not reach (eyes); drain out of (eyes); drift into (eyes); drop from (eyes); emanate from (eyes); enter (eyes); erase (lines) from (eyes); etch (lines) around (eyes); fade from (eyes); fade out of (eyes); fill (eyes); filter into (eyes); flare in (eyes); flash in (eyes); flash through (eyes); flee from (eyes); flicker in/into (eyes), flit through (eyes); flood (eyes); fog (eyes); form (lines) at (the corners) of (eyes); form in (eyes); glaze (eyes); gleam in (eyes); glimmer in (eyes); glitter in (eyes);

267

glow in (eyes); grow in (eyes); harden (eyes); haunt (eyes); ignite in (eyes); increase in (eyes); invade (eyes); is back in (eyes)*; is evident in (eyes)*; jump into (eyes); kindle in (eyes); leave (eyes); lift from (eyes); light (eyes); linger in (eyes); mirror in (eyes); move through (eyes); narrow (eyes); pucker (eyes); reflect in (eyes); remain in (eyes); resonate from (eyes); return to (eyes); round (eyes); run through (eyes); seep into (eyes); settle in (eyes); shadow (eyes); shine in (eyes); shoot through (eyes); show in (eyes); slide from (eyes); slide into (eyes); slip into (eyes); smolder in (eyes); soften (eyes); steal into (eyes); stretch (eyes); sweep into (eyes); swirl around in (eyes); tighten (lines) about (eyes); tighten (skin) around (eyes); touch (eyes); turn (eyes) (almost black); twinkle in (eyes); vanish from (eyes); widen (eyes).

Face as Object

add (a decade) to (face); add (lines) to (face); add (years) to (face); animate (face); appear in (face); appear on (face); begin to form on (face); bloom across (face); bloom on (face); blossom on (face); break out on (face); burn in (face); carve (harsh lines) on (face); carve (lines) across (face); carve in (deep lines) on (face); cast (shadows) over (face); change on (face); chase (itself) across (face); chase across (face); clear from (face); close over (face); cloud (face); color (face); come (back) into (face); come onto/to (face); come over (face); consume (face); contort (face); cover (face); crease (face); creep across (face); creep into (face); creep over (face); crinkle (face); cross (face); cross over (face); cut (harsh lines) into (face); darken (face); dart across (face); dash across (face); deepen (lines) in (face); descend over (face); descend upon (face); disappear from (face); dissipate from (face); do not leave (face); do not lift from (face); dominate (face); drain from (face); drain out of (face); drift across (face); drift over (face); drop from (face); ease from (face); edge across (face); edge over (face); erase (years) from (face); etch (face); etch (lines) across (face); etch across (face); fade from (face); fall away from (face); fall over (face); feel (stiff) on (face); fill (face); flame on (face); flash across (face); flash over (face); flee (face); flee from (face); fleet across (face); flick over (face); flicker across (face); flicker on (face); flicker over (face); flit across (face); flit over (face); float across (face); flood (face); form on (face); freeze on (face); gentle (harsh planes) of (face); go from (face); grip (face); hold (face) hostage; inch across (face); is back on (face)*; is carved into (face)*; is carved on (face)*; is clamped to (face)*; is fixed upon (face)*; is imprinted on (face)*; is mirrored on (face)*; is painted across (face)*; is painted on/upon (face)*; is pasted on (face)*; is pinned to (face)*; is planted on (face)*; is plastered across (face)*; is plastered on (face)*; is reflected on (face)*; is set on (face)*; is stamped on (face)*; is wiped clean from (face)*; is wiped from (face)*; is wiped off (face)*; leap onto (face); leave (face); leech (the color) from (face); lift from (face); light (face); light up (face); line (face); linger on (face); mar (face); materialize on (face); move across (face); move over (face); pass across (face); pass over (face); pinch (face); play across (face); play over (face); pucker (face); race across (face); rack (face); recede from (face); remain on (face); rest on (face); return to (face); rip across (face); ripple across (face); roll over (face); savage (face); scrunch up (face); settle across (face); settle on (face); settle over (face); shadow (face); show on (face); shut down (face); skirt (its way) across (face); skitter across (face); slide across (face); slide over (face); slip across (face); slip from (face); slip over (face); smooth over (taut lines) of (face); soften (face); soften (hard contours) of (face); soften (harsh lines) on (face); spread across (face); spread over (face); steal across (face); steal over (face); streak (face); stretch across (face); suffuse (face); sweep across (face); sweep over (face); take over (face); tauten (face); tense (face); tighten (face); tighten on (face); touch (face); transform (face); traverse (face); turn (face) (stony); twist (face); twist across (face); vanish from (face); warm (face); wash across (face); wash over (face); waver on (face); wrinkle (face).

Features as Object

alter (features); animate (features); appear on (features); carve (features) into (granite); change (features); chase across (features); close over (features); cloud (features); come into (features); come over (features); contort (features); cover (features); crease (features); creep across (features); cross (features); cross over (features); darken (features); descend on (features); distort (features); dominate (features); drift across (features); drift over (features); ease out of (features); etch (features); fall over (features); flash across (features); flash over (features); flicker across (features); flit across (features); flow over (features); form on (features); form over (features); freeze (features); go over (features); harden (features); is carved in/into (features)*; is carved on (features)*; is chiseled into (features)*; is etched on/onto/upon (features)*; is reflected upon (features)*; is stamped on (features)*; leave (features); lift (features); light (features); make (features) harsh; make (features) lighten; mar (features); mask (features); move over (features); overcome (features); overspread (features); pass across (features); pass over (features); pinch (features); play across (features); play over (features); remain on (features); settle across (features); settle on (features); settle over (features); shadow (features); shape (features); shrink (features); slide across (features); slip over (features); soften (features); spread over (features); stamp (features); steal across (features); steal over (features); strain (features); suffuse (features); sweep over (features); take hold of (features); take over (features); tauten (features); tense (features); tighten (features); touch (features); transform (features); twist (features); wash over (features).

Forehead as Object

crease (forehead); ease (lines) on (forehead); etch (deep lines) across (forehead); furrow (creases) across (forehead); furrow (forehead); pucker (forehead).

Lips as Object

begin to settle about (lips), belie (compressed lips); curl up (one corner) of (lips); draw (lips) back; fill out (lips); make (lips) flatten; make (lips) part; pinch (lips); play across (lips); play around (lips); play on (lips); pucker (lips); pull (lips) down; pull (lips) tight; purse (lips); rest on (lips); settle on (lips); slip over

269

(lips); tighten (lips); touch (lips); tug at (lips); twist (lips); waver on (lips); wobble on (lips).

Mouth as Object

alter (shape) of (mouth); appear around (mouth); bring (a quirk) to (corners) of (mouth); cling about (mouth); come to (mouth); compress (mouth); create (deep grooves) by (mouth); creep across (mouth); cross (mouth); curl (mouth); curve (mouth); deepen (lines) about (mouth); deepen (lines) by (mouth); deepen around (mouth); engrave (deep lines) beside (mouth); etch (lines) around (mouth); expose (a faint dimple) at (corner) of (mouth); find (its way) to (mouth); go from (mouth); harden (mouth); pull at (corners) of (mouth); round (mouth); seal (mouth) shut; settle about (mouth); settle on (mouth); shape (mouth); show in (lines) at (sides) of (mouth); soften (mouth); thin (mouth); tighten (lines) at (corners) of (mouth); tilt (corners) of (mouth); touch (mouth); tug at (corners) of (mouth); tug downward(s) (corners) of (mouth); turn (mouth) down; turn (mouth) into (a thin line); turn down (corners) of (mouth).

1.5 - Verbs: Expression as Object

Brow or Character as Subject

(I) knit (brow) into (an expression)*; (I) pull down (brow) in (an expression)*; contract in (an expression); crinkle into (an expression); dip in (an expression); furrow in (an expression); go up in (an expression); narrow in (an expression); raise in (an expression); rise in (an expression); shoot upward(s) in (an expression); wrinkle with (an expression).

Character (I / He / She) as Subject

adopt (an expression); affect (an expression); assume (an expression); attempt (an expression); bear (an expression); cast (an expression) at (him); cast (him) (an expression); conceal (an expression); conjure (an expression); contrive (an expression); cut (him) (an expression); dart (him) (an expression); don (an expression); face (him) with (an expression); fake (an expression); feign (an expression); flash (an expression) at (him); flash (an expression) over (shoulder); flash (him) (an expression); flick (him) (an expression); fling (him) (an expression); force (an expression); form (an expression); give (an expression); give (him) (an expression); hide (an expression); hold (his attention) with (an expression); level (an expression) on (him); look at (him) with (an expression); maintain (an expression); make (an expression); manage (an expression); manufacture (an expression); marshal (an expression); mask (an expression); match (his expression)*; meet (his expression)*; mirror (his expression)*; muster (an expression); offer (him) (an expression); present (him) with (an expression); produce (an expression); pull (an expression); put on (an expression); retain (an expression); send (an expression) (his way); send (an expression) over (shoulder); send (him) (an expression); shoot (an expression) at (him); shoot (him) (an expression); show (an expression); show (him) (an expression); slant (him) (an expression); slide (an expression) toward(s) (him); slide (him) (an expression); slip (him) (an expression); spare (him) (an expression); sport (an expression); strike (him) with (an expression); summon (an expression); surprise (him) with (an expression); tease (him) with (an expression); throw (him) (an expression); toss (an expression) over (shoulder); toss (him) (an expression); try (an expression); turn (an expression) on (him); turn (an expression) toward(s) (him); wear (an expression).

Eyebrows / Brows or Character as Subject

(I) arch (eyebrows) in (an expression)*; (I) draw down (eyebrows) in (an expression)*; (I) lower (eyebrows) in (an expression)*; (I) raise (eyebrows) in (an expression)*; (I) school (eyebrows) into (an expression)*; alter into (an expression); arch in (an expression); arch upward(s) in (an expression); come together in (an expression); crease in (an expression); crimp in (an expression); descend in (an expression); dip in/into (an expression); drag together in (an expression); draw into (an expression); draw together in (an expression); draw up in (an expression); draw upward(s) in (an expression); flick upward(s) in (an expression); fly up in (an expression); furrow in (an expression); go up in (an expression); hold (an expression); jerk up in (an expression); knot in (an expression); lift in (an expression); lift with (an expression); lower in (an expression); lower to hide (an expression); meet over (bridge of nose) in (an expression); narrow in (an expression); peak in (an expression); pull high together in (an expression); pull low in (an expression); pull together in (an expression); raise in (an expression); rise in (an expression); rise in/into (an expression); shoot sky-high in (an expression); shoot up in (an expression); slant in (an expression); slant upward(s) in (an expression); snap together in (an expression); take on (an expression); tip in (an expression); twitch into (an expression); twitch together in (an expression); wiggle together in (an expression); wing upward(s) in (an expression).

Eyes as Subject

adopt (an expression); alter in (an expression); appraise (him) with (an expression); are aglow with (an expression)*; are alight with (an expression)*; are alive with (an expression)*; are bleak with (an expression)*; are bright with (an expression)*; are dark with (an expression)*; are fixed in (an expression)*; are half closed in (an expression)*; are half shut in (an expression)*; are intense with (an expression)*; are laced with (an expression)*; are lacking in (expression)*; are luminous with (an expression)*; assume (an expression); bear (an expression); become stricken with (an expression); begin to follow (him) with (an expression); blaze with (an expression); blink (an expression); blink closed in (an expression); bore into (his) with (an expression); brim with (an expression); burn into (him) with (an expression); burn with (an expression); carry (an expression); cast (an expression); change to (an expression); close in (an expression); close with (an expression); cloud with (an expression); come to rest on (him) with (an expression); come together in (an expression); come up to (his) in (an expression); contain (an expression); cool to (an expression); crease

271

into (an expression); crinkle into (an expression); crinkle with (an expression); darken with (an expression); dart to (him) with (an expression); deepen in (an expression); develop (an expression); dim with (an expression); drop in (an expression); fan out with (an expression); fill with (an expression); fix on (his) with (an expression); fix upon (him) with (an expression); flare with (an expression); flash in (an expression); flick into (an expression); flick over (him) with (an expression); flicker to (his) with (an expression); flicker with (an expression); flutter half-shut in (an expression); flutter open with (an expression); fly open with (an expression); focus on (him) with (an expression); follow (him) with (an expression); gain (an expression); gaze up with (an expression); glaze with (an expression); gleam in (an expression); gleam with (an expression); glimmer with (an expression); glint at (him) with (an expression); glisten with (an expression); glitter with (an expression); glow with (an expression); harden in (an expression); harden with (an expression); hold (an expression); hold (him) with (an expression); light up with (an expression); linger on (him) with (an expression); lock on/onto (his) with (an expression); lock with (his) in (an expression); look at (him) with (an expression); look into (his) with (an expression); lower to hide (an expression); meet (his) with (an expression); move over (him) with (an expression); narrow in (an expression); narrow in/into (an expression); narrow on (him)with (an expression); narrow with (an expression); open in (an expression); open to reveal (an expression); open wide in (an expression); open wide with (an expression); open with (an expression); possess (an expression); provide (an expression); rake (him) with (an expression); regard (him) with (an expression); round in (an expression); round with (an expression); run over (him) with (an expression); screw up in (an expression); sear over (him) in (an expression); search (his) with (an expression); seek (his) with (an expression); shift to (his) in (an expression); shimmer with (an expression); shine with (an expression); shut in (an expression); skim over (him) with (an expression); smolder with (an expression); snap with (an expression); soften in/into (an expression); spark with (an expression); sparkle with (an expression); squeeze shut in (an expression); study (him) with (an expression); survey (him) with (an expression); sweep over (him) with (an expression); thin with (an expression); train on (him) with (an expression); turn on (him) with (an expression); twinkle with (an expression); warm with (an expression); watch (him) with (an expression); wear (an expression); widen in (an expression); widen in/into (an expression); widen with (an expression); wrinkle up with (an expression).

Face or Character as Subject

(I) arrange (an expression) on (face)*; (I) bring (an expression) to (face)*; (I) display (an expression) on (face)*; (I) fix (an expression) on/to (face)*; (I) force (an expression) onto (face)*; (I) have (an expression) on (face)*; (I) keep (an expression) on (face)*; (I) leave (an expression) on (face)*; (I) paint (an expression) on (face)*; (I) paste (an expression) on/onto (face)*; (I) pin (an expression) on/to (face)*; (I) plant (an expression) on (face)*; (I) plaster (an expression) on (face)*; adopt (an expression); alter to (an expression); assume (an expression); attain (an expression); beam at (him) with (an expression); bear (an expression); begin to take on (an expression); betray (a flicker) of (expression); bloom into (an expression); break into (an expression); burn with (an expression); carry (an expression); change in (an expression); change to (an expression); cloud in (an expression); collapse into (an expression); constrict in (an expression); contort in/into (an expression); contort with (an expression); convulse in (an expression); crease in/into (an expression); crease up in (an expression); crease with (an expression); crinkle into (an expression); crinkle up in (an expression); crumple in upon (itself) in (an expression); crumple into (an expression); crunch into (an expression); crystallize into (an expression); curl into (an expression); curve into (an expression); darken in/into (an expression); darken with (an expression); dissolve into (an expression); distort into (an expression); draw in/into (an expression); droop in (an expression); drop in (an expression); ease into (an expression); erupt into (an expression); etch into (an expression); fade into/to (an expression); fall into (an expression); fill with (an expression); flood with (an expression); form (an expression); freeze in/into (an expression); give way to (an expression); glitter with (an expression); glow with (an expression); go rigid in (an expression); harden into (an expression); have (an expression); hold (an expression); iron (itself) into (an expression); is alive with (an expression)*; is arranged in (an expression)*; is carved into (an expression)*; is clamped into (an expression)*; is composed into (an expression)*; is drawn into (an expression)*; is fixed in (an expression)*; is frozen in (an expression)*; is gripped with (an expression)*; is hard with (an expression)*; is illuminated with (an expression)*; is lined with (an expression)*; is lost in (an expression)*; is schooled into (an expression)*; is set in/into (an expression)*; is shrouded with (an expression)*; is stamped with (an expression)*; is taut with (an expression)*; is tight with (an expression)*; is white with (an expression)*; lift into (an expression); lift with (an expression); light up in (an expression); light up with (an expression); light with (an expression); lighten into (an expression); lock in/into (an expression); melt into (an expression); mirror (his expression)*; modify into (an expression); narrow to (an expression); pinch into (an expression); possess (an expression); pucker in/into (an expression); pull (itself) into (an expression); rearrange (itself) into (an expression); reassemble (itself) into (an expression); redden in (an expression); relax in/into (an expression); relax into (an expression); respond with (an expression); return to (an expression); reveal (an expression); sag into (an expression); screw up in/into (an expression); scrunch in (an expression); scrunch up in/into (an expression); seize in (an expression); settle (back) into (an expression); shine with (an expression); show (an expression); shut down in (an expression); slant in (an expression); smooth into (an expression); sober into (an expression); soften in/into/to (an expression); soften into (an expression); soften with (an expression); sport (an expression); stretch into (an expression); switch to (an expression); tighten in/into (an expression); tighten with (an expression); transform into (an expression); twist in/into (an expression); twist with (an expression); wear (an expression).

Features or Character as Subject

(I) school (features) into (an expression)*; acquire (an expression); adjust into (an expression); are cast in/into (an expression)*; are composed in (an expression)*; are drawn in/into (an expression)*; are fixed in (an expression)*; are pulled into (an expression)*; are set in/into (an expression)*; are set with (an expression)*; are shadowed with (an expression)*; are stamped with (an expression)*; are tight with (an expression)*; arrange (themselves) into (an expression); assemble into (an expression); assume (an expression); clamp into (an expression); contort in/into (an expression); crease into (an expression); crumple (back) into (an expression); draw into (an expression); fall into (an expression); firm into (an expression); flutter in (an expression); form (an expression); freeze in/into (an expression); harden into (an expression); hold (an expression); lock in (an expression); mold in (an expression); morph into (an expression); realign (themselves) into (an expression); rearrange (themselves) in (an expression); relax into (an expression); reshape (themselves) into (an expression); retain (an expression); reveal (an expression); scrunch into (an expression); settle (back) into (an expression); shift in/into (an expression); soften in/into (an expression); soften with (an expression); take on (an expression); tighten in (an expression); tilt in (an expression); transform into (an expression); twist in/into (an expression); wear (an expression).

Forehead as Subject

crease in (an expression); furrow in (an expression); pucker in (an expression); wrinkle in (an expression); wrinkle with (an expression).

Lips or Character as Subject

(I) draw (lips) together in (an expression)*; (I) press (lips) into (an expression)*; (I) press (lips) together in (an expression)*; (I) school (lips) into (an expression)*; are drawn back from (teeth) in (an expression)*; are pressed down in (an expression)*; are pulled downward(s) in (an expression)*; are set in (an expression)*; are turned up at (corners) in (an expression)*; clamp together in (an expression); compress in (an expression); crook upward(s) in (an expression); curl back into (an expression); curl in/into (an expression); curve downward(s) in (an expression); curve in/into (an expression); curve upward(s) in (an expression); draw back in (an expression); draw together in (an expression); droop at (one corner) in (an expression); drop open in (an expression); fall open in (an expression); flatten into (an expression); form (an expression); hint at (an expression); lift in (an expression); part in (an expression); part with (an expression); press together in (an expression); purse in/into (an expression); purse together in (an expression); quirk in/into (an expression); quirk up in (an expression); shape into (an expression); thin in/into (an expression); tighten in (an expression); tug down in (an expression); twist in/into (an expression); twitch in/into (an expression).

Mouth as Subject

clamp (tight) in (an expression); clamp in (an expression); come down in (an expression); compress in (an expression); contort into (an expression); curl in/into (an expression); curl up into (an expression); curve downward(s) in (an expression); curve in/into (an expression); curve with (an expression); draw into (an expression); drift to (an expression); droop in (an expression); drop open in (an expression); fall open in (an expression); firm in (an expression); form (an expression); give (an expression); go down at (corners) in (an expression); hang slack in (an expression); harden with (an expression); have (an expression); is agape in (an expression)*; is drawn (tight) in (an expression)*; is drawn up on (one side) into (an expression)*; is fashioned in (an expression)*; is lifted to form (an expression)*; is parted in (an expression)*; is pulled down in (an expression)*; is pulled into (an expression)*; is pulled inward(s) in (an expression)*; is set in/into (an expression)*; is shaped in (an expression)*; is skewed in (an expression)*; is stretched into (an expression)*; kick up in (an expression); lift in (an expression); move in (an expression); open in (an expression); open wide in (an expression); pucker in (an expression); purse into (an expression); quirk at (corners) in (an expression); quirk in/into (an expression); quirk up at (one side) in (an expression); quirk with (an expression); reform into (an expression); shift into (an expression); slacken in (an expression); soften into (an expression); straighten into (an expression); stretch in/into (an expression); thin into (an expression); thin to (an expression); tighten into (an expression); tighten with (an expression); tilt into (an expression); tug down at (corners) in (an expression); turn down at (corners) in (an expression); turn down in (an expression); twist (sideways) in (an expression); twist downward(s) in (an expression); twist in/into (an expression); twist with (an expression); twitch in/into (an expression); twitch with (an expression).

Nose as Subject

crinkle in (an expression); lift in (an expression); scrunch up in (an expression); wrinkle in/into (an expression); wrinkle up with (an expression).

USAGE EXAMPLES

At her sharp inhale, a smug expression crept over Ken's face.

He looked at her with an expression of pained reproach.

Simon's blank expression gave her the answer.

Her father's expression had hardened.

The utter seriousness of his expression gave her pause.

Also by Dahlia Evans

The Body Thesaurus – A Fiction Writer's Sourcebook of Words and Phrases to Describe Characters

"The Ultimate Thesaurus That Helps Fiction Writers Describe Characters With Ease!"

If you're like most writers, you get sick and tired of endlessly searching thesauri looking for that perfect word to describe your character's physical appearance or the way they move their body. Wouldn't it be easier to have a book that gives you all these words without the hassle? If you answered *'yes'*, then this book is for you!

Dahlia Evans has compiled a thesaurus specifically aimed at describing a character's physical appearance and movement. This unique sourcebook is filled to the brim with words and phrases gathered from thousands of published novels. Now, you will have no problem conjuring up words and phrases like a magician, bringing your prose to life.

Inside You'll Discover:

* An exhaustive list of over 30,000 words and phrases describing each part of the body.

* 40 chapters, with each one including a list of adjectives, verbs, and noun phrases for that particular body part.

* Numerous example sentences showing many of these words in use.

* And best of all, words and phrases are sorted alphabetically, as well as by part of speech.

The Body Thesaurus is the ultimate fiction writer's companion; a resource that you'll want to keep close by for all your future writing projects.

Made in the USA
Middletown, DE
07 September 2023

38188953R00175